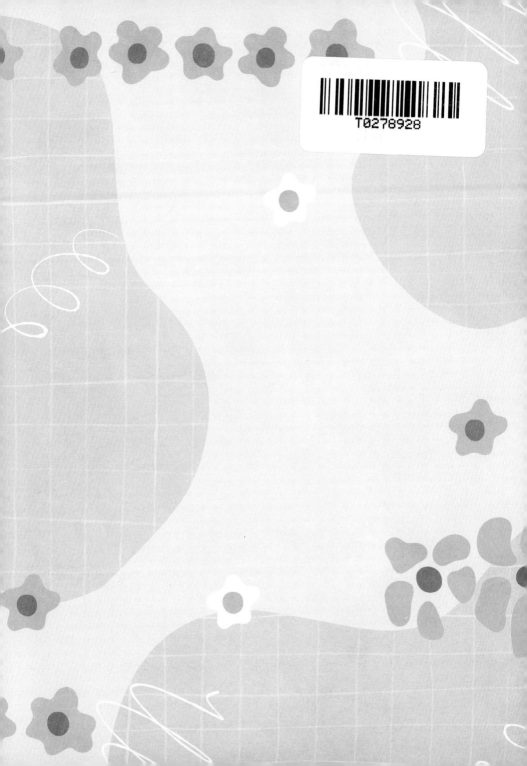

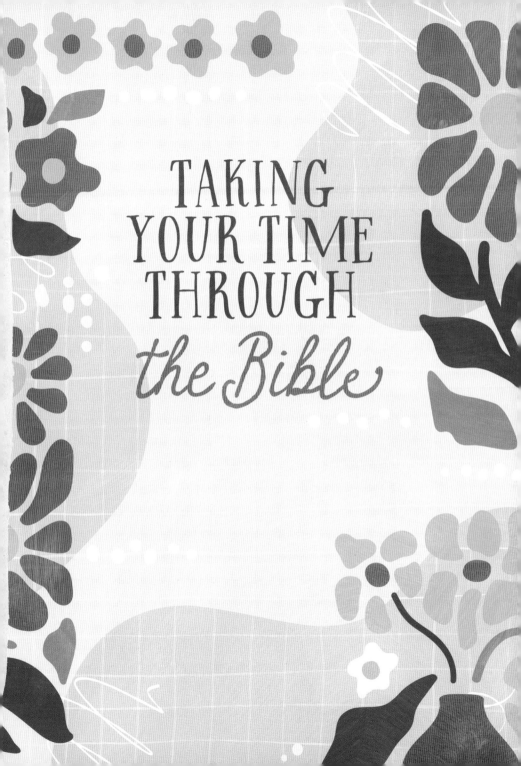

# TAKING YOUR TIME THROUGH

## the Bible

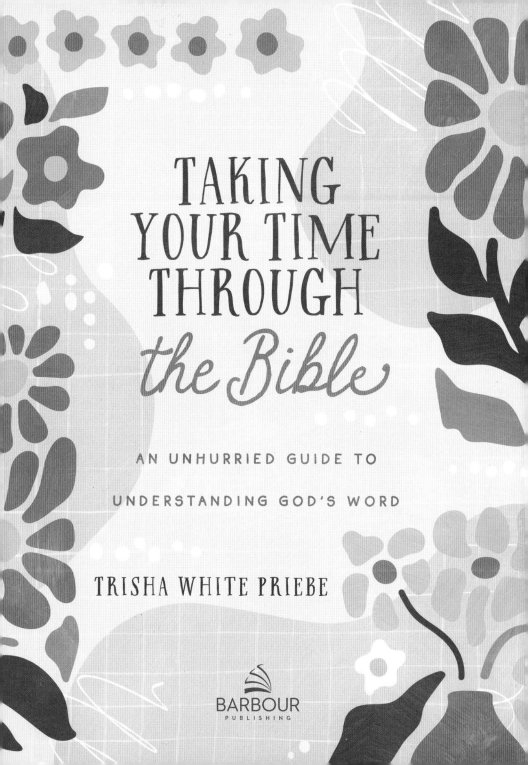

# TAKING YOUR TIME THROUGH the Bible

AN UNHURRIED GUIDE TO

UNDERSTANDING GOD'S WORD

TRISHA WHITE PRIEBE

**BARBOUR**
PUBLISHING

© 2025 by Barbour Publishing, Inc.

ISBN 979-8-89151-010-4

Cover design: Greg Jackson, Thinkpen Design

Published by Barbour Publishing, Inc., 1810 Barbour Drive, Uhrichsville, Ohio 44683, www.barbourbooks.com

*Our mission is to inspire the world with the life-changing message of the Bible.*

 Member of the
Evangelical Christian
Publishers Association

Printed in China.

# TAKING YOUR TIME THROUGH
## *the Bible*

It's great to read through the Bible in a year—but it's even better to slow down and savor your time in God's Word.

When your life feels rushed, this unique Bible reference will offer the tools and the encouragement you need to simply relax with God and His Word.

The beautifully designed pages that follow provide just enough information to guide you into scripture, which you are then encouraged to read and contemplate at your own pace. In *Taking Your Time through the Bible*, you'll find

- brief book and chapter summaries for context and clarity;

- thoughtful questions to help you focus on the Bible's text;

- "learn more" references to direct you to related passages of scripture; and

- encouraging prompts that continually redirect your thoughts to the main topic—knowing God through His Word.

So find a comfortable spot with your Bible. Go slow, be intentional, and read and pray and think and learn. Take your time with this unhurried guide to God's Word, and eagerly anticipate what He will teach you!

With heartfelt gratitude to
Faith White and Gail Priebe,
two faithful mothers
whose love of God
and the scriptures
has helped shaped my own.

# GENESIS

*God creates the world and chooses a special people.*

## SETTING THE STAGE

The Bible's first words are simple yet profound: "In the beginning God. . ." (1:1). No need for a grand introduction or a detailed backstory. Genesis never *explains* God; it simply *assumes* His existence. And the assumption is clear: God is, was, and forever will be.

Chapters 1 and 2 describe how God created the universe without any fancy scientific blueprint or drawn-out construction plan. He simply started speaking: "God said. . .and it was so" (1:6-7, 9, 11, 14-15).

Humans, however, were something altogether different—the only part of God's creation not brought into existence using words. Instead, "God formed man from the dust of the ground and breathed into his nostrils the breath of life" (2:7). Then woman was crafted from one of man's ribs. Humanity became God's masterpiece, made in His image and displaying His divine creativity.

These first two humans, Adam and Eve, were the only two people to know a perfect world, but they soon ruined paradise by disobeying God at the encouragement of a "subtle" (3:1) serpent.

Sin cast humanity into a moral freefall, and eventually, the world's first child (Cain) murdered his brother (Abel). People ultimately became so evil that God chose to flood the whole earth, saving only the righteous Noah and his family along with an ark full of animals.

Once the earth had been repopulated, God chose a man named Abram to be patriarch of a specially blessed people. These people were later called "Israel," the alternative name of Abram's grandson Jacob.

Genesis ends with Jacob's son Joseph, through a miraculous chain of events, ruling in Egypt—thus setting up the events of the following book of Exodus.

## GOOD TO KNOW

Though the author of Genesis is not identified, the book is traditionally attributed to Moses. He lived around the 1400s BC, but the events of Genesis date to the very beginning of time.

*Reading the Bible isn't a race. Let the pages unfold at a pace that allows your spirit to breathe.*

## GENESIS 1

In six days, God brings the entire universe and its many wonders to life. All three persons of the Trinity are active in creation (1:26). Human beings—made in the image of God—are the culmination of creation, which God deems "very good."

*What do you enjoy most about God's creation?*

## GENESIS 2

Sabbath, a weekly day of rest, is woven into the DNA of creation, reflecting the fact that God intentionally paused after six days of creation. The mysterious beauty of Adam and Eve's "one flesh unity" is explained in greater detail.

*How is observing the Sabbath a countercultural act today?*

## GENESIS 3

Eve is tempted and disobeys God's singular rule—not to eat the fruit of one specific tree in the garden. She offers the fruit to Adam, who also eats, and the consequences roll in like thunder. Adam and Eve are permanently evicted from the garden, the gates are closed, death is introduced, and the ground is cursed. Yet God already has a plan to account for their sin.

*Why did Adam and Eve disobey God? Why do we?*

## GENESIS 4

Adam and Eve begin having children. Their oldest son, Cain, in a fit of jealousy over his unaccepted offerings to God, kills his brother Abel. Although the Ten Commandments won't arrive for many centuries, Cain knows murder is wrong. He becomes a wanderer, but God mercifully marks Cain. This reminds us of God's unfailing care after our own poor choices.

*How does the story of Cain show the seriousness of sin?*

## Take Your Time and Learn More

- **In the beginning:** JOHN 1:1–5
- **Sabbath rest for God's people:** HEBREWS 4:1–11
- **Temptation:** JAMES 1:13–15
- **Firstborn:** COLOSSIANS 1:15–20

*The greatest truths in scripture are often revealed in the unhurried moments.*

## GENESIS 5

Tracing the roots from Adam to Noah, this genealogy—and all the family lineages listed throughout scripture—remind us that every single person created by God has a purpose and a story. One story of significance: Enoch. The Bible's brief but powerful passage about Enoch says he "walked with God, and he was not, for God took him" (5:24).

*If your life with God were described in a single sentence, what would it be?*

## GENESIS 6

Humanity is growing increasingly wicked, and God now regrets creating humans. Choosing to spare Noah and his family due to their righteousness, God uses the word *covenant* for the first time (6:18). He instructs Noah to build an ark—a giant boat—one and a half football fields long, six interstate lanes wide, and four stories tall.

*How do you choose to live righteously in a world where evil is prevalent?*

## GENESIS 7

God instructs Noah to enter the ark with his family and pairs of every animal. And then, 1,656 years after creating Adam, God spectacularly floods the earth for forty days and nights. Every living thing outside the ark dies: only Noah and those who are with him survive (7:23).

*How does Noah's faith challenge you to trust God when His instructions don't make sense?*

## GENESIS 8

The ark comes to rest on the mountains of Ararat, and Noah sends out a series of birds to find dry land. A dove returns with an olive leaf, and God tells Noah it is time to leave. So Noah and his family exit the ark, build an altar, and worship the Lord.

*What are you currently waiting on God's timing for?*

## Take Your Time and Learn More

- Enoch: HEBREWS 11:5
- Universal unrighteousness: ROMANS 3:10–25
- Noah: HEBREWS 11:7
- Burnt offerings: LEVITICUS 1:3–17

*Bible study is truly a lifelong journey.*
*Relax and enjoy the trip.*

## GENESIS 9

Everything on earth has changed. God tells Noah's family to have children, and He promises never again to destroy the earth with a flood. Noah's sons are blessed, but Ham's disrespect leads to a curse on his son Canaan. Noah lives 350 years after the flood, and then he dies.

*When have you witnessed God's faithfulness in a season of change?*

## GENESIS 10

Often called the "Table of Nations," this remarkable list traces the origins of various people groups. It begins with Noah's sons and includes their languages and territories—all of which will be verified through modern archaeology. God's faithfulness exists on every page.

*What does the diversity of nations and languages teach you about God's creativity?*

## GENESIS 11

The people of Babel—a name for the early city of Babylon—begin building a tower to make their name great. So God saves them from themselves by confusing their language and scattering them across the earth. This is the first recorded attempt by the Babylonians to rebel against God.

*How do you know if your ambition is pleasing God or simply self-promoting?*

## GENESIS 12

God tells a childless old man named Abram to leave his country and his father's household and go "to a land that I will show you" (12:1). God also makes a covenant with Abram. He promises to bless him, make him a great nation, and benefit all nations through him. Abram obeys.

*Are you willing to step out in faith and obedience,*
*even if it means leaving your comfort zone?*

### Take Your Time and Learn More

- Rainbow: REVELATION 10:1
- Genealogy of Noah: 1 CHRONICLES 1:4–23
- Babel: LUKE 1:51
- Genealogy of Abram (later called Abraham): MATTHEW 1:1–2

*Try to forget the demands of life for a while.*
*You're spending quality time with God.*

## GENESIS 13

Abram and his nephew Lot journey together until conflicts erupt among their herders. Abram suggests they part ways and graciously allows Lot to choose his portion of the land. Lot selects the fertile plains of Jordan, leaving Abram with the rest. God reaffirms His promise to bless Abram and his descendants.

*How much patience, humility, and grace do you show when handling conflict?*

## GENESIS 14

Abram rescues Lot, who had been captured during a war between regional kings. He then encounters and receives a blessing from Melchizedek, who is both a king and a priest—a rare combination that foreshadows Jesus. Abram refuses the spoils offered by the king of Sodom, demonstrating trust in God's provision.

*In what areas might you trust God's provision more fully?*

## GENESIS 15

God reassures Abram about His promise of descendants and land. And Abram, despite being an old man, believes God. Consistent with the rest of scripture, God counts Abram's belief—not his rituals or sacrifices—as righteousness (15:6). God then confirms His promise to Abram with a special type of covenant.

*What is a promise God has made to you that you can honor by believing?*

## GENESIS 16

Unable to bear children, Abram's wife, Sarai, takes matters into her own hands. She gives her maidservant, Hagar, to Abram as a surrogate. When Hagar conceives, Sarai is harsh and Hagar flees. God's tenderness is revealed: His covenant commitment isn't to Hagar, yet He pursues her (16:6–13). Hagar returns and gives birth to Ishmael.

*When you have an unmet desire, do you patiently trust or creatively scheme?*

## Take Your Time and Learn More

- Conflict resolution: ROMANS 12:17–19
  - Melchizedek: HEBREWS 7:11–22
- Abraham's faith: HEBREWS 11:8–19
  - Hagar: GALATIANS 4:24–25

# Good things come to those who wait—on the Lord, that is.

## GENESIS 17

God's name *El Shaddai*—the God who satisfies—is first used (17:1). God reaffirms His covenant with Abram, renaming him Abraham and promising to make him the father of many nations. God also institutes circumcision as a sign of this covenant. Sarai becomes Sarah, and God promises her a son, Isaac, through whom the covenant will be established.

*How well do you trust God to meet your needs and fulfill His promises in your life?*

## GENESIS 18

Three visitors—one of whom is the Lord—come to Abraham, and Abraham shows good hospitality. Over dinner, the guests promise that Sarah will soon give birth to a son. Sarah, being ninety years old, laughs in disbelief. Abraham intercedes for Sodom, bargaining with God not to destroy the city if even ten righteous people can be found there.

*How comfortable are you with welcoming people into your home and practicing hospitality?*

## GENESIS 19

God can't find ten righteous men in Sodom, so He destroys the city along with neighboring Gomorrah. Lot's family is spared, though, as angels warn Lot to flee. His wife looks back and turns into a pillar of salt. Lot escapes to Zoar, where his daughters—apparently believing they are the last people on earth—get him drunk to conceive children. This leads to the births of Moab and Ammon.

*What might God want you to leave behind so that you can follow Him completely?*

## GENESIS 20

While sojourning in Gerar, Abraham fearfully claims that Sarah is his sister. King Abimelech takes the beautiful woman with intentions to marry her, but God warns him in a dream and closes all the wombs in his household. Abimelech rebukes Abraham and returns Sarah unharmed. Abraham prays for Abimelech, and God heals him and his household.

*Have you ever been tempted to compromise your integrity in challenging situations? What happened?*

## Take Your Time and Learn More

- Circumcision: Romans 4:9–12
- Sarah: Romans 9:9
- Sodom and Gomorrah: 2 Peter 2:6–9
- Repeated deception: Genesis 26:6–11

*The Bible is countercultural, and so is Bible study.*
*There's no need to rush through this.*

## GENESIS 21

Finally, the long-awaited Isaac is born, fulfilling God's twenty-five-year-old promise. Sarah, who once laughed in disbelief, now laughs with joy (21:6). Ishmael, now fourteen years old, is sent away with Hagar, but God will protect them. King Abimelech and Abraham make a covenant of peace, and Abraham lives a long time in the land of the Philistines.

*How does God's faithfulness to Abraham encourage you to trust God's promises to you?*

## GENESIS 22

God tests Abraham's faith, asking him to offer his only son, Isaac, as a sacrifice. Abraham obeys, believing God will provide (22:8). At the last moment, God does provide a ram for the offering. This event foreshadows God's ultimate sacrifice of His own Son, Jesus, and demonstrates Abraham's unwavering trust and obedience to God's commands.

*Has God ever called you to sacrifice something dear? How did you respond?*

## GENESIS 23

Sarah dies at age 127 in Hebron. Abraham mourns her, and the Hittites generously offer him a burial site for Sarah. He buys the cave of Machpelah and buries her there. This marks the first land Abraham owns in Canaan, beginning the fulfillment of God's promise (17:8).

*What does the Hittites' generosity teach you about how to treat strangers in need?*

## GENESIS 24

Abraham is getting old and wants to find a wife for Isaac—specifically one from among his people. Abraham sends out a servant to seek a woman, and God's faithfulness becomes evident when the man returns with Isaac's distant cousin Rebekah. Isaac joyfully receives Rebekah and loves her (24:67). God's covenant with Abraham's descendants continues.

*How do you trust God's guidance when seeking important decisions for your life?*

### Take Your Time and Learn More

- Hagar and Sarah: GALATIANS 4:21–31
- Abraham and Isaac: JAMES 2:21–24
- Machpelah: ACTS 7:16
- Journey to find a wife: GENESIS 29:1–30

*God speaks in the quiet moments.*
*Approach His Word with calm expectation.*

## GENESIS 25

Abraham marries Keturah and has six more sons. But he gives everything he has to Isaac—the child of God's promise—before dying at age 175. Isaac and Rebekah give birth to twins—Esau and Jacob—whose relationship is marked from the beginning by conflict and competition. Esau foolishly sells his birthright to Jacob for a bowl of stew.

*How do you safeguard your important relationships from jealousy and competition?*

## GENESIS 26

History repeats itself as Isaac lies about Rebekah being his sister and not his wife. Even so, God protects and blesses Isaac abundantly. In spite of opposition, Isaac digs wells and makes peace with the Philistines. God reaffirms His covenant with Isaac, even as Esau causes "grief of mind to Isaac and to Rebekah" (26:35).

*Have you ever allowed fear of man, instead of trust in God, to guide your decisions? What happened?*

## GENESIS 27

Old and blind, Isaac knows he needs to bless his oldest son, Esau. But Rebekah schemes for her favorite son, Jacob, to receive the blessing instead. Disguised as Esau, Jacob deceives Isaac—meaning Jacob now owns Esau's birthright *and* blessing. Because of Esau's fury, Jacob realizes he'll need to leave home to save his life.

*How does manipulation ultimately insult God's goodness?*

## GENESIS 28

Isaac blesses Jacob and instructs him not to marry a Canaanite woman. So Jacob begins a journey to find a wife from his mother's people. One night, he dreams of a ladder reaching up to heaven. God reaffirms the covenant He had made with Abraham and Isaac, promising to bless Jacob and his descendants. When he wakes, Jacob vows to serve God.

*What events in your life have served as catalysts to draw you closer to God?*

## Take Your Time and Learn More

- Esau's birthright: HEBREWS 12:16–17
- Similar deception: GENESIS 12:10–20
- Jacob over Esau: MALACHI 1:2–3
- Jacob's ladder: JOHN 1:51

*Before you read, pray. Ask God to*
*speak His truth to your spirit.*

## GENESIS 29

Jacob meets a beautiful shepherdess named Rachel at a well in Haran. He agrees to work seven years for her father in order to marry her. But just as Jacob deceived Esau with a false identity, so Laban deceives Jacob by giving Rachel's older sister, Leah, to Jacob. Jacob then works seven more years for Rachel.

*Do you believe God is able to use even your sins to*
*accomplish His good will for your life? How?*

## GENESIS 30

Nobody benefits from Laban's deception. Jacob hates Leah, and the sibling rivalry between the sisters creates ongoing tension and strife. Unable to conceive, Rachel gives her servant to Jacob to bear sons. Seeing this, Leah gives her servant to Jacob, bringing more sons. Finally, Rachel gives birth to a son, Joseph. Jacob decides it's time to return home.

*In what ways can you please God when others treat you unfairly?*

## GENESIS 31

After twenty years of mistreatment and deception, Jacob decides to leave Laban's household. God directs him to return with his family to Canaan, but before he leaves, Rachel steals her father's household idols. Laban pursues Jacob and searches for the idols but never finds them. After a heated exchange, Jacob and Laban agree to go their separate ways.

*How do Christians today mix worldly "idols" with Christian beliefs?*

## GENESIS 32

Jacob sends messengers ahead to tell Esau of his return. They return saying Esau is coming to meet him with four hundred men. Afraid, Jacob sends everyone ahead and stays alone. That night, Jacob wrestles with the angel of God, refusing to let go until he receives a blessing. Jacob is renamed Israel, and God reiterates the name change in Genesis 35.

*How do you handle situations where you fear potential conflict?*

### Take Your Time and Learn More

- Jacob's time in Aram: HOSEA 12:12
- Sons of Jacob: 1 CHRONICLES 2:1–2
- God's protection of Jacob: PSALM 105:12–15
- Testing by God: PSALM 17:3

*Don't hurry, don't worry. God's Word provides everything you need for living well.*

## GENESIS 33

Jacob sees Esau coming with four hundred men—just as the messengers said—and it looks like Esau may finally take revenge on Jacob for the stolen birthright and blessing. Instead, Esau "ran to meet him and embraced him and fell on his neck and kissed him. And they wept" (33:4). In gratitude, Jacob builds an altar and worships the God of Israel.

*How do asking for and receiving forgiveness both require humility?*

## GENESIS 34

Jacob and Leah's daughter, Dinah, is raped by Shechem, a Hivite prince. Shechem then asks Jacob and his sons for permission to marry Dinah. Jacob's sons are angry, but they agree to the marriage. . .under the condition that all Hivite men be circumcised. Then, while the men are recovering, Dinah's brothers Simeon and Levi kill all the males of the city.

*What is the difference between justice and revenge?*

## GENESIS 35

Jacob returns to Bethel, where he had the dream of a ladder to heaven (Genesis 28). God reaffirms His covenant and officially changes Jacob's name to Israel. A sad series of events occurs: Rachel dies giving birth to Benjamin, Reuben (Jacob's firstborn) sleeps with his father's concubine, and Isaac (Jacob and Esau's father) dies at age 180.

*In what ways can you cultivate a greater sense of reverence and awe for God?*

## GENESIS 36

Esau, also known as Edom, settles in the hill country of Seir, and his family grows. This further fulfills God's promises to Abraham regarding the multiplication of his descendants. Also, it distinguishes Esau's lineage from the lineage of Jacob, who now inherits the covenant blessings.

*How might these genealogies inspire you to trust God's sovereignty over your own legacy?*

## Take Your Time and Learn More

- Reconciliation with a brother: MATTHEW 5:23–24
- Vengeance for rape: 2 SAMUEL 13
- Jacob's journey to Bethel: HOSEA 12:4–5
- Esau's descendants: OBADIAH 1–6

*God loves it when you read and study His Word.*

## GENESIS 37

Joseph is Jacob's favorite son, which creates problems. A jealousy-fueled series of events leads to Joseph's brothers selling him into slavery. The brothers cover Jacob's robe in goat's blood to deceive Jacob into thinking Joseph had died. This ironically parallels the time Jacob used his brother's cloak and a slaughtered goat to portray himself as Esau to his father.

*How do you cultivate a heart of contentment when you're tempted with jealousy?*

## GENESIS 38

Judah—Jacob and Leah's fourth son—marries a Canaanite and has three sons: Er, Onan, and Shelah. When Er dies childless, Judah asks Onan to marry the widow and fulfill the duty of carrying on the family line. He refuses and is killed by God, so Tamar disguises herself and tricks Judah into sleeping with her. Tamar becomes pregnant with twins by her father-in-law.

*Tamar is one of the few women listed in Jesus' genealogy. Does that change how you see her?*

## GENESIS 39

Joseph is sold into slavery in Egypt and serves in Potiphar's house. Despite temptation from the master's wife, Joseph remains faithful to God by refusing her sexual advances. This leads to false accusations of assault, and Joseph is imprisoned. God blesses him, however, and he gains favor—even in prison.

*How does Joseph's story encourage you to stay faithful to God no matter what?*

## GENESIS 40

Joseph interprets dreams for Pharaoh's cupbearer and baker while all three are imprisoned. Both dreams foreshadow the men's fates: the cupbearer will be restored to his position, but the baker will be executed. Joseph demonstrates his gift of dream interpretation and continues trusting God despite his difficult circumstances.

*Do you trust in God's timing and purpose, even when it seems others have forgotten you?*

## Take Your Time and Learn More

- Joseph's life: ACTS 7:8–14
- Judah and Tamar in genealogy of Christ: MATTHEW 1:3
- Joseph's time in Egypt: PSALM 105:17–19
- Remembering those in prison: HEBREWS 13:3

*Reading the Bible isn't a race. Let the pages unfold
at a pace that allows your spirit to breathe.*

## GENESIS 41

Pharaoh dreams of seven fat cows devoured by seven lean cows, and seven plump ears of grain consumed by seven thin ears. Joseph explains there will be seven years of plenty followed by seven years of famine. In appreciation, Pharaoh elevates Joseph—now thirty years old—to be Egypt's second-in-command to prepare for the coming crisis.

*How does this promotion prove God's kindness not only
to Joseph but to Egypt, God's enemy?*

## GENESIS 42

Famine prompts Jacob's sons—Joseph's brothers—to journey to Egypt to buy grain. Joseph oversees grain sales, and he recognizes his brothers immediately. The men bow to Joseph, fulfilling his prophetic dream. Joseph tests his brothers by accusing them of spying, detains Simeon, and demands the others return with their youngest brother.

*How has God graciously worked through situations
in your life that felt unfair at the time?*

## GENESIS 43

The famine persists in Canaan, prompting Jacob's sons to return to Egypt to buy grain. Judah pledges to protect Benjamin, convincing a hesitant Jacob to let him go. In Egypt, Joseph invites them into his home for a meal, seating them from oldest to youngest at his table. The brothers are understandably amazed (43:33).

*In what specific ways does Joseph's story remind you that God is working in all things?*

## GENESIS 44

Joseph devises a way to test his brothers' integrity: he plants a silver cup in Benjamin's sack, framing him for theft. When the brothers are "caught," Judah displays a changed heart by pleading for Benjamin's release. Whereas Judah once suggested the brothers kill Joseph, he now offers himself as a slave in Benjamin's place.

*How is Judah a picture of Christ in this chapter (specifically in verse 33)?*

## *Take Your Time and Learn More*

- Dream interpretation: DANIEL 2:1–30
- Joseph as deliverer: ACTS 7:9–14
- Showing kindness to foreigners: DEUTERONOMY 10:17–19
- Forgiveness: MATTHEW 6:14–15

*The greatest truths in scripture are often*
*revealed in the unhurried moments.*

## GENESIS 45

Overcome with emotion, Joseph finally reveals his identity. He assures his brothers of God's sovereignty. It's been more than twenty years since they've seen each other, and Jacob's sons are stunned. Joseph sends for their father, instructing the entire family to return with him to Egypt. When he hears the news about Joseph, Jacob will be just as shocked as his sons had been.

*When have you experienced unexpected reconciliation or forgiveness in a relationship?*

## GENESIS 46

Jacob and his family move to Egypt due to the famine. Jacob has now been humbled by life, and God reassures him in a vision that this is the right decision. In Egypt, Joseph reunites with his father. Pharaoh welcomes the family and offers them the best of Egypt. They settle in Goshen, and Joseph helps them adjust.

*How have you handled seasons of major change?*
*Could you sense God working in the background?*

## GENESIS 47

Joseph brings his family before Pharaoh, securing their settlement in Goshen. The famine worsens, and Joseph implements a system to exchange land and labor for food, which consolidates Pharaoh's power. Despite the hardship, the Israelites thrive in Goshen, demonstrating God's provision. Jacob lives in Egypt seventeen years.

*How has God met your unfaithfulness with His faithfulness,*
*as He did with Jacob's family?*

## GENESIS 48

Jacob blesses Joseph's sons, Ephraim and Manasseh. And despite Joseph's attempt to correct him, Jacob intentionally blesses Ephraim, the younger, over Manasseh, the elder. This reflects a recurring theme in scripture: God does what is least expected, blessing individuals according to His purposes rather than human conventions.

*How might God's pattern of unlikely blessings challenge your understanding of merit?*

### *Take Your Time and Learn More*

- Joseph's faith: HEBREWS 11:22
- Jacob's sons in the wilderness: NUMBERS 26:5–51
- Joseph's family in Egypt: JOSHUA 24:1–4
- Ephraim: JEREMIAH 31:9

*Bible study is truly a lifelong journey.*
*Relax and enjoy the trip.*

## GENESIS 49

Jacob, now 147 years old, gathers his sons to give prophetic blessings. Judah receives the prominent blessing—the royal lineage, ultimately fulfilled in Christ, will come through him. Jesus will be called "the Lion of the tribe of Judah" (Revelation 5:5). Having lived a full life, Jacob then dies.

*How does Jacob's gradual change from deceitful to wise*
*reflect our own sanctification process?*

## GENESIS 50

Joseph grieves the death of his father and fulfills the old man's wish to be buried in Canaan. Interestingly, Jacob is buried with his less-loved wife, Leah. Joseph's brothers fear retribution now that their father is dead, but Joseph assures them, "God meant it [their bad behavior] for good" (50:20). Joseph dies at age 110 and is buried in Egypt.

*How does Joseph's story encourage you to forgive those who have wronged you?*

## Take Your Time and Learn More

- Jacob's blessing: HEBREWS 11:21
- Joseph's burial request: EXODUS 13:19

# EXODUS

*God establishes His covenant and guides*
*His people to the promised land.*

## SETTING THE STAGE

Exodus, the second book of the Bible, picks up where Genesis ends—with Jacob leading his family down to Egypt to be saved by Joseph during the famine. Nearly four hundred years pass in the span of the first chapter, and the new story of Exodus begins with the words, "Now there arose a new king over Egypt who did not know Joseph" (1:8).

What a poignant reminder that all human leaders—good or bad—are eventually forgotten, but the name of the Lord endures forever.

In His kindness, God chose Abraham's family to be His people and to represent His blessing to the world. But now, this "new king over Egypt" is threatened by the people of Israel (1:9). So he brutally enslaves them while simultaneously attempting to destroy them (1:13-16).

But God always maintains a fierce commitment to His chosen people.

Demonstrating His delight in using the unexpected to accomplish the extraordinary, God raises up a tongue-tied, reluctant leader named Moses to deliver an entire nation from bondage (4:10).

What follows is an exciting series of events that evidence God's power and presence. From the burning bush to the ten powerful plagues, from the parting of the Red Sea to the provision of manna and quail, from the Ten Commandments to the pillar of cloud and fire—God proves He is "merciful and gracious, longsuffering, and abundant in goodness and truth" toward His dearly beloved people (34:6).

This much is abundantly clear: God *always* keeps His word.

## GOOD TO KNOW

Author is not stated but traditionally attributed to Moses. In Exodus 34:27 God tells Moses, "Write these words," and Jesus quotes from Exodus as "the book of Moses" (Mark 12:26). Written around the mid-1400s BC.

*Try to forget the demands of life for a while.*
*You're spending quality time with God.*

## EXODUS 1

Four hundred years after Genesis ends, the Israelites have multiplied greatly in Egypt, alarming the new Pharaoh. Worried the Israelites could rise up to fight him, Pharaoh enslaves them and orders the death of all male Hebrew infants. The God-fearing midwives disobey the order, so Pharaoh decrees that all newborn Hebrew boys be thrown into the Nile.

*How does fear  when left unchecked—often lead to sin and poor decision-making?*

## EXODUS 2

Jochebed, a Hebrew woman, births a baby boy and hides him, eventually placing him in a basket in the Nile. Pharaoh's daughter discovers the baby, takes him in as her own son, and names him Moses. When he's grown, Moses kills an Egyptian for beating a Hebrew. Then he flees to Midian, where he marries Zipporah.

*In what ways do you already see God's providence at work in Moses' life?*

## EXODUS 3

Moses encounters God in a burning bush on Mount Horeb. God reveals Himself as the God of Abraham, Isaac, and Jacob, and He says His name is I AM THAT I AM. He commissions Moses to deliver the Israelites from Egypt, but Moses isn't convinced he's the right person for the job. God assures him of His presence and promises to be with him every step of the way.

*God uses broken people, and Moses is no exception.*
*Why should this encourage you?*

## EXODUS 4

God equips Moses for his appointed mission despite his doubts. God demonstrates His power to Moses through signs: turning his staff into a snake and making his hand leprous, then immediately healing him. Reluctantly, Moses accepts the task of leading Israel out of Egypt. Excuses, after all, are an insult to the God who has called him.

*Have you ever had doubts about your God-given role?*
*What do you do with such doubts?*

## Take Your Time and Learn More

- Moses' birth: HEBREWS 11:23–27
- Moses kills an Egyptian: ACTS 7:23–29
- Moses' faith: HEBREWS 11:24–29
- Reluctant public speaker: JEREMIAH 1:4–10

*Good things come to those who wait—on the Lord, that is.*

## EXODUS 5

Moses and his God-appointed spokesman—his brother, Aaron—go to Pharaoh to demand the Israelites be allowed to worship in the wilderness. Pharaoh reacts by increasing the people's workload, causing them to complain to Moses. Moses appeals to God for help, but the situation actually worsens.

*Have oppositions or setbacks ever made it difficult for you to obey God with confidence?*

## EXODUS 6

God reassures Moses of His faithfulness, promising to deliver the Israelites from slavery. Despite Moses' initial doubts, God reaffirms His covenant with Abraham, Isaac, and Jacob. Moses and Aaron relay God's message to the people, but the Israelites' spirits remain crushed by bondage, making it difficult to believe freedom is possible.

*What can you do now to prepare for times when life feels too hard to be hopeful?*

## EXODUS 7

Moses and Aaron confront Pharaoh. First, they turn Aaron's staff into a snake, but Pharaoh's heart remains hard when his sorcerers are able to mimic the miracle. (God's enemies love to counterfeit His work, but they cannot stand in His way.) Next, Moses and Aaron turn the water in the Nile to blood. Pharaoh is still unfazed.

*God's patience is on display in this chapter. How have you witnessed His patience firsthand?*

## EXODUS 8

God sends plagues of frogs and gnats to Egypt as signs of His power. In response, Pharaoh promises to let the Israelites go—but then his heart is hardened and he reneges. Swarms of flies bring destruction and disease, but Pharaoh remains defiant. Still, God is patient with Pharaoh, just as He is with sinners.

*How can you discern between genuine repentance and brief compliance—in yourself and others?*

## *Take Your Time and Learn More*

- Oppressed Israelites in Egypt: ACTS 7:17–19
- Events leading up to the Exodus: ACTS 7:34–36
- Miraculous signs and wonders in Egypt: PSALM 78:43–51
- Future judgments and plagues: REVELATION 16

*The Bible is countercultural, and so is Bible study.*
*There's no need to rush through this.*

## EXODUS 9

God sends a plague of livestock disease, followed by boils and then hail and fire upon Egypt. All of these plagues confirm God's supremacy over creation. But despite these displays of power—plus ongoing, clear warnings by God through Moses and Aaron—Pharaoh persists in disobedience, prolonging the suffering of everyone under his leadership.

*How did the plagues serve as both acts of judgment and opportunities for repentance?*

## EXODUS 10

God sends locusts (the eighth plague), which devastate crops and bring economic ruin to Egypt. So Pharaoh summons Moses and Aaron. But despite his temporary concessions, he ultimately refuses to release the Israelites. Pharaoh's defiance is intensifying as the consequences grow harsher, demonstrating the human heart's fierce rebellion against God's authority.

*How does sincerely acknowledging God's authority cultivate humility?*

## EXODUS 11

God communicates the tenth and final plague: the death of every firstborn. The Lord warns, "There shall be a great cry throughout all the land of Egypt, such as there has not been before, nor shall there be anything like it again" (11:6). God tells Moses to prepare the Israelites to leave, and He hardens Pharaoh's heart.

*Do you believe God is as sovereign today as He was in ancient Egypt? Why or why not?*

## EXODUS 12

God institutes the Passover, which will mark Israel's liberation from Egypt 430 years after they arrived. God commands the Israelites to sacrifice a lamb, spread its blood on the doorposts, and eat a very specific meal. This event will become central to Judaism and will foreshadow Christ's sacrifice. The tenth plague strikes at midnight, and two to three million Israelites flee Egypt.

*How does the Passover represent both justice and mercy?*

## Take Your Time and Learn More

- God's sovereignty over natural elements: JOB 37:6–13
- God's superiority over false gods: PSALM 96:4–5
- God's righteous judgment: PSALM 9:1–4
- Jesus as the Passover Lamb: 1 CORINTHIANS 5:7–8

*God speaks in the quiet moments.*
*Approach His Word with calm expectation.*

## EXODUS 13

God instructs Moses to consecrate all the firstborn to Him as a reminder of His mighty act. Moses then recounts to the people God's instructions for observing the Feast of Unleavened Bread. It is important to God—and therefore to Moses—that the Israelites remember their deliverance from Egypt. They begin their journey toward the Promised Land.

*In what ways do you actively remember and celebrate God's deliverance in your life?*

## EXODUS 14

Pharaoh pursues Israel. Trapped between the Red Sea and the approaching Egyptian army, Moses reassures the Israelites that God will make a way. God parts the sea and the Israelites cross on dry ground. Then the sea returns on the pursuing Egyptians, who all drown. As a result, Israel fears God and trusts Moses. . .for now.

*How does God's parting of the Red Sea encourage you*
*to trust Him when you feel trapped?*

## EXODUS 15

This chapter records the song of the redeemed after the Israelites have crossed the Red Sea. Together, the Israelites praise God for delivering them from the Egyptians. Next, Miriam leads the women in praising God for His power, victory, and faithfulness: "Sing to the LORD, for He has triumphed gloriously" (15:21).

*How do you cultivate a spirit of gratitude for God's answers to your prayers?*

## EXODUS 16

The Israelites grumble against Moses and Aaron, craving better food in the wilderness. So God provides manna and quail. He tells them not to hoard but to trust His daily provision. Whenever they disobey, the food spoils. God establishes Sabbath observance, providing double portions of the food beforehand.

*Have you ever moved from gratitude to grumbling in a moment? Why or why not?*

## Take Your Time and Learn More

- Declaration of devotion to God: DEUTERONOMY 4:6–9
- God's power over mighty waters: ISAIAH 43:16–19
- Song of salvation and victory: PSALM 118:14–16
- Bread of Life: JOHN 6:30–35

*Before you read, pray. Ask God to*
*speak His truth to your spirit.*

## EXODUS 17

The Israelites continue journeying through the wilderness. They quarrel with Moses over water, so God generously provides it from a rock. Later, they battle the Amalekites, whom God promises to destroy for attacking His people. (Other than a brief note in Psalms, the Amalekites disappear after 1 Chronicles.) Through every difficulty, God is faithful to His covenant promise.

*How does grumbling reveal our true attitude toward God's provision?*

## EXODUS 18

Moses' father-in-law, Jethro, comes to the wilderness for a visit. After observing Moses, Jethro advises him to delegate leadership responsibilities. Moses wisely heeds this counsel, appointing capable leaders over smaller groups. This decision eases Moses' burden and ensures more efficient justice for millions of Israelites. Jethro then returns to his home in Midian.

*How do you discern between helpful and unhelpful counsel?*

## EXODUS 19

The Israelites arrive at Mount Sinai, the mountain of God. Nobody but Moses is allowed to climb it. God instructs Moses to prepare the people for His presence. Then He hands down laws and promises to make them a kingdom of priests and a holy nation if they obey. The people agree to do as God says.

*How would an understanding of God's holiness change the*
*way you approach Him in prayer and worship?*

## EXODUS 20

God gives the Ten Commandments to Moses on Mount Sinai. The first four are about vertical relationship—expressing the way God's people should honor Him. The last six are about horizontal relationship—expressing the way God's people should honor others. All ten commandments will shape Israel's identity.

*How was it gracious of God to give the Ten Commandments to His people?*

## Take Your Time and Learn More

- Call to worship and obey God: PSALM 95:6–7
- The importance of wise counsel: PROVERBS 15:22
- The chosen people, the royal priesthood: 1 PETER 2:9–10
- The greatest commandments: MATTHEW 22:34–40

*Don't hurry, don't worry. God's Word provides
everything you need for living well.*

## EXODUS 21

Moses continues outlining God's laws and expectations for His people. He gives specific instructions regarding Hebrew servants, individuals' rights, penalties for various offenses, and restitution for injuries. The laws emphasize justice and fairness in social interactions, providing an important framework for order and accountability within the community.

*Many of God's laws in Exodus protect the vulnerable.
What does this say about God's heart?*

## EXODUS 22

Moses continues communicating God's laws. These laws emphasize honesty, compassion, and fairness and cover such topics as property damage, theft, restitution, justice, lending practices, and reverence for God's authority. And as always, they show careful attention to the most vulnerable.

*God gave Israel 613 laws. How does this prove His concern for every aspect of our lives?*

## EXODUS 23

Moses continues communicating God's instructions. He ordains three feasts—Unleavened Bread, Harvest, and Ingathering—that are all intended to remind Israel of God's provision. And all of His instructions protect His people from Satan's subtle deception and division. God promises to bless His people for their obedience and lead them safely to the Promised Land.

*How can you regularly and intentionally honor God's protection and provision?*

## EXODUS 24

After the Israelites promise to do what God commands, Moses and the elders ascend Mount Sinai at God's invitation. They witness His glory "like devouring fire on the top of the mountain" (24:17). God then invites Moses to ascend the mountain for forty days and forty nights. He leaves Aaron and Hur in charge.

*Does picturing God's glory as a consuming fire alter
your views about His power and holiness?*

## Take Your Time and Learn More

- Retaliation: MATTHEW 5:38–39
- Restitution: LUKE 19:8
- What God requires of His people: MICAH 6:8
- The covenant's significance: HEBREWS 9:18–22

*God loves it when you read and study His Word.*

## EXODUS 25

God gives Moses specific instructions for building the tabernacle (the sacred dwelling place for God among His people) as well as the ark of the covenant, the table of the Presence, and the golden lampstand. God wants the Israelites to use the items they plundered from the Egyptians (Exodus 12:35–36) to create these sacred objects.

*How does it reflect God's heart that He planned a place to dwell among His people?*

## EXODUS 26

God continues giving careful instructions for building the tabernacle. The tabernacle's design reflects His desire for order, which emphasizes the reverence and care required to commune with Him. The tabernacle is a continuation of God's plan to restore fellowship broken by sin.

*How does the tabernacle resemble today's church? How does it differ?*

## EXODUS 27

God communicates instructions for the bronze altar, the court of the tabernacle, and the oil for the lamp. The altar, made of acacia wood overlaid with bronze, is where sacrifices will be offered. The court, enclosed by curtains, will serve as a sacred space for worship and communion with God.

*God is concerned with the smallest details.*
*How does this reflect His interest in your life?*

## EXODUS 28

God details the garments for Aaron and his sons, the priests. These intricately designed garments symbolize their "set-apartness" for service in the tabernacle. Even the bells on the hems of their robes serve an important purpose. Each piece is carefully described with specific materials and adornments, emphasizing the dignity of their role before God and Israel.

*God is determined to dwell among His people. How is this His greatest gift?*

## Take Your Time and Learn More

- Jesus as High Priest: HEBREWS 8:1–6
- Believers' access to God: HEBREWS 10:19–22
- God in the details of our lives: LUKE 12:4–7
- Qualifications and role of the high priest: HEBREWS 5:1–4

*Reading the Bible isn't a race. Let the pages unfold at a pace that allows your spirit to breathe.*

## EXODUS 29

God gives instructions for consecrating the priests and the altar. He details His expectations for sacrifices (including the sin offering, burnt offering, and grain offering), for anointing the priests with oil, and for preparing the priests' clothing. Aaron and his sons will be consecrated, symbolizing their dedication to God and their important role as mediators.

*Why would it have been both humbling and frightening to be selected as priests in the tabernacle?*

## EXODUS 30

God gives instructions for building the altar of incense and the bronze "laver" (basin) for washing. (Note: being washed will be an important theme throughout scripture.) God specifies the ingredients for the anointing oil and the incense, emphasizing their sacredness. He also institutes a type of atonement tax to be gathered during each census.

*What does God's chosen term "mercy seat" (30:6) reveal about His character?*

## EXODUS 31

God tells Moses He has appointed Bezalel and Aholiab to lead the craftsmanship of the tabernacle. He emphasizes the importance of the Sabbath, declaring it a sacred sign between Himself and His people. Finally, God gives Moses two tablets inscribed by His own finger.

*Do you believe God has given you what you need to obey Him, as He did for Bezalel and Aholiab (31:6)? Why or why not?*

## EXODUS 32

Moses has now been on Mount Sinai for nearly six weeks, and the Israelites have grown impatient. Despite promising to obey, they demand Aaron make a god for them. So he collects their jewelry and fashions a golden calf, which the people worship. God's anger burns hot, and Moses pleads for mercy. Moses descends Mount Sinai, shatters the tablets, and confronts the people.

*What is the link between impatience and unbelief?*

## Take Your Time and Learn More

- Mediation and access to God: HEBREWS 10:19–22
- Incense before God: PSALM 141:2
- Importance of the Sabbath: ISAIAH 58:13–14
- Golden calf: DEUTERONOMY 9:7–21

*The greatest truths in scripture are often*
*revealed in the unhurried moments.*

## EXODUS 33

Because of the Israelites' sin, God tells Moses that He is withdrawing His presence from them. Moses intercedes, and God graciously agrees to continue accompanying the people to the Promised Land. Moses then asks to see God's glory, and God reveals a part of His goodness. But He mercifully shields Moses from His full glory.

*What does Moses' insistence that God accompany them*
*reveal about his understanding of God?*

## EXODUS 34

God tells Moses to return to Mount Sinai for new tablets of the Ten Commandments. God reveals His character as "merciful and gracious, longsuffering" (34:6). Moses' face shines after meeting with God, so he'll have to wear a veil to avoid frightening the people. God establishes laws about worship, the Sabbath, and the feasts.

*How have you seen God as "merciful and gracious, longsuffering" in your life?*

## EXODUS 35

Moses assembles the Israelites and communicates God's instructions to them. He describes the Sabbath regulations and contributions for the tabernacle construction. He tells those "of a willing heart" (35:5) to gather materials and skilled workers. So the people voluntarily—perhaps enthusiastically—offer gold, silver, fabrics, and expertise for God's work.

*How do you think the golden calf incident influenced the Israelites' eagerness to work?*

## EXODUS 36

"The people are bringing much more than enough for the service of the work" (36:5). The Israelites follow God's instructions, building the sanctuary and its furnishings with precision and excellence. Their willingness to contribute demonstrates their commitment to honor God's presence among them. No doubt they understand they had almost lost that presence.

*How can you use your talents to eagerly contribute to God's work today?*

## Take Your Time and Learn More

- Desire for God's presence: PSALM 27:7–9
- Covenant renewal: DEUTERONOMY 10:12–13
- Generous support of the tabernacle: 1 CHRONICLES 29:9
- Cheerful giving: 2 CORINTHIANS 9:6–7

*Bible study is truly a lifelong journey.
Relax and enjoy the trip.*

## EXODUS 37

Redundantly—but not without purpose—the specific details for creating the ark of the covenant, the mercy seat, the table of showbread, the golden lampstand, and the anointing oil are listed. We see firsthand that the Israelites who rebelled against God five chapters ago are now following God's instructions meticulously. For good or bad, hearts change quickly.

*What role should attention to detail and excellence play in worship and service to God?*

## EXODUS 38

Construction continues: the altar of burnt offering, the laver of bronze, the court, and the gate of the court are built as God instructed. Every detail of the tabernacle—its furnishings and rituals—foreshadows a new covenant and a high priest who will come and make every broken thing right (Hebrews 9:1-10:18).

*Sacrifices teach continual surrender. How do you incorporate surrender into your worship?*

## EXODUS 39

Aaron's priestly garments are made according to God's instructions, and "all the work of the tabernacle. . .was finished" (39:32). So the Israelites (very possibly holding their breath) present the pieces to Moses. Mirroring God's work in creation, Moses sees all that was made and blesses it as good. Now it must be assembled.

*How does the Israelite tabernacle bring humanity a step closer to restoring what was broken in Eden?*

## EXODUS 40

It's been a year since Israel left Egypt. Now the tabernacle is assembled. Moses anoints it with oil and consecrates Aaron and his sons as priests. God's glory fills the tabernacle, where He will dwell among His people. Resting over it is the cloud of the Lord by day and His fire by night.

*The God of the tabernacle lovingly leads you today. How does that deepen your understanding of Him?*

## Take Your Time and Learn More

- Construction of a temple: 1 KINGS 6
- The bronze altar and articles for worship: 2 CHRONICLES 4
- Meticulous craftsmanship: 1 CHRONICLES 22:14–16
- The glory of the Lord fills the temple: 1 KINGS 8:10–11

# LEVITICUS

*God creates a way for sinful people to live in His presence.*

## SETTING THE STAGE

The third book, Leviticus, is a handbook for how to approach a holy God. Not because God is a tyrannical dictator but because He desires to make a way for sinful humans to live in His perfect presence.

At any point since Genesis 3, God could have scrapped the entire human race because of sin. But in addition to being holy and just, God is also kind and compassionate.

For the Israelites, God's chosen people, to be able to come into His Holy presence, sin must be addressed and atoned for through an intricate system of sacrifices and rituals outlined in the law.

Leviticus emphasizes the seriousness of sin and the need for purification. The book's meticulous list of sacrifices and rituals is not just a system of tedious protocols; it's a profound recognition that sin creates a barrier between a holy God and unholy people. The sacrificial system is a tangible way for the Israelites to acknowledge their sin, seek forgiveness, and restore their relationship with God.

At first glance, Leviticus might seem to be a complex rulebook; in reality, it's a symphony of God's grace and justice—an invitation for humanity to live in harmony with God. For the Israelites (and for us), Leviticus is a reminder that despite sin's inescapable consequences, God has provided a way for restoration.

What an example of His mercy!

## GOOD TO KNOW

Author not stated but traditionally attributed to Moses. Written approximately the mid-1400s BC.

*Try to forget the demands of life for a while.*
*You're spending quality time with God.*

## LEVITICUS 1

Moses outlines the regulations for burnt offerings, an important aspect of Israelite worship. The offering (taken from cattle, sheep, or goats) represents a voluntary act of devotion and atonement for sin. The animal has to be without blemish, symbolizing purity and sincerity in worship. The animal is to be slaughtered, its blood sprinkled around the altar.

*Why is it helpful to see how God required His chosen people to approach Him?*

## LEVITICUS 2

Moses details the regulations for grain offerings (fine flour, unleavened cakes, or roasted grain), which symbolize thanksgiving and dedication to God. The offerings are to be seasoned with salt, signifying the covenant relationship. Oil and frankincense are also added, representing God's presence and acceptance. A portion is burned, while the rest belongs to the priests.

*What does the detailed nature of these instructions reveal about God's character?*

## LEVITICUS 3

Moses lists regulations for peace offerings, symbolizing fellowship with and gratitude to God. These offerings can be from unblemished cattle, sheep, or goats. The offering is to be slaughtered, its blood sprinkled around the altar. The fat portions and kidneys are burned on the altar, while the breast and right thigh are given to the priests.

*Why is it significant that two of the five offerings*
*are intended to show gratitude to God?*

## LEVITICUS 4

Moses addresses offerings for unintentional sins. If the anointed priest or the entire community sins, a young bull must be offered. Leaders must offer a male goat, while individuals must sacrifice a female goat or lamb. If one is unable to offer a goat or lamb, two turtledoves or pigeons can be given. If those are unattainable, a grain offering is acceptable.

*Why must all individuals—regardless of status—atone for their sins?*

## Take Your Time and Learn More

- Living sacrifices: ROMANS 12:1–2
- Sacrifices of praise: HEBREWS 13:15–16
- Peace offering: EPHESIANS 2:13–14
- Atonement: HEBREWS 9:22

*Good things come to those who wait—on the Lord, that is.*

## LEVITICUS 5

Moses clarifies various sins (failure to testify, unintentional impurity, and careless vows) that require a sin offering for atonement. The sin must be confessed and an animal must be offered. If one is unable to afford a standard animal offering, less costly alternatives will suffice.

*God makes provision for those who can't afford traditional offerings. How does this reflect His character?*

## LEVITICUS 6

Moses explains restitution for wrongs committed against others, detailing procedures for those who steal, deceive, or wrongfully acquire property. He outlines the requirements for the burnt offering, grain offering, and sin offering. He also provides instructions for the ordination of priests and the continual burning of the altar fire.

*Why should a sin against a neighbor (6:2) result in a trespass offering made to God?*

## LEVITICUS 7

Moses expands on the laws for the trespass offering and the peace offering. He outlines specific instructions for handling and consuming sacrifices, emphasizing the distinction between holy and common. He also clarifies the portions of the offerings allocated to the priests and their families. He emphasizes that the sacrifices must be promptly consumed.

*How does the provision for sacrifices demonstrate God's compassion and grace?*

## LEVITICUS 8

Moses describes the ordination ceremony for Aaron and his sons as priests—a significant event for Israel. Moses anoints the tabernacle and its vessels with oil, symbolizing consecration. Aaron and his sons undergo purification rituals, signifying their readiness for service. They are clothed in priestly garments, and the blood of sacrifices is applied to their bodies and clothing.

*Why does Israel need a mediator to represent them before God?*

## *Take Your Time and Learn More*

- Atonement for sins: 1 JOHN 1:9
- Reconciliation: MATTHEW 5:23–24
- Fellowship with God: 1 CORINTHIANS 10:16–17
- Bloodshed for forgiveness: HEBREWS 9:22

*The Bible is countercultural, and so is Bible study.*
*There's no need to rush through this.*

## LEVITICUS 9

Following God's instructions, Aaron offers the first sacrifices. These include a sin offering, a burnt offering, and a peace offering. As the tabernacle is consecrated, the glory of the Lord appears to the people, affirming His acceptance of their worship. Fire from the Lord consumes the offerings on the altar, signifying His approval.

*Why would the priests have to make offerings for themselves before making them for the people?*

## LEVITICUS 10

Moses recounts the tragic deaths of Nadab and Abihu, Aaron's sons, who offer unauthorized fire before the Lord. God responds with fire, consuming them instantly. This story illustrates both the seriousness of approaching God with reverent obedience and the consequences of disregarding God's holiness by acting presumptuously in His presence.

*Is God required to accept everything we offer Him?*

## LEVITICUS 11

Moses explains dietary laws, distinguishing between clean and unclean animals. Land animals must have a split hoof and chew the cud to be considered clean, while sea creatures require fins and scales. Winged insects are permissible if they have jointed legs. These regulations promote health and illustrate the importance of honoring God in every aspect of life.

*Why would God expect people to obey laws they do not fully understand?*

## LEVITICUS 12

Moses addresses purification rituals following childbirth, distinguishing between the birth of a son and a daughter. After giving birth, the mother is ceremonially unclean for a prescribed period. Afterward, she offers a sacrifice at the tabernacle, signifying her purification and reintegration into the community.

*What does Joseph and Mary's offering (Leviticus 12:8; Luke 2:22–24) reveal about them?*

### Take Your Time and Learn More

- Purity required for atonement: 1 PETER 1:18–19
- The temple of God: 1 CORINTHIANS 3:16–17
- Separation from the unclean: MARK 7:14–23
- Purification of Jesus: LUKE 2:21–24

*God speaks in the quiet moments.*
*Approach His Word with calm expectation.*

## LEVITICUS 13

Moses outlines laws that will prevent the spread of skin diseases—specifically leprosy. Priests diagnose skin conditions based on various symptoms (swelling, scabs, and sores) and determine whether individuals are clean or unclean. This chapter prescribes procedures for isolating infected individuals from the community and monitoring their condition.

*In what ways can leprosy in this chapter serve as a picture for sin?*

## LEVITICUS 14

Moses gives the law of the leper's cleansing. It involves two birds, cedarwood, scarlet yarn, and hyssop—symbolizing purification and renewal. The priest examines the individual outside the camp, pronounces the person clean, then performs a ceremony that signifies restoration to the community and fellowship with God.

*Since the Bible gives no record of a leper ever being healed by natural means, why are these laws given?*

## LEVITICUS 15

Moses shares the laws concerning bodily discharges, distinguishing between clean and unclean. He addresses various situations—male and female discharges, chronic conditions, and issues related to childbirth and sexual activity. He outlines purification rituals, emphasizing the importance of hygiene and purity.

*How do these laws demonstrate God's concern for the physical well-being of His people?*

## LEVITICUS 16

Moses describes the Day of Atonement, the most solemn day on the Israelite calendar. Aaron, the high priest, enters the Holy Place once per year to make atonement for the people's sins. He sacrifices a bull for his own sin and a goat for the people's sin. A second goat—the scapegoat—symbolically carries the sin away.

*How does the Day of Atonement illustrate God's justice and mercy at the same time?*

### Take Your Time and Learn More

- Jesus' compassion and authority over sickness:
  MATTHEW 8:1–4
- Cleansing and restoration: MARK 1:40–45
- Bodily discharges: MARK 5:25–34
- One sacrifice for all: HEBREWS 9:11–14

*Before you read, pray. Ask God to*
*speak His truth to your spirit.*

## LEVITICUS 17

Moses focuses on regulations regarding the proper handling of animal sacrifices and the significance of the blood. He emphasizes that all animal sacrifices must be brought to the tabernacle, prohibiting offerings outside its confines. The blood represents life, so consumption of blood is strictly forbidden.

*Why is it significant that blood was necessary to make atonement (17:11)?*

## LEVITICUS 18

Moses outlines laws prohibiting incest, adultery, and other forms of sexual immorality. He emphasizes the sanctity of marriage and the importance of maintaining purity in relationships. These laws underscore the significance of honoring God's design for sexuality instead of conforming to the evil practices of one's culture (18:24–26).

*Are you tempted to conform to cultural pressures? Why or why not?*

## LEVITICUS 19

Moses outlines several laws and principles intended to guide the Israelites in righteous living. This chapter covers reverence for parents, honesty in business dealings, care for the poor and vulnerable, fair treatment of laborers, and respect for the disabled. It also addresses idolatry, occult practices, and justice in the legal system.

*Why is "Love your neighbor as yourself" (19:18) one of the key commands?*

## LEVITICUS 20

Moses continues sharing regulations about various offenses and their corresponding penalties. He reiterates the seriousness of idolatry, witchcraft, and sexual immorality, instituting severe consequences—including death—for those who engage in them. He shares the importance of holiness and total obedience to God's commands.

*Do you think God cares as much about the way you*
*live your life as He did the Israelites?*

## Take Your Time and Learn More

- Sanctity of blood: HEBREWS 9:22
- Sexual purity: 1 CORINTHIANS 6:18–20
- Compassion in relationships: MATTHEW 22:37–40
- Penalties for sin: ROMANS 6:23

*Don't hurry, don't worry. God's Word provides
everything you need for living well.*

## LEVITICUS 21

Moses provides the guidelines for the conduct of priests, emphasizing their unique role as mediators between God and His people. Priests must maintain a higher standard of purity and avoid certain defilements, including contact with the dead. This chapter outlines requirements for physical blemishes—ensuring priests present themselves as worthy representatives of God.

*What does it mean, practically speaking,
to keep from profaning God's name (21:6)?*

## LEVITICUS 22

Moses continues detailing regulations, focusing on the priests' and sacrificial animals' purity requirements. He emphasizes the need for the priests to maintain ceremonial cleanliness and avoid defilement so that their offerings will be acceptable to God. This chapter addresses various scenarios in which individuals may be disqualified from participating in certain practices.

*How do the unblemished sacrifices point to the future sacrifice in Jesus (John 1:29)?*

## LEVITICUS 23

Moses outlines Sabbath practices and the feasts that the Israelites will observe as sacred occasions. These include Passover, the Feast of Unleavened Bread, the Feast of Firstfruits, the Feast of Weeks, the Feast of Trumpets, the Day of Atonement, and the Feast of Tabernacles. Each feast commemorates key events in Israel's history and celebrates God's faithfulness.

*How do you think special days served to strengthen Israel's appreciation for God?*

## LEVITICUS 24

Moses outlines additional laws, promises, and warnings. First, he talks about the oil for the lampstand and showbread in the tabernacle. Then he details the penalty for blasphemy and the restitution for various offenses. Moses recounts an incident in which a blasphemer curses God and is subsequently stoned to death.

*In what specific ways can you honor and respect God's name?*

### Take Your Time and Learn More

- Regulations for priestly conduct: Ezekiel 44:15–16
- Mercy over ritual observance: Matthew 12:1–8
- Appointed feasts: Colossians 2:16–17
- Consecrated bread: Matthew 12:3–4

*God loves it when you read and study His Word.*

## LEVITICUS 25

Moses explains five land laws involving the Sabbath year and the Year of Jubilee. These laws emphasize rest, restoration, and redemption. Every seventh year is to be a Sabbath year—the land is left fallow, debts are forgiven, and Hebrew slaves are released. The Year of Jubilee, occurring every fifty years, returns land to the original owner.

*The Israelites observed regular rhythms to remember God. Do you have any rhythms like this?*

## LEVITICUS 26

Moses outlines six conditions of blessing and consequence. God promises abundant blessings—rain, harvest, peace, and His presence—for the obedient. Disobedience results in various punishments—including disease, famine, defeat in battles, and exile. Moses warns the people against idolatry and disobedience while offering hope for restoration through repentance.

*What do you do when obedience to God's commands conflicts with societal expectations?*

## LEVITICUS 27

Moses addresses the value of people, animals, and property dedicated to God as vows or offerings. He outlines the regulations for redeeming these offerings if they cannot be fulfilled or are deemed unsuitable. He emphasizes the principle of consecration and the importance of fulfilling commitments to the Lord.

*What does it look like today to give your best to God?*

### Take Your Time and Learn More

- The acceptable year of the Lord: LUKE 4:18–19
- Blessings for obedience: DEUTERONOMY 28:1–14
- Consecration: ROMANS 12:1–2

# NUMBERS

*God and His promises remain faithful even when His people fail.*

## SETTING THE STAGE

After receiving the law in Leviticus and spending a year at Mount Sinai, the Israelites are finally ready to set out on their journey through the wilderness toward the Promised Land. The excitement is palpable; this is the moment they've waited for since leaving Egypt.

The opening chapter of Numbers begins with a census—the people are being numbered, revealing the vastness of God's chosen people. This is where the book gets its name.

The Levitical priesthood is established, as are laws about how the twelve tribes will be arranged in their camp. Laws from Leviticus are further developed.

And finally, it is time to go. In chapter 10, the cloud of God's presence moves from the tabernacle and begins leading the children of Israel out of Sinai into the wilderness.

Almost immediately, the Israelites are unhappy. They're hungry. They're thirsty. So they begin complaining that they want to go back to Egypt (11:5).

The God who rescued them from Pharoah's brutality is understandably angry. In response to the Israelites' sin, God delivers a difficult but merciful indictment: they will wander in the wilderness for forty years until they die, and only their children will enter the Promised Land (14:33).

Amid miracles and rebellions over the next four decades, the Israelites will experience both God's provision and His discipline, and their arduous journey will serve as a testing ground for their faith and obedience.

This wilderness narrative illustrates the complexities of human nature, the consequences of disobedience, and God's enduring commitment to His covenant people.

## GOOD TO KNOW

Author not stated but traditionally attributed to Moses. Written approximately 1400 BC.

*Reading the Bible isn't a race. Let the pages unfold*
*at a pace that allows your spirit to breathe.*

## NUMBERS 1

The book opens with the Israelites being numbered in preparation for their journey to the Promised Land. God commands Moses and Aaron to count all military-age men from each tribe (except the Levites) who will serve the tabernacle. This census ensures tribal organization.

*The phrase, "The LORD spoke to Moses" appears fifty times in Numbers.*
*What does this tell you about God's leadership of Israel?*

## NUMBERS 2

Each tribe is assigned a specific location and standard under which to camp, forming a structured and organized layout around the tabernacle. The chapter details the positioning of the tribes according to their ancestral relationships. This arrangement not only serves practical purposes but symbolizes the central role of worship for the Israelites.

*Why is unity so important—then and now—in carrying out God's commands?*

## NUMBERS 3

God designates the Levites, specifically the descendants of Aaron, to serve as priests and assistants in the tabernacle. This chapter lists the duties of the Levitical families—including the care and transportation of the tabernacle, its furnishings, and the preparation of sacrifices. Finally, it details the redemption of the firstborn Israelites.

*Why did God choose the tribe of Levi for the service of the tabernacle?*

## NUMBERS 4

Moses continues detailing the responsibilities of the Levites regarding the tabernacle. The chapter outlines the meticulous procedures both for transporting and caring for the furnishings and for dismantling, wrapping, and transporting the various pieces of the tabernacle during their journeys. Only the Levites are permitted to handle these holy objects.

*What does the precision of God's instructions here tell you about His view of worship?*

### Take Your Time and Learn More

- Individual contribution: EXODUS 30:11–16
- Unity and diversity: 1 CORINTHIANS 12:12–31
- Eternal priesthood: HEBREWS 7:11–24
- Duties of the Levites: 1 CHRONICLES 23:24–32

*The greatest truths in scripture are often*
*revealed in the unhurried moments.*

## NUMBERS 5

God gives Moses laws concerning purity, suspected infidelity or wrongdoing within marriage, offenses committed against others, and procedures for testing and resolving allegations. These laws emphasize justice, accountability, and integrity in the community.

*Why do you think Numbers 5:6 says sinning against people impacts one's relationship with God?*

## NUMBERS 6

The Lord gives Moses laws regarding the Nazirite vow, a voluntary act of devotion to God taken by individuals seeking special consecration for a specific period. Nazirite vow takers must not drink wine or strong drink, cut their hair, or approach corpses. Upon completing the vow, they offer sacrifices to God in gratitude.

*Why do spiritual discipline and commitment to God require personal sacrifice?*

## NUMBERS 7

Moses records the offerings brought by the "princes" (leaders) of the twelve tribes of Israel for the dedication of the tabernacle. Each prince presents identical offerings over twelve days, representing the unity and equality among the tribes in their devotion to God. At this point in history, the Israelites are wholeheartedly committed to worshipping God.

*Why is it important that all the tribes participate in setting up and giving to the tabernacle?*

## NUMBERS 8

Moses describes the consecration of the Levites for service in the tabernacle. They are commanded to cleanse themselves with water, shave, and offer sacrifices to God. The Levites are set apart to assist the priests, serving from ages twenty-five to fifty, and are given specific duties related to the tabernacle's care and transportation.

*Why might God have required that Levite service fall between the ages of twenty-five and fifty?*

## Take Your Time and Learn More

- Woman caught in adultery: JOHN 8:1–11
- Paul's vow: ACTS 21:17–26
- Joyful and sacrificial giving: 2 CORINTHIANS 8:1–5
- Ministry service: 2 TIMOTHY 2:24–26

*Bible study is truly a lifelong journey.*
*Relax and enjoy the trip.*

## NUMBERS 9

Moses writes about the Passover, which is to be celebrated on the fourteenth day of the first month. Those unable to participate at the appointed time (due to either impurity or travel) can celebrate it one month later.

*How can you ensure you are as attentive to God's guidance as the Israelites were to the movement of His cloud and fire?*

## NUMBERS 10

God instructs Moses to make two silver trumpets to summon the congregation, signal movement, and call for battle. The Israelites then leave Sinai, the cloud guiding their journey. God faithfully leads His people as they journey toward the Promised Land.

*The Israelites have matured into an organized nation since leaving Egypt. In what ways has your spiritual walk matured?*

## NUMBERS 11

The Israelites complain. The wilderness is difficult, and they miss the food they enjoyed in Egypt. Moses cries out to God, who responds by providing quail to satisfy the people's craving for meat. However, the abundance of quail leads to a plague among the people. Moses appoints seventy elders to share the burden of leadership.

*Why does discontentment ultimately reflect a lack of gratitude and trust in God's provision?*

## NUMBERS 12

Miriam and Aaron (Moses' siblings) criticize Moses for marrying a Cushite woman. God summons the three to the tabernacle, where He rebukes Miriam and Aaron and affirms Moses' unique relationship with Himself. Miriam is struck with leprosy, but Moses intercedes for her. Miriam is miraculously healed and restored seven days later.

*How do you distinguish between constructive feedback and self-righteous complaints?*

## *Take Your Time and Learn More*

- Passover Lamb: 1 CORINTHIANS 5:7–8
- Trumpet of God: 1 THESSALONIANS 4:16–17
- Israelites' experience in the wilderness: 1 CORINTHIANS 10:1–13
- Unity among God's people: GALATIANS 3:28

*Try to forget the demands of life for a while.*
*You're spending quality time with God.*

## NUMBERS 13

Moses sends twelve spies to explore Canaan. After forty days, they return with reports of the land's abundance. . .but also of its intimidating inhabitants and fortified cities. Caleb and Joshua encourage their fellow spies to trust God's promise, but the other spies refuse.

*Why do you think the spies focus more on Canaan's difficulties than its blessings?*

## NUMBERS 14

The Israelites weep, wishing they had died in Egypt. Moses intercedes, pleading for God's mercy, but God is angry and decrees that nobody from the current generation (except Caleb and Joshua) will enter the Promised Land. Instead, they will wander the wilderness for forty years—one year for each day the spies explored Canaan.

*How do you cultivate a heart that trusts God, regardless of circumstances or peer pressure?*

## NUMBERS 15

Even as the Israelites demonstrate unbelief, God graciously gives them directions for how they will act when they eventually receive the Promised Land. So Moses outlines laws regarding offerings, sacrifices, and unintentional sins. Israel needs to be reminded in this moment of their need for atonement and gratitude.

*Why is repentance so critical to the Christian life?*

## NUMBERS 16

Three Israelite men—Korah, Dathan, and Abiram—lead a rebellion against Moses. Consequently, the earth swallows them while fire kills their followers. The next day, the Israelites accuse Moses and Aaron of killing the Lord's people, so God sends a plague that is only halted when Aaron intercedes.

*What is the right response to a leader whom God has appointed?*

## *Take Your Time and Learn More*

- Caleb's faithfulness and courage: JOSHUA 14:6–14
- Rebellion of the Israelites: HEBREWS 3:7–19
- Importance of obeying God's commands: JOHN 14:15–17
- Consequences of rebellion: JUDE 11–15

*Good things come to those who wait—on the Lord, that is.*

## NUMBERS 17

In response to Korah's rebellion, God commands Moses to collect a staff from each of the tribes—including Aaron's—and place it in the tabernacle. The next day, Aaron's staff has ripened with buds, blossoms, and almonds—signifying God's choice. This miracle silences further complaints and confirms Aaron's authority.

*How does God's budding-rod miracle demonstrate His patience and compassion?*

## NUMBERS 18

This chapter elaborates on the duties and privileges of the Levites—specifically the descendants of Aaron, the priests. They are assigned to assist the priests in the tabernacle, performing various tasks related to its maintenance and offerings. God does this as an act of kindness to Aaron and his sons.

*Why is the inheritance of Aaron and his sons (18:20) the greatest inheritance of all?*

## NUMBERS 19

Moses explains the ordinance of the red heifer, a sacrifice used for purification from ceremonial uncleanness due to contact with death. A red heifer without blemish is slaughtered, its blood sprinkled before the tabernacle seven times. The entire animal is then burned. This process foreshadows Christ's ultimate sacrifice, which cleanses us from sin and death.

*Uncleanness cannot correct itself.*
*Why is this spiritual truth so important to understand?*

## NUMBERS 20

Miriam dies and is buried. The Israelites complain about lack of water in the wilderness. Moses and Aaron seek God's guidance, and He instructs them to speak to a rock to bring forth water. Moses strikes the rock in anger, and water gushes out abundantly. God rebukes Moses and Aaron for their lack of faith, declaring they will not enter the Promised Land. Aaron dies.

*Why is disobedience so deeply offensive to God?*

## Take Your Time and Learn More

- **Authority of God's Word:** HEBREWS 4:12–13
  - **Ultimate mediator:** HEBREWS 7:11–28
  - **Perfect cleansing:** HEBREWS 9:13–14
  - **Living water:** 1 CORINTHIANS 10:1–4

*The Bible is countercultural, and so is Bible study.*
*There's no need to rush through this.*

## NUMBERS 21

The Israelites continue journeying through the wilderness, meeting various enemies. They defeat the Canaanites but complain about the lack of food and water. God sends venomous serpents as punishment, and many people die. The people repent, and God instructs Moses to create a bronze serpent, offering healing to those who look at it. The Israelites conquer several cities.

*How would you define "grumbling against God's provision" today?*

## NUMBERS 22

Balak, king of the Moabites, is afraid of Israel's growing power, so he seeks the help of the false prophet Balaam to curse Israel. Balaam refuses at first, but he eventually agrees. However, an angel blocks his path, and Balaam's donkey miraculously speaks. Balaam repents.

*What do you think motivated Balaam to agree to the king's plan?*

## NUMBERS 23

Instead of cursing Israel, Balaam blesses Israel three times. Despite King Balak's frustration, Balaam explains that he is unable to change God's intentions—His blessing cannot be revoked, and Israel's future is secure. God is committed to His chosen people, so His promises are sure.

*What does this story teach about God's control even over pagan kings?*

## NUMBERS 24

Balaam continues blessing Israel despite Balak's insistence on cursing them. Inspired by God, Balaam delivers four poetic prophecies. He describes Israel as a lion and prophesies of a coming king from Israel, symbolized by a star rising out of Jacob. Balaam reaffirms his inability to speak contrary to God's command.

*Can God still work through unwilling or unlikely individuals to accomplish His plans? Why or why not?*

## Take Your Time and Learn More

- Bronze serpent: JOHN 3:14–15
- Balaam: 2 PETER 2:15–16
- Enduring fame and influence: PSALM 72:17
- Christ as star: REVELATION 22:16

*God speaks in the quiet moments.*
*Approach His Word with calm expectation.*

## NUMBERS 25

Israel begins indulging in idolatry and sexual immorality with Moabite women. God is angry and sends a deadly plague that claims the lives of twenty-four thousand Israelites. Phinehas, Aaron's grandson, zealously intervenes by executing an Israelite man and his Midianite companion. This halts the plague.

*How can you keep from gradually slipping into spiritual idolatry as the Israelites did?*

## NUMBERS 26

After the plague has killed twenty-four thousand, Moses counts the Israelites again. This census numbers all military-age men (except for the Levites, who are listed separately). God continues to prove His faithfulness by preserving His people and fulfilling His promises.

*What other reasons might God have had for the Israelites to be counted at the beginning and end of the wilderness journey?*

## NUMBERS 27

The daughters of Zelophehad appeal to Moses and the assembly for inheritance rights since their father had no sons. God affirms their right to inherit, establishing a precedent for Israelite inheritance laws. God instructs Moses to appoint Joshua as his successor who will lead the people into the Promised Land.

*How did Moses lead the Israelites by example when God announced His decision about Joshua?*

## NUMBERS 28

Moses details the regulations for daily, weekly, monthly, and annual offerings presented at the tabernacle. He specifies the required animals, grain offerings, and drink offerings for each occasion, highlighting the importance of regular worship and observance of God's appointed times.

*How do the specific instructions about these offerings reflect God's nature?*

## Take Your Time and Learn More

- Moabite women: 1 CORINTHIANS 10:8
- Census data: 1 CHRONICLES 23:2–4
- Daughters of Zelophehad: JOSHUA 17:4
- Redemption: HEBREWS 10:1

*Before you read, pray. Ask God to
speak His truth to your spirit.*

## NUMBERS 29

Moses continues sharing God's instructions for offerings and feasts. He emphasizes the importance of observing these appointed times with meticulous adherence to God's commands. Obeying these instructions is the way Israel will show their dedication to maintaining their covenant relationship with God.

*How do you make a priority of thanksgiving, dedication,
and celebration in your spiritual life?*

## NUMBERS 30

Moses addresses the law of vows made by individuals, specifically focusing on women. A woman's vow could be nullified or confirmed by her father or husband if he objected on the day he heard it. If a husband remained silent, the vow stood. A widow or divorced woman was bound by her own vows.

*How do you think these regulations may have safeguarded ancient Israelite women?*

## NUMBERS 31

Midian is judged for helping lead Israel astray and seducing them into idolatry. Led by Phinehas and Eleazar, the Israelites defeat the Midianites, killing everyone but the virgin girls and plundering the livestock and possessions. Moses concludes with instructions for purifying the soldiers and dividing the spoils of war.

*The consequence for sin in this story often bothers readers more than the sin. Why?*

## NUMBERS 32

The tribes of Reuben and Gad ask Moses for permission to settle on the east side of the Jordan River, where they found land for their livestock. Moses initially rebukes them, remembering the previous generation's repeated faithlessness. They assure Moses of their commitment, so he agrees on the condition they keep their word.

*What can happen when personal priorities override the
collective mission of a home or church?*

## Take Your Time and Learn More

- Ultimate sacrifice: HEBREWS 10:1–10
- Seriousness of promises to God: MATTHEW 5:33–37
- Battle against the Midianites: JUDGES 7
- Settlement of the Promised Land: JOSHUA 22:1–9

*Don't hurry, don't worry. God's Word provides
everything you need for living well.*

## NUMBERS 33

Moses records a summary of the Israelites' journey from Egypt to Moab, detailing each campsite along the way. He catalogs the significant locations and events during their forty years of wilderness wandering. God faithfully guides and protects His people throughout their journey despite their disobedience and grumbling.

*Can you think of a time God was faithful to you
in the face of your own disobedience?*

## NUMBERS 34

The Israelites prepare to enter the Promised Land, and Moses describes the territory they will inherit upon entering Canaan. He outlines the regions allotted to each tribe, providing a clear demarcation of their respective inheritances. By establishing these boundaries, God fulfills His promise to Abraham, Isaac, and Jacob in accordance with His covenant.

*How should God's record of keeping His promises
influence our response to doubt or fear?*

## NUMBERS 35

Moses elaborates on the cities given to the Levites, which become the six cities of refuge. When someone unintentionally causes a death, these sanctuary cities will protect that person from those who seek vengeance. Moses emphasizes the importance of justice and mercy, ensuring fair treatment for both the victim's family and the accused.

*What can you learn about God's character from His institution of the cities of refuge?*

## NUMBERS 36

Moses addresses concerns raised by the daughters of Zelophehad regarding marriage outside their tribe. To preserve tribal inheritances, God commands that women marry within their tribe to prevent land from being transferred between tribes. And with that, the book of Numbers is complete.

*Why is trusting God's timing and direction often so difficult?*

### Take Your Time and Learn More

- Israel's journey: 1 CORINTHIANS 10:1–4
- Allocation of land to the tribes: JOSHUA 14:1–5
- Cities of refuge: JOSHUA 20:1–6
- Daughters of Zelophehad: JOSHUA 17:3–6

# DEUTERONOMY

*God will keep His covenant and rescue His people.*

## SETTING THE STAGE

Deuteronomy is Moses' farewell address to the children of Israel as they prepare to enter the Promised Land. Because of Moses' disobedience and ensuing failure to uphold God's holiness before the people at Meribah-Kadesh (Numbers 20:1-13), he will not be entering with them.

In a series of passionate speeches, Moses recaps the Israelites' journey, emphasizes the importance of obeying God, and warns against idolatry.

As an old man who has seen many things and desperately wants the next generation to do better, he calls out, "Hear, O Israel: The LORD our God is one LORD. And you shall love the LORD your God with all your heart and with all your soul and with all your might" (6:4-5). Moses then passes the leadership baton to Joshua and blesses the tribes.

In chapter 32, Moses climbs Mount Nebo. From its heights, God graciously shows him the entire land that He had promised to give the descendants of Abraham.

Moses—after leading the Israelites through the wilderness, receiving the law on Mount Sinai, and interceding for the people countless times—dies on that mountain. God buries him in an undisclosed location.

The final verses of Deuteronomy record that there has never been a prophet like Moses—someone with whom God spoke face to face and who performed mighty signs and wonders before the people (34:10-12).

Moses' invitation in Deuteronomy to pursue wholehearted commitment to God remains as relevant to us today as it was to the Israelites as they prepared to step into their long-awaited inheritance.

## GOOD TO KNOW

Authorship traditionally attributed to Moses, an idea supported by Deuteronomy 31:9: "Moses wrote this law and delivered it to the priests. . .and to all the elders of Israel." Chapter 34, recording Moses' death, was probably recorded by his successor, Joshua. Written approximately 1400 BC.

# God loves it when you read and study His Word.

## DEUTERONOMY 1

The Promised Land is in sight. Moses speaks to Israel, reflecting on their journey and urging them to obey God. He laments their forty years of wandering brought on by sin. . .but he recognizes that God has remained faithful. Moses urges the people to trust God as they face Canaan. Despite his own exclusion from entering the land, Moses emphasizes God's justice and mercy.

*Why is it impossible for God to turn a blind eye to sin?*

## DEUTERONOMY 2

Moses continues recounting Israel's journey, highlighting their dependence on God's provision as they defeated kings and secured provision for survival in the wilderness. Moses recalls God's gracious protection and guidance, reminding Israel of their covenant relationship. He gives various instructions for how to interact with neighboring nations.

*How do you distinguish between necessary conflicts and conflicts you should avoid?*

## DEUTERONOMY 3

Moses recounts Israel's victories. He highlights God's provision and the fulfillment of His promises to the Israelites. Moses reflects on his own inability to enter the Promised Land due to his past disobedience. However, he appoints Joshua as his successor, encouraging him and the people to fearlessly possess the land.

*How does Moses' humble acceptance of his punishment prove his unwavering faith in God?*

## DEUTERONOMY 4

Moses, having reminded Israel of their past failures against God in the wilderness, now wants to remind them to obey God in the Promised Land. He warns against idolatry and reminds the people of their covenant at Mount Sinai. He emphasizes the importance of passing down God's laws and teaching God's deeds to future generations.

*What does it mean to seek God "with all your heart" (4:29) today?*

## Take Your Time and Learn More

- Refusal to enter the Promised Land: NUMBERS 13–14
- Edomites: NUMBERS 20:14–21
- Moses' punishment: NUMBERS 27:12–14
- Ten Commandments: EXODUS 19–20

*Reading the Bible isn't a race. Let the pages unfold
at a pace that allows your spirit to breathe.*

## DEUTERONOMY 5

Moses reminds the Israelites of the Ten Commandments and their importance for covenant relationship with God. At this point, the covenant was originally made with the previous generation of Israelites, so Moses reminds the people that this is their covenant too. Obedience to God will be the foundation of their relationship with Him.

*What does it mean—then and now—to have no other gods before the Lord (5:7)?*

## DEUTERONOMY 6

Love is one of the great themes in Deuteronomy. Moses emphasizes Israel's duty to love and obey God wholeheartedly. He instructs them to diligently teach God's commandments to their children, integrating them into every aspect of daily life. He reminds them to remember their history, remaining loyal to God and avoiding all other gods.

*Why do you think Moses stressed the importance of
loving God with heart, soul, and strength?*

## DEUTERONOMY 7

Moses reminds the Israelites of their unique role as God's chosen people. He instructs them to utterly destroy the Canaanite nations—warning against marrying the Canaanites or worshiping their gods. He assures the people of God's faithfulness and promises blessings for loyalty—such as victory and prosperity. God's past faithfulness should motivate their future obedience.

*What are some reasons we so easily forget what God has done in the past?*

## DEUTERONOMY 8

Moses reminds the people of the importance of remembering God's provision and remaining faithful in times of prosperity. He reminds Israel of how God humbled and tested them in the wilderness, providing manna to teach dependence on Him. He warns against forgetting God's blessings in the Promised Land or falling into pride and disobedience.

*How can prosperity and success lead a person to forget God?*

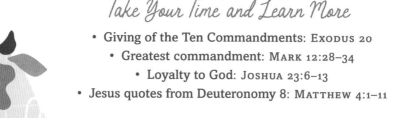

## Take Your Time and Learn More

- Giving of the Ten Commandments: Exodus 20
  - Greatest commandment: Mark 12:28–34
    - Loyalty to God: Joshua 23:6–13
- Jesus quotes from Deuteronomy 8: Matthew 4:1–11

*The greatest truths in scripture are often
revealed in the unhurried moments.*

## DEUTERONOMY 9

Moses recounts Israel's sad history of rebellion (including the golden calf incident), reminding the people of God's faithfulness despite their disobedience. He attributes their ability to enter the Promised Land not to their righteousness but to God's covenant faithfulness. God is leading Israel to do something they can only accomplish by trusting Him.

*How does remembering (not dwelling on) our mistakes help us appreciate God's grace?*

## DEUTERONOMY 10

When Moses angrily broke the first tablets of the Ten Commandments, it was a clear representation of Israel's breaking God's law. Now Moses recounts how he received new tablets afterward, and he reminds the people of the importance of fearing and obeying God wholeheartedly.

*What characteristics or behaviors exemplify devotion to God?*

## DEUTERONOMY 11

Moses commands the people to love God and heed His Word. Loving God is not an impulse or a feeling—it's a choice. Moses reminds the Israelites that blessings come from obedience. . .and consequences from disobedience. He encourages Israel to teach God's laws to future generations and to remain steadfast in their commitment to Him.

*Why would Moses keep emphasizing the need to teach God's laws to future generations?*

## DEUTERONOMY 12

Moses instructs the people about true worship, which is primarily concerned with what pleases God. So Moses commands the Israelites to destroy pagan altars and worship only at God's chosen sanctuary. He warns them against following the pagan practices of neighboring nations, and he outlines regulations for offerings and sacrifices, calling for rejoicing in God.

*How do you ensure that your worship pleases God?*

## Take Your Time and Learn More

- Golden calf: EXODUS 32
- Giving of the Ten Commandments: EXODUS 20:1–17
- Wholehearted devotion: DEUTERONOMY 6:4–9
- Instructions for sacrifices: EXODUS 20:24–26

*Bible study is truly a lifelong journey.*
*Relax and enjoy the trip.*

## DEUTERONOMY 13

Moses challenges the people to use discernment, warning against false prophets and idolatry. He tells the people not to listen to those advocating worship of other gods, even if they seem to perform miracles. He instructs Israel to remain loyal to the one true God and to reject any teaching that deviates from God's revealed truth.

*How do you discern between truth and error when listening to religious teachers?*

## DEUTERONOMY 14

Moses outlines dietary and tithing laws for Israel—designating what they should and shouldn't eat and how they should designate a portion for the Levites, widows, orphans, and sojourners. This chapter highlights the sanctity of Israel as God's chosen people, encouraging them to maintain purity and generosity.

*How does setting aside a portion for the disadvantaged reflect God's heart?*

## DEUTERONOMY 15

Moses introduces laws regarding the cancelation of debts and the release of Hebrew slaves. By God's design, Israel was always to loan money, understanding that debts would be forgiven every seven years. God consistently commands open-handed, compassionate generosity toward the poor. Israel was liberated from Egypt and now must extend similar kindness to others.

*Does God's generosity to you motivate you to show generosity to others?*

## DEUTERONOMY 16

Moses outlines regulations for three annual feasts: the Passover, the Feast of Weeks, and the Feast of Tabernacles. Israel must celebrate these feasts with joy and gratitude, reflecting on God's deliverance and provision. Moses instructs Israel to include everybody. He also tells them to appoint judges who will show justice and impartiality in legal matters.

*Why is the combination of celebration and remembrance vital in the Christian life?*

## Take Your Time and Learn More

- Warning against false prophets: 1 John 4:1–3
- Dietary laws: Leviticus 11
- Generosity and compassion: Luke 6:34–35
- Passover and Feast of Unleavened Bread: Exodus 12

*Try to forget the demands of life for a while.*
*You're spending quality time with God.*

## DEUTERONOMY 17

Moses establishes principles for Israel's governance, emphasizing justice and obedience to God's law. He mandates the execution of those found guilty of idolatry, and he outlines procedures for seeking legal judgments. He warns against excess, restricting kings from accumulating wealth or marrying many wives. A king's obligation is to diligently study and follow God's law.

*Why do you think kings specifically were warned against accumulating wealth or wives?*

## DEUTERONOMY 18

Moses says Levites and priests are to be faithfully supported by the gifts and offerings of God's people. He prohibits Israel from practicing pagan rituals, divination, and sorcery—they should instead rely solely on God's guidance. Moses predicts a future prophet's arrival and warns against false prophets in the meantime.

*How concerned should Christians be about our culture's normalization of pagan beliefs?*

## DEUTERONOMY 19

Moses outlines laws concerning the cities of refuge. He designates three cities—centrally located and with accessible roads—ensuring justice and protection for those who accidentally cause someone's death. He stresses the importance of impartial justice, condemns false witnesses, and commands thorough investigation. He reflects God's concern for justice and righteousness.

*How does the Psalms' description of God as "our refuge" parallel these cities of refuge?*

## DEUTERONOMY 20

Moses provides instructions for Israel's conduct in warfare, commanding them not to fear what other militaries fear (numbers, equipment, strategy) because God's presence will be with them. He exempts people from fighting for various reasons, and he outlines regulations for how to treat conquered people—including destroying the Canaanites for their rampant corruption.

*What does God's command to destroy the Canaanites say about His attitude toward evil?*

## Take Your Time and Learn More

- Desire for a king: 1 SAMUEL 8
- Peter quotes from Deuteronomy 18: ACTS 3:22–23
- Cities of refuge: NUMBERS 35
- Warfare and trust in God's deliverance: 2 CHRONICLES 20:1–30

*Good things come to those who wait—on the Lord, that is.*

## DEUTERONOMY 21

Moses addresses various social and legal matters in Israel. He provides guidelines for handling unsolved murders, orders Israel to treat captured women with dignity, and outlines inheritance rights for firstborn sons. He also addresses the discipline of rebellious grown children and the treatment of executed criminals.

*Do you believe justice and compassion are at odds with each other? Why or why not?*

## DEUTERONOMY 22

Moses continues sharing various social and ethical laws for Israel. He addresses matters like returning lost property, caring for livestock, and maintaining clear gender distinctions. He prohibits sexual immorality—including adultery and rape—and stipulates penalties for offenders. He emphasizes the importance of sexual purity and integrity within the community.

*What happens when a community or culture doesn't regard sin seriously?*

## DEUTERONOMY 23

Moses explains that illegitimate descendants, those with specific physical defects, and people from certain nations are forbidden in the Lord's assembly. He prohibits practices such as prostitution and charging interest to people in need. He also stresses the importance of fulfilling vows made to God.

*What are examples of vows to God today—and why are they never a small thing?*

## DEUTERONOMY 24

Moses covers a range of social and legal regulations for Israel. He addresses issues such as divorce, remarriage, and the treatment of newlywed couples. He prohibits various injustices, mandates fair treatment of workers, and emphasizes generosity. He says in closing, "You shall remember that you were a bondman in the land of Egypt" (24:22).

*Why would Israelites behave differently if they remember their history as slaves in Egypt?*

## Take Your Time and Learn More

- Treating women with dignity: LUKE 10:38–39
  - Marriage and divorce: MATTHEW 19:3–9
- Keeping oaths and vows: MATTHEW 5:33–37
  - Sanctity of marriage: MATTHEW 5:31–32

*The Bible is countercultural, and so is Bible study.*
*There's no need to rush through this.*

## DEUTERONOMY 25

Moses prescribes consequences for various offenses (while prohibiting excessive punishment) and mandates fairness in legal disputes. He commands levirate marriage, where a brother marries his deceased brother's widow to ensure her welfare and preserve the family line. He condemns dishonesty and instructs Israel to judge Amalek.

*How does preventing excessive punishment provide insight into God's character?*

## DEUTERONOMY 26

Moses explains the law of offering firstfruits and tithes to God upon entering the Promised Land. He instructs Israel to express gratitude for God's deliverance from Egypt and His provision of the Promised Land. Moses then gives them words to say in declaration of God's faithfulness to His promises. He reminds Israel to follow God's commands diligently.

*How can you establish intentional reminders of what God has done for you?*

## DEUTERONOMY 27

Moses is finished sharing commands. Now he simply encourages Israel to obey. He tells them to set up stones on Mount Ebal in the Promised Land and clearly inscribe the law on them. He instructs them to build an altar of uncut stones and offer sacrifices. He then lists curses for various sins, highlighting the severity of disobedience.

*Why do you think Moses keeps returning to the themes of obedience and disobedience?*

## DEUTERONOMY 28

Moses outlines blessings for obedience and curses for disobedience. Obedient Israelites will be blessed in every way. But if they disobey, they will experience diseases, defeat, and exile. Moses urges the people to choose life by obeying God, again warning against idolatry and disobedience. He describes in detail the consequences of turning away from God.

*What are some benefits of collective responsibility?*

## Take Your Time and Learn More

- Marriage and the resurrection: MATTHEW 22:23–33
- Tithes and offerings: MALACHI 3:8–10
- Renewal of the covenant: JOSHUA 8:30–35
- Blessings of obedience and vice versa: GALATIANS 3:10–14

*God speaks in the quiet moments.*
*Approach His Word with calm expectation.*

## DEUTERONOMY 29

Because most of the people who had made the covenant with God in Horeb died in the wilderness, Moses now reconfirms the covenant with this new generation of Israelites. Moses reminds them of God's deliverance from Egypt and His faithful provision in the wilderness. He urges them to remain faithful to God with their whole hearts.

*What accountability do you have in your life to be faithful to God?*

## DEUTERONOMY 30

Through inspiration by God, Moses knows that the Israelites will experience both blessings and curses for their obedience and disobedience in the years ahead. So he outlines their path to repentance, restoration, and faithfulness. He assures the people of God's nearness and accessibility, encouraging them to choose life by loving and obeying God with sincere hearts.

*Why must the consequences for not following God be so severe?*

## DEUTERONOMY 31

After leading Israel for forty years, Moses transfers his leadership to Joshua. Despite his impending death, Moses reassures Israel of God's presence and faithfulness. Moses commissions Joshua to lead Israel into the Promised Land, encouraging the people to remain steadfast. He then assembles the elders of the tribes to issue one final warning.

*How do Moses' memories influence the tone and content of his final appeals?*

## DEUTERONOMY 32

Moses sings a song contrasting God's faithfulness with Israel's rebellious history. The song warns of the consequences of forsaking God and emphasizes His justice and mercy. He predicts Israel's future punishment and restoration. That same day, God tells Moses it is time for him to die.

*How can you prevent yourself from becoming complacent in your relationship with God?*

### Take Your Time and Learn More

- Covenant renewal: JOSHUA 24:1–28
- Call to choose life: ROMANS 10:6–13
- Transition of leadership to Joshua: JOSHUA 1
- Warning and judgment: LUKE 19:41–44

## DEUTERONOMY 33

Moses chooses to bless the Israelites one more time. He praises God's role as their refuge and calls upon the Lord to bless and protect each tribe. Moses highlights the unique qualities and roles of each tribe and concludes his blessing with hope. His job as their leader is done.

*How does Moses' language and imagery in this chapter*
*suggest his affection for the Israelites?*

## DEUTERONOMY 34

God shows one final grace to Moses—allowing him to see the Promised Land while standing on the peak of Mount Nebo. Then, at age 120, Moses dies and God buries him. Joshua succeeds the great leader, and the book of Deuteronomy concludes by commending Moses' job as a prophet—unparalleled in his relationship with God.

*Why do you think God chose to keep the location of Moses' burial unknown?*

## Take Your Time and Learn More

- Blessings before death: GENESIS 49
- Leading the Israelites into the Promised Land: JOSHUA 1

# JOSHUA

*God is willing and able to give victory against all odds.*

## SETTING THE STAGE

The book of Joshua picks up where Deuteronomy left off, continuing the story of the Israelites' journey to the Promised Land. Now led by Joshua, Moses' successor, they cross the Jordan River. God's guidance and power is proved again by the miraculous fall of Jericho, a city with formidable walls. They face various battles and witness divine intervention ensuring their victory.

The book of Joshua also recounts the faithfulness of Rahab, a prostitute whose faith in the God of Israel (2:11) leads her to courageously hide the Israelite spies. Rahab will eventually become an ancestor to David and ultimately to Jesus, highlighting the inclusiveness of God's redemptive plan.

Near the end of the book, the Israelites take possession of the Promised Land. "Not any good thing that the LORD had spoken to the house of Israel failed; all came to pass" (21:45).

Joshua addresses the people of Israel with two final speeches similar in style and content to what Moses shared at the end of his life. He recounts God's lavish generosity throughout their long history and instructs the people to stay faithful to the one true God.

He leaves them with a choice: "Choose for yourselves this day whom you will serve, whether the gods that your fathers served who were on the other side of the flood, or the gods of the Amorites, in whose land you dwell. But as for me and my house, we will serve the LORD" (24:15).

Afterward, Joshua, the servant of the Lord, dies at age 110.

## GOOD TO KNOW

Authorship traditionally attributed to Joshua himself, except for the final five verses (24:29–33), which describe Joshua's death and legacy. Written approximately 1375 BC.

*Don't hurry, don't worry. God's Word provides everything you need for living well.*

## JOSHUA 1

God commissions Joshua to lead the Israelites into the Promised Land after Moses' death. God tells Joshua to "be strong and very courageous" (1:7)—echoed by God's people later in the chapter and throughout biblical history. Joshua instructs the Israelites to prepare to cross the Jordan River to inherit the land God promised their ancestors.

*What does it look like for you to be strong and courageous in the face of difficult tasks?*

## JOSHUA 2

Joshua sends two spies to Jericho, the first city across the border into the Promised Land, to get a good view of the city's layout. Rahab, a Canaanite prostitute, fears God and helps the spies in exchange for sparing her family when Jericho falls.

*How do the mentions of Rahab in Hebrews 11:31, James 2:25, and Matthew 1:5 challenge your concept of worthiness?*

## JOSHUA 3

The Israelites prepare to cross the Jordan River into the Promised Land. Joshua urges the people to sanctify themselves ahead of a miraculous intevention by God the next day. Led by priests carrying the ark, the Jordan River stops flowing, allowing the Israelites to cross on dry ground.

*Have you ever stepped out to obey God in faith despite your fears?*

## JOSHUA 4

After crossing the Jordan on dry ground, they obey God by setting up twelve stones of remembrance to memorialize His faithfulness and power. This ensures that future generations of Israelites will remember the miraculous event and fear the Lord their God forever.

*In what practical ways are you ensuring that future generations will remember God's significant works in your life?*

## Take Your Time and Learn More

- Joshua is commissioned to lead: DEUTERONOMY 31
- Rahab's faith: HEBREWS 11:31
- Crossing of the Red Sea: EXODUS 14
- Memorializing events: EXODUS 12

# God loves it when you read and study His Word.

## JOSHUA 5

For the first time as a nation, the Israelites enter the Promised Land. In obedience to God, the Israelite men are circumcised and all Israelites celebrate the Passover. On the first day they have access to local food, the manna stops. Joshua is then visited by the angel of God.

*Manna is evidence of God's perfect provision. How is God's perfect provision shown in your life?*

## JOSHUA 6

Israel marches around the city of Jericho for seven days, and Jericho's walls fall. Israel defeats Jericho unconventionally—without any military force—and only Rahab and her family are spared and welcomed as Israelites (6:25). Joshua clearly warns the Israelites not to plunder the city for themselves but to take only silver, gold, bronze, and iron for the treasury.

*Do you struggle to obey any of God's commands whenever they seem unconventional?*

## JOSHUA 7

Joshua sends men to fight the people of Ai, but Israel suffers a surprising defeat. God says it's because someone sinned by plundering things from Jericho. God holds the nation of Israel corporately responsible (7:1, 11). Israel learns the importance of obedience and the severity of sin. Achan is found guilty and punished by death.

*Have you ever suffered the penalty for someone else's sin? How did it impact your view of sin?*

## JOSHUA 8

After being defeated by Ai, Joshua devises a military strategy with God's help. Israel ambushes Ai, luring its army away. Ai is captured and burned, its king executed. Afterward, Joshua builds an altar on Mount Ebal, fulfilling Moses' command (Deuteronomy 27:4-8). Israel worships God, and Joshua reads aloud every word of the law given by God to Moses.

*How does Israel's defeat of Ai reflect God's heart for forgiveness and restoration?*

## Take Your Time and Learn More

- Institution of the Passover: Exodus 12
- Fall of Jericho: Hebrews 11:30
- Sin in the community: 1 Corinthians 5
- Blessings and curses: Deuteronomy 27–28

*Reading the Bible isn't a race. Let the pages unfold
at a pace that allows your spirit to breathe.*

## JOSHUA 9

Joshua is deceived into making a covenant with his enemies, the Gibeonites. After learning he was deceived, Joshua still honors his covenant, demonstrating the importance of keeping promises. Instead of killing the Gibeonites as they deserve, Joshua assigns them to labor in the service of the temple—God's enemies serve God's purposes.

*Where else in the Bible did God use evil actions to accomplish good purposes?*

## JOSHUA 10

Five Amorite kings unite to attack Gibeon for making peace with Israel. But Joshua leads a surprise attack, and God causes hailstones to kill more enemies than Israel's swords do. Joshua prays for the sun and moon to stand still, allowing Israel to achieve a decisive victory over their enemies. God gives Israel six more cities in southern Canaan.

*Have you ever asked God for something impossible,
knowing everything is possible with Him?*

## JOSHUA 11

Various kings and armies unite against Israel, but Joshua persistently obeys God, leading the Israelites to victory. (Note: the people who are destroyed in these chapters are God's enemies.) Canaan's northern region is conquered, and the land is divided among the tribes. God fulfills His promise to give Israel this land.

*Not one word of God's promise to Moses fails (11:23).
What promises of God are you trusting?*

## JOSHUA 12

This chapter recounts Israel's victories under Moses and Joshua over the kings east and west of the Jordan River. It includes a roster of the conquered kings—including those of Jericho, Ai, and the southern Canaanite cities. This list is meant to highlight God's faithfulness in fulfilling His promises of land inheritance to Israel. God always keeps His promises.

*How can you intentionally remember past victories from God in your life?*

### Take Your Time and Learn More

- Discernment: 2 CORINTHIANS 11:13–15
- Victory over forces of darkness: LUKE 10:18–20
- God's protection: PSALM 46
- Victories of the Israelites: DEUTERONOMY 2:26–37

*The greatest truths in scripture are often
revealed in the unhurried moments.*

## JOSHUA 13

Joshua is old—it's been forty-five years since he and Caleb first spied out the land. Joshua receives instructions from God to divide the remaining unconquered land among the tribes, and he obeys. (Note: Because the tribe of Levi was appointed to serve as priests, they receive no land inheritance. God is their inheritance.)

*What are some benefits of long lists of unfamiliar names?*

## JOSHUA 14

Caleb, now eighty-five, reminds Joshua of God's promise for his inheritance. He requests the land of Hebron, promised by Moses. Caleb recounts his faithfulness and willingness to conquer giants. So Joshua blesses Caleb and gives him Hebron, fulfilling God's promise. (Note: Hebron is where Abraham, Sarah, and their ancestors are buried [Genesis 23:19, 25:10].)

*What are you waiting on God for right now?*

## JOSHUA 15

This chapter details the land allotment for the tribe of Judah, including its southern borders extending to the wilderness of Zin. Caleb, from the tribe of Judah, receives Hebron as Moses promised. Caleb says whoever helps him conquer the city of Kiriath-sepher can marry his daughter. His nephew Othniel conquers it.

*God meticulously made these land allotments.
How careful is He in providing for believers today?*

## JOSHUA 16

This chapter describes the borders of the tribe of Ephraim (descendants of Joseph), which extend from the Jordan River to the Mediterranean Sea. The people struggle to fully conquer their allotted land, highlighting the ongoing tension between possessing and occupying the Promised Land.

*How are trust and obedience related?*

## Take Your Time and Learn More

- Allocation of land: JOSHUA 21
- Caleb's steadfast faith and obedience: NUMBERS 14:6–9
- Boundaries and allotments of land: JUDGES 1
- Descendants of Ephraim: 1 CHRONICLES 7:20–29

*Bible study is truly a lifelong journey.*
*Relax and enjoy the trip.*

## JOSHUA 17

This chapter details the land allotment for the tribe of Manasseh (more descendants of Joseph). This tribe complains about the size of their allotment, so Joshua instructs them to clear the forests and expand their territory. They don't seem to appreciate this answer. Also, like previous tribes, they fail to drive out the Canaanites completely, leading to ongoing conflict.

*How does discontentment hinder our ability to see and appreciate God's goodness?*

## JOSHUA 18

The entire Israelite community assembles at Shiloh to erect the tabernacle, signifying God's presence among them in the Promised Land. This important occasion marks a pivotal transition from wilderness wanderings to settled life, anchoring their identity and covenant with God. Land allotment is then detailed for the tribe of Benjamin.

*The tabernacle was located in a central region, accessible to all tribes. How significant is this?*

## JOSHUA 19

Land is allotted to the final six tribes of Israel, each receiving what God commanded through Joshua. The Israelites then give Joshua an inheritance as well, and all of these allotments reflect God's faithfulness as He fulfils His promises to each tribe. Each tribe's land will become the foundation for its identity and inheritance.

*How has God recently displayed His faithful provision in your life?*

## JOSHUA 20

After all the land is finally distributed to the tribes, God establishes several cities of refuge throughout the Promised Land. These cities are similar to safehouses, where someone who accidentally commits manslaughter can live without fear of retribution.

*How do cities of refuge reflect God's heart for redemption?*

## Take Your Time and Learn More

- Justice and fairness in distribution: NUMBERS 27:1–11
- Meticulous fulfillment of God's land promises: NUMBERS 34
- Equitable distribution: NUMBERS 26:52–56
- Cities of refuge: NUMBERS 35

*Try to forget the demands of life for a while.
You're spending quality time with God.*

## JOSHUA 21

As the priestly tribe entrusted with serving the tabernacle (something like today's church leaders), the Levites are given forty-eight cities throughout the tribes. The final verse of this chapter says, "Not any good thing that the LORD had spoken to the house of Israel failed; all came to pass" (21:45).

*Can you think of some significant promises God has kept in your life?*

## JOSHUA 22

The eastern tribes return home after helping conquer the land. Misunderstandings arise over a huge structure they build on the west side of the Jordan. The western tribes believe the structure is an altar to a false god, and they're ready to fight. Clarification is made and tensions are resolved. The incident demonstrates how quickly disunity can change things.

*How can pride get in the way of handling misunderstandings?*

## JOSHUA 23

Nearing death, Joshua gathers all of Israel's leaders. As with Moses' final message to the people, Joshua urges the leaders to be faithful to God. He warns against idolatry and disobedience (which carry inevitable consequences) and reminds the Israelites that God has given them everything they need to obey.

*Joshua tells the leaders, "Cling to the LORD your God"
(23:8). What does this look like today?*

## JOSHUA 24

Joshua gathers all the tribes and recounts God's faithfulness throughout their history. He famously says, "Choose for yourselves this day whom you will serve" (24:15). Israel chooses God. Joshua then dies at age 110. The bones of Joseph, brought up from Egypt, are buried in Shechem. Eleazar the high priest also dies. The Israelites enter a new era.

*How does remembering the past strengthen our trust in God for the future?*

### *Take Your Time and Learn More*

- Levitical cities: 1 CHRONICLES 6:54–81
- Unity and cooperation: NUMBERS 32
- Farewell addresses: DEUTERONOMY 6–11
- Responsibility to God: DEUTERONOMY 7:6–11

# JUDGES

*Humans are capable of horrific sin when they disobey God.*

## SETTING THE STAGE

Judges, the seventh book in the Bible, records a tumultuous period in Israel's history following their conquest of the Promised Land. Within its pages, we see a cycle of sin, oppression, repentance, and deliverance. . .over and over again.

After Joshua's death—and despite his warning—Israel falls into a pattern of disobeying God and worshipping idols. In response, God allows neighboring nations to oppress His people.

Judges is aptly named for the leaders God raises to deliver His people in times of crisis—among them are Deborah, Gideon, and Samson. These judges rule the tribes before the nation of Israel is ruled by kings.

After each judge's death, the cycle begins again, with Israel falling into disobedience, idol worship, and oppression.

As tempting as it may be to point a finger of judgment at God's chosen people, the question remains: Who among us *hasn't* experienced our own cycle of messing up, feeling the weight of it, begging for mercy, and discovering grace? The Israelites are simply a study in human nature.

Judges highlights the consequences of moral and spiritual failure. . .as well as the significance of repentance and mercy.

Following a string of disturbing incidents, the book of Judges concludes with these heartbreaking words: "In those days there was no king in Israel. Every man did what was right in his own eyes" (21:25).

But even in this book brimming with failure, God remains committed to saving His people—so the stage is being set for the grand fulfillment of God's covenant promises.

## GOOD TO KNOW

Author unknown; some suggest the prophet Samuel. Written approximately 1050 BC, covering events that occurred as far back as 1375 BC.

*Good things come to those who wait—on the Lord, that is.*

## JUDGES 1

After Joshua's death, the tribes of Israel inquire of God. Because they have failed to obey His covenant, pockets of Canaanites still need to be driven out of the Promised Land. God appoints Judah to lead the charge, but the Israelites continue to hedge on full obedience to God's commands.

*Are you ever content to practice only partial obedience to God's commands? Why or why not?*

## JUDGES 2

The generation after Joshua will fail to follow God for two big reasons: First, their fathers didn't appoint new leaders. Second, their fathers failed to teach them what God had done for them. So they stray, and God raises up judges to deliver them. Thus begins the cycle of disobedience, oppression, repentance, deliverance, and peace.

*How can this section of the Bible motivate you to teach the children in your life about God?*

## JUDGES 3

God leaves a handful of Canaanites in the land to test the Israelites' faithfulness. Israel fails—engaging in intermarriage with the Canaanites and worshipping Canaanite gods. So God sells the Israelites into slavery as He warned. A cycle of disobedience, consequences, and deliverance occurs over nearly one hundred years and three judges.

*Canaanite gods can't save the Israelites. What modern objects of trust are equally as worthless?*

## JUDGES 4

God raises up Deborah, a judge who honors Him and obeys His commands. She summons Barak to lead the army against Jabin's commander, Sisera. Barak hesitates, so Deborah accurately predicts that a woman will defeat Sisera. Jael is that woman, killing Sisera with a tent peg and a hammer. Israel triumphs.

*What does Deborah's successful leadership of Israel imply about God's view of women?*

## Take Your Time and Learn More

- Full and active obedience: JOHN 8:28–29
- Warning about turning from God: JOSHUA 24:1–28
- Command to destroy the Promised Land's inhabitants: DEUTERONOMY 7
- Barak's faith: HEBREWS 11:32–34

*The Bible is countercultural, and so is Bible study.
There's no need to rush through this.*

## JUDGES 5

Deborah and Barak sing a victory song, praising God for defeating Sisera's army. They recount the battle's events and honor everyone who participated. Deborah contrasts the faithfulness of Israel's allies with the choices of Meroz, a group that did not come to the aid of God's people. Israel will now experience peace for forty years.

*God seems to enjoy raising up unexpected leaders.
Why do such people bring God glory?*

## JUDGES 6

Oppressed by Midian after falling into unfaithfulness again, the Israelites call out to God. So God sends a prophet and appoints a new judge. Gideon is a fearful man—the weakest member from the weakest clan in his tribe. He's surprised God wants him to lead an army. Gideon tests God with fleeces, but the Lord is faithful.

*How is God glorified by calling a self-proclaimed weakling to do His work?*

## JUDGES 7

Gideon and thirty-two thousand men set out for battle. But then God tells Gideon the army is too big and sends most of the men home—leaving only three hundred. Using unconventional tactics and weapons (including jars, trumpets, and torches), Israel wins the battle. More than one hundred thousand Midianites die, leaving no doubt that the decisive victory belongs to God.

*God repeatedly demonstrates His patience with Gideon.
How has God done the same for you?*

## JUDGES 8

Israel's fearful fifth judge, Gideon, morphs from insecure to arrogant—making threats, killing kings, and avenging brothers. But nowhere is God included in these decisions. Gideon collects the people's gold jewelry and fashions a priestly ephod for himself—violating God's commands— and all Israel worships it. Gideon dies, and the Israelites return to idol worship.

*Why is idolatry so attractive to the human heart?*

## Take Your Time and Learn More

- Another victory song: EXODUS 15
- An invitation to lead: EXODUS 3
- Unconventional deliverance: EXODUS 14
- Golden earrings requested: EXODUS 32:1–4

*God speaks in the quiet moments.*
*Approach His Word with calm expectation.*

## JUDGES 9

Gideon is gone, so his son Abimelech kills seventy brothers (from many mothers) to become king. One brother, Jotham, escapes, warning the leaders of Shechem about the consequences of making Abimelech king. Jotham's warnings are ignored, and Abimelech rules. (Note: Abimelech killed his brothers *on* a stone and was then killed *by* a stone.)

*God's justice is on display in these messy chapters, but so is His patience. How so?*

## JUDGES 10

The Israelites fall headfirst into apostasy again, worshipping seven different groups of gods. So God sells them into the hands of the Philistines and Ammonites for eighteen years. Distressed, the Israelites cry out to God for help. He rebukes them for disobeying, but—tender to their misery (10:16)—delivers them.

*Are there any idols (things the heart treasures over God) in your life?*

## JUDGES 11

The Israelites hastily appoint Jephthah to lead them in a war against the Ammonites. Jephthah makes a rash vow to God—promising to sacrifice whatever comes out of his house first if Israel wins. Israel *does* win, and Jephthah's only child (a daughter) excitedly runs to meet him.

*Leviticus 5:4–6 provides a way out of a foolish oath.*
*Why might Jephthah have failed to pursue it?*

## JUDGES 12

The Ephraimites, always looking for a fight, are upset because Jephthah didn't call them to go to war. So they challenge him, leading to the first battle between the tribes of Israel. Jephthah's tribe of Gilead wins, largely through a creative test involving accents and pronunciation. Jephthah rules for six years before he dies.

*When interacting with someone who enjoys conflict,*
*do you engage or try to de-escalate? Why?*

### *Take Your Time and Learn More*

- Power struggle: 2 SAMUEL 2
- Idolatry: 1 SAMUEL 7
- Jephthah's faith: HEBREWS 11:32
- Civil war: 1 KINGS 12

*Before you read, pray. Ask God to*
*speak His truth to your spirit.*

## JUDGES 13

The Israelites are under Philistine subjection. An angel appears to the barren wife of Manoah to announce she will conceive a son—a Nazirite dedicated to God. Samson will be Israel's thirteenth judge and will deliver Israel from the Philistines. Samson is born and grows up.

*How has God shaped history through the rulers He's raised up?*

## JUDGES 14

Samson has little regard for the God of Israel. Infatuated with a Philistine woman, Samson wants to marry her despite his parents' objections. At the wedding feast, he poses a riddle to the guests then leaves town to keep a promise. So the bride's father gives her to one of the groomsmen to marry instead.

*Does God's choice to work through leaders like Samson indicate He endorses all their actions?*

## JUDGES 15

Samson angrily seeks revenge after his wife is given away. He captures three hundred foxes, ties torches to their tails, and releases them into the Philistines' fields, destroying their crops. In response, the Philistines burn Samson's former bride and her father. Enraged, Samson slaughters a thousand Philistines with the jawbone of a donkey.

*Does revenge bring long-term satisfaction? Why or why not?*

## JUDGES 16

Samson falls in love with another Philistine, Delilah, who is bribed to discover the secret of his strength. Samson admits that his strength lies in his uncut hair, so Delilah secretly cuts it. The Philistines capture Samson, gouge out his eyes, and imprison him. When his hair grows back, he collapses a temple during a festival, killing himself and many Philistines.

*Are you surprised Samson is included in Hebrews 11, the faith chapter (verse 32)? Why or why not?*

## Take Your Time and Learn More

- Another miraculous birth and special calling: LUKE 1:13–20
- Deception and betrayal in marriage: GENESIS 38
- Revenge: ROMANS 12:19
- Humiliation and suffering: MATTHEW 27:27–31

*Don't hurry, don't worry. God's Word provides*
*everything you need for living well.*

## JUDGES 17

A man named Micah confesses to stealing silver from his mom. Micah returns the money and his mother says she dedicates it to the Lord—but uses the silver to fashion an idol. Micah builds a private temple for the idol and hires a Levite to be his personal priest. He is confident God will prosper him as a result.

*How often do people today reduce God to a means of securing*
*success or protection? Have you ever done that?*

## JUDGES 18

The tribe of Dan needs a new place to settle, so they send scouts to find land. The scouts encounter Micah's temple. They steal everything and coerce the Levite to come serve as their priest. The tribe then burns the peaceful city of Laish to the ground, killing everyone, and renames the city "Dan."

*Why does a weakened relationship with God often lead*
*to a weakened relationship with people?*

## JUDGES 19

A Levite and his concubine are traveling and stay overnight at an old man's home in the territory of Benjamin. While there, wicked men demand the right to rape the Levite. He forces his concubine into their hands, and they abuse her until morning, when she dies on the doorstep. The Levite then chops her body into twelve pieces and sends one to each of the tribes.

*Why does abandoning God's commands often lead*
*to a breakdown in ethical behavior?*

### Take Your Time and Learn More

- Corruption of true worship: 1 KINGS 12:25–33
- Prophecy of the Danites' future: GENESIS 49:16–17
- Consequences of rampant sin: GENESIS 19

*God loves it when you read and study His Word.*

## JUDGES 20

Representatives from the eleven tribes—excluding Benjamin—gather to discuss the injustice done to the concubine. They demand the tribe of Benjamin hand over the criminals, but the order is refused. So the tribes prepare for Israel's first civil war. After three battles, the tribe of Benjamin is almost completely exterminated.

*What is the right response when loyalty conflicts with justice?*

## JUDGES 21

Israel mourns for the tribe of Benjamin, but they also vow not to give their daughters in marriage to Benjamin's men. Not wanting the tribe to completely die out, they devise a plan for Benjamin's men to abduct women from a feast to the Lord at Shiloh, reassuring the angry fathers that their daughters will save the tribe. Sadly, Israel's own worst enemy has become *Israel*.

*Why do bad decisions so easily ripple into more bad decisions?*

## Take Your Time and Learn More

- Consequences of disobedience: JOSHUA 7
- Survival insurance: DEUTERONOMY 25:5–10

# RUTH

*God is always at work behind the scenes to*
*accomplish His good purposes.*

## SETTING THE STAGE

The book of Ruth tells a short but beautiful story about a mother-in-law, Naomi, and her daughter-in-law Ruth. It weaves together themes of loyalty, providence, and the extraordinary ways God works through ordinary people.

In four chapters, Ruth invites us to reflect on one critically important question: Is God actively involved in the details of our lives. . .even the painful ones?

Through a set of difficult circumstances—including famine, loss, widowhood, relocation, and uncertainty—the book of Ruth reminds us that God is continuously unfolding His perfect redemptive plan, sometimes in the unlikeliest of ways.

In a tangible expression of this reality, the book of Ruth concludes with a genealogy, revealing Ruth to be the great-grandmother of King David, whom we'll meet soon.

Through her relation to King David, Ruth is a direct ancestor of Christ, making her a notable character in the broader story of God's redemptive plan as it unfolds through the generations leading to the birth of the Messiah.

Even as Ruth was searching for hope for her family, God was working in Ruth's life to create hope for the world.

## GOOD TO KNOW

Author not stated; some suggest Samuel. Ruth probably lived around 1100 BC.

*Reading the Bible isn't a race. Let the pages unfold at a pace that allows your spirit to breathe.*

## RUTH 1

During the time of the judges, Elimelech and his wife (Naomi) and their sons move to Moab to escape a famine. After settling, the sons do what Moses warned against—marry women who worship other gods. Over time, Elimelech and his sons die, bereaving Naomi. But she returns to Bethlehem with her daughter-in-law Ruth.

*How does Ruth's unusual choice to stay with her mother-in-law show God's grace in their lives?*

## RUTH 2

Ruth goes to work in the field of a wealthy man, relying on God's law that Israelites must not reap the perimeters of their field so the poor can gather along the edges. It happens that the landowner is a relative of Naomi. Seeing Ruth's unselfish care for her mother-in-law, Boaz leaves extra grain for her. Ruth returns home with plenty.

*What does God's law in Leviticus 19:9–10 reveal to us about His heart for people in need?*

## RUTH 3

Naomi instructs Ruth to seek Boaz's favor. And Boaz, acknowledging Ruth's virtue, promises to redeem her. But there's a problem: according to the law of Levirate marriage (Deuteronomy 25:5–10), another man has the first right to marry Ruth. Boaz promises to find an answer.

*Each detail of Ruth's story is for her good. How do you see God's faithful design in your life?*

## RUTH 4

Boaz, the kinsman-redeemer, takes Ruth as his wife, redeeming Elimelech's land and upholding Naomi's inheritance. Through their marriage, Ruth bears a son named Obed, who will become the grandfather of King David. . .and thus an ancestor of Jesus.

*Boaz was the son of Rahab (Matthew 1:5), the Canaanite prostitute who sheltered the spies. What does this tell you about God's heart for outsiders?*

## Take Your Time and Learn More

- Care for widows: DEUTERONOMY 14:29
- Gleaning: LEVITICUS 19:9–10
- Characteristics of an excellent wife: PROVERBS 31:10–31
- Ruth and Boaz in the genealogy of Christ: MATTHEW 1:1–17

# 1 SAMUEL

*God opposes the proud and exalts the humble.*

## SETTING THE STAGE

The book of 1 Samuel records a pivotal transition in Israel's history as it shifts from the era of the judges to the establishment of a king.

But first, the book begins with Hannah, a barren woman who desperately wants a child and fervently prays for one at the tabernacle. In her prayer, she vows to God that if He gives her a son, she will give him back all the days of his life (1:11).

God graciously answers her request with a son named Samuel, who will serve in the house of the Lord under the guidance of Eli the priest. In response to God's kindness, Hannah offers a prophetic prayer that fits 1 Samuel's theme: *God opposes the proud and exalts the humble.*

Israel faces many internal and external challenges. The Philistines, specifically, pose a significant and ongoing threat: in a pivotal moment, the ark of the covenant—representing God's presence, relationship, guidance, and power—is captured. This signifies the spiritual decline of Israel.

In response to the Israelites' outspoken desire for a king to lead them (8:19-20), God leads Samuel to anoint Saul, a tall, handsome man from the tribe of Benjamin (9:2).

Saul is initially successful in his military campaigns, but he later disobeys God so flagrantly that it becomes clear his dynasty will not endure.

First Samuel ends true to Hannah's prayer: proud Saul is brought low, and humble David is exalted. Now the stage is set for the reign of Israel's greatest king.

## GOOD TO KNOW

Author not stated. Samuel himself was likely involved, though some of 1 Samuel occurs after the prophet's death. Written approximately 1100-1000 BC.

*The greatest truths in scripture are often revealed in the unhurried moments.*

## 1 SAMUEL 1

We are introduced to the family of Elkanah, who has two wives—Peninnah (who has children) and Hannah (who is barren). Grieved for her childlessness, Hannah prays fervently to God at the tabernacle, vowing to dedicate her child to Him if He gives her a son. God graciously hears her prayer and gives her a baby, Samuel.

*What are some obstacles you face in maintaining a consistent, fervent prayer life?*

## 1 SAMUEL 2

Hannah's prayer of gratitude in this chapter is often compared to Mary's song (Luke 1:46-55) since they share many similarities. Both are referred to as *magnificats* because they magnify the Lord. Hannah leaves Samuel at the temple to serve God. We learn about the corrupt behavior of Eli's sons and the rebuke Eli receives as a result.

*Consider an answer to prayer (past or present)
for which you can magnify God today.*

## 1 SAMUEL 3

Samuel—likely a preteen—is serving under Eli's guidance when he hears God calling him during the night. Initially mistaking the voice for Eli's, Samuel learns to respond, "Speak, Lord, for Your servant hears" (3:9). God reveals to Samuel His plan to judge Eli's household. Then "Samuel grew, and the Lord was with him" (3:19).

*What does Samuel's call indicate about the value
and potential of children in God's eyes?*

## 1 SAMUEL 4

Israel faces a devastating defeat against the Philistines, leading to the loss of many lives. Despite the Israelites' arrogant attempts to use the ark of the covenant as a lucky charm for victory, God allows it to be taken, signaling His judgment against Israel for their disobedience and idolatry. Eli and both of his sons die.

*Why are religious symbols never a substitute for genuine faith?*

### Take Your Time and Learn More

- Miraculous birth of another forerunner: Luke 1:5–25, 57–58
- God's greatness that lifts the lowly: Psalm 113
- Calling of God: Jeremiah 1
- Lamenting Israel's defeat and humiliation: Psalm 44:9–16

*Bible study is truly a lifelong journey.*
*Relax and enjoy the trip.*

## 1 SAMUEL 5

The Philistines place the captured ark of the covenant in the temple of their god Dagon. The next morning, the statue of Dagon has fallen on its face before the ark. The morning after that, Dagon is destroyed. God afflicts the Philistines with tumors, spreading panic throughout the Philistine cities.

*God will not be anybody's trophy. How do people try to use Him for their own agendas today?*

## 1 SAMUEL 6

Seven months after taking the ark of the covenant, the Philistines decide to send it back to Israel. Along with guilt offerings as a gesture of appeasement, they send the ark over the Philistine border on a cart pulled by cows. Some of the Israelites fail to honor the sanctity of the ark, leading to the deaths of seventy men.

*What does the ark of the covenant teach you about God's holiness?*

## 1 SAMUEL 7

Samuel calls the Israelites to repent and turn back to God. They gather at Mizpah, where Samuel prays and confesses on their behalf. When the Philistines learn of this assembly, they decide to attack, but God intervenes powerfully, giving Israel a decisive victory. Samuel sets up a stone of remembrance and calls it Ebenezer. Peace returns to Israel.

*What role does repentance play in the restoration of Israel's relationship with God?*

## 1 SAMUEL 8

The elders of Israel tell Samuel they want a king to rule over them just like the other nations. Samuel is rightfully upset, but he consults God, who tells Samuel to listen to the people. Samuel warns the Israelites of the consequences of having a king, but they insist. So God will give them a king.

*Why do you think the idea of having a king was so attractive to the Israelites?*

## Take Your Time and Learn More

- God's power over all nations: EXODUS 7–12
- Holiness due to God's presence: EXODUS 19–20
- Choose whom you will serve: JOSHUA 24:14–15
  - God's instructions concerning kingship: DEUTERONOMY 17:14–20

*Try to forget the demands of life for a while.*
*You're spending quality time with God.*

## 1 SAMUEL 9

Saul is a young man from the tribe of Benjamin who is sent by his father to search for some lost donkeys. After an unsuccessful search, Saul's servant suggests seeking help from Samuel. Meanwhile, God informs Samuel that Saul is coming. . .and that he's been chosen to lead Israel.

*Saul is described as tall and handsome. Why do humans value external appearance so much?*

## 1 SAMUEL 10

Samuel privately anoints Saul as king over Israel, then gives Saul specific signs that will confirm to him that he is God's choice as king. Each sign comes to pass. Despite his initial reluctance, Saul begins to fulfill his role as king under Samuel's guidance.

*What does Israel's willingness to install a king (despite Samuel's warnings) say about their priorities?*

## 1 SAMUEL 11

Saul proves to be a good military leader, defeating the Ammonites and earning the widespread admiration of the Israelites. He humbly begins his reign as a strong and capable leader chosen by God. The Israelites make him their king in Gilgal—the place Israel camped upon entering the Promised Land.

*Can you think of a location where God has done significant things for you?*

## 1 SAMUEL 12

Samuel gives a farewell address to the Israelites, recounting God's abundant faithfulness to them from Egypt until now. He calls them to acknowledge their wrongdoing in asking for a king and warns of the consequences if they fall away. He also assures the people that God will continue to be with them if they remain faithful.

*Why is it tempting to look to human leaders to accomplish what God alone can do?*

### Take Your Time and Learn More

- Another handsome man: 1 KINGS 1:5–6
- Anointing of a king: 1 SAMUEL 16:1–13
- Humble leadership: MARK 10:44–45
- Farewell address: JOSHUA 24

# Good things come to those who wait—on the Lord, that is.

## 1 SAMUEL 13

Though Saul's reign begins promisingly, his leadership quickly deteriorates. He intrudes into the priest's office and impatiently offers a sacrifice to God. So Samuel rebukes him, declaring that Saul's kingdom will not endure due to his disobedience. The Philistine threat intensifies, and Israel's military situation worsens.

*How does impatience reveal a lack of trust in God's timing and ability?*

## 1 SAMUEL 14

Jonathan, Saul's son, initiates a daring attack against the Philistine garrison. Despite the odds, God grants Jonathan and the Israelites victory, leading to great confusion and panic among the Philistines. Saul makes a rash oath that almost leads to Jonathan's death. Saul's reign is marked by constant warfare on every side.

*How do you discern when it's appropriate to act boldly and when it's wise to wait for guidance?*

## 1 SAMUEL 15

God instructs Saul to completely destroy the Amalekites and their possessions as punishment for their past sin against Israel. Saul only partially obeys, sparing the Amalekite king, Agag, and the best of the livestock. Samuel rebukes Saul and kills Agag, and 1 Samuel 15:35 says, "The LORD regretted that He had made Saul king over Israel."

*Have you ever prioritized sacrifice over obedience to God's commands? If so, how?*

## 1 SAMUEL 16

In preparation for raising up the next king of Israel, God instructs Samuel to go to Bethlehem and anoint one of Jesse's sons. After examining each of them, Samuel anoints the youngest—an insignificant shepherd named David. Afterward, Saul struggles with an evil spirit and calls David to play music for him in his court.

*Why is it encouraging that God looks at hearts rather than outward appearances?*

## Take Your Time and Learn More

- Samuel's instruction to Saul to wait: 1 SAMUEL 10:8
- Victory with a small band of men: JUDGES 7
- God honors those who honor Him: 1 SAMUEL 2:30
- Samuel's anointing of Saul: 1 SAMUEL 10:1

*The Bible is countercultural, and so is Bible study.*
*There's no need to rush through this.*

## 1 SAMUEL 17

The famous story of David and Goliath unfolds. The giant Philistine champion challenges the Israelites, and the shepherd boy David defeats him with a sling and stone. This victory illustrates David's humble trust in the God of Israel and marks a pivotal moment in Israel's history.

*Why do many people focus on the human heroism here*
*and overlook God's power and faithfulness?*

## 1 SAMUEL 18

Saul gradually declines in every way while David steadily rises in influence and power. As David wins more and more battles, he gains attention and praise. Saul is jealous and plots against David, hoping to eliminate him as a threat. But David continues to serve faithfully. Many of his psalms are linked to this period of his life.

*Why is jealousy so harmful?*

## 1 SAMUEL 19

Saul's jealousy intensifies, and he orders his son Jonathan and all his servants to kill David. But Jonathan delights in David and warns him (19:2). David flees and stays one step ahead of Saul. Multiple times, the king sends messengers to kill David, but he always escapes.

*Three times in this chapter, David is protected from Saul.*
*How have you seen God's protection in your life?*

## 1 SAMUEL 20

Jonathan's loyalty to David is clear despite his father's opposition. This is profound because Jonathan is the heir to Saul's throne. If anyone should hate David, it should be Jonathan. The two friends devise a plan to communicate Saul's intentions, and David flees when it becomes clear the king is determined to kill him.

*What can you learn from Jonathan about being a good friend?*

## Take Your Time and Learn More

- God's deliverance through unlikely means: JUDGES 6–7
  - David's humility: 1 SAMUEL 16:6–13
  - David hunted by Saul: PSALM 59
  - Trust amid adversity: PSALM 56

*God speaks in the quiet moments.*
*Approach His Word with calm expectation.*

## 1 SAMUEL 21

David is alone, running for his life. First, he seeks refuge in a place called Nob with Ahimelech the priest. Pretending to be on a secret mission for Saul, David receives consecrated bread and Goliath's sword. David then flees to Achish, the king of Gath, where he pretends to be a madman in order to avoid harm.

*How does this chapter impact your understanding of David's psalms?*

## 1 SAMUEL 22

David flees to the cave of Adullam to escape Saul's pursuit. His family and others join him. King Saul, obsessed and paranoid, bribes his servants to be loyal to him. Then he condemns the innocent priests who helped David, killing eighty-five of them. One priest, Abiathar, escapes to join David.

*Have you ever seen power and pride destroy a person? Why does this happen?*

## 1 SAMUEL 23

David seeks God's guidance regarding the Philistine threat to the city of Keilah. Despite the risks, David leads his men to defend the city, defeating the Philistines. Saul, hearing of David's whereabouts, sets out to capture him. Learning of Saul's plans, David flees to the wilderness. Jonathan—Saul's son and David's friend—reassures David of God's protection.

*How do you make sure God is guiding your daily decisions?*

## 1 SAMUEL 24

David finds Saul in a cave. Despite his men's urging for him to kill Saul, David instead cuts off a piece of Saul's robe as evidence of his restraint. . .and then regrets this minor act against the king. David confronts Saul and calls on God to judge between them. Saul promises to stop pursuing David.

*Can you think of a time you showed mercy and*
*forgiveness to someone who wronged you?*

## Take Your Time and Learn More

- Jesus references 1 Samuel 21: MATTHEW 12:1–8
- God cares for the suffering: MATTHEW 5:3–10
- David trusts God for protection and deliverance: PSALM 31
- Showing kindness to enemies: PROVERBS 25:21–22

*Before you read, pray. Ask God to
speak His truth to your spirit.*

## 1 SAMUEL 25

Samuel dies, and Israel—who didn't seem to honor him in his life—mourns for him in his death. David encounters Nabal, a wealthy but foolish man who denies him and his men hospitality. David plans revenge, but Nabal's wife, Abigail, intervenes with wisdom and humility, averting disaster. When Nabal dies suddenly, David marries Abigail.

*Are you surprised that Samuel's death gets only one verse? Why or why not?*

## 1 SAMUEL 26

Saul pursues David, and David and his men encounter Saul's camp while he sleeps. David again refrains from causing harm. Instead, David takes Saul's spear and water jar as evidence of his opportunity to hurt the king. David confronts Saul, reiterating his innocence and loyalty. Again, Saul promises to stop pursuing him.

*How does David's respect for Saul impact your views on dealing with ungodly authority?*

## 1 SAMUEL 27

Feeling threatened by Saul, David seeks refuge among the Philistines. He settles in Gath under King Achish's protection, accompanied by his men and their families. David deceives Achish, claiming to raid Israelite territories while secretly attacking other nations instead. Achish trusts David and gives him a city in which to live.

*What were some of the risks David took in seeking refuge among the Philistines?*

## 1 SAMUEL 28

Saul, desperate for guidance before battle, asks a medium to bring up Samuel's spirit, violating God's command against communicating with the dead. Samuel rebukes Saul and foretells the imminent, fatal consequences of his rebellion against God. Saul is deeply troubled.

*Why is desperation typically a poor ingredient in decision-making?*

## Take Your Time and Learn More

- Love for enemies: MATTHEW 5:43–48
- Turning the other cheek: MATTHEW 5:38–39
- The heart displayed in actions: PROVERBS 27:19
- Seeking forbidden guidance: DEUTERONOMY 18:9–14

*Don't hurry, don't worry. God's Word provides
everything you need for living well.*

## 1 SAMUEL 29

David and his men prepare to fight alongside the Philistines against Israel. While Achish has no problem with David, the Philistine commanders distrust David's loyalty and insist that he and his men return home. David protests but ultimately complies, sparing himself from fighting against his own people.

*How was the Philistine commanders' mistrust of David actually a gift?*

## 1 SAMUEL 30

David and his men go back to their home among the Philistines. But when they reach their town of Ziklag, they find it's been burned down by the Amalekites, who have taken the women and children captive. Distressed, David seeks God's guidance and pursues the Amalekites, rescuing their captives and recovering their plunder.

*How does David's generosity in victory reveal his character and his faith in God?*

## 1 SAMUEL 31

The Philistines defeat Israel in battle, resulting in the deaths of Saul and his three sons—including Jonathan. The book concludes with the tragic aftermath of the battle, where the Philistines desecrate the bodies of Saul and his sons. This marks the end of Saul's reign as king, setting the stage for David's ascent to the throne.

*How do you think David grappled with both relief and sorrow after this battle?*

## Take Your Time and Learn More

- God intervenes to prevent sin: GENESIS 20
- Praise to God for deliverance: PSALM 34
- Death of Saul and his sons: 1 CHRONICLES 10

# 2 SAMUEL

*Though human leaders fail, God will send
a future King to rule perfectly.*

## SETTING THE STAGE

The book of 2 Samuel tells the story of King David's reign. Building on the events of 1 Samuel, this book chronicles David's ascent to the throne, his triumphs, his challenges, and the establishment of Jerusalem as the capital city.

In this book, Jerusalem becomes both the political and religious center of the kingdom—made most evident when the ark of the covenant is triumphantly returned to the city.

Though David is largely successful as king, he is also plagued by deep personal and moral errors. Most notably, he fails Bathsheba and Uriah when he destroys their marriage covenant and takes the man's life. The prophet Nathan confronts David, leading to his repentance and God's forgiveness—though the consequences of his actions are severe.

The last half of the book documents David's struggles within his own family—conspiracy, deception, rape, revolt, and the untimely deaths of three of his children (12:18; 13:32; 18:14).

Second Samuel concludes with David's song of thanksgiving, which expresses gratitude for God's faithfulness and reflects on David's journey from shepherd to king.

David's imperfections point to the hope of God's promise to send a future king who will rule the world perfectly. . .and eternally.

## GOOD TO KNOW

Author unknown but not Samuel—since the events of the book take place after his death. Some suggest Abiathar the priest (15:35). Written approximately 1010–970 BC, the reign of King David.

## God loves it when you read and study His Word.

### 2 SAMUEL 1

An Amalekite arrives at David's camp claiming to have killed Saul in battle. He presents Saul's crown and armlet, likely expecting a reward. Instead, David executes the Amalekite for presuming to kill God's anointed. He then grieves Saul and Jonathan's deaths, lamenting Israel's loss: "How the mighty have fallen!" (1:19).

*How does David's reaction to the news of Saul's death demonstrate his character?*

### 2 SAMUEL 2

David is anointed king over the tribe of Judah while Ish-bosheth, Saul's son, reigns over the rest of Israel. Abner, Saul's commander, supports Ish-bosheth's rule. A conflict ensues, resulting in a battle at Gibeon. Abner's forces defeat those of David's commander, but the casualties are heavy on both sides—illustrating the fragmentation of Israel after Saul's death.

*How do you discern God's direction when faced with uncertainty or multiple options?*

### 2 SAMUEL 3

Conflict between the houses of Saul and David escalates. Abner, once Saul's commander, defects to David's side and negotiates to unite all Israel under David's kingship. However, Joab, David's commander, resents Abner's killing of his brother in battle. Joab murders Abner to avenge his brother's death. David mourns Abner and declares his innocence in the killing.

*How does pursuing justice differ from seeking revenge?*

### 2 SAMUEL 4

Ish-bosheth, Saul's son and the king of Israel, is assassinated by two of his own commanders. They bring his head to David, likely expecting a reward, but David condemns their actions and executes them. He does not want to benefit from political murders. This chapter marks the end of Saul's dynasty.

*How did the assassins underestimate David's loyalty to God and to the house of Saul?*

## Take Your Time and Learn More

- **Death of Saul and his sons:** 1 SAMUEL 31
- **David rises as king:** 1 CHRONICLES 11–12
- **David's descendants:** 1 CHRONICLES 3
- **Saul's descendants:** 1 CHRONICLES 8

*Reading the Bible isn't a race. Let the pages unfold*
*at a pace that allows your spirit to breathe.*

## 2 SAMUEL 5

All the tribes of Israel unite under David, who is anointed king. He will reign for forty years. David captures the stronghold of Jerusalem, making it his capital and naming it "the city of David." He builds up the city and expands his influence, supported by God's guidance and blessings. The Philistines attack, but David defeats them with God's help.

*Why is waiting on God's timing so difficult?*

## 2 SAMUEL 6

David attempts to bring the ark of the covenant to Jerusalem. During the journey, a man named Uzzah touches the ark to steady it, and God strikes him dead. Fearing God's wrath, David temporarily stops the procession, leaving the ark in the house of Obed-edom. David later resumes the journey, this time following God's instructions for transporting the ark.

*What does the story of Uzzah teach us about God's holiness versus our good intentions?*

## 2 SAMUEL 7

David wants to build a temple to honor God, but the Lord responds—through the prophet Nathan—that David will not be the one to build it. Instead, a descendant of the king will. God then makes a covenant with David, promising him a descendant who will establish an everlasting kingdom. David responds with humility and gratitude.

*Have you ever shared David's desire to do something special for God? How did it turn out?*

## 2 SAMUEL 8

David continues expanding his kingdom through military conquests, establishing Israel's dominance in the region. He also strengthens his administration, appointing officials to govern various aspects of the kingdom. Through David, God is establishing Israel as a powerful and prosperous nation.

*David's victories came from God's power (8:14).*
*How much of your success do you attribute to God?*

### Take Your Time and Learn More

- David captures Jerusalem: 1 CHRONICLES 11:4–9
- David brings the ark of the covenant to Jerusalem: 1 CHRONICLES 13–16
- God's covenant with David: PSALM 89
- David's victories: 1 CHRONICLES 18

*The greatest truths in scripture are often revealed in the unhurried moments.*

## 2 SAMUEL 9

David seeks to show kindness to anyone remaining from Saul's household. He discovers Mephibosheth, Jonathan's disabled son, and welcomes him to live in Jerusalem. David also grants him land and invites him to dine regularly at the king's table. This act of grace demonstrates David's commitment to honor his friendship and covenant with Jonathan.

*How does David's kindness to Mephibosheth illustrate God's care for the weak and fatherless?*

## 2 SAMUEL 10

David sends messengers to offer condolences to Hanun—the new king of the Ammonites—upon his father's death. Suspecting David's messengers of espionage, Hanun humiliates them, leading to conflict. The Ammonites join the Syrians in preparation for battle against Israel. Despite initial setbacks, Israel emerges victorious.

*How can we "seek peace and pursue it" (Psalm 34:14) while handling misunderstandings?*

## 2 SAMUEL 11

David commits a terrible sin against God and against Bathsheba, the wife of Uriah the Hittite (one of David's loyal soldiers). Bathsheba becomes pregnant, prompting David to scheme to cover up his adultery by bringing Uriah back from the battlefield to sleep with his wife. When Uriah refuses to go home, David orchestrates the man's death in battle.

*What role do rationalization, deception, and self-justification play in sin?*

## 2 SAMUEL 12

Nathan the prophet confronts David about his sin by telling him a parable of a rich man who stole a poor man's beloved lamb. This prompts David's indignation, and Nathan famously responds, "You are the man!" (12:7). David immediately and sincerely repents. God forgives him. . .but also pronounces heavy consequences.

*What does David's prayer of repentance in Psalm 51 tell you about the way he viewed this sin?*

## *Take Your Time and Learn More*

- Grace, forgiveness, and restoration: LUKE 15:11–32
  - David and the Ammonites: 1 CHRONICLES 19
- David's sin against God and Bathsheba: PSALM 51
  - Repentance and God's mercy: PSALM 32

*Bible study is truly a lifelong journey.*
*Relax and enjoy the trip.*

## 2 SAMUEL 13

As another devastating consequence of David's sin, Amnon—David's son—lusts after his half sister Tamar and devises a plan to rape her. Despite her pleas, Amnon assaults Tamar, then rejects her. Tamar's full brother Absalom, consumed by anger, orchestrates Amnon's murder. David grieves deeply over Amnon's death while Absalom flees to escape punishment.

*Amnon had received evil counsel. How do you decide whose advice to take?*

## 2 SAMUEL 14

Joab, David's commander, hatches a plan to reconcile David with his estranged son Absalom. He hires a wise woman to act out a story, appealing to David's sense of justice and mercy. David agrees to pardon Absalom, who is allowed to return to Jerusalem. . .but not to see David. Absalom's return signals a tentative reconciliation, but tensions continue.

*Why does culture idolize physical appearance (14:25)? How much does this affect you?*

## 2 SAMUEL 15

Absalom sneakily undermines his father's reign by winning the hearts of the Israelites. Once he is confident of his popularity, he conspires to overthrow David, garnering support for his rebellion. David, aware of Absalom's plot, flees Jerusalem with his household, showing his humility and trust in God's sovereignty.

*Why is unchecked ambition dangerous in the life of any leader?*

## 2 SAMUEL 16

As David flees Jerusalem, a Benjamite named Shimei curses and throws stones at him, blaming him for Saul's downfall. David restrains his men from retaliating. Meanwhile, Absalom enters Jerusalem. Hushai, David's loyal counselor, fakes allegiance to Absalom to undermine his counsel. Absalom publicly sleeps with David's concubines to assert his authority.

*How does mistreatment actually present you with opportunities to glorify God?*

## Take Your Time and Learn More

- Violence and revenge for rape: GENESIS 34
- Forgiveness and restoration: MATTHEW 18:21–35
- Betrayal by someone close: PSALM 41
- Suffering and persecution: MATTHEW 26:67–68

*Try to forget the demands of life for a while.*
*You're spending quality time with God.*

## 2 SAMUEL 17

Absalom's rebellion escalates as Ahithophel (one of David's advisers) encourages Absalom to pursue and defeat David immediately. Hushai—loyal to David—suggests a delay, and Absalom listens, providing David an opportunity to escape. David and his followers cross the Jordan River, avoiding Absalom's pursuit.

*How do you decide when to follow or reject someone's counsel?*

## 2 SAMUEL 18

David's forces engage in battle against Absalom's army. Despite David's instructions to deal gently with Absalom, Joab kills him in the forest of Ephraim. Absalom's death signals the end of his rebellion, bringing David a bittersweet victory. News of Absalom's death devastates David, who grieves the loss of his son.

*How do you reconcile David's love for Absalom despite his betrayal?*

## 2 SAMUEL 19

Joab rebukes David for mourning Absalom's death, urging him to acknowledge and appreciate the loyalty of his supporters who risked their lives in battle for him. David heeds this advice and returns to Jerusalem as king.

*How can a small, trusted circle of friends and mentors help*
*you stay accountable in your obedience to God?*

## 2 SAMUEL 20

Sheba—a troublemaker from the tribe of Benjamin—rebels against David's rule, leading many Israelites to desert David. David orders his commander to gather troops and quell the rebellion, but his commander delays and is killed. Joab rallies David's forces, kills Sheba, and restores peace.

*Is peace ever not costly?*

### Take Your Time and Learn More

- God's counsel: PROVERBS 21:30
- Wayward children: LUKE 15:11–32
- Division within families: MATTHEW 10:34–37
- Loyalty and betrayal: MATTHEW 26:47–50

# *Good things come to those who wait—on the Lord, that is.*

## 2 SAMUEL 21

A famine strikes Israel due to Saul's earlier mistreatment of the Gibeonites. David inquires of the Gibeonites about restitution, and they demand the execution of seven of Saul's descendants. David agrees, sparing Mephibosheth but handing over the others. David buries the bones of Saul and Jonathan, as well as those of the executed descendants, in Saul's family tomb.

*What can we learn from the way David balances competing interests?*

## 2 SAMUEL 22

David offers a song of praise and thanksgiving to God for delivering him from his enemies and granting him victory. He reflects on his past trials and acknowledges God's strength, protection, and faithfulness throughout his life. David also describes God's majestic power, depicting Him as a rock, fortress, and deliverer.

*Is it truly possible to show gratitude to God in all circumstances? Why or why not?*

## 2 SAMUEL 23

David's final words are recorded, reflecting on his life and reign as king of Israel. These aren't his deathbed words, but they express his heart near the end of his life. He acknowledges God's role in his accomplishments and blessings, and he reminisces about his valiant warriors, recounting their courage and loyalty.

*Are you surprised David is called a man after God's own heart? Why or why not?*

## 2 SAMUEL 24

Against Joab's advice, David numbers the army and thus angers God. Consequently, a plague kills seventy thousand Israelites. David repents, acknowledging his sin and pleading for mercy. God instructs David to build an altar on Araunah the Jebusite's threshing floor to stop the plague.

*Can you think of any time in the Bible when David doesn't genuinely repent after sinning?*

## Take Your Time and Learn More

- Gibeonite deception: JOSHUA 9–10
- God's deliverance: PSALM 18
- Desire for a righteous ruler: PSALM 72
- David's census of Israel: 1 CHRONICLES 21

# 1 KINGS

*Though God is merciful, His justice demands
consequences for disobedience.*

## SETTING THE STAGE

First Kings details the reigns of several important kings in Israel and Judah, highlights the construction of the temple in Jerusalem, and covers the ministry of the prophets Elijah and Elisha.

The book begins with David's last days (1:1–2:11) and documents Solomon's ascension to the throne. Solomon's reign—at least early on—will be characterized by wisdom, peace, and prosperity.

One of Solomon's most notable accomplishments is the construction of the Jerusalem temple, a magnificent structure that becomes the central place of worship for the Israelites.

Following Solomon's death (11:43), his son Rehoboam assumes the throne. But the kingdom is soon divided, setting the stage for ongoing political and religious turmoil.

Throughout 1 Kings, the role of the prophets becomes more prominent. Elijah, for example, confronts Baal worship in a dramatic series of events, and his successor, Elisha, continues his ministry.

The book also details the long line of monarchs in Israel and Judah who come after David. These include King Ahab and Queen Jezebel, whose reign is marked by rebellion against God, and Jehoshaphat, who is righteous.

This collection of stories provides a brief but comprehensive view of this critical period in Israel's history.

## GOOD TO KNOW

Author not stated and unknown; one early tradition claimed Jeremiah wrote 1 and 2 Kings. Covering events from about 970 to 850 BC, 1 Kings was probably written after the Babylonian destruction of Jerusalem in 586 BC.

*The Bible is countercultural, and so is Bible study.
There's no need to rush through this.*

## 1 KINGS 1

David is ready to transition power to his son Solomon. While only in his seventies at this point, David has lived many lifetimes and seems older than his years. As he nears death, his son Adonijah attempts to seize the throne, prompting Bathsheba and the prophet Nathan to intervene. They ensure that Bathsheba's son Solomon is anointed king.

*Can you think of a situation in your life in which humility changed the outcome?*

## 1 KINGS 2

David—Israel's greatest human king—knows he will die soon, so he gives his final charge to Solomon. He urges him to obey God's commands and enact justice. He tasks Solomon with avenging past wrongs and eliminating potential threats to his rule. And then David dies "at a good old age, full of days, riches, and honor" (1 Chronicles 29:28).

*How do you prioritize obedience in your daily walk with God?*

## 1 KINGS 3

In a dream, God appears to Solomon and asks him what he desires. Solomon requests wisdom rather than long life, wealth, or power, so God grants him everything. Solomon uses his wisdom to solve the mystery of two women claiming the same baby. The new king suggests splitting the baby in two, revealing the true mother's love.

*How much do you value wisdom compared to wealth and success?*

## 1 KINGS 4

Solomon's reign is characterized by wisdom, prosperity, and organization. He appoints twelve governors to oversee Israel's regions, ensuring efficiency. His administration thrives, with ample provisions for his household and the people. Visitors flock to see his wisdom and insight, and Israel flourishes under his rule.

*Is there anything in your life you need to ask God for greater wisdom to handle?*

## Take Your Time and Learn More

- Transitioning power to Solomon: 1 CHRONICLES 22–29
- David's final charge to Solomon: 1 CHRONICLES 28–29
- Solomon's request to God: 2 CHRONICLES 1
- Solomon's wisdom: 2 CHRONICLES 9

*God speaks in the quiet moments.*
*Approach His Word with calm expectation.*

## 1 KINGS 5

Solomon prepares to build the temple. He sends a message to King Hiram of Tyre, requesting cedar and cypress trees and skilled workers for the project. Hiram agrees, and a treaty is formed between the two kingdoms. Solomon mobilizes a massive workforce consisting of tens of thousands of laborers, plus stonecutters and carpenters.

*What might God be leading you to do for Him in this season of your life?*

## 1 KINGS 6

The temple construction—Solomon's grand project—begins. The temple's particulars are meticulously detailed, including its cedar wood paneling and stone masonry. Inside is the Most Holy Place, which contains the ark of the covenant. Construction on this huge project lasts seven years, and its completion represents a milestone in Israel's history.

*How can you cultivate a spirit of perseverance in pursuing God's calling for your life?*

## 1 KINGS 7

Solomon continues his ambitious building projects, constructing his own palace and the House of the Forest of Lebanon. The palace features luxurious materials, showcasing Solomon's wealth and power. Additionally, Solomon builds a porch of pillars and the Porch of Judgment, where he administers justice.

*What would those who know you best say is your biggest priority?*

## 1 KINGS 8

Solomon dedicates the newly completed temple with a grand ceremony. He gathers Israel's leaders, priests, and people to bring the ark of the covenant into the Most Holy Place. He offers a fervent prayer that acknowledges God's faithfulness. The temple fills with God's glory, signifying His presence among His people. Solomon then urges obedience to God's commands.

*What does it mean to have a heart "perfect with the LORD" (8:61)?*

## Take Your Time and Learn More

- Solomon prepares to build the temple: 2 CHRONICLES 2
- Construction of the temple: 2 CHRONICLES 3
- The grandeur of Solomon's buildings: 2 CHRONICLES 4
- Dedication of the temple: 2 CHRONICLES 5–7

*Before you read, pray. Ask God to*
*speak His truth to your spirit.*

## 1 KINGS 9

Twenty-four years after ascending the throne, Solomon completes the temple and palace—his greatest accomplishment. God appears to him a second time, reaffirming His covenant. Solomon gives twenty cities to Hiram as compensation for the materials used in the construction. He also enslaves the remnants of the Canaanites.

*How easy is it to take the wisdom in God's Word for granted? Why?*

## 1 KINGS 10

The Queen of Sheba visits Solomon, drawn by his fame concerning the name of the Lord. Impressed by his wisdom, wealth, and splendor, she offers him gifts and praises God. Solomon answers her tough questions and shares his wisdom. The chapter describes Solomon's immense wealth—including gold, precious stones, and rare treasures.

*How can you recognize if you are beginning to drift from God's commands?*

## 1 KINGS 11

Despite God's warnings, Solomon succumbs to idolatry after marrying many foreign women who lead him astray. He builds altars to their gods, angering the true God and violating His commands. God punishes Solomon by raising adversaries against him, including Hadad, Rezon, and Jeroboam. After forty years as king, Solomon dies.

*How does Solomon's life prove that wisdom doesn't always come with age?*

## 1 KINGS 12

Following Solomon's death, his son Rehoboam becomes king. When the northern tribes request lighter burdens than those imposed by Solomon, Rehoboam ignores the elders' counsel and listens instead to peers. A rebellion led by Jeroboam divides the kingdom. Jeroboam rules the northern tribes (still known as Israel) and Rehoboam rules only Judah and Benjamin.

*How many cross-generational relationships do you have with women in your church family?*

## Take Your Time and Learn More

- God's response to Solomon's prayer dedicating the temple: 2 CHRONICLES 7
- Queen of Sheba's visit: 2 CHRONICLES 9:1–12
- Solomon's later perspective: ECCLESIASTES 1
- Rehoboam's disastrous choice: 2 CHRONICLES 10

*Don't hurry, don't worry. God's Word provides
everything you need for living well.*

## 1 KINGS 13

A prophet speaks against King Jeroboam's altar in Bethel, predicting its destruction by a coming descendant of David named Josiah. Jeroboam attempts to seize the man, but his hand withers. The man of God restores Jeroboam's hand and refuses his hospitality, obeying God's command not to eat or drink in Bethel. He is later deceived into disobeying, resulting in his death by a lion.

*Have you ever listened to the lies of this world over the Word of God? What happened?*

## 1 KINGS 14

Jeroboam's son Abijah is sick, prompting the king to send his wife in disguise to seek guidance from Ahijah the prophet. Despite this deception, the prophet reveals God's judgment upon Jeroboam's dynasty for its idolatry. Abijah dies, fulfilling the prophecy. Jeroboam's reign is marked by strife and idolatry, leading to his eventual downfall.

*What are some cultural idols you need to guard against in your own life?*

## 1 KINGS 15

In Judah, Abijam succeeds Rehoboam as king, but he continues the idolatry. Asa succeeds Abijam and brings reform to Judah, removing idols and pagan practices. Despite his father's errors, Asa's heart remains devoted to God, resulting in peace and prosperity during his reign.

*Does your heart genuinely desire to do what is right? Why or why not?*

## 1 KINGS 16

A series of kings rules over Israel. Baasha's reign is full of idol worship. Elah is assassinated by Zimri, who reigns for only seven days before committing suicide. Omri establishes the capital in Samaria. His son (Ahab) succeeds him, marries Jezebel, and introduces Baal worship. Less than a century after David's death, Ahab becomes the most wicked king in Israel.

*What might this story tell you about the modern cultural and political environment?*

### Take Your Time and Learn More

- Fulfillment of the prophecy against Jeroboam's altar: 2 KINGS 23:15–20
- Rehoboam's reign: 2 CHRONICLES 12
- Asa's reign: 2 CHRONICLES 14–16
- Political and spiritual developments during this period: 2 CHRONICLES 17–21

*God loves it when you read and study His Word.*

## 1 KINGS 17

During a time of drought and famine in Israel, God commands His prophet Elijah to hide by the brook Cherith, where ravens bring him food. When the brook dries up, God sends Elijah to a widow in Zarephath and provides for them miraculously during the famine. Elijah resurrects the widow's son, demonstrating God's power and faithfulness.

*Why do you think God often uses unlikely people to demonstrate His glory? Have you ever seen this personally?*

## 1 KINGS 18

Elijah confronts King Ahab and the prophets of Baal on Mount Carmel. He challenges them to a showdown to prove the true God. Baal's prophets fail to summon fire, but God answers Elijah's prayer with consuming fire, vindicating His supremacy. Elijah orders the prophets' execution then prays for rain to end the drought. God sends a torrential downpour.

*When was the last time you asked God to do something big?*

## 1 KINGS 19

After defeating the prophets of Baal, Elijah flees Queen Jezebel's threats. Exhausted and discouraged, he prays for death, but God provides food, water, and rest. Strengthened, Elijah travels to Horeb, where God appears in a gentle whisper—not in the wind, earthquake, or fire. God reassures Elijah that he's not alone.

*Why do people look for God's presence in extraordinary moments but miss it in quiet ones?*

## 1 KINGS 20

Ben-hadad, king of Syria, besieges Samaria. Despite his initial hesitance, Ahab, king of Israel, defeats him twice with God's help. Ben-hadad regroups. . .but again faces defeat. Seeking peace, he strikes a treaty with Ahab. A prophet rebukes Ahab for sparing Ben-hadad's life.

*Why would God work even through bad people?*

## Take Your Time and Learn More

- Elijah and the widow: LUKE 4:24–26
- Elijah's prayer: JAMES 5:17–18
- Spiritual warfare, despair, and God's sustaining presence: PSALM 42
- Siege of Samaria: 2 KINGS 6:24–7:20

*Reading the Bible isn't a race. Let the pages unfold at a pace that allows your spirit to breathe.*

## 1 KINGS 21

Naboth, a vineyard owner, refuses to sell his ancestral land to greedy King Ahab. Jezebel, Ahab's wife, arranges for Naboth to be falsely accused and subsequently executed. Ahab seizes the vineyard. God sends Elijah to confront Ahab for his wickedness, prophesying judgment on him and his household. Ahab humbles himself, and God delays the judgment

*How can you guard against greed?*

## 1 KINGS 22

King Ahab of Israel seeks the support of Judah's King Jehoshaphat in reclaiming Ramoth-gilead from Aram. Jehoshaphat suggests consulting prophets. False prophets predict victory, but a true prophet warns of defeat. Ahab disregards the true prophet, leading to his own death in battle. . .just as the real prophet foretold.

*How can you discern truth from falsehood in your daily life?*

## Take Your Time and Learn More

- Prophecy against those who covet and seize fields unjustly: MICAH 2:1–2
- Ramoth-gilead: 2 CHRONICLES 18

# 2 KINGS

*God moves among individuals and nations to accomplish His will.*

## SETTING THE STAGE

Second Kings continues the historical narrative of Israel and Judah, picking up where the events of 1 Kings left off. It begins with the final days of the prophet Elijah and the beginning of Elisha's ministry.

The consistent themes of idolatry and rebellion dominate the book. Despite the clear commands of God against worshipping other gods, many of the kings and the majority of the people continue to indulge in the worship of foreign deities. They erect altars and high places to honor these false gods, leading to the collapse of both Israel and Judah.

Two significant events in this book include the fall of the northern kingdom of Israel to the Assyrians (leading to the scattering of the ten tribes), and the eventual capture of Jerusalem by the Babylonians.

Prophets such as Elisha, Isaiah, and Jeremiah play a key role—offering guidance, delivering warnings, and communicating messages from God. They consistently warn against disobedience and call people to repentance.

Second Kings concludes with the Babylonian exile, demonstrating the significance of faithfulness to God's covenant, the consequences of idolatry and disobedience, and the role of the prophets in communicating God's messages to His people.

Above all, it is clear that God desires His people to align themselves with His purposes.

## GOOD TO KNOW

Author not stated and unknown; one early tradition claimed Jeremiah wrote 1 and 2 Kings. Covering about three hundred years from the 800s BC on, 2 Kings was probably written sometime after the Babylonian destruction of Jerusalem in 586 BC.

*The greatest truths in scripture are often revealed in the unhurried moments.*

## 2 KINGS 1

King Ahaziah of Israel is injured in a fall in his home. He seeks counsel from the god Baal-zebub as to whether he will recover. Elijah intercepts the messengers, proclaiming God's judgment on Ahaziah's apostasy. Ahaziah sends two groups of men to arrest Elijah, but they are burned with fire from heaven. A third group is spared; Elijah predicts Ahaziah's death, which happens shortly.

*Where are you most likely to turn in the first moment of trouble?*

## 2 KINGS 2

Elijah knows his time is short, but his successor Elisha refuses to leave his side. Elisha inherits Elijah's mantle. In front of other prophets, Elisha proves his anointing by parting the Jordan River with Elijah's cloak. As they cross over, a chariot of fire separates the men. Elijah ascends to heaven in a whirlwind. When young men mock Elisha, they are punished by bears.

*Why is discipleship and mentorship so important in the Christian life?*

## 2 KINGS 3

Jehoram is now king of Israel. Joined by Judah's King Jehoshaphat and the king of Edom, they march against Moab. Hindered by a lack of water, they seek Elisha's guidance. Elisha agrees to intervene for Jehoshaphat's sake. God provides water, fulfilling Elisha's prophecy. However, Moab's king sacrifices his own son, invoking God's wrath.

*How does a lack of prayer indicate what we think about God's ability to meet our needs?*

## 2 KINGS 4

Elisha performs several miracles. He aids a widow in debt, multiplying her oil to sell it and pay off creditors. He grants a barren couple a son, fulfilling their longing for a child. Later, the child suddenly dies, but Elisha resurrects him. In Gilgal, he purifies a deadly stew and feeds a hundred prophets.

*Is it hard for you to ask for help when you need it? Why or why not?*

## Take Your Time and Learn More

- Calling down fire from heaven: LUKE 9:51–56
- Visible manifestation of God's presence: LUKE 9:28–36
- Jehoshaphat's alliance: 2 CHRONICLES 20
- Multiplying a small amount of food: MARK 6:30–44

*Bible study is truly a lifelong journey.*
*Relax and enjoy the trip.*

## 2 KINGS 5

Naaman, a Syrian military commander, suffers from leprosy. A captive Israelite servant suggests he seek healing from Elisha. Initially reluctant, Naaman follows Elisha's instructions and bathes in the Jordan. . .and is healed. He gratefully offers wealth to Elisha, who refuses. Elisha's servant, however, covets the reward and deceitfully takes it. He gets leprosy as punishment.

*How can our expectations sometimes interfere with a blessing God has planned for us?*

## 2 KINGS 6

Elisha helps expose Syrian military plans to the king of Israel, thwarting their attacks. When Syria's king learns of Elisha's role, he dispatches a formidable army to capture him. Elisha prays, and God strikes the army with blindness. Elisha leads them into Israel, but instead of executing them, he throws a feast.

*How can you show kindness this week because of the kindness God has shown you?*

## 2 KINGS 7

Elisha prophesies an imminent end to the famine in Samaria. Four lepers, desperate for food, stumble upon the deserted Syrian camp, finding it filled with provisions. They share the news with the city, leading to a rush and confirming Elisha's prophecy. Food prices plummet as the famine ends. However, an officer who doubted Elisha's prophecy is trampled to death.

*Do you ever struggle to believe God's promises? Why?*

## 2 KINGS 8

Elisha predicts seven years of famine; afterward, he restores a Shunammite woman's land that she had left behind in search of food. King Jehoram of Judah, hearing of Elisha's miracles, asks about his own illness. Elisha prophesies Jehoram's death and Hazael's ascension as king of Syria. Jehoram's son Ahaziah reigns in Judah but walks in his father's wicked ways.

*Is there anyone in your community with a specific need that you could help meet?*

## Take Your Time and Learn More

- Healing of Naaman: LUKE 4:27
- Prayer for eyes to be opened: EPHESIANS 1:18–23
- Healing of lepers: LUKE 17:11–19
- Restoring what was lost: 2 KINGS 4:8–37

*Try to forget the demands of life for a while.
You're spending quality time with God.*

## 2 KINGS 9

Elisha anoints Jehu as king of Israel. Divinely tasked with wiping out Ahab's evil lineage, Jehu conspires with fellow officers to swiftly eliminate King Joram and Jezebel's son Ahaziah. He then confronts Jezebel's eunuchs, leading to Jezebel's death as she is thrown from a window and trampled by horses. Jehu eradicates Ahab's descendants, fulfilling Elijah's prophecy.

*Where do you see wickedness or untruth creeping into the church today? What can you do?*

## 2 KINGS 10

King Jehu continues eliminating the house of Ahab. He gathers Baal worshippers under the pretense of honoring Baal. . .then slaughters everyone and demolishes their temple. Despite his zeal for God, Jehu fails to abolish the golden calves in Bethel and Dan. However, as a reward for executing judgment on Ahab, God promises Jehu four generations on the throne.

*Can you think of anything in your life that is displeasing to God and in need of elimination?*

## 2 KINGS 11

Judah's king, Ahaziah, is mortally wounded in a battle with Jehu's forces. Athaliah, the mother of Ahaziah, begins wiping out the entire family line. But a relative hides baby Joash and his nurse from Athaliah's massacre. Six years later, Queen Athaliah is killed, and King Joash of Judah begins to reign at age seven.

*Is there any area of your life you need to recommit to God?*

## 2 KINGS 12

Joash becomes king of Judah and initiates repairs to the temple that was damaged during Athaliah's reign. The temple repairs are made by freewill offerings and honest workmen. Joash pleases God as long as the priest Jehoida instructs him. But then Jehoida dies, and Joash starts listening to bad counsel. After reigning forty years, he's assassinated by two officials.

*Who in your life consistently influences you to please God?*

## Take Your Time and Learn More

- God's judgment on unrighteous rulers: REVELATION 19:11–21
- Jehu: HOSEA 1:4–5
- Reign of Athaliah and ascension of Joash: 2 KINGS 11
- Joash in Judah: 2 CHRONICLES 24

*Good things come to those who wait—on the Lord, that is.*

## 2 KINGS 13

King Jehoahaz reigns in Israel and continues the idolatry of Jeroboam. Israel suffers under Hazael's oppression, but Jehoahaz seeks God's mercy, prompting Him to deliver Israel from their enemies. Elisha dies, but his influence continues even in death. Though Israel's disobedience persists, so does God's compassion.

*Whose life still deeply impacts your own, even though that person is now with God?*

## 2 KINGS 14

Amaziah becomes king of Judah, initially obeying God's commands. But he does not tear down the high places of false worship. Amaziah defeats the Edomites but provokes Israel's King Jehoash in battle, leading to a devastating defeat. Amaziah is captured, Jerusalem's walls are breached, and Jehoash plunders the temple and takes hostages. Amaziah is killed and his son Azariah becomes king.

*Why does God maintain the line of David despite so many kings' unfaithfulness?*

## 2 KINGS 15

Azariah (Uzziah) is sixteen when he begins reigning in Judah. He initially pleases God but later becomes prideful, receiving leprosy as divine punishment. Various kings rise and fall, each judged by their adherence to God's commands. In Israel, Jeroboam II's reign brings temporary prosperity despite idolatry, but political instability ensues with various assassinations.

*Why does pride lead to bad decisions?*

## 2 KINGS 16

Ahaz inherits the throne of Judah, ruling in disobedience to God. He adopts pagan practices, sacrificing his son and desecrating the temple. Ahaz allies with Assyria against Israel and Syria but faces Assyrian dominance and oppression. Despite Ahaz's unfaithfulness, God preserves Judah for the sake of His covenant with David. Ahaz dies and his son Hezekiah replaces him.

*How much partnership should Christians allow themselves with unbelievers?*

### Take Your Time and Learn More

- Consequences of rejecting God's prophets:
  2 CHRONICLES 36:15–21
- Time of Jeroboam II: AMOS 1:1
- Vision during the reign of King Uzziah: ISAIAH 6
- Prophecy of the coming Messiah
  given to King Ahaz: ISAIAH 7

*The Bible is countercultural, and so is Bible study. There's no need to rush through this.*

## 2 KINGS 17

Israel's disobedience culminates in God's judgment. Hoshea, the last king of Israel, is seized by Shalmaneser, king of Assyria. This chapter traces Israel's history of rebellion—from Jeroboam's golden calves to the foreign gods. Despite warnings, Israel persists in rejecting God. This was not what God intended when He delivered His people from Egypt.

*What things in your life compete against your love for God?*

## 2 KINGS 18

Hezekiah ascends the throne in Judah, exhibiting faithfulness to God. The new king smashes all the high places, the Asherah poles, and Moses' bronze snake that people have been worshipping. An enemy commander mocks Hezekiah's trust in God, but Isaiah prophesies Assyria's defeat. Hezekiah seeks Isaiah's counsel, and God defeats Assyria to save Jerusalem.

*How can good things (like Moses' bronze snake) become evil when misprioritized?*

## 2 KINGS 19

Assyria's king, Sennacherib, mocks God's power and demands Hezekiah's surrender. Hezekiah seeks Isaiah's counsel, who assures him of God's intervention and Sennacherib's demise. Hezekiah then prays earnestly in the temple, pleading for God's deliverance. That night, God decimates Assyria's army. Sennacherib's sons kill him while he worships his god, Nisroch.

*Have you ever found that focusing on God makes your problems seem smaller?*

## 2 KINGS 20

Hezekiah is sick and facing death. He prays for healing, and God gives him fifteen more years of life. Hezekiah's miraculous recovery prompts a visit from envoys of Babylon's king, to whom Hezekiah flaunts his treasures. Isaiah foretells Babylon's future conquest of Judah.

*Why does a personal walk with God matter until the very last breath?*

## *Take Your Time and Learn More*

- **Consequences of idolatry:** JEREMIAH 3:6–10
- **Assyrian invasion of Judah:** ISAIAH 36–37
- **King Hezekiah's prayer:** ISAIAH 37:14-20
- **Hezekiah's miraculous recovery:** ISAIAH 38

*God speaks in the quiet moments.*
*Approach His Word with calm expectation.*

## 2 KINGS 21

Manasseh becomes king of Judah, reigning for fifty-five years. He commits egregious sins, rebuilding high places, worshipping foreign gods, and even sacrificing his own son in the fire. His idolatry leads Judah astray, provoking God's anger. Despite warnings, Manasseh persists in evil. His reign epitomizes apostasy, defying God's covenant and leading Judah into spiritual decay. His evil son Amon then rules for two years.

*Do you think spiritual decay typically happens incrementally or all at once? Why?*

## 2 KINGS 22

Amon's son Josiah becomes king of Judah at age eight. He reigns righteously, seeking God's guidance. As the temple is being renovated, the high priest Hilkiah discovers the Book of the Law. Josiah reads it and realizes Judah's departure from God's commands. Josiah institutes reforms, purging idolatry and renewing the nation's covenant with God.

*How did love of God's Word change Josiah's life and leadership? How is it changing yours?*

## 2 KINGS 23

Josiah makes sweeping reforms to remove idolatry from Judah. He destroys altars, idols, and cultic practices—renewing his covenant with God. He reinstates Passover and purges the land of mediums and spiritists. He destroys the high places. He removes pagan priests and demolishes their sites. He dies at age thirty-nine in a battle with Egypt.

*Josiah stubbornly obeys God in an evil age. How can you commit to do the same?*

## Take Your Time and Learn More

- Manasseh's evil deeds: JEREMIAH 7:1–15
- Reign of Josiah: 2 CHRONICLES 34
- Celebration of Passover: 2 CHRONICLES 35:1–19

*Before you read, pray. Ask God to*
*speak His truth to your spirit.*

## 2 KINGS 24

Nebuchadnezzar of Babylon invades Judah, leading King Jehoiakim into submission. Jehoiakim rebels and dies during Nebuchadnezzar's reign. Then Nebuchadnezzar carries off temple items, officers, fighting men, skilled workers, and artisans—leaving only the poorest people to work in the fields. This chapter marks the beginning of Judah's captivity.

*Do you think God is any less offended today by idolatry and disobedience? Why or why not?*

## 2 KINGS 25

Zedekiah, the newest king in Judah, is captured and his sons are killed. Nebuzaradan, a Babylonian officer, ransacks Jerusalem—destroying the temple, other buildings, and city walls, and deporting most citizens to Babylon. Only a small remnant remains. This chapter marks Judah's downfall, fulfilling Jeremiah's prophecies of exile.

*Why is there always hope for followers of Jesus, no matter how bad things get?*

## Take Your Time and Learn More

- Prophecy of seventy years of captivity: JEREMIAH 25
  - The siege and fall of Jerusalem: JEREMIAH 52

# 1 CHRONICLES

*Obedience to God brings blessing,*
*and disobedience brings judgment.*

## SETTING THE STAGE

The name *Chronicles* refers to the historical account or record of events in chronological order, so it makes sense that 1 Chronicles begins with the most extensive collection of genealogies recorded in the Bible.

These genealogies trace the descendants of Adam to the twelve tribes of Israel, emphasizing the genealogy of David and establishing him in the line of Jesus. These genealogies also provide a sense of continuity throughout scripture.

Much of 1 Chronicles records the reign of David (chapters 11–29), but unlike the parallel accounts in 2 Samuel and 1 Kings, 1 Chronicles focuses on David's positive achievements, emphasizing his righteousness and devotion to God. The book specifically highlights David's zeal for worship and his preparation for the building of the temple.

First Chronicles includes specific details about the organization of the Levitical priesthood, with emphasis on the worship practices, highlighting the importance of following God's prescribed methods for approaching Him.

The book concludes with David charging Solomon to be faithful to God and to carry out the construction of the temple exactly as God instructed. David's death (29:28) sets the stage for the subsequent book of 2 Chronicles, which will record the reigns of various kings and the exile.

## GOOD TO KNOW

Author not stated but traditionally attributed to Ezra the priest. Covers the history of Israel from about 1010 BC (the death of King Saul) to about 970 BC (the death of King David).

*Don't hurry, don't worry. God's Word provides everything you need for living well.*

## 1 CHRONICLES 1

First Chronicles begins with a detailed genealogy from Adam to Abraham, lists the sons of Noah and the descendants of Abraham, then includes Esau and the Edomite kings. This chapter establishes the Israelites' historical lineage, highlighting their unique place in God's covenantal plan.

*Do you think God had a plan for every person on this list? Why or why not?*

## 1 CHRONICLES 2

The genealogy shifts to the descendants of Israel (Jacob), beginning with Jacob's sons. It focuses on Judah's lineage, tracing it to King David. The chapter also mentions Caleb's descendants, who receive a special inheritance for their faithfulness. This chapter highlights the continuity of God's covenant promises and the importance of faithful individuals in shaping Israel's future.

*How does the record of Jacob's lineage illustrate God's long-term plan for His people?*

## 1 CHRONICLES 3

The genealogy continues, focusing on the descendants of David, Israel's most celebrated king. It lists David's sons born in Jerusalem—including Solomon—as well as others born to his wives and concubines. In spite of David's flaws, his descendants form the royal line of Judah, culminating in the birth of Jesus, the Messiah.

*In what ways does Jesus' kingship differ from His ancestor David's?*

## 1 CHRONICLES 4

The focus now shifts to the descendants of Judah. Notably, the chapter highlights the prayer of Jabez, whose name means "sorrow" or "pain." He prays for blessing and protection, invoking God's favor. Jabez's prayer serves as a focal point amid the genealogical lists. The chapter records various clans and cities associated with the tribe of Judah.

*Jabez was not afraid to pray boldly. For what are you praying boldly today?*

### Take Your Time and Learn More

- Genealogy from Adam to Noah: GENESIS 5
  - Genealogy of David: RUTH 4:18–22
  - Genealogy of Jesus: MATTHEW 1:1–17
- Territory allotted to Judah: JOSHUA 15:20–32

*God loves it when you read and study His Word.*

## 1 CHRONICLES 5

The genealogies continue with the descendants of Reuben, Gad, and the half-tribe of Manasseh. Although Reuben was Jacob's firstborn, his birthright was given to Joseph's sons due to his transgression of defiling his father's bed. Though these tribes are skilled at battle, they are eventually exiled by the Assyrians due to their disobedience and idolatry.

*When have you cried out to God in a crisis? What happened?*

## 1 CHRONICLES 6

The genealogy of the Levites, the priestly tribe, is detailed. The chapter traces their lineage from Levi, the son of Jacob, through Aaron, the first high priest. It lists the various roles and responsibilities of the Levites in the worship and service of God. Notable names such as Moses, Aaron, and Samuel appear in this genealogy.

*Why do you think God wanted the Levites to be scattered among the other tribes of Israel?*

## 1 CHRONICLES 7

The genealogy continues, focusing on the descendants of Issachar, Benjamin, Naphtali, Manasseh, Ephraim, and Asher. It records the lineages of various clans within these tribes, detailing their numbers and territories. This chapter contributes to the broader narrative by meticulously describing Israel's tribal genealogies and their settlement in the Promised Land.

*What short description could be attached to your name in a genealogy someday?*

## 1 CHRONICLES 8

The genealogy continues, focusing on the tribe of Benjamin. It includes notable names such as King Saul—the first king of Israel—and his descendants. The chapter also lists the inhabitants of Gibeon alongside Benjamin's lineage. Additionally, it mentions the sons of Ehud, a judge of Israel, and the various towns and villages associated with the tribe.

*What role does understanding the past play in impacting the future?*

### Take Your Time and Learn More

- Tribe of Manasseh: GENESIS 48
- Levites: NUMBERS 3
- Territory of Manasseh: JOSHUA 17
- Tribe of Benjamin: JUDGES 3:15–30

*Reading the Bible isn't a race. Let the pages unfold
at a pace that allows your spirit to breathe.*

## 1 CHRONICLES 9

The genealogical records continue, detailing the Israelites' return to Jerusalem after the Babylonian captivity. This chapter lists the priests, Levites, and temple servants. Notable names—such as King Saul's descendants and gatekeepers—are mentioned, highlighting the restoration of community life following the exile.

*Who in your personal genealogy has been important in your life?*

## 1 CHRONICLES 10

This chapter recounts the tragic downfall and death of Saul, Israel's first king. Following a devastating defeat by the Philistines on Mount Gilboa, Saul and his sons are killed in battle. The Israelites flee their cities, and the Philistines occupy them. Saul's story serves as a sobering reminder of the importance of faithful obedience to God.

*How does King Saul's life serve as a cautionary tale?*

## 1 CHRONICLES 11

David is anointed king over all Israel, fulfilling God's promise. His reign begins in Hebron, where his mighty men pledge their loyalty. David marches into Jerusalem, defeats it, and takes up residence in the fortress—calling it the city of David. His army grows and he rises to power, establishing Israel's prominence.

*In what area of your life do you need more humble courage?*

## 1 CHRONICLES 12

David's growing army gains support from various tribes and regions. Men from all over Israel come to pledge allegiance to him, including warriors from Benjamin, Gad, and Manasseh. This chapter lists the numbers and capabilities of these valiant fighters, describing their military strength and loyalty to David. Under David's leadership, Israel is unified.

*What can you do to increase the spirit of unity in your church and Christian community?*

## Take Your Time and Learn More

- After the exile: NEHEMIAH 11
- Death of Saul and his sons: 1 SAMUEL 31
- David's kingdom: 2 SAMUEL 5
- Transition of power from Saul to David: 2 SAMUEL 2–4

*The greatest truths in scripture are often*
*revealed in the unhurried moments.*

## 1 CHRONICLES 13

David resolves to bring the ark of the covenant to Jerusalem, recognizing its central importance to Israel's worship. However, he consults leaders instead of seeking God's guidance on the proper method, and they transport the ark on a cart, contrary to the Lord's instructions. As they journey, the oxen stumble and Uzzah reaches out to steady the ark, resulting in his death.

*Why are good intentions not the same as true obedience?*

## 1 CHRONICLES 14

This chapter recounts David's marriages and the births of his children, including sons who would become leaders in Israel. Notably, David seeks God's guidance before engaging in military campaigns, leading to victories over the Philistines. Jerusalem is established as Israel's political and religious center under David's rule.

*How often do you seek God's guidance before making decisions? Why?*

## 1 CHRONICLES 15

David again prepares to bring the ark of the covenant to Jerusalem, this time seeking God's guidance and following His instructions. Learning from his mistakes, David ensures the ark is carried by Levites on poles, as commanded by God. Israel celebrates the return of the ark to Jerusalem.

*Do you think God still cares as much today about how His orders are followed?*

## 1 CHRONICLES 16

The ark is brought to Jerusalem amid great rejoicing and sacrifices. David commissions a psalm of thanksgiving, appointing Asaph and his musicians to lead the worship. The psalm recounts God's mighty deeds and faithfulness to Israel throughout history.

*What has God done in your past that you can praise and thank Him for today?*

## Take Your Time and Learn More

- Consequences of mishandling the ark of the covenant: 2 SAMUEL 6:6–7
- David's reign: 2 SAMUEL 5
- The ark of the covenant returns to Jerusalem: 2 SAMUEL 6:12–19
- Israel's worship of God: PSALM 105

*Bible study is truly a lifelong journey.*
*Relax and enjoy the trip.*

## 1 CHRONICLES 17

David cannot understand why he lives in a nice house while the ark sits in a tent. He expresses his desire to build a permanent temple, but God reveals through the prophet Nathan that David's son will fulfill this task. Instead, God promises David an everlasting dynasty, establishing his royal lineage forever. David responds with humility and gratitude.

*Have you ever wanted to do more for God than He had called you to do? How did that play out?*

## 1 CHRONICLES 18

David's reign is marked by military success and expansion of Israel's territory. David defeats and subdues neighboring nations—including the Philistines, Moabites, and Syrians—establishing Israel's dominance in the region. David gathers great wealth from the spoils of war, which he dedicates to the Lord. David is a powerful and respected king.

*What does David's life indicate about the connection between humility, obedience, and success?*

## 1 CHRONICLES 19

David tries to show kindness to Hanun, the king of Ammon, but is repaid with suspicion and hostility. Hanun's advisers convince him that David's emissaries are spies, leading to their humiliation and mistreatment. Enraged, David mobilizes Israel's army to confront the Ammonites and their allies. The ensuing battle results in a decisive victory for Israel.

*Why are misunderstandings so dangerous—and how do you seek to avoid them?*

## 1 CHRONICLES 20

This chapter continues to detail David's military campaigns and victories. His conquests highlight his military skill and the fulfillment of God's promises of victory to Israel. David is a mighty warrior-king, establishing Israel's dominance over neighboring nations during his reign.

*What makes a person truly successful?*

## Take Your Time and Learn More

- Davidic covenant: 2 SAMUEL 7
- David's military victories: 2 SAMUEL 8
- David and the Ammonites: 2 SAMUEL 10
- David and a giant: 1 SAMUEL 17

*Try to forget the demands of life for a while.*
*You're spending quality time with God.*

## 1 CHRONICLES 21

Disregarding God's command, David takes a census of his troops. Joab—David's commander—protests the decision, but David persists. Consequently, God sends a plague that kills thousands of Israelites. David repents, acknowledges his sin, and pleads for God's mercy. God instructs David to purchase the threshing floor of Araunah to offer sacrifices and halt the plague.

*How has God been merciful to you in spite of your sin?*

## 1 CHRONICLES 22

Though he is prohibited from building it himself, David prepares for the construction of the temple. He gathers resources and instructs his son Solomon on how to undertake the task. David also encourages Solomon to seek wisdom and understanding. David provides vast amounts of gold, silver, and other materials for the temple's construction.

*How does David's willingness to support Solomon in building the temple reflect his character?*

## 1 CHRONICLES 23

David appoints his son Solomon as king and organizes the Levites for service in the temple. He divides them into various categories—including musicians, gatekeepers, and overseers. David then assigns specific roles and responsibilities to each Levitical clan, ensuring the orderly administration of worship in the sanctuary.

*How can you purposely make more time for prayer in your daily routine?*

## 1 CHRONICLES 24

David organizes the priests into divisions for their service in the temple. This chapter lists the names of the priestly families and their responsibilities—ensuring that the duties of the temple are carried out efficiently and fairly among the priests.

*Are all services performed for God meaningful, regardless of size? Why or why not?*

### *Take Your Time and Learn More*

- Consequences of David's sin: 2 SAMUEL 12:13–25
- David's preparations for building the temple: 1 KINGS 5
- Responsibilities of the priesthood: NUMBERS 18
- The priesthood: LEVITICUS 8–9

*Good things come to those who wait—on the Lord, that is.*

## 1 CHRONICLES 25

David appoints musicians from the Levites to serve in the temple, assigning them roles in leading worship through song. This chapter lists the names of the appointed musicians, along with their sons. Music and praise are important parts of Israel's worship.

*How are you using your unique, God-given talents to serve Him and your local church?*

## 1 CHRONICLES 26

David appoints gatekeepers from the Levites to guard the entrances of the temple and the treasuries. The gatekeepers are organized into divisions, each assigned specific duties and responsibilities. This chapter lists the names of the gatekeepers and their jobs, highlighting their role in maintaining order and security within the sanctuary.

*What are some of the responsibilities God has entrusted to you to do for Him?*

## 1 CHRONICLES 27

David organizes Israel's army—twelve divisions (of twenty-four thousand soldiers each) who serve one month out of the year. David appoints leaders over specific tribes, each responsible for managing different aspects of the nation—such as agriculture, finances, and royal household affairs. David appoints his brothers and sons to key positions.

*What are some traits of true servant leadership?*

## Take Your Time and Learn More

- Role of music in worship: 1 CHRONICLES 16:42
- Levitical duties in service to the temple: 1 CHRONICLES 23:2–5
- Census of Israel: NUMBERS 1

*The Bible is countercultural, and so is Bible study.*
*There's no need to rush through this.*

## 1 CHRONICLES 28

David addresses the assembly of Israel before his death, declaring Solomon his successor and charging him to build the temple. David recounts God's covenant promises, emphasizing the importance of obedience, and provides detailed instructions and plans for the temple's construction. David encourages Solomon to obey God all the days of his life.

*What are you doing to leave a legacy of loving God to future generations?*

## 1 CHRONICLES 29

David gathers Israel's leaders to contribute to the temple's construction. He leads by example, offering vast amounts of precious materials. The people respond by contributing enthusiastically. David praises God for their generosity, acknowledging that all wealth and honor come from Him. The book concludes with Solomon's anointing and David's death.

*Why is leading by example always better than just speaking words?*

### Take Your Time and Learn More

- David's instructions to Solomon to build the temple: 1 CHRONICLES 22:6–16
- David's preparations for building the temple: 1 CHRONICLES 22:14–19

# 2 CHRONICLES

*God's perfect purposes for His people are
displayed through human history.*

## SETTING THE STAGE

Picking up where the last book left off, 2 Chronicles begins with Solomon's reign, focusing on the construction and dedication of the temple in Jerusalem. Upon the building's completion, Solomon "knelt down on his knees before all the congregation of Israel and spread out his hands toward heaven" and prayed (6:13).

Solomon's prayer at the dedication emphasizes the importance of the temple as the place of worship and the importance of seeking God's guidance.

Continuing on, the book chronicles the reigns of various kings in Judah, evaluating each one based on his faithfulness to God and commitment to worship. Second Chronicles consistently distinguishes between kings who follow David's example and those who deviate from the path of righteousness, leading to the growth or decline of the kingdom.

Notable kings in this book include Asa, Jehoshaphat, Joash, Hezekiah, and Josiah. The book focuses strongly on these kings' efforts to restore proper worship.

Second Chronicles covers the Babylonian exile and concludes with the decree of Cyrus that allows the exiled Israelites to return to their land. The narrative ends on a hopeful note, emphasizing God's faithfulness and ability to restore.

## GOOD TO KNOW

Author not stated but traditionally attributed to Ezra the priest. Covers Israelite history from about 970 BC (the accession of King Solomon) to the 500s BC (when exiled Jews returned to Jerusalem).

*God speaks in the quiet moments.*
*Approach His Word with calm expectation.*

## 2 CHRONICLES 1

Solomon consolidates his reign and allies himself with Egypt by marrying Pharaoh's daughter. God appears to Solomon in a dream, offering to give him whatever he desires. Solomon humbly requests wisdom to govern Israel justly. Pleased with his humility, God not only gives him wisdom, but also riches and honor.

*Why did it show humility on Solomon's part to ask God for wisdom?*

## 2 CHRONICLES 2

Solomon begins preparations for the temple. He asks Hiram, king of Tyre, for skilled craftsmen and materials for the construction. Hiram agrees to supply cedar and cypress timber from Lebanon and to send a skilled craftsman. Solomon mobilizes a vast labor force—thirty-six hundred overseers, seventy thousand burden bearers, and eighty thousand stonecutters.

*Is bigger always better in service to God? Why or why not?*

## 2 CHRONICLES 3

Solomon begins the construction of the temple on Mount Moriah—on the threshing floor his father, David, had purchased. The king builds the temple according to the specifications laid out by David and guided by God. This chapter describes the temple's dimensions and layout. Solomon seeks to honor God through the construction of a magnificent edifice.

*Why do you think God has left us with such detailed specifications for the temple?*

## 2 CHRONICLES 4

This chapter lists the many furnishings for the temple, meticulously crafted according to God's specifications. The workers—supervised by Solomon and overseen by Hiram's skilled craftsman—complete the intricate work. The construction of the temple reflects Solomon's commitment to excellence in honoring God's presence.

*Why does God deserve excellence in everything we do for Him?*

## Take Your Time and Learn More

- Solomon's request for wisdom: 1 Kings 3:4–15
- Solomon's preparations to build the temple: 1 Kings 5
- Construction of Solomon's temple: 1 Kings 6
- Furnishings of Solomon's temple: 1 Kings 7:13–51

*Before you read, pray. Ask God to
speak His truth to your spirit.*

## 2 CHRONICLES 5

Solomon brings the ark of the covenant into the newly completed temple. The priests and Levites sanctify themselves for the occasion, and the ark is placed in the Most Holy Place. As the priests leave the temple, a cloud fills the house, signifying God's presence. Solomon addresses the assembly, praising God for His faithfulness and promising to uphold His covenant.

*When was the last time you praised and worshipped God privately?*

## 2 CHRONICLES 6

Still addressing the assembly gathered for the dedication of the temple, Solomon offers a heartfelt prayer, acknowledging God's faithfulness to fulfill His promises and expressing gratitude for the completion of the temple. Solomon prays for God's continual presence and favor among His people. Solomon intercedes for the nation, seeking forgiveness for sin.

*Why is it immportant that Solomon—not a priest—offered this prayer?*

## 2 CHRONICLES 7

Following Solomon's prayer, fire descends from heaven, consuming the sacrifices on the altar, and the glory of the Lord fills the temple. The people bow in worship before God's presence. God promises to bless the land if His people remain faithful, but He warns of consequences for disobedience. Solomon dedicates the temple with a grand fourteen-day feast.

*How faithfully do you pray for your leaders?*

## 2 CHRONICLES 8

Solomon continues consolidating his reign and strengthening Israel's infrastructure. He builds fortified cities to improve the borders and maintain control over the land. He secures Jerusalem, expands its territory, establishes commercial partnerships, and appoints officials. He also ensures that the religious feasts and sacrifices are honored.

*Solomon takes Pharaoh's daughter as his wife—do you think he consulted God first?*

### *Take Your Time and Learn More*

- Dedication of Solomon's temple: 1 KINGS 8:62–66
- Solomon's prayer: 1 KINGS 8:22–53
- God's glory fills the temple: 1 KINGS 8:10–13
- Solomon's reign: 1 KINGS 9–11

*Don't hurry, don't worry. God's Word provides
everything you need for living well.*

## 2 CHRONICLES 9

The queen of Sheba visits Solomon. Drawn by his fame and impressed by his wisdom, she marvels at God's blessings upon his kingdom. Solomon and the queen exchange gifts, and she returns home. Solomon's wealth continues to increase. He dies at the end of this chapter, and his son Rehoboam succeeds him.

*How do you "keep your heart" (Proverbs 4:23) as Solomon instructed?*

## 2 CHRONICLES 10

After Rehoboam becomes king, the people seek relief from heavy taxation and labor burdens. Rehoboam consults with elders and young advisers. The elders advise him to show humility and serve the people, while the young advisers urge him to maintain Solomon's harsher policies. Rehoboam follows the advice of his peers, turning up the workload and pressuring the people.

*Why are "yes men" dangerous? And why is consulting them foolish?*

## 2 CHRONICLES 11

Rehoboam's unwise leadership decisions have created division. Facing rebellion from the northern tribes, Rehoboam fortifies Judah's defenses. He also heeds the word of the prophet Shemaiah, preventing a potential conflict with the tribes of Israel. Despite the division, the Levites and those loyal to God remain steadfast in their allegiance to the house of David.

*Rehoboam had eighteen wives, plus concubines—how does
this show the effect of a parent's example?*

## 2 CHRONICLES 12

Rehoboam forsakes God's laws, and Egypt invades. Egypt conquers Jerusalem, seizing treasures from the temple and royal palace. The prophet Shemaiah warns Rehoboam and the leaders of Judah, acknowledging their repentance. In response, God relieves them from total destruction. Rehoboam reigns for seventeen years, but his time is marked by apostasy and conflict.

*Is anything or anyone standing in the way of your full commitment to God?*

### Take Your Time and Learn More

- Queen of Sheba's visit: 1 KINGS 10:1–13
- Division of the kingdom: 1 KINGS 12:16–20
- Rehoboam's reign: 1 KINGS 12:1–24
- Consequences of Rehoboam's disobedience: 1 KINGS 14:21–30

*God loves it when you read and study His Word.*

## 2 CHRONICLES 13

Abijah, Rehoboam's son, ascends to the throne of Judah. He confronts Jeroboam—king of Israel—over his rebellion and idolatry. In a powerful speech, Abijah asserts Judah's loyalty to God. Despite having fewer troops, Abijah trusts in God's promise to preserve David's descendants. A battle ensues, and God graciously gives Judah the victory.

*What do you do when you feel overpowered by temptation?*

## 2 CHRONICLES 14

Abijah dies, and Asa succeeds his father as king of Judah. Seeking to restore faithfulness to God, he removes pagan idols and altars, commanding Judah to seek the Lord wholeheartedly. He fortifies cities and builds up defenses. Facing an invasion by a vast Ethiopian army, Asa cries out to God for help. In response, God grants victory.

*Can a Christian succeed at anything without prayer? Why or why not?*

## 2 CHRONICLES 15

The prophet Azariah encourages Asa to seek God and warns of the consequences of forsaking Him. Asa removes more idols and renews the covenant with God. He gathers the people to Jerusalem, where they offer sacrifices and renew their commitment to serve God. Asa even deposes his grandmother, Maacah, for her idolatry. The nation experiences peace and prosperity.

*Why is absolute surrender necessary, yet so hard?*

## 2 CHRONICLES 16

Asa enters into a treaty with Ben-hadad, king of Aram, seeking his help against Baasha, king of Israel. Hanani the seer rebukes Asa for relying on a foreign power instead of trusting God. Asa responds by imprisoning Hanani and oppressing some of the people. Asa rules forty-one years before dying with a "severe" disease in his feet (2 Chronicles 16:12).

*Practically speaking, what does it look like to trust God and not your own strength?*

## Take Your Time and Learn More

- Abijah's reign: 1 KINGS 15:1–8
- Asa's reign: 1 KINGS 15:11–14
- Asa's obedience to God: 1 KINGS 15:9–15
- Asa and Baasha: 1 KINGS 15:16–24

*Reading the Bible isn't a race. Let the pages unfold at a pace that allows your spirit to breathe.*

## 2 CHRONICLES 17

King Jehoshaphat succeeds his father, Asa, as king of Judah and follows God's commands. He strengthens the kingdom's defenses, appoints officials, and sends Levites to teach the law throughout Judah. Jehoshaphat's reign sees prosperity and respect from neighboring nations. The people follow his example, worshipping God earnestly.

*How is true and genuine worship an antidote to sin?*

## 2 CHRONICLES 18

Jehoshaphat allies with Ahab, king of Israel, by marrying his daughter. Ahab seeks a joint military campaign against Ramoth-gilead and asks for Jehoshaphat's support. Jehoshaphat insists on consulting prophets, who prophesy defeat. Ignoring this warning, Ahab leads the battle, disguising himself and endangering Jehoshaphat's life. Ahab dies from a random arrow.

*Why are people so easily offended by God's truth?*

## 2 CHRONICLES 19

After narrowly escaping death in battle alongside Ahab, Jehoshaphat returns to Jerusalem, where he is rebuked for helping the ungodly. Jehoshaphat appoints judges throughout Judah, instructing them to fear God and act with integrity and impartiality. He establishes a high court in Jerusalem to handle cases involving priests, Levites, and rulers.

*Why does living uprightly require courage?*

## 2 CHRONICLES 20

An army of Moabites and Ammonites wages war against Judah. Jehoshaphat seeks God's help and leads Judah in fasting and prayer. Jehoshaphat and the people worship God, and the next day, they witness the enemy's miraculous defeat. Judah celebrates with praise and plunder.

*What does it say to us that Jehoshaphat and the people worship God before their victory?*

## Take Your Time and Learn More

- Jehoshaphat's righteous rule: 1 KINGS 22:41–50
  - Ahab's final battle: 1 KINGS 22:1–40
    - Righteous judgment: PSALM 82
- Confidence in God's victory: ROMANS 8:31

*The greatest truths in scripture are often*
*revealed in the unhurried moments.*

## 2 CHRONICLES 21

Jehoshaphat dies, and his son Jehoram becomes king of Judah. He rules wickedly, murdering his brothers and leading Judah astray through idol worship like the kings of Israel. Despite God's warnings, Jehoram refuses to repent. He dies painfully, afflicted with a severe bowel disease. The city does not mourn.

*Have you ever been tempted to compromise because it*
*seemed rational in the moment? What happened?*

## 2 CHRONICLES 22

Jehoram's youngest son, Ahaziah, becomes king of Judah and follows in his father's wicked ways—influenced by the counsel of his mother, Athaliah. Anointed by God, Jehu executes judgment and kills Ahaziah. In retaliation, Athaliah starts killing the royal heirs. However, Joash—Ahaziah's infant son—is rescued and hidden in the temple by Jehoiada the priest.

*Why does power so easily corrupt people?*

## 2 CHRONICLES 23

Jehoiada the priest anoints young Joash, Ahaziah's surviving son, as king. Jehoiada then orchestrates a coup against Athaliah, the usurper queen, leading to her execution. The temple is cleansed of idolatry, and Joash assumes the throne. Under Jehoiada's guidance, Judah enjoys a period of restoration and renewal. Joash's reign marks a return to worshipping God.

*How much impact can one person who's determined to obey God make today?*

## 2 CHRONICLES 24

Joash becomes king of Judah at age seven, reigning in Judah under the guidance of Jehoiada the priest. Together, they repair the temple and restore proper worship. Joash commands the Levites to collect offerings for temple repairs, but after Jehoiada's death, Joash abandons the Lord's house and worships idols. The chapter ends with Joash's assassination.

*Who are you listening to and allowing yourself to be influenced by?*

### Take Your Time and Learn More

- Jehoram's reign: 2 KINGS 8:16–24
- Athaliah's coup: 2 KINGS 11:1–16
- Jehoiada the priest: 2 KINGS 11
- Joash's reign: 2 KINGS 12

*Bible study is truly a lifelong journey.*
*Relax and enjoy the trip.*

## 2 CHRONICLES 25

Amaziah—Joash's son—succeeds him as king of Judah. He reigns with initial devotion to God. A prophet warns Amaziah against relying on foreign help, but Amaziah ignores it. He brings back idols and worships them, angering God. He challenges Joash—king of Israel—to battle. . .and is defeated. Amaziah rules for twenty-nine years but ends his reign in disgrace.

*Why does great personal defeat often seem to happen after great personal victory?*

## 2 CHRONICLES 26

Amaziah's son, Uzziah, becomes king of Judah at age sixteen. He seeks God's guidance and prospers, winning battles and fortifying Jerusalem. But pride leads to his downfall. He enters the temple to burn incense—a task reserved for priests. The priests confront him, but Uzziah becomes angry. God strikes him with leprosy, forcing him to live in isolation until he dies.

*How can you actively guard your heart from pride?*

## 2 CHRONICLES 27

Uzziah's son Jotham succeeds his father as king of Judah. He reigns for sixteen years, ruling with righteousness and devotion to God. Jotham fortifies cities in Judah and defeats the Ammonites. His reign sees prosperity and stability because he walks steadfastly with the Lord.

*What does it look like today to walk steadfastly with God?*

## 2 CHRONICLES 28

Ahaz becomes king of Judah, ruling wickedly by worshipping idols and sacrificing his children to false gods. God allows Judah to be defeated by the northern kingdom and the Syrians, resulting in captivity and significant loss of life. Ahaz seeks help from Assyria but is met with further disaster. The prophet Oded rebukes Ahaz for betraying his own people.

*Why does God want us to turn to Him first when we're in need?*

## Take Your Time and Learn More

- King Amaziah: 2 KINGS 14:1–22
- King Azariah (Uzziah): 2 KINGS 15:1–7
- King Jotham: 2 KINGS 15:32–38
- King Ahaz: 2 KINGS 16

*Try to forget the demands of life for a while.*
*You're spending quality time with God.*

## 2 CHRONICLES 29

Ahaz's son Hezekiah becomes king of Judah and immediately takes action to restore worship in the temple. He gathers the priests and Levites, urging them to consecrate themselves and the sanctuary. They cleanse the temple of idols and impurities. The temple's doors are opened, and the priests can't handle all the sacrifices that are brought.

*Why do you think so many sacrifices are brought to*
*the temple under Hezekiah's leadership?*

## 2 CHRONICLES 30

Hezekiah invites all of Judah and Israel to join in the Passover celebration—which they do with great enthusiasm, resulting in a massive assembly. Despite initial skepticism and logistical challenges, the Passover is celebrated with great joy and unity, marking a significant return to God among the people. The celebration lasts an additional seven days.

*Why does genuine worship of God result in true joy?*

## 2 CHRONICLES 31

After the Passover celebration, Hezekiah leads Judah in further reforms. He reestablishes the priests and Levites in their duties and provides for their support through tithes and offerings. The people respond generously, bringing abundant contributions for the temple and the priests. His dedication to worship and obedience to God's commands leads to blessings on the nation.

*Hezekiah doesn't coast—he continues pushing for*
*greater change. How can you do the same?*

## 2 CHRONICLES 32

Sennacherib, king of Assyria, invades Judah and besieges Jerusalem. Hezekiah prepares for the attack by repairing the city's defenses and encouraging the people to trust in God. Sennacherib sends a message challenging Judah's faith, but Hezekiah prays for deliverance and God sends an angel to strike down the Assyrian army. Hezekiah dies and his son Manasseh succeeds him.

*Why does spiritual growth also come with spiritual warfare? How can you prepare?*

## Take Your Time and Learn More

- King Hezekiah's reign: 2 KINGS 18:1–3
- Hezekiah's religious reforms: 2 KINGS 18:4–8
- Another revival of proper worship: 2 KINGS 23:1–27
- Assyrian invasion: 2 KINGS 18:13–19:37

# Good things come to those who wait—on the Lord, that is.

## 2 CHRONICLES 33

Manasseh rules wickedly, promoting idol worship and even erecting pagan altars in the temple. God sends warnings, which Manasseh ignores. So God allows Assyria to capture Manasseh and take him as prisoner to Babylon. He repents, and God restores him to the throne. Then he leads Judah in worshipping the Lord. After Manasseh dies, his evil son Amon rules for two years.

*How is it encouraging that God hears humble prayers even from wicked kings?*

## 2 CHRONICLES 34

Amon's son Josiah is eight when he becomes king of Judah, and he reigns righteously. He restores worship and repairs the temple. After discovering the Book of the Law, he repents, reinstating the covenant and urging the people to follow God's commands. He removes idolatry and celebrates a Passover unlike any since the time of the judges.

*What does idolatry look like in our Western culture today?*

## 2 CHRONICLES 35

Josiah prepares for the Passover, following the law meticulously. He provides generous offerings, inspiring the people to do the same. The priests and Levites fulfill their duties faithfully, conducting the Passover celebration according to God's commands. Josiah ignores the warning of Egypt's Pharaoh, joins battle against him, and is mortally wounded.

*How can you discern between genuine warnings and false alarms?*

## 2 CHRONICLES 36

Successive kings have led Judah in rebellion against God. Despite prophetic warnings, they persist in idolatry and disobedience. Now Judah's downfall culminates as it is defeated by Babylon. Nebuchadnezzar captures Jerusalem, destroys the temple, and exiles people to Babylon for seventy years. After exile, Cyrus of Persia allows the Jews to return and rebuild their temple.

*Why must a longsuffering, merciful God also punish sin?*

## Take Your Time and Learn More

- King Manasseh: 2 KINGS 21:1–18
- King Josiah: 2 KINGS 22
- Passover celebrated: 2 KINGS 23:21–23
- Fall of Jerusalem: 2 KINGS 24:18–25:30

# EZRA

*God moves the hearts of rulers to accomplish His will.*

## SETTING THE STAGE

The book of Ezra is set about fifty years after the Babylonians destroyed Jerusalem and the temple and took many of the Israelites into exile. It begins with Cyrus, the king of Persia, being moved by God (1:1) to issue a decree allowing the Israelites to return to their homeland and rebuild their temple.

The book highlights God's divine orchestration of events, fulfilling Jeremiah's prophecy that the exiles would one day return to Jerusalem. King Cyrus's decree marks the beginning of the fulfillment of this promise, demonstrating God's sovereignty over the affairs of nations and His faithfulness to His promises.

So the exiles return with great excitement. After some initial setbacks and discouragement, the construction of the temple resumes. Soon its completion is celebrated with the dedication of the altar and the observance of the Passover.

The second half of the book introduces Ezra, after whom the book is named. Ezra is a priest, scribe, and skilled teacher of the law. His job: to ensure that the Israelites follow God's commandments. Given Israel's history, this will be no small feat.

But God is faithful. Ezra leads a spiritual and moral reform, and the Israelites respond with a commitment to obey God's law.

The themes of return, restoration, and revival are central to Ezra, reflecting a period of renewed commitment to God after a challenging exile.

## GOOD TO KNOW

Author not stated but traditionally attributed to Ezra the priest (7:11). Written approximately 530 BC to the mid-400s BC.

*The Bible is countercultural, and so is Bible study.*
*There's no need to rush through this.*

## EZRA 1

God moves Cyrus, king of Persia, to issue a decree allowing the Jews to return to Jerusalem and rebuild the temple. Cyrus acknowledges God's sovereignty and instructs the Israelites to reconstruct the temple, providing resources and returning sacred articles taken from the original temple by Nebuchadnezzar. The restoration of Jerusalem has begun.

*Today, God dwells in the hearts of His people. How is the condition of your heart before God?*

## EZRA 2

This chapter includes a detailed list of the exiles who return from Babylon to Jerusalem to rebuild the temple following Cyrus's decree. The list includes the number of people from each family, their lineage, and the areas from which they come. The people offer voluntary contributions for the reconstruction of the temple and the restoration of worship.

*Is God prompting you to contribute something—time, energy, resources—to His work?*

## EZRA 3

The returning exiles gather in Jerusalem and begin rebuilding the altar on its original site. They reinstate daily sacrifices, following the law of Moses. The foundation of the new temple is laid. However, older exiles who remember Solomon's temple weep at the sight of this new foundation, realizing its comparative modesty. Still, the people praise God for His faithfulness.

*Are you living with any regrets that you need to give to God?*

## EZRA 4

Enemies of the returning exiles oppose the rebuilding efforts, seeking to halt the construction of the temple in Jerusalem. They create fear by making bribes, lodging accusations, and writing letters accusing the Israelites of rebellion. King Artaxerxes orders the temple construction to cease, and it remains halted until the second year of Darius's reign.

*Has there ever been a time when you were steadfast in the face of opposition? What happened?*

## Take Your Time and Learn More

- Cyrus's proclamation: 2 CHRONICLES 36:22–23
  - Return of the exiles: NEHEMIAH 7
  - First temple construction: 1 KINGS 6
  - Sorrow and longing: PSALM 137

*God speaks in the quiet moments.*
*Approach His Word with calm expectation.*

## EZRA 5

The prophets Haggai and Zechariah encourage Jewish leaders Zerubbabel and Jeshua to resume temple construction. Despite opposition, the returning exiles start building again. Adversaries of the project send a letter to King Darius asking him to search the royal records to see if Cyrus has indeed authorized the temple construction.

*How do you respond to discouragement about a task God has set before you?*

## EZRA 6

Darius investigates and finds Cyrus's decree affirming the rebuilding. So Darius not only commands the continuation of construction but also orders funding from the royal treasury. The temple is finished with joyful celebration, and offerings are presented according to the law of Moses. The exiles keep the Passover, rejoicing in their newfound freedom and restored worship.

*Why does joy come after obedience to God?*

## EZRA 7

During the reign of Artaxerxes, Ezra—a Levite—arrives in Jerusalem from Babylon. Skilled in the law of Moses, he receives permission from the king to teach and enforce it among the Israelites. Ezra's mission is to bring order to Judah, promoting righteousness according to God's law. Artaxerxes supports Ezra with resources for the temple and for worship.

*What proofs of God's generous provision—spiritual or material—can you thank Him for today?*

## EZRA 8

Ezra organizes a return to Jerusalem from Babylon. He ensures that everyone is accounted for—especially the Levites and priests. Fearing attacks on the journey, Ezra proclaims a fast and prays for protection. God answers by granting them safe passage. Arriving in Jerusalem, they deliver the offerings and treasures for the temple.

*In what specific, practical ways do you depend on God for protection?*

### Take Your Time and Learn More

- A call to temple construction: HAGGAI 1
- Royal building permit: 2 CHRONICLES 36:22–23
- Daniel's prayer for the restoration of Jerusalem: DANIEL 9:1–19
- Prayer for protection: PSALM 91

## EZRA 9

Ezra learns that many Israelites have married foreign wives, violating God's command. Deeply distressed, Ezra tears his garments and mourns before God, confessing the people's sins and acknowledging God's righteousness. Despite the people's unfaithfulness, Ezra also recognizes God's mercy in allowing a remnant to return to Jerusalem. He pleads for forgiveness.

*Why are we often most vulnerable to temptation right after a victory?*

## EZRA 10

A crowd of Israelites gathers in Jerusalem to weep with Ezra, acknowledging their sin. Ezra urges them to repent and separate from their foreign wives and children. The assembly agrees, and a plan is devised to address the issue. Representatives from each family oversee the process, and everyone who has married a foreign wife needs to end the relationship.

*Why are pagan influences—then and now—so catastrophic to true faith and worship?*

## Take Your Time and Learn More

- Prayer for forgiveness and restoration: DANIEL 9:1–19
- Collective confession and repentance: NEHEMIAH 9

# NEHEMIAH

*God protects His people, who—in response—*
*should be faithful to worship and obey.*

## SETTING THE STAGE

The book of Nehemiah focuses on the efforts of Nehemiah, a cupbearer to King Artaxerxes of Persia, in leading the rebuilding of Jerusalem's walls and the community's spiritual restoration.

Nehemiah's story unfolds following the return of the Israelites from Babylonian captivity.

The book opens with Nehemiah receiving news about the distressed condition of Jerusalem, specifically the broken-down walls and gates (1:3) that are leaving the city vulnerable to attack. Grieved by this news, Nehemiah asks King Artaxerxes for permission to return to Jerusalem and help rebuild. The king agrees.

Arriving in Jerusalem, Nehemiah faces opposition almost immediately. But despite the challenges, he organizes the people, assigns specific tasks, and works diligently to rebuild the walls and gates in a remarkably short period.

With the walls rebuilt, the focus shifts to spiritual renewal, and the people of Israel respond by repenting and committing to follow God's commands.

In addition to rebuilding the walls and gates, Nehemiah accomplishes many important tasks in this book—including influencing officials and nobles to cancel the debts of the poor, reviewing the genealogies of the returned exiles, reinstating the use of the tithe, and reestablishing sabbath observance.

The book concludes with a simple but powerful prayer from Nehemiah: "Remember me, O my God, for good!" (13:31).

## GOOD TO KNOW

Contains "the words of Nehemiah" (1:1), though Jewish tradition says those words were put on paper by Ezra. Written approximately 445 BC.

*Don't hurry, don't worry. God's Word provides
everything you need for living well.*

## NEHEMIAH 1

Nehemiah, a cupbearer for the king of Persia, hears about Jerusalem's distress and the broken walls. He mourns, fasts, and prays fervently for God's favor, confessing Israel's sins and his own. Nehemiah appeals to God for mercy, recalling His promises to restore His people if they repent. He wants to return to Jerusalem to help rebuild the walls.

*Why is it helpful to focus on God's attributes while praying?*

## NEHEMIAH 2

Nehemiah is sad. King Artaxerxes asks why, and Nehemiah shares his concern for Jerusalem's desolation. Moved by Nehemiah's distress, the king permits him to return to Jerusalem to rebuild the city's walls. Nehemiah requests letters for safe passage and materials from the king's forest. Nehemiah arrives in Jerusalem and gathers people to start rebuilding.

*How long do you think Nehemiah's prayer (verse 4)
was? What does this say about prayer?*

## NEHEMIAH 3

The rebuilding of Jerusalem's walls begins under Nehemiah's leadership. The reconstruction effort is organized and systematic. Priests, goldsmiths, and rulers contribute to the restoration, highlighting the unity and community effort involved. Despite opposition from neighboring adversaries, the people remain focused and diligent in their work.

*What specific gifts has God given you that could be
used to serve others in your local church?*

## NEHEMIAH 4

Sanballat and Tobiah try stopping construction on the walls by mocking and threatening Nehemiah and the workers. Nehemiah responds by praying for strength and assigning guards to protect the builders. Despite threats, the work continues, with half the workers laboring and the other half standing guard. Nehemiah encourages the people to trust God.

*How does God want you to respond to negative events or criticism from others?*

### Take Your Time and Learn More

- Confession, repentance, and intercession: DANIEL 9:1–19
- God fulfills His purposes through human agents: EZRA 7
  - Division of tasks: 1 CHRONICLES 9
  - Opposition to rebuilding: EZRA 4

*God loves it when you read and study His Word.*

## NEHEMIAH 5

Internal conflicts arise among the Jews due to economic oppression. Nehemiah learns that some wealthy Jews are exploiting their poorer brothers, charging exorbitant interest rates and enslaving them. Nehemiah confronts these individuals, demanding they stop. He sets an example of lending to the needy without interest. The wealthy Jews agree, and the exploitation stops.

*Is it ever right for you to accept less than what you deserve? Why or why not?*

## NEHEMIAH 6

Sanballat, Tobiah, and Geshem try to distract Nehemiah from completing the wall. They invite Nehemiah to a meeting, intending to harm him. When Nehemiah refuses, Sanballat sends false prophets to intimidate Nehemiah. Still, he remains steadfast, praying for strength, discernment, and God's justice. Despite pushback, the wall is completed in just fifty-two days.

*What is currently a greater threat to your obedience to God: opposition or distraction?*

## NEHEMIAH 7

Now that the wall is completed, Nehemiah appoints Hanani and Hananiah to safeguard Jerusalem. He also appoints gatekeepers, singers, and Levites for service in the temple. Nehemiah requests the genealogical records to identify those who returned from exile. He then assembles the people and reads the records to ensure the integrity of the community.

*How can you strengthen your commitment to your God-given responsibilities?*

## NEHEMIAH 8

Ezra reads the law of Moses to those gathered in Jerusalem's square. The people respond with reverence, standing to hear the Word of God from morning until midday. Ezra and other Levites interpret the law, helping the people understand its meaning. Upon hearing the law's demands, the listeners weep but are encouraged to rejoice. They celebrate the Feast of Tabernacles.

*How can you guard against apathy toward God's Word?*

## Take Your Time and Learn More

- Care for materially poor: LEVITICUS 25
- Consequences of deceit: PROVERBS 19:9
- Return of the exiles: EZRA 2
- Public reading of the law: DEUTERONOMY 31:9–12

*Reading the Bible isn't a race. Let the pages unfold
at a pace that allows your spirit to breathe.*

## NEHEMIAH 9

The Israelites gather to confess their sins and recount God's faithfulness throughout their history. The Levites lead in prayer, acknowledging God's sovereignty, mercy, and covenant faithfulness. They recount God's acts of deliverance, provision, and discipline, affirming His righteousness and forgiveness. The assembly pledges to renew their covenant with Him.

*Why did the Israelites place such importance on passing
down their stories to future generations?*

## NEHEMIAH 10

The people—including leaders, priests, Levites, and heads of households—make a binding agreement to uphold God's law. They pledge to follow the law of Moses, committing to separate themselves from foreign influences and observe the Sabbath and other practices. They vow to care for the temple and obey God's commands.

*Why does it sometimes take negative experiences to refocus our attention on God?*

## NEHEMIAH 11

The leaders cast lots to determine who will live in Jerusalem, since the city needs inhabitants to ensure its security and vitality. Some willingly volunteer to dwell in Jerusalem, while others are chosen. This chapter lists the names of those selected to live there. Residents are necessary to maintain a strong presence in the city of God.

*Has God ever asked you to give up a comfort in order to serve Him? What happened?*

## Take Your Time and Learn More

- God's faithfulness despite people's disobedience: EXODUS 34
- Renewal of the covenant: DEUTERONOMY 29
- Resettlement: 1 CHRONICLES 9

*The greatest truths in scripture are often*
*revealed in the unhurried moments.*

## NEHEMIAH 12

Nehemiah lists the priests and Levites who returned with Zerubbabel. He organizes a dedication ceremony for the rebuilt walls of Jerusalem. Two processions are led by priests, singers, and musicians—walking in opposite directions along the top of the wall. Nehemiah appoints leaders to oversee the contributions for the priests and Levites, ensuring their care.

*Is celebration—corporate or personal—a regular part*
*of your worship to God? Why or why not?*

## NEHEMIAH 13

After returning to Babylon, Nehemiah hears about various violations of God's law in Jerusalem. So he returns to confront the offenders and cleanse the temple. He reinstates use of the tithe, reestablishes the Sabbath ordinance, and rebukes men who have married foreign women. He restores order, maintains Jerusalem's sanctity, and preserves the identity of God's people.

*What responsibility do you think Christians have to keep each other accountable?*

### Take Your Time and Learn More

- **Music and worship:** 1 CHRONICLES 25
- **Need for repentance and reform:** MALACHI 3

# ESTHER

*Even when God seems hidden, He is still*
*working and protecting His people.*

## SETTING THE STAGE

The book of Esther is set in the Persian Empire during the reign of King Ahasuerus (also called Xerxes). It tells the exciting story of Esther, a Jewish orphan who is raised by her cousin Mordecai.

The book is unique because it never mentions the name of God, though the story underscores God's gracious providence in preserving His people. Look for God in the book of Esther, and you will find Him everywhere.

The story of Esther is broken into three main parts:

- ❖ Esther becomes queen.

- ❖ Esther helps deliver her people from destruction.

- ❖ The Jews take revenge on their enemies.

The most pivotal and well-known verse of the book is 4:14: "For if you altogether remain quiet at this time, then relief and deliverance shall arise for the Jews from another place, but you and your father's house shall be destroyed. And who knows whether you have come to the kingdom for such a time as this?"

A slow reading of the book reveals a gripping narrative of intrigue, danger, and divine intervention. It highlights the courage of people like Esther and Mordecai and reminds us that God is always working behind the scenes to accomplish His good purposes.

## GOOD TO KNOW

Author not stated but perhaps Ezra or Nehemiah. Written approximately 486–465 BC, during the reign of King Ahasuerus of Persia. Esther became queen around 479 BC.

*Bible study is truly a lifelong journey.*
*Relax and enjoy the trip.*

## ESTHER 1

King Ahasuerus (also known as Xerxes) throws two extravagant feasts lasting 187 days. On the last day, he calls Queen Vashti to appear before his guests to show off her beauty. Vashti refuses, and the furious king has her dethroned.

*How can humility help us resist the human urge to seek validation through external recognition?*

## ESTHER 2

Ahasuerus, on the hunt for Vashti's replacement, holds a contest. Esther is a beautiful Jewish orphan being raised by Mordecai. Posing as a Persian, she hides her Jewish identity and the king chooses her to be the new queen. In a separate incident, Mordecai saves the king's life from a murder plot.

*How do you see God at work in the events of this story, even though His name is not mentioned?*

## ESTHER 3

The king promotes one of his officials named Haman (a descendent of the ancient Canaanites) to the highest position in his kingdom. Full of himself, Haman demands everybody bow to him. Mordecai the Jew refuses, so Haman angrily decides to kill all the Jews. Ahasuerus carelessly approves the plan, and a date is set for the Jewish extermination.

*Why does power and authority so easily corrupt leaders?*

## ESTHER 4

Mordecai is distressed to learn of Haman's evil plan. He knows Esther is the Jewish people's only hope, so he urges her to talk to King Ahasuerus and reveal her Jewish heritage. There is risk in approaching the king uninvited, but Esther courageously says, "If I perish, I perish" (4:16).

*How can you better steward what God has given you to impact others for good?*

### Take Your Time and Learn More

- Extravagant feast by a king: DANIEL 5
- Preparation to meet a redeemer: RUTH 3
- Faithfulness in the face of persecution: DANIEL 3
- Fasting, prayer, and seeking God's intervention: 2 CHRONICLES 20

*Try to forget the demands of life for a while.*
*You're spending quality time with God.*

## ESTHER 5

Esther goes to see the king, who graciously extends his golden scepter. Esther invites Ahasuerus and Haman to a banquet. . .then invites them back to a second one the next day. Leaving the event, Haman again sees Mordecai in the street. And again, Mordecai refuses to bow. "Full of indignation" (5:9), Haman orders gallows to be built for hanging Mordecai in the morning.

*Why is anger typically a bad ingredient in decision-making?*

## ESTHER 6

The same evening, Ahasuerus struggles to sleep. He has the royal chronicles read to him, and hears how Mordecai had foiled an assassination plot and saved his life. The incident had escaped the king's memory, so in the morning, he instructs Haman to honor Mordecai. The uptight official must lead his enemy around the city on a royal horse.

*How does this chapter illustrate the fleeting nature of worldly power and honor?*

## ESTHER 7

Esther hosts her second banquet for King Xerxes and Haman. After the feast, she tells the king about her Jewish identity and reveals Haman's evil plot to exterminate her people—including Mordecai, who saved the king's life. Ahasuerus is furious and orders Haman to be hanged on the gallows built for Mordecai.

*Was there ever a time when obedience to God required you to act courageously in spite of fear? What happened?*

## Take Your Time and Learn More

- Courage in the face of persecution: DANIEL 6
  - Elevation of the righteous: DANIEL 2
- God's judgment on the wicked: DANIEL 5

*Good things come to those who wait—on the Lord, that is.*

## ESTHER 8

Haman is dead, but the king's decree to kill the Jews still exists. Esther pleads with Ahasuerus to revoke his decree, but a royal law can't be reversed. Thinking creatively, the king commissions Mordecai to create a counter-decree, enabling the Jews to defend themselves. Even before the day arrives, the Jews rejoice.

*How does this story of sin and deliverance remind you of the gospel?*

## ESTHER 9

The day of the king's original decree arrives, and the Jewish people triumph over their enemies, resulting in widespread celebration and the establishment of the commemorative Feast of Purim. Esther's plea for deliverance works better than she could have imagined. Her people will live.

*Why is it often easier to see God's sovereignty in a story like Esther's. . .but not in our own?*

## ESTHER 10

Esther's final chapter is a short epilogue in which Mordecai is elevated to second-in-command under Ahasuerus. But instead of using his power for evil, Mordecai "seek[s] the well-being of his people" (10:3). He and Esther represent God's providential care for His exiled people.

*God's providence is present on every page of every story. How have you experienced this providence?*

## Take Your Time and Learn More

- Royal decree that brings deliverance: EZRA 6:1–15
  - Victory for God's people: EXODUS 17:8–16
    - Authority and influence: 1 KINGS 4

# JOB

*God is good and can be trusted, even if we
live with unanswered questions.*

## SETTING THE STAGE

The book of Job is a profound exploration of human suffering, divine sovereignty, and the nature of faith. Classified as wisdom literature, it seeks to answer the age-old question: Why does God allow suffering and evil in the world? It also challenges the simplistic correlation between righteousness and prosperity.

In the first verse of the book, we meet Job—a wealthy and upright man living in the land of Uz. Unbeknownst to Job, God and Satan discuss Job's faithfulness. God ultimately permits Satan to afflict Job with unimaginable loss and suffering. . .while preserving his life.

The majority of the book records the dialogue and debate between Job and his three friends—Eliphaz, Bildad, and Zophar. They initially come to comfort Job but end up discussing the nature of suffering and God's justice in a deeply unhelpful way.

Job understandably wants an audience with God, and God responds to Job out of a whirlwind. Though God never directly answers Job's questions, He does offer a series of rhetorical questions that highlight His wisdom, creativity, and power that's evident in the natural world. This response humbles Job, and God chooses to restore Job's fortune, doubling his previous blessings.

In the end, Job finds a renewed sense of purpose and a greater understanding of God's majesty.

## GOOD TO KNOW

Author not stated. Date is unclear, but many believe Job is one of the oldest stories in the Bible, perhaps from approximately 2000 BC.

*The Bible is countercultural, and so is Bible study.*
*There's no need to rush through this.*

## JOB 1

Job is a blameless and upright man living in Uz. Though he doesn't know it, a conversation about him is taking place in heaven. Satan challenges God's praise of Job, claiming the man only serves God because of His many blessings. So God allows Satan to test Job's faith by afflicting him with loss and suffering. Job remains faithful.

*How does Job's response to suffering challenge your ability to trust God during trials?*

## JOB 2

Satan challenges God's assessment of Job again, prompting another test. This time, Job is afflicted with painful sores from his head to his feet (2:7). Job's wife urges him to curse God and die, but Job remains steadfast. Three of Job's friends arrive and sit in silence with him. Job wrestles with his anguish and God's justice.

*God limits Satan's actions in this story. What does this teach you about God's role in trials?*

## JOB 3

Job laments the day he was born, and he longs to die. He asks questions that have no easy answers—like, "Why did I not die from the womb?" (3:11)—and he expresses extreme despair. His words reveal the depth of his suffering, highlighting the profound agony of his situation.

*Have you ever found it hard to balance your questions for God with your trust in His goodness?*

## JOB 4

The kindest thing Job's friends did for him was sit in silence (2:13). But now they begin to speak. Accusing Job of weak faith, Eliphaz asserts that suffering is a consequence of sin: "Who ever perished, being innocent?" (4:7). Grossly oversimplifying the complexities of suffering, Eliphaz urges Job to repent, believing restoration will follow.

*How do you ensure that your responses to others' suffering reflect Christlike compassion?*

*Take Your Time and Learn More*

- Testing and the response of faith: LUKE 22:31–34
- Steadfastness in the face of suffering: 1 PETER 5
- Deep anguish: PSALM 88
- Suffering and its role in spiritual growth: JAMES 1:2–12

*God speaks in the quiet moments.*
*Approach His Word with calm expectation.*

## JOB 5

Eliphaz continues talking. . .and what he says is not entirely wrong. He urges Job to seek God and trust His wisdom, but he also continues to assert that suffering comes from sin. No doubt genuinely believing he's offering wise counsel, Eliphaz advises Job to repent in order to restore blessings and peace. And Job lets him talk.

*How do you respond to unhelpful counsel from friends and family?*

## JOB 6

Job responds to Eliphaz, saying he feels abandoned by his friends and by his God. He questions the value of his suffering and seeks understanding for his pain, but he receives only criticism and disappointment. Poignantly, he says, "To him who is afflicted pity should be shown from his friend. But he forsakes the fear of the Almighty" (6:14).

*In times of suffering, do you find it difficult to be honest with God and others? Why or why not?*

## JOB 7

Job continues his response, lamenting his suffering and the brevity of human life. He compares his days on earth to those of a hired worker, longing for relief from his pain. He questions God's attention to human suffering and pleads for death as a release from his torment.

*How do you reconcile your own suffering with your understanding of God's character?*

## JOB 8

Bildad, another of Job's friends, speaks. He insists that God justly rewards the righteous. Like Eliphaz before him, Bildad isn't entirely wrong. But even when he begins a thought correctly, he typically ends it horribly. Bildad too has an oversimplified understanding of God's retribution and blessing.

*Have you ever felt that prosperity proves faith and suffering proves a lack of faith? Is that true?*

## Take Your Time and Learn More

- Calling out to God in times of trouble: PSALM 34
- Desire to flee from trouble: PSALM 55
- Brevity of human life: PSALM 90
- God's eternal perspective: PSALM 147:5

*Before you read, pray. Ask God to*
*speak His truth to your spirit.*

## JOB 9

Job responds by acknowledging God's total supremacy and his own insignificance by comparison. He laments his inability to argue his case with God, longing for a mediator to plead his innocence. He feels trapped between trusting God's justice and witnessing his own suffering.

*How does Job's struggle affect your own understanding of God's purposes in pain?*

## JOB 10

Job continues his response, but he addresses God this time. Feeling abandoned and unfairly targeted, he wrestles with the Lord's justice. Despite his despair, Job pleads for God's understanding, hoping for relief from his anguish and a chance to plead his case before God. He knows he's hiding no obvious sin (10:7).

*Do you often bring your feelings to God in prayer, or do you tend to internalize them? Why?*

## JOB 11

Zophar, another friend, rebukes Job, accusing him of speaking falsely about God's justice. Like the other men before him, Zophar presumes to know God's motives and thoughts. Zophar insists Job repent in order to restore his fortunes. He warns Job of God's retribution for the wicked and commends His blessings for the righteous.

*Why is it tempting to rush to shallow conclusions when we're faced with suffering?*

## JOB 12

Feeling the weight of his pain, Job rebukes his friends for their lack of understanding. He recognizes God's wisdom and His sovereignty over all creation. Job knows God's mercy is his only hope. He maintains his faith even as he seeks understanding in the mysteries of suffering.

*How do the responses of Job's friends demonstrate the impact of our words on those who suffer?*

## Take Your Time and Learn More

- Humanity's humble position before God: PSALM 8
- God's intimate involvement in human life: PSALM 139
- Seeking wisdom and guidance from God: PROVERBS 3
- God's sovereignty over human arrogance: PSALM 94

*Don't hurry, don't worry. God's Word provides everything you need for living well.*

## JOB 13

Job continues to defend his integrity to his friends. He expresses frustration with their lack of wisdom and accuses them of being deceptive. Job fiercely maintains his trust in God with the words, "Though He slay me, I will still trust in Him" (13:15). Even as he grieves, Job's faith outshines his confusion.

*What can Job's friends teach us about the superiority of God's wisdom over people's?*

## JOB 14

Job reflects on the brevity of life, comparing it to a flower that withers and a shadow that fades. He longs for relief from his suffering, and he questions whether there is hope after death. But even in his honest complaints, Job acknowledges that God—not Satan—is sovereign over the length of life (14:5).

*How does considering eternity affect the way you think about the hard parts of your life?*

## JOB 15

Eliphaz gets a second chance to speak, and he doubles down on his original message. In addition to insisting that Job's suffering is due to a specific sin, he accuses Job of arrogance. Eliphaz again urges Job to repent and return to God, believing that's the only way to end his suffering.

*Do you listen to your friends' advice (whether good or bad) with humility, or do you immediately become defensive? Why?*

## JOB 16

Job's friends are miserable comforters, and he finally tells them so. He feels not only attacked by God but abandoned by everyone else. He still maintains his innocence and longs for justice. His anguish deepens, but his faith remains.

*What are some of the best ways you've felt supported during seasons of intense suffering?*

## Take Your Time and Learn More

- God's nearness to those who seek Him: PSALM 139
- Human mortality: PSALM 90
- Righteousness versus wickedness: PSALM 1
- Seeking God's intervention: PSALM 69

*God loves it when you read and study His Word.*

## JOB 17

Beginning with "My breath is corrupt. My days are extinct" (verse 1), Job continues to express his despair, feeling as though his hopes are dashed. He laments his suffering and his friends' lack of support. He longs for vindication and assurances of God's presence, but he finds no comfort in his current pain.

*This book was written thousands of years ago. Why are Job's words still relatable?*

## JOB 18

The dialogue between Job and his friends continues. Bildad rebukes Job, accusing him of arrogant words and suggesting (again) that Job's suffering is due to his own wickedness. He correctly portrays the fate of the wicked as darkness, destruction, and terror. . .but then unnecessarily warns Job to repent in order to avoid the same future.

*How do these discourses illustrate the importance of reading scripture in context?*

## JOB 19

Job responds to Bildad's accusations, expressing deep sadness. Yet—almost as if he can't help it—Job continues speaking eternal truth about God. He articulates a profound sense of hope in the midst of his suffering, saying, "I know that my Redeemer lives and that He shall stand at the latter day on the earth" (19:25).

*Why do you think Job could speak such powerful truth about God in his worst moments?*

## JOB 20

In Zophar's final speech, he continues his condemnation by vividly describing the fleeting nature of wealth and the severity of God's judgment on the unrighteous. And again, he warns Job of the consequences of sin.

*What can these conversations teach you about the importance of depending on God rather than seeking validation from people?*

## Take Your Time and Learn More

- Trust in God's deliverance: PSALM 31
- God's justice: PSALM 73
- Hope of ultimate vindication: PSALM 22
- Consequences of righteous and wicked behavior: PSALM 37

*Reading the Bible isn't a race. Let the pages unfold*
*at a pace that allows your spirit to breathe.*

## JOB 21

Job refutes the idea that God rewards the faithful with prosperity and punishes the wicked with hardship. He creates a long list of good things that can happen to wicked people. The assumption, of course, is that if good things happen to wicked people, bad things can happen to faithful people.

*Why is it so deeply embedded in our minds that only*
*good things will happen to good people?*

## JOB 22

Eliphaz shares his final words with Job, accusing him of hiding sin and insisting that Job's suffering is the result of his wickedness. He urges Job to repent, promising restoration if he returns to God. He confidently claims that the righteous prosper while the wicked suffer, and he uses this belief to justify his accusations against Job.

*What are the dangers of always linking suffering to personal sin, as Eliphaz does here?*

## JOB 23

Job desperately wants to plead his case directly before God's judgment seat (23:3). He's looking for reasons for his afflictions and the assurance that he has not sinned against God. He says, "But He knows the way that I take. When He has tested me, I shall come forth as gold" (23:10). Though his friends don't understand him, Job believes that God does.

*Is it possible to question God's ways while still trusting His plans? Why or why not?*

## JOB 24

Job questions why the wicked seem to prosper while the vulnerable remain oppressed. To Job, God seems indifferent to those who exploit the helpless. He wants answers for God's silence. Job notes the disparity between the prosperous wicked and the suffering righteous.

*Have you ever struggled to reconcile God's silence with His*
*goodness? Where have you taken these struggles?*

## *Take Your Time and Learn More*

- Apparent prosperity of the wicked and suffering of the righteous: PSALM 73
- God's presence in every aspect of life: PSALM 139
- Guidance during times of trial: PSALM 23
- Plight of the innocent: PSALM 10

145

*The greatest truths in scripture are often
revealed in the unhurried moments.*

## JOB 25

Bildad gives his final speech to Job. He talks about God's supremacy over humanity, emphasizing that no one can be righteous before the Lord. Bildad says humans are flawed compared to God. And while his words aren't untrue, they aren't particularly helpful or encouraging to Job, who is in pain. Like the other men, he oversimplifies the nature of suffering.

*Why do Bildad's words ultimately fall short of what Job needs to hear?*

## JOB 26

Job responds to Bildad by acknowledging God's sovereignty. He praises God's power, wisdom, and control over creation, aacknowledging the limitations of human understanding in comprehending the complexity of God's plans. Job seems to understand what his friends do not: there is great mystery in suffering. God alone knows the reasons for every season of suffering.

*How can acknowledging God's control over the world
be helpful to you during your suffering?*

## JOB 27

Continuing his discourse with his friends, Job asserts his integrity. While he never claims to be sinless, he also knows his current suffering isn't due to any particular sin. He knows the wicked will face judgment, but he also reaffirms his righteousness and his trust in God's justice.

*Why do you think God included the details of Job's
difficult conversations with his friends?*

## JOB 28

Still speaking to the three friends, Job talks about the mystery of wisdom, comparing its value to precious metals and gems. He says God alone gives wisdom and that man's search for wisdom leads ultimately to the fear of the Lord. (Note: Solomon, the wisest man who ever lived, will much later echo many of the same thoughts in his writing.)

*Do you believe wisdom can be gained without experiencing suffering? Why or why not?*

## Take Your Time and Learn More

- Humility of humanity before God: PSALM 8
- God's majesty and work in the world: PSALM 104
- Ultimate reward of the righteous and
  downfall of the wicked: PSALM 9
- The importance of seeking wisdom: PROVERBS 2

*Bible study is truly a lifelong journey.*
*Relax and enjoy the trip.*

## JOB 29

Job reflects on his past. He remembers being in positions of leadership and having compassion on the oppressed. These memories—while good—seem to intensify his current suffering. His lament reveals his profound loss and his desire for things to be what they once were.

*In 29:1-4, Job describes his relationship with God.*
*How does your relationship with God compare?*

## JOB 30

Job continues by contrasting his previous life of honor with his current state of humility. Lamenting his ongoing suffering, he feels rejected by society and afflicted by God. His anguish is palpable as he struggles to understand why his former life has been replaced with this one. Job has so many unanswered questions.

*What do you do with the big unanswered questions in your life?*

## JOB 31

Again, Job proclaims his innocence to his friends and details his commitment to living righteously. Specifically, he denies lust, dishonesty, adultery, and mistreatment of servants—then he appeals to God's judgment against his accusers. At last, Job is finished talking to his friends.

*How can you live with the tension between sadness and faith in God's goodness?*

## JOB 32

A fourth man, Elihu, has been listening to the discussion between Job and his three friends. Frustrated, the young man speaks—but it is more of an angry outburst. He too will only pour salt in the wound of Job's suffering. Later, Elihu will even claim to speak on God's behalf (Job 36:2).

*Elihu says age doesn't always equal wisdom, nor does*
*youth indicate foolishness. Do you agree?*

### Take Your Time and Learn More

- Reflection on prosperity: PSALM 112
- Profound despair during intense suffering: PSALM 88
- Integrity before God: PSALM 101
- Importance of listening to wise counsel: PROVERBS 18

*Try to forget the demands of life for a while.*
*You're spending quality time with God.*

## JOB 33

Elihu rebukes Job for accusing God of injustice. He urges Job to repent to avoid further suffering. And though Elihu indicates the importance of humility, he lacks humility when he says, "Remain silent, and I shall teach you wisdom" (33:33). Elihu sets the stage for God's eventual response.

*Job's friends are often right about God and wrong about Job. What does this teach you about people's sincere efforts to counsel the suffering?*

## JOB 34

Elihu accuses Job of speaking without knowledge. Claiming to speak on behalf of God's righteousness, Elihu challenges Job's righteousness. He declares (as the other men did previously) that God punishes the wicked and rewards the righteous (34:11). Elihu rejects Job's claims of innocence and urges him to humbly submit to God's wisdom and sovereignty.

*Are unfair rebukes more painful when coming from fellow believers? Why or why not?*

## JOB 35

Elihu rebukes Job for speaking rashly. He challenges Job's claim of righteousness, adding a layer to the ongoing debate by suggesting that righteousness benefits humans more than it benefits God. He suggests God is not affected by human behavior. Like the other friends, Elihu uses perceived truths about God to crush Job.

*Do you agree with Elihu (35:6–8) that our behavior affects other people more than it does God?*

## JOB 36

Elihu continues his speech by saying, "Bear with me a little" (36:2)—ironic, since Job has been patiently bearing with Elihu since chapter 32. Warning against rebellion, Elihu urges Job to trust God's righteousness. He emphasizes the importance of repentance and submission to God's discipline, promising restoration if Job humbles himself before God.

*How do we see "the patience of Job" in this discussion with his friends?*

## Take Your Time and Learn More

- Restoration of relationship with God: Psalm 32
- Importance of aligning with God's truth: Psalm 119
- God's justice: Psalm 37
- God's compassion and mercy toward His creation: Psalm 103

## Good things come to those who wait—on the Lord, that is.

### JOB 37

Elihu concludes his speech by extolling God's majesty through the wonder of nature, specifically seen in storms. He correctly says, "God thunders marvelously with His voice. He does great things, which we cannot comprehend" (37:5). Elihu emphasizes God's control and encourages Job to consider God's greatness and submit to His sovereignty.

*During difficult seasons, does nature encourage you? Why or why not?*

### JOB 38

Finally, God speaks, responding to Job out of a whirlwind. He first establishes His character, since everything else is secondary. He probes Job's understanding of creation and sovereignty, implying the limitations of human strength and wisdom. God is responding to Job's questions, even if He doesn't answer them. God speaks; Job listens.

*How does pondering God's total control provide comfort in times of uncertainty or suffering?*

### JOB 39

God continues to speak. After establishing His character, He communicates His omnipotence. He talks about the instincts and behaviors of various animals, emphasizing His wisdom in their design and care. In each example, He illustrates His authority over all aspects of the natural world, affirming His unmatched wisdom and power. There is no one like God.

*What can you learn about God's character from the way He responds to Job?*

### JOB 40

Continuing to speak, God challenges Job's understanding of His justice and power by asking if Job "contends with the Almighty" (40:2). For the first time since God began asking Job questions, Job answers. In humility he says, "Behold, I am vile. What shall I answer You?" (40:4). So God resumes His questioning.

*How is God's response to Job so much more helpful and holy than the response of Job's friends?*

## Take Your Time and Learn More

- God's power and sovereignty over creation: PSALM 29
  - God's wisdom and authority in shaping and sustaining the world: PSALM 104
- God's providential care for His creation: PSALM 147
  - God's incomparable greatness: ISAIAH 40

*The Bible is countercultural, and so is Bible study.
There's no need to rush through this.*

## JOB 41

God concludes His questions by depicting the mighty Leviathan, a creature of awe-inspiring strength. The description of this creature serves to highlight God's incomprehensible power and authority over all things. He can control what is most formidable and intimidating. God beautifully and rightfully says, "Whatever is under the whole heaven is Mine" (41:11).

*Does it help you to recognize that everything in the world belongs to God? Why or why not?*

## JOB 42

Job humbly acknowledges God's sovereignty and repents of his complaints. But God never rebukes Job; rather, He strongly rebukes Job's friends. God then doubly restores everything Job lost—except his children. (Some scholars believe this is because those children would be restored to Job in eternity.) Job's suffering is redeemed, and he lives 140 more years.

*How is God's heart for restoration on display in this story?*

### Take Your Time and Learn More

- God's authority over and supremacy over all creation: PSALM 74
- Suffering, humility, and restoration: JAMES 5

# PSALMS

*God wants and welcomes our worship—*
*lament, praise, faith, and hope.*

## SETTING THE STAGE

The book of Psalms is a much-loved and dearly treasured collection of 150 poetic and lyrical writings. They come from many different periods in Israel's history and span the full range of themes and emotions.

Given its many literary devices (such as parallelism, imagery, metaphor, and hyperbole) as well as its rich and beautiful descriptions of our relationship with God, this book is often called the hymnbook or prayer book of the Bible. Christians often turn to the Psalms during their highest and lowest moments in life since the book has something helpful to offer in every situation.

Collectively, the book of Psalms accomplishes three main objectives.

First, it serves as a guide for worship and prayer. Many of the psalms provide an accessible and tangible language for individuals and communities to communicate with God.

Second, the book of Psalms offers biblically saturated language for lament and comfort. The psalm writers demonstrate that it is acceptable to bring our honest questions to God, and they show us how to do it. They also provide a comprehensive resource for finding hope and comfort in life's most difficult moments.

Third, Psalms contains an abundance of wisdom and instruction. As part of the Bible's wisdom literature, the psalms offer insight into righteous living, fear of God, and pursuit of holiness.

The psalms are timeless and transparent, as relevant today as they were when they were written.

## GOOD TO KNOW

Various authors, with nearly half of the psalms attributed to David. Other names noted include Solomon, Moses, Asaph, Ethan, and the sons of Korah. Many psalms don't mention an author. Written approximately the 1400s BC (Moses' time) through the 500s BC (the time of the Jews' Babylonian exile).

*God speaks in the quiet moments.*
*Approach His Word with calm expectation.*

## PSALM 1

The righteous delight in God's law, meditating on it day and night. Like trees planted by a stream of water, they are nourished by God's Word. It upholds and sustains them. And this delight informs everything they do. The wicked, on the other hand, are like chaff—blown away by the wind—fleeting and worthless and ultimately destined for destruction.

*Do your closest relationships draw you closer to God or lead you away from Him?*

## PSALM 2

The nations are rebelling against God and against the new king—likely David. Despite the people's plotting, God establishes His reign and warns the people to submit, emphasizing His sovereignty and the futility of opposing His rule. Even still, God is gracious, and there are blessings for those who take refuge in Him.

*How strongly do you feel pressured by culture to conform to worldly perspectives?*

## PSALM 3

This psalm is the first of thirteen linked to a specific event in David's life. It also contains the first occurrence of the word *Selah*. David wrote this prayer during a time of deep distress while fleeing from his son Absalom. He expresses lament over his enemies and hope in the Lord.

*When you're unable to sleep because of anxious thoughts, how often do you talk to God about it?*

## PSALM 4

David writes this evening hymn to express his persistent trust in God in the midst of adversity. He is confident God won't abandon him in his darkest moments. Specifically, David draws attention to the one blessing that nothing (or nobody) can steal from him: his peace (4:8). David's confidence in God is directly linked to his ability to rest.

*How is internal peace from God different than external peace from circumstances?*

### Take Your Time and Learn More

- Trees planted by water: JEREMIAH 17:7–8
- Peter and John quote from Psalm 2: ACTS 4:23–26
- David's reliance on God in times of trouble: 2 SAMUEL 15–18
- Trust and reliance on God in times of trouble: PHILIPPIANS 4:6–7

*Before you read, pray. Ask God to*
*speak His truth to your spirit.*

## PSALM 5

Deeply ingrained in ancient Israel's view of God is the truth that He hates all evil. So in this psalm, David appeals to God in prayer by repeatedly acknowledging the Lord's loathing of sin and calling on His justice to make things right. David understands that his enemies' actions against him are ultimately rebellion against God (5:10).

*What does It look like—practically and generally—to seek refuge in God each day?*

## PSALM 6

David writes this psalm during a time of intense personal distress. Remember, the psalms are poetry, so the writers often use hyperbole to make a point (see 6:5). Ultimately, David knows—despite his weakness and suffering—that God will deliver him. So he places his confidence in the Lord.

*Why is it important to always read Bible verses in context?*

## PSALM 7

This psalm is the first in a series (7, 27, 31, 34, 52) by David during his time as a fugitive. It is a lament—a plea for justice and protection. David begs God for vindication, asking that the wicked be caught in their own schemes while the righteous be preserved by the Lord's steadfast love.

*Have you ever chosen to trust God's judgment rather than seek revenge? If so, how did it go?*

## PSALM 8

David marvels at God's majesty in creation, contrasting God's glory with man's insignificance. Yet in spite of human frailty, God chooses to love and care for the people He created. David's natural response is "How excellent is Your name in all the earth!" (8:9).

*Do you ever ponder the fact that the God who holds the stars in place also cares about every detail of your life?*

## Take Your Time and Learn More

- Prayers of the righteous: PROVERBS 15:29
- Jesus' use of hyperbole: MARK 9:43–49
- God's righteous judgment: ROMANS 2:5
- Hebrews quotes from Psalm 8: HEBREWS 2:5–9

*Don't hurry, don't worry. God's Word provides
everything you need for living well.*

## PSALM 9

David praises God's justice, celebrating His righteous judgment against his enemies. David recounts God's gracious deliverance and refuge in times of trouble, no doubt reminding himself why he can trust in God's unfailing protection now and in the future.

*David opens the psalm by writing, "I will praise You, O LORD, with my whole heart;
I will show forth all Your marvelous works" (9:1). For what can you thank God today?*

## PSALM 10

This psalm is a lament over the wickedness and arrogance of evildoers who oppress the vulnerable. The psalmist cries out to God, questioning His apparent silence in the face of injustice. Yet even as the wicked say, "God has forgotten" (10:11), David answers by expressing confidence in God's faithful character.

*Are you ever tempted to believe "God has forgotten"?
How can you remind yourself otherwise?*

## PSALM 11

Likely written when David was being hunted by Saul, this psalm expresses trust in God's protection. The larger theme is God's provision for the righteous when they are mistreated by the wicked. God sees, knows, and cares. So David is certain his confidence in God can withstand trials.

*Have you ever trusted God through mistreatment instead of
taking matters into your own hands? How did it go?*

## PSALM 12

The psalmist expresses his frustration over the prevalence of deceit and flattery. He laments the lack of truthful people and the abundance of liars. In contrast, the psalmist praises God's faithfulness, expressing absolute confidence that His words are always pure and true.

*Why is it so important for Christians to consistently speak the truth?*

### Take Your Time and Learn More

- God's righteous rule over the nations: REVELATION 19:1–3
- True religion cares for the vulnerable: JAMES 1:27
- Trusting God's wisdom: PROVERBS 3:5–6
- Purity of God's Word: PROVERBS 30:5

*God loves it when you read and study His Word.*

## PSALM 13

Four times David cries, "How long?" He questions God's apparent silence. David's raw honesty and deep faith are on display; still, David ends the psalm singing to the Lord "because He has dealt bountifully with me" (13:6). Even before David receives what he requests, he praises the God who provides.

*What are you waiting on God for today?*
*Can you praise Him now for an answer yet to come?*

## PSALM 14

This psalm paints a bleak picture of the godless. It is nearly identical to Psalm 53, and Romans 3:10-12 references it while describing humanity's sinful condition. Despite the prevailing wickedness of the human heart, David expresses a confident belief that "the LORD is his refuge" (14:6) and will restore the fortunes of His people.

*Are you ever discouraged by the world's wickedness*
*and injustice? How do you find hope?*

## PSALM 15

The one who dwells in God's presence is filled with integrity, righteousness, truthfulness, and justice. This person honors his commitments, speaks honestly, and lends to people in need without exploiting them. While moral living does not earn salvation, authentic Christian living glorifies God and leads to deeper communion with Him.

*How diligent are you in fulfilling your promises and honoring your word as sacred?*

## PSALM 16

This psalm is a declaration of trust and confidence in God's protection, provision, and presence. The psalmist acknowledges God as the source of all blessings and delight. He rejects idolatry and finds contentment, confidence, and joy in God alone.

*How does this psalm challenge our cultural mind-set of happiness and fulfillment?*

## Take Your Time and Learn More

- Lament in suffering: LAMENTATIONS 3:55–58
- Paul quotes from Psalm 14: ROMANS 3:10–12
- Living a life of moral integrity: MICAH 6:8
- Peter quotes from Psalm 16: ACTS 2:25–28

*Reading the Bible isn't a race. Let the pages unfold at a pace that allows your spirit to breathe.*

## PSALM 17

David prays for God's vindication against his enemies. He appeals to God's righteousness, asking for protection from wicked men and expressing confidence in God's deliverance. He contrasts his integrity with the deceit of his enemies, and he seeks refuge in God's unfailing love, anticipating His gracious intervention.

*David relied on God as his best and only option. In what situation do you need to do the same?*

## PSALM 18

David writes this psalm on the day God gloriously rescued him from the hand of all his enemies—specifically Saul. David clearly testifies to God's goodness and faithfulness through his trials. He knows God is the only source of anything good in his life.

*When has God graciously delivered you from a difficult trial? How did this change your relationship with Him?*

## PSALM 19

Many consider Psalm 19 to be the most beautiful psalm, combining powerful metaphorical language with profound biblical theology. It begins with a declaration of God's glory and concludes with a prayer for acceptance of the psalmist's words and thoughts. It highlights the way God's creation and His Word reveal His character and guide His people.

*How do you cultivate obedience to God in a world that glorifies different priorities?*

## PSALM 20

This psalm is a prayer for victory, specifically during times of war or conflict. The psalmist acknowledges that victory and protection ultimately come from God, who offers unfailing support to His people.

*Do you believe God influences the outcomes of modern-day conflicts? Why or why not?*

## Take Your Time and Learn More

- Jesus' prayer for deliverance: MATTHEW 26:36–46
- Song of thanksgiving: 2 SAMUEL 22
- God's glory in creation: ROMANS 1:18–23
- Reliance on God's power over human strength: ISAIAH 31:1

*The greatest truths in scripture are often
revealed in the unhurried moments.*

## PSALM 21

While Psalm 20 *asks* for victory, Psalm 21 *celebrates* victory. It is a song of thanksgiving and praise for God's blessings. The psalm alludes to a better King (Christ) and His coming kingdom, and it concludes with a vow of continued praise and trust in God's unfailing support.

*Do you naturally recognize God's role in your successes,
or do you point to your own effort?*

## PSALM 22

Psalms 22, 23, and 24 form a trilogy. Psalm 22 depicts the good shepherd giving His life for His sheep, Psalm 23 illustrates the great shepherd caring tenderly for His sheep, and Psalm 24 demonstrates the chief shepherd returning as King of glory to reward His sheep. These beautiful psalms foreshadow Christ's suffering and the glorious redemption it will bring.

*How does considering God as your shepherd encourage you during difficult seasons?*

## PSALM 23

Just as a good shepherd cares for his sheep, so God tenderly cares for His people. It is His joy to provide His children with guidance, provision, and protection. The psalmist David finds comfort and reassurance in God's presence, even when facing danger and adversity. Trusting in the great shepherd's care, David experiences peace and contentment.

*How does this psalm shape your understanding of God's
character and your relationship with Him?*

## PSALM 24

God is the sovereign Creator and King over all creation. He is holy and should be approached with "clean hands and a pure heart" (24:4) as we celebrate His glory and acknowledge His power. The psalmist David calls for the gates to be lifted for this King of glory to enter, affirming God's eternal reign and supreme authority.

*How can you cultivate a deeper reverence for
God in your thoughts, words, and actions?*

## Take Your Time and Learn More

- God's faithfulness to His anointed: 2 SAMUEL 7:1–17
  - Jesus' crucifixion: MATTHEW 27:35–56
  - The good shepherd: JOHN 10:11–18
  - Entrance of the King: REVELATION 19:11–16

*Bible study is truly a lifelong journey.*
*Relax and enjoy the trip.*

## PSALM 25

This psalm is a prayer, written by David for guidance, forgiveness, and deliverance. When he says, "For Your name's sake" (25:11), he's appealing to God's character and reputation, asking God to act according to His own glory and honor rather than human merit. David humbly admits his faults, demonstrating that confession of sin shows great wisdom.

*How is it encouraging that those who fear God have the deepest relationship with Him (25:14)?*

## PSALM 26

David is suffering as a result of unfair circumstances, so he seeks vindication before God. He doesn't deny he's a sinner, but he denies that his current trouble is due to specific sin in his life. This psalm emphasizes the importance of living a life of integrity and seeking God's guidance when being mistreated.

*Do you regularly examine your life? How can that help to maintain your integrity?*

## PSALM 27

Some scholars believe David wrote this psalm of lament while hiding in the wilderness. But far more than safety from those seeking to kill him, David wants God's nearness, asking only that he may dwell with God all the days of his life (27:4).

*How do you cultivate confidence in God's protection in the midst of difficult circumstances?*

## PSALM 28

While the circumstances behind this psalm are unclear, Psalm 28 is attributed to David. Pleading for God's help, he appeals to God's justice to intervene against the wicked and reward them according to their deeds. He concludes the psalm with a declaration of trust and a call to worship God forever.

*How persistent are you in praying for God's intervention in your life and in the lives of others?*

## Take Your Time and Learn More

- Prayer for guidance: PSALM 86:11
- Heart examination: PSALM 139:23–24
- Confidence in God's protection: PSALM 62:1–2
- God is a stronghold: PSALM 18:2

*Try to forget the demands of life for a while.*
*You're spending quality time with God.*

## PSALM 29

This psalm glorifies God's majestic power, depicted through the imagery of thunder. It emphasizes His supremacy over creation, inviting the reader to "give to the LORD the glory due to His name" (29:2). But not only is He a God of power, He's a God of peace (29:11). He is truly worthy to be praised!

*How much do you incorporate praise for God's*
*name into your daily prayers and worship?*

## PSALM 30

This psalm is bookended with praise, opening with "I will extoll You" and ending with "I will give thanks to You forever." David acknowledges God's faithfulness in turning his mourning into dancing and clothing him with joy. He celebrates God's power to rescue and restore, inviting others to thank God too.

*Do you boast about God? What could you tell someone*
*today about God's faithfulness to you?*

## PSALM 31

Bookending this lament with praise, David expresses wholehearted confidence in God. It is David's personal experience with God over the years that now enables him to trust God with his life. So he commits to praising God even as he waits for Him to act on his behalf.

*How can the ways God has helped you in the past*
*encourage you to trust Him in the future?*

## PSALM 32

There is blessing for those whose sins are forgiven and whose guilt is covered by God. The psalmist reflects on the misery of trying to hide sin, acknowledging the freedom that results from confession. There is joy in the forgiveness and peace that come from being reconciled to God.

*Have you ever felt the weight of unconfessed sin. . .followed*
*by the freedom of confessing it to God?*

## Take Your Time and Learn More

- Worship and reverence due to God: 1 CHRONICLES 16:29
- Gratitude and praise: ISAIAH 12:1
- Help and deliverance from enemies: LAMENTATIONS 3:55–57
- Paul quotes from Psalm 32: ROMANS 4:7–8

*Good things come to those who wait—on the Lord, that is.*

## PSALM 33

This psalm invites the reader to praise God, giving specific reasons why God is worthy of this praise—namely, His Word is trustworthy and His actions are just. The psalmist urges righteous living, recognizing God's watchful care over those who fear Him and hope in His steadfast love (33:18). When people fail to praise God, they contradict their very purpose.

*Reflect on a time God demonstrated His faithfulness by clearly intervening in your life.*

## PSALM 34

This chapter is an acrostic poem, meaning each verse begins with successive letters of the Hebrew alphabet. And all of them celebrate God's faithfulness. David recounts his deliverance and affirms God's gracious care for the righteous. He acknowledges that God's protection and provision are for those who seek Him.

*Could you note twenty-six ways God has blessed you, beginning with each letter of the alphabet?*

## PSALM 35

David's prayer in this psalm uses military language. Phrases such as "take hold of shield and buckler" and "draw out also the spear" depict a battle scene in which David calls on God to fight on his behalf, defend his innocence, and bring judgment on his enemies.

*What biblical examples demonstrate the benefits of being still and letting God fight the battle?*

## PSALM 36

This psalm contrasts the arrogance, deceitfulness, and wickedness of the ungodly with the steadfast love, faithfulness, and righteousness of God. The psalmist finds refuge in God's protection, celebrating His abundant blessings and seeking His guidance and salvation from evildoers.

*For what can you thank God that illustrates His abundant provision and blessing in your life?*

## Take Your Time and Learn More

- The eternal nature of God: PSALM 90:2
- God is good: 1 PETER 2:3
- Treatment of enemies: MATTHEW 5:44
- The depravity of sinners: ROMANS 3:10–18

*The Bible is countercultural, and so is Bible study.*
*There's no need to rush through this.*

## PSALM 37

Here David writes a wisdom psalm—contrasting life and death, wisdom and folly, reward and punishment. He begins by urging the faithful not to worry about the apparent success of the wicked. Without God, their accomplishments are fleeting. Ultimately, God will uphold the righteous and reward their faithfulness.

*How do you resist the temptation to envy the successes of those who disobey God?*

## PSALM 38

In this psalm, David calls out to God for healing from physical and spiritual pain. Scholars believe David is now dealing with an illness or disease. Not all disease, of course, can be attributed to personal sin, but David has reason to believe God is disciplining him. He is overwhelmed and wants nothing more than renewed fellowship with God.

*How do you incorporate confession and repentance into your daily faith walk?*

## PSALM 39

The psalmist David reflects on the brevity of life and the frailty of humanity. He wrestles with the limitations of human existence, contemplating the fleeting nature of time and the inevitability of death. Even in this introspection, the psalmist seeks God's guidance, acknowledging his need for wisdom in navigating life's challenges.

*How should the Christian's perspective on life differ from the world's?*

## PSALM 40

This psalm, written by David, is a song of praise and thanksgiving based on God's past acts of faithfulness and deliverance. We will see verses 13-17 again—nearly verbatim—in Psalm 70. David responds to God's gracious salvation by expressing his wholehearted desire to do the Lord's will.

*When have you intentionally taken a few minutes just to consider what God has done for you? How did that go?*

## Take Your Time and Learn More

- Inheritance of the earth: MATTHEW 5:5
- Deep distress and cry for mercy in times of affliction: PSALM 6:1
- Brevity of life: JAMES 4:14
- Hebrews quotes from Psalm 40: HEBREWS 10:5-7

*God speaks in the quiet moments.*
*Approach His Word with calm expectation.*

## PSALM 41

This psalm expresses gratitude for God's blessings and contains a prayer for healing and restoration from illness. God's promises to His children are always trustworthy, even in moments of pain. Psalm 41:9 appears to reference Jesus' betrayal, using nearly identical words to John 13:18–19. God cares deeply about His own.

*Have you ever faced betrayal? If so, how did you rely on God for help and healing?*

## PSALM 42

Likely written by an Israelite in exile, this psalm contains a beautiful metaphor of a deer panting for water, illustrating the psalmist's deep thirst for God. Unable to visit the temple for worship, the writer expresses longing and sorrow, reminding himself to "hope in God, for I shall yet praise Him" (42:11).

*Have you ever been unable to worship with fellow believers for a while? How did that affect you?*

## PSALM 43

This psalm is a continuation of Psalm 42. Many Bible scholars believe these two psalms should actually be treated as one. The psalmist continues expressing a desire for justice, asking God to defend him against his enemies. Despite feeling overwhelmed, the psalmist preaches truth to himself (43:5), choosing to hope in God.

*In moments of pain, are you more likely to listen to your dark thoughts or speak truth to them?*

## PSALM 44

This psalm is a national lament after defeat in battle. The psalmist expresses distress over God's apparent abandonment of Israel. He remembers that God once faithfully delivered them. . .yet they're now experiencing defeat and humiliation. The psalm ends with a plea for God to intervene and deliver His people from their enemies.

*Do you believe God's silence is always a sign of His anger or discipline? Why or why not?*

## Take Your Time and Learn More

- Betrayal and loyalty: JOHN 13:18
- Longing and thirst: ISAIAH 55:1
- Hope in God: ROMANS 15:13
- Overwhelming victory through God: ROMANS 8:37–39

*Before you read, pray. Ask God to*
*speak His truth to your spirit.*

## PSALM 45

This psalm is a majestic and celebratory poem—often considered a royal psalm or a song meant to be sung at a royal marriage. It begins with praise for the king and concludes with a blessing for his reign. Along with the next two psalms, it foreshadows Christ and His bride, the church.

*How can you cultivate a spirit of celebration in your worship and service to God?*

## PSALM 46

This psalm is a powerful expression of confidence in God during chaos. The references to God as a "refuge" and "fortress" inspired Martin Luther's famed sixteenth-century hymn, "A Mighty Fortress Is Our God." The psalm concludes with a call to "be still and know that I am God" (46:10)—a beautiful reminder of God's authority over all things.

*How does "Be still" challenge our tendency to rely on*
*our own strength and understanding?*

## PSALM 47

This psalm exalts God as the supreme ruler over all nations. It calls for joyful praise and shouts of triumph while acknowledging His sovereignty. The sons of Korah celebrate God's reign, highlighting His victory over the earth's rulers and the chosen inheritance for His people. It concludes with a resounding invitation to worship.

*How does considering God's sovereignty over all nations*
*alter your perception of world events?*

## PSALM 48

This psalm celebrates the unmatched glory and security of Zion, the beautiful city of God, and serves as a reminder of God's faithfulness to His people throughout history. It encourages believers to trust God's protection and rejoice in His presence. God's people have so many reasons to praise Him, and this psalm is a good start.

*How do you prioritize praise and worship amid*
*the busyness and challenges of daily life?*

## Take Your Time and Learn More

- Hebrews quotes from Psalm 45: HEBREWS 1:8–9
- Peace and security: ISAIAH 2:2–4
- God's universal kingship: EPHESIANS 1:20–22
- New Jerusalem: REVELATION 21:22–23

*Don't hurry, don't worry. God's Word provides
everything you need for living well.*

## PSALM 49

This psalm addresses the universal reality of death and the fleeting nature of wealth and worldly success. No amount of money can secure salvation in the face of death; though unfortunately, riches can sometimes give people a false sense of security. The psalmist then shifts his focus to the hope found in trusting God—which extends long beyond the grave.

*Why is it actually a blessing from God that riches cannot redeem?*

## PSALM 50

Some Israelites have started viewing the sacrificial system as a spiritual speeding ticket—a price to be paid to do whatever they want. But the psalmist rebukes the wicked who hypocritically offer sacrifices while lacking true obedience. God isn't primarily interested in sacrifices—He's most interested in hearts (1 Samuel 15:22).

*How are Christians today tempted to engage in
religious rituals devoid of genuine obedience?*

## PSALM 51

This psalm is David's heartfelt plea for forgiveness and restoration after he sinned against Bathsheba and experienced the prophet Nathan's rebuke. David is deeply aware that he has offended God, so he desperately seeks the Lord's mercy. He expresses contrition, longs for a new heart, and affirms God's desire for genuine repentance and a restored relationship.

*Do you believe genuine repentance necessarily leads to a changed life? Why or why not?*

## PSALM 52

David denounces the deceit and wickedness of Doeg, the man who massacred eighty-five priests at Saul's command (1 Samuel 21–22). David contrasts Doeg's deceit with God's justice, emphasizing the eventual downfall of the wicked. Rehearsing these truths about God leads David to trust God's future protection.

*How can you practice preaching truth to yourself, like
David did, when you're discouraged?*

## Take Your Time and Learn More

- Human mortality: ECCLESIASTES 12:7
  - Righteous living: MICAH 6:6–8
- Forgiveness and renewal: 1 JOHN 1:9
  - Pursuing goodness: 1 PETER 2:1–3

*God loves it when you read and study His Word.*

## PSALM 53

Nearly identical to Psalm 14, this psalm declares humanity's universal rebellion against God—emphasizing the foolishness of denying His existence and living apart from His commands. The psalmist portrays a corrupt society in which evildoers oppress the righteous, and he calls on God to restore His people and bring salvation.

*How often do you pray for those who deny God's existence or rebel against Him?*

## PSALM 54

David begs God for protection against his enemies, acknowledging God as a helper and praising His faithfulness. While seeking vindication and salvation from those who oppose him, David trusts in God's ongoing deliverance. Even before being delivered, David promises to offer gratitude and praise to God for His goodness and rescue.

*Have you experienced God's deliverance in a difficult situation? How did it impact your faith?*

## PSALM 55

This psalm flows out of deep despair. David longs for relief from his enemies, including a trusted friend who has now turned against him. Though David never reveals the identity of the betrayer, he says they shared sweet fellowship together in the house of God. He ends the psalm by saying, "But I will trust in You."

*Why does betrayal from friends typically cut more deeply than attacks from enemies?*

## PSALM 56

David consistently reminds himself of what is true and eternal. Throughout the psalm, he fixes his eyes on God in the midst of his troubles. He reminds himself that God is aware of his struggles and keeps every human tear in a bottle (56:8). Not one moment of fear or grief escapes God's notice.

*Do you take comfort in knowing God sees, cares, and keeps track of your tears?*

### *Take Your Time and Learn More*

- Human sinfulness and the need for redemption: ROMANS 3:10–12
- God delivers David: 1 SAMUEL 23:19–29
- Trust and reliance on God: 1 PETER 5:7
- Trust in God despite threats from enemies: MATTHEW 10:28

*Reading the Bible isn't a race. Let the pages unfold at a pace that allows your spirit to breathe.*

## PSALM 57

This psalm is a plea for God's protection. David wrote these words while fleeing for his life from Saul. Yet even while facing significant threats from his enemies, David still praises God. The threat is great, but David's God is greater, so David prays for deliverance and worships God.

*If we're unable to praise God during difficult times, what might that indicate about our priorities?*

## PSALM 58

Likely written during the later years of Saul's reign when David was still in exile, David cries for justice against unjust leaders. This is one of many "imprecatory" psalms in which David unapologetically pleads for God to bring judgment on the wicked. Despite the prevalence of evil, David trusts in God's ultimate justice.

*In what ways do you think God's judgment differs from human justice?*

## PSALM 59

David was inspired to write this psalm when Saul jealously sent men to wait outside his home to assassinate him (1 Samuel 19:11-16). Thankfully, with the help of his wife, David escaped. He acknowledges God's protection and vows to praise Him. Despite the ongoing threats from his enemies, David remains confident in God's faithfulness.

*How confident are you of God's faithfulness to you? Why?*

## PSALM 60

This psalm begins with a desperate cry to God for help after experiencing defeat in battle. The land is now destroyed by invaders, and the situation is dire. David recounts God's past faithfulness, and he prays for God's favor and deliverance. David knows "it is He who shall trample down our enemies" (60:12).

*When you face deep discouragement, where do you go to find strength?*

## Take Your Time and Learn More

- David encounters Saul in the cave: 1 SAMUEL 24
  - Treatment of enemies: MATTHEW 5:44
  - Paul quotes from Psalm 59: ROMANS 3:13–18
  - God's help in battle: 2 SAMUEL 8:13–14

*The greatest truths in scripture are often
revealed in the unhurried moments.*

## PSALM 61

David wants God's presence, protection, and refuge. He says, "From the ends of the earth I will cry to You" (61:2)—in other words, "I'll pray here in the middle of nowhere." The psalmist acknowledges God as his rock, recognizing His sovereignty and unfailing love. David famously and beautifully cries, "Lead me to the rock that is higher than I" (61:2)

*How can you make praise and thanksgiving a daily habit as David does (61:8)?*

## PSALM 62

David expresses unwavering confidence in God as the ultimate source of his security and salvation. David emphasizes the importance of trusting in God alone rather than relying on human strength or worldly wealth. Despite ongoing adversity—perhaps including being a fugitive from Saul at this time—David is steadfast in his faith.

*How do you guard your heart against trusting in your financial situation?*

## PSALM 63

David is likely living in the wilderness as he writes these words, comparing his longing for God to a "dry and thirsty land where there is no water" (63:1). He reflects on past experiences with God's power and presence, seeking Him earnestly in prayer and worship. Despite facing ongoing threats, David finds satisfaction and joy in God.

*In what ways can experiencing a trial feel like living in a wilderness?*

## PSALM 64

David describes his enemies' evil, ongoing plots against him. People literally want to destroy him. However, David knows God will always ultimately turn the tables in the end, vindicating His own. So David praises and acknowledges God's sovereign rule over all the earth.

*How does the certainty of God's justice encourage you
whenever you see the world's injustice?*

## Take Your Time and Learn More

- Security in the midst of life's storms: MATTHEW 14:22–33
- Trust and confidence in God's unfailing love: ISAIAH 26:3–4
- Spiritual satisfaction: JOHN 6:35
- Viscious words: JAMES 3:8–10

*Bible study is truly a lifelong journey.*
*Relax and enjoy the trip.*

## PSALM 65

David celebrates God's abundant blessings and His sovereignty over creation. Sometimes God communicates through big displays—like His many miracles for Israel. But more often, He illustrates His power in nature, from majestic mountains to roaring seas, faithfully reminding His people that He is their Creator and Sustainer. God is worthy of all worship and praise.

*When have you seen God's power displayed in nature? How did that affect you?*

## PSALM 66

This psalm records a song of praise and thanksgiving for God's mighty deeds. The psalmist calls everyone to worship God, recounting God's awesome works and salvation. God turned the sea into dry land, demonstrating His power over creation. The psalmist reflects on personal experiences of God's faithfulness, acknowledging deliverance and answered prayers.

*Psalm 66:5 says, "Come and see the works of God."*
*What has God done for you this week?*

## PSALM 67

This psalm is a prayer for God's blessing and salvation to be known among all the nations. The psalmist prays for God's favor, asking for His face to shine upon them so that His way may be known on earth and His salvation may be received among all nations. The psalmist anticipates universal praise and worship of God.

*How can you contribute to making God known on earth (67:2)?*

## PSALM 68

This psalm recounts Israel's journey from Egypt to the Promised Land—recalling God's triumph over His enemies, His provision for the needy, and His presence among His people. The psalmist calls for praise, acknowledging God's sovereignty and urging all nations to worship Him.

*God is father to the fatherless and judge of widows (68:5).*
*What does this reveal about His character?*

### Take Your Time and Learn More

- God's provision and sustenance: MATTHEW 6:26
- Testing and purification: 1 PETER 1:7
- Every nation, tribe, people, and language: REVELATION 7:9–10
- Paul quotes from Psalm 68: EPHESIANS 4:8

*Try to forget the demands of life for a while.*
*You're spending quality time with God.*

## PSALM 69

David begs for God's deliverance from overwhelming distress. He describes being submerged in deep waters, overwhelmed by enemies, and stung by betrayal from loved ones. Still, he maintains his trust in God, appealing for salvation and rescue. The psalm ends with a determined decision to praise and magnify God (69:30).

*What enables the psalmist to shift so easily from lament to praise (69:29-30)?*

## PSALM 70

In this short but powerful psalm, David begs God to hurry and help—to confound and shame those who seek his harm. David roots his request in deep dependence on God's steadfast love and faithfulness. He demonstrates reliance on God's timely intervention and steadfast presence in times of trouble.

*When we need help fast, why is it easier to turn to people rather than God?*

## PSALM 71

The writer of this psalm is believed to be elderly, and the psalm contains a prayer for old age. The psalmist expresses confidence in God's faithfulness, having trusted Him since youth. Through trials, the psalmist seeks refuge in God's steadfast love, desiring to proclaim God's power to another generation.

*How can you proclaim God's goodness and power to younger generations?*

## PSALM 72

This royal psalm, attributed to Solomon, includes a prayer for a righteous king. It describes the ideal reign of a king who rules with justice, protecting the afflicted and delivering the needy. Ultimately, it reflects the hope for a kingdom ruled by God—embodying justice, mercy, and righteousness for all people.

*How often do you pray for your leaders? Do you believe prayer impacts their decisions?*

## Take Your Time and Learn More

- Zeal for God's house: JOHN 2:17
- Urgency and prayer for deliverance: MATTHEW 26:38–39
- God's faithfulness in old age: ISAIAH 46:4
- Everlasting reign: LUKE 1:32–33

*Good things come to those who wait—on the Lord, that is.*

## PSALM 73

This psalm was written by Asaph—a worship leader and prophet during King David's reign. It answers the age-old question of why the wicked prosper while the righteous suffer. While Asaph is initially confused, he eventually understands the fleeting nature of their success, the certainty of their final judgment, and the eternal blessings awaiting the righteous.

*Why is it ultimately illogical to envy the success of the wicked?*

## PSALM 74

Asaph laments the destruction of Jerusalem's temple. He begs for God's intervention, recalling His past deliverance and appealing to His covenant faithfulness. Asaph urges God to remember His people and act decisively against their enemies. He longs for the day God's glory will be displayed again in Zion.

*When or where have you felt spiritual desolation and a longing for God's glory to be restored?*

## PSALM 75

Asaph praises God as the righteous judge who upholds justice. The psalm begins with thanksgiving, declaring God's name and wonderful deeds. Asaph then recounts God's sovereign rule, stating that He "puts down one and sets up another" (75:7). Asaph warns the arrogant not to exalt themselves or rely on their own strength.

*Does this psalm challenge your understanding of success and achievement?*

## PSALM 76

Asaph exalts God's unmatched power and victory, emphasizing His control over the nations. He praises God's presence in Jerusalem and His power in defeating the enemies. God breaks the weapons of war and brings peace to the earth. Truly, God is "terrifying to the kings of the earth" (76:12).

*How does recognizing your limitations and weaknesses honor God?*

## Take Your Time and Learn More

- Apparent prosperity of the wicked: Job 21:7–15
- Devastation and desolation: Lamentations 2:1–9
- God's authority and judgment: Daniel 2:20–21
- God's glorious triumph over enemies: Revelation 19:11–16

*The Bible is countercultural, and so is Bible study.*
*There's no need to rush through this.*

## PSALM 77

Asaph wrestles with doubts and questions during a season of distress, believing God is being unresponsive to his prayers. Asaph then reflects on God's past faithfulness, regaining his hope and confidence in God's presence and guidance. Asaph's journey from despair to devotion demonstrates the connection between remembrance and trust.

*What mighty deed has God worked in your own life*
*to prove His unfailing love and power?*

## PSALM 78

In the longest of the historical psalms, Asaph recounts Israel's history, emphasizing God's faithfulness despite their disobedience. He calls people to remember and teach future generations about God's mighty works—from the Exodus to the establishment of David's kingdom (which is happening at the time of writing). His point is clear: learn from history.

*Why do you think the Israelites continued to sin despite witnessing God's many miracles?*

## PSALM 79

Asaph laments the desolation of Jerusalem and the defilement of the temple by foreign invaders. He cries out to God for mercy, acknowledging the severity of Israel's sin and the resulting devastation. Instead of "Why?" he asks, "How long?" Asaph appeals to God's reputation and begs for Him to avenge His people's suffering.

*When praying about a tragedy, what's the difference between "How long?" and "Why?"*

## PSALM 80

Asaph begs for God's restored favor upon Israel—symbolized as a vineyard. God is angry with His people and opposed to their prayers, so Asaph pleads with God to shine His face upon them and restore their relationship. Three times Asaph asks God, "Restore us again"—the final time appealing specifically to Yahweh, the covenant name of God.

*What can you learn about Israel's relationship with*
*God from the metaphor of the vineyard?*

## Take Your Time and Learn More

- God's deliverance and faithfulness: ISAIAH 43:16–19
- Warning against disobedience: 1 CORINTHIANS 10:1–12
- A plea for intervention and mercy: JOEL 2:17
- Total dependance on God's care: JOHN 15:1–6

*God speaks in the quiet moments.*
*Approach His Word with calm expectation.*

## PSALM 81

Asaph writes this call to worship to be sung or read at a feast, likely the Feast of Tabernacles. He celebrates God as Israel's deliverer and provider, calling Israel to remember and obey. He recalls God's rescue from Egypt, inviting Israel to rejoice in their liberation. Despite Israel's long history of disobedience, God longs to bless them.

*God faithfully keeps His promises, so why do you think people struggle to trust Him?*

## PSALM 82

Asaph writes this psalm about God's jurisdiction over everything and everyone. God is the presiding judge over every human being. The final words of the chapter say, "You shall inherit all nations" (82:8). This is good news for people outside God's chosen Israel. God paid the ultimate price to make this inheritance possible.

*Why is it characteristic of the wicked to prey upon the poor and needy (82:4)?*

## PSALM 83

Asaph writes this imprecatory psalm, calling on God to bring literal harm on Israel's enemies who conspire to destroy God's people. Asaph lists various nations plotting harm, and he seeks God's judgment upon them. Ultimately, Asaph wants the enemies to be defeated so that they will be forced to acknowledge God as "Most High over all the earth" (83:18).

*Do you think it is ever right to pray an imprecatory prayer today?*

## PSALM 84

One of the most beautiful psalms in the Bible, Psalm 84 was written by one or more sons of Korah. In Numbers 16, Korah led a rebellion with 250 leaders against Moses while in the wilderness, and God destroyed them. Korah's line continued though (Numbers 26:9–11), and this psalm rings with delight in God and His mercy.

*How have you experienced God as a "sun and shield" (84:11) in your life?*

### Take Your Time and Learn More

- Call to worship and obey: Exodus 20:2–17
- Jesus quotes from Psalm 82: John 10:34–36
- Plea for God's intervention: 2 Chronicles 20:1–30
- Longing for God: Matthew 5:6

*Before you read, pray. Ask God to speak His truth to your spirit.*

## PSALM 85

This psalm, a prayer of the returned exiles, reflects on God's past favor and mercy toward Israel and expresses hope for restoration and forgiveness. The psalmist—believed to be from the sons of Korah—acknowledges God's wrath and the consequences of Israel's sin. Yet remembering God's past goodness, he asks for restoration and revival.

*When has God shown mercy to you?*
*Does remembering His mercy Inspire hope for the future?*

## PSALM 86

Known as "a prayer of David," this psalm is a heartfelt plea for God's mercy, protection, and guidance. Though scholars are unable to pinpoint the circumstances surrounding this psalm, David is clearly asking for mercy because he is completely dependent on God. As in other psalms, David declares his unwavering trust in God's sovereignty.

*David gives thanks to God with his whole heart (86:12).*
*What can you thank God for today?*

## PSALM 87

This psalm celebrates Zion, God's chosen city, as the birthplace of God's people. It extols Zion's glorious status and significance, describing the honor bestowed on it by God, who loves and cherishes its inhabitants. Even foreigners and distant nations recognize Zion's special place in God's plan.

*How does your relationship with God bring joy and celebration into your life?*

## PSALM 88

This psalm is one of the most profound expressions of lament in the Bible. The writer feels abandoned by God and overwhelmed by suffering. He pleads for God's attention but feels unheard and forsaken. Despite this distress, the psalmist determines to be faithful to God, acknowledging Him as the only refuge.

*Do you ever struggle to be honest with God about your pain and doubts?*

## Take Your Time and Learn More

- God's promise to forgive: Isaiah 40:1–2
- God's compassion: Exodus 34:6–7
- City of God: Galatians 4:26
- Abandonment and isolation: Lamentations 3:1–20

*Don't hurry, don't worry. God's Word provides
everything you need for living well.*

## PSALM 89

This psalm is attributed to Ethan the Ezrahite—described in 1 Kings 4:31 as famous for his wisdom. Here he praises God's steadfast love and promises to David, declaring His power and authority over all creation. Despite setbacks, God's covenant remains forever unbroken. Ethan acknowledges Israel's suffering but trusts in God's eventual deliverance and restoration.

*What are some specific examples of God's faithfulness in your own past?*

## PSALM 90

This is the only song of Moses in the psalms, though there are two others recorded in scripture (Exodus 15, Deuteronomy 32). Scholars believe this psalm may have been written either when Moses struck the rock (Numbers 20:1-13) or when Miriam and Aaron died. Moses reflects on the eternal nature of God and the brevity of human life.

*How can understanding the brevity of life lead to greater wisdom?*

## PSALM 91

This beautiful psalm has reassured believers for centuries with its promises of safety for those who dwell in God's presence. God will fiercely protect His people, so believers have no need to fear the night. Psalm 91 offers comfort to anyone seeking refuge in the Almighty during life's darkest trials.

*Is there an area of your life filled with stress or worry that you need to entrust to God?*

## PSALM 92

Psalm 92 is a song for Sabbath. The psalmist celebrates God's righteousness, declaring His works to be great and worthy of praise. This psalm contrasts the fate of the righteous—who flourish like trees—with the destiny of the wicked—who will be destroyed. Praising God is important, especially during times of worship and rest.

*Do you prioritize Sabbath rest as a means of honoring God
and refreshing your soul? Why or why not?*

## Take Your Time and Learn More

- God's covenant faithfulness: 2 SAMUEL 7:12–16
- Eternal perspective of time: 2 PETER 3:8–9
- Satan quotes from Psalm 91: LUKE 4:9–12
- Rejoicing in the Lord: ISAIAH 61:10

*God loves it when you read and study His Word.*

## PSALM 93

This psalm contains three simple but powerful messages: the Lord reigns, His throne is secure, and His decrees are very trustworthy. The psalmist encourages readers to trust in God's steadfastness. He assures them that God reigns supreme over all things, offering comfort and confidence in times of uncertainty.

*Why is living independently of God actually bondage rather than freedom?*

## PSALM 94

The psalmist cries out for justice in the face of oppression and wickedness. He appeals to God as the righteous judge who will avenge the innocent and punish the wicked. Ultimately, the psalmist understands that vengeance belongs to God and that He will uphold justice for His people.

*Why is it wise on multiple levels to leave vengeance to God?*

## PSALM 95

This psalm is a call to worship and obedience, exhorting believers to do three important things: sing to the Lord, worship, and bow down. They should not harden their hearts like the Israelites did in the wilderness.

*What are the benefits of community worship?*

## PSALM 96

This psalm is a hymn of praise that honors God's greatness and glory among the nations. The psalmist calls for singing a new song to the Lord, declaring His marvelous works and salvation. He invites everyone to join in worshipping God—"For the LORD is great and greatly to be praised" (96:4).

*How do you protect your worship of God from becoming monotonous or routine?*

## Take Your Time and Learn More

- God's universal reign: REVELATION 19:6
- God's judgment: ROMANS 12:19
- Hebrews quotes from Psalm 95: HEBREWS 3:7–11
- Song of thanksgiving: 1 CHRONICLES 16:23–31

*Reading the Bible isn't a race. Let the pages unfold*
*at a pace that allows your spirit to breathe.*

## PSALM 97

The psalmist exalts God's sovereignty and righteousness, rejoicing in His reign over the earth. The author uses phrases found in other Old Testament passages, including the imagery of clouds and thick darkness surrounding God's presence, the reference to worthless idols, and the idea of God delivering His people from the hand of the wicked.

*How do you feel about your own sin? Does it disgust you or are you more likely to make excuses for it?*

## PSALM 98

This is the only psalm in scripture with the simple title "A psalm"—no other explanation is given. It's a hymn of praise celebrating God's salvation and victory. The psalmist calls for joyful singing and music-making to the Lord, acknowledging His wonderful works among the nations. Even creation joins the chorus as the rivers clap their hands and the hills sing for joy.

*Why must our praise and worship for God never be silent?*

## PSALM 99

The psalmist exalts God's sovereignty and holiness; he also recalls God's justice and mercy in responding to and forgiving His people. He cites specific examples of God's faithful servants— Moses, Aaron, and Samuel—who interceded on Israel's behalf. God's power and authority are unmatched.

*Why is God gracious to welcome and respond to the prayers of His children?*

## PSALM 100

This psalm is a joyful call to worship and thanksgiving. The psalmist urges all the earth to shout joyfully to the Lord, serving Him with gladness and entering His presence with singing. Believers are invited to enter God's gates with thanksgiving and His courts with praise, recognizing His enduring love and faithfulness.

*God will be faithful to you forever. How is that good news today?*

## Take Your Time and Learn More

- Christ as the conquering King: REVELATION 19:11–16
  - Joy and praise: LUKE 2:10–14
  - God's holiness: EXODUS 19:16–20
  - Worship: EPHESIANS 5:19–20

*The greatest truths in scripture are often
revealed in the unhurried moments.*

## PSALM 101

David pledges to live blamelessly and wisely, resolving to lead with integrity and avoid wickedness and evil influences. He commits to maintaining a pure heart and surrounding himself with people who walk uprightly. He vows to uphold justice and root out wickedness from his kingdom. His goals: moral integrity, righteous leadership, and godly personal conduct.

*If your integrity is measured by who you are at home, who are you?*

## PSALM 102

This psalm is a prayer of distress and hope from an afflicted individual, likely in exile. The psalmist cries out to God in anguish, feeling abandoned. He describes his deep suffering, physical ailments, and ongoing loneliness. Yet amid this despair, the psalmist affirms God's eternal nature and power. He finds encouragement in God's promise to restore Zion.

*How does it encourage you that God never changes?*

## PSALM 103

This psalm is a hymn of praise and thanksgiving for God's abundant mercy and compassion. Scholars believe this psalm was written by David in his later years because of his deep personal gratitude for God's gift of forgiveness. As an old man, David would surely understand that "the LORD is merciful and gracious, slow to anger and abundant in mercy" (103:8).

*How have you personally experienced God's steadfast love?*

## PSALM 104

This psalm is a majestic hymn of praise celebrating God's creation and providence. The psalmist marvels at God's wisdom and power displayed in the natural world—from the heavens to the earth. He describes God's role as Creator and Sustainer of all life, providing for the needs of every living creature.

*How does creation point you to the greatness of God?*

## Take Your Time and Learn More

- Integrity and righteousness: 1 SAMUEL 16:7
- The eternal nature of Christ: HEBREWS 1:10–12
- Renewal: ISAIAH 40:28–31
- God's sovereignty over creation: GENESIS 1

*Bible study is truly a lifelong journey.*
*Relax and enjoy the trip.*

## PSALM 105

Psalms 105 and 106 seem to be two sides of the same coin. Psalm 105 tells the story of God's faithfulness to Israel—from Abraham to the Exodus—while Psalm 106 tells the sad story of Israel's repeated failure and unfaithfulness. This psalm recounts Israel's journey out of slavery in Egypt, highlighting God's deliverance and provision.

*How has God recently been faithful to you?*

## PSALM 106

In the previous psalm, readers are invited to "remember [God's] marvelous works that He has done" (105:5); in this psalm, Israel has apparently forgotten them. This psalm recounts Israel's history of rebellion, disobedience, idolatry, and ingratitude. Despite their unfaithfulness, God's compassion endures, and He repeatedly rescues them from trouble.

*Why is it so easy to forget what God has done for us in the past?*

## PSALM 107

This psalm is a hymn of thanksgiving for God's steadfast love and deliverance. Specifically, the psalmist shows God as Savior to four groups of people: wanderers, the imprisoned, the sick, and the storm-tossed. Each time they cry out to God in distress, He responds with mercy, rescuing them from their troubles.

*Can you think of a time God specifically rescued you in response to your cry? What happened?*

## PSALM 108

This psalm beautifully compiles sections from two other psalms. Verses 1–5 resemble Psalm 57:7–11, and verses 6–13 resemble Psalm 60:5–12. This psalm is a prayer of confidence and praise. It combines elements of trust and petition, calling believers to proclaim God's glory and to trust in His victory over adversity.

*What in your life currently requires courage?*

## Take Your Time and Learn More

- God's covenant with Israel: GENESIS 12:1–3
  - God's mercy: NEHEMIAH 9:16–31
    - Redemption: LUKE 15:11–32
  - Standing against evil: EPHESIANS 6:10–18

*Try to forget the demands of life for a while.*
*You're spending quality time with God.*

## PSALM 109

This psalm of David is considered to be the strongest of his imprecatory psalms. He appeals to God for justice against his enemies, recounting their malicious actions and deceitful words. He calls for God's retribution, describing the suffering inflicted by those who hate Him. David expresses righteous anger and a plea for deliverance.

*Is there a hurt or grievance in your life that you need to surrender to God?*

## PSALM 110

Psalm 110 is one of the most quoted portions of the Old Testament in the New Testament—with as many as twenty-seven direct quotations and allusions. The psalmist declares God's decree to exalt the Messiah to His right hand, where He will rule in power. The Messiah is portrayed as a victorious warrior, defeating His enemies and establishing His kingdom.

*Is it comforting or frustrating to you that God is in control?*

## PSALM 111

Psalm 111 is an acrostic poem, arranged according to the Hebrew alphabet. Each line after the opening, "Praise the LORD," begins with a successive letter of the alphabet, praising God's greatness and faithfulness. The psalmist exalts God's works and attributes, declaring His righteousness, grace, and compassion.

*What do you have to praise the Lord for today?*

## PSALM 112

Whereas the previous psalm describes God, this psalm describes the one who fears God. This person is prosperous and compassionate, trusting in God even in darkness. His heart is steadfast in faith. He is generous and just, filled with integrity. The psalmist contrasts this person's security with the fate of the wicked, who will be brought to ruin.

*What has shaken you? How have you found God to be your rock?*

### Take Your Time and Learn More

- Response to enemies: MATTHEW 5:44
- Hebrews quotes from Psalm 110: HEBREWS 5:6
- Fear of the Lord: PROVERBS 1:7
- Trusting God's wisdom: JAMES 1:5

*Good things come to those who wait—on the Lord, that is.*

## PSALM 113

Scholars believe Psalms 113–118 were sung during Passover celebrations. . .and were likely sung by Jesus and His disciples on the night He was betrayed. The psalmist rightly declares that God's name should be blessed from sunrise to sunset. His glory and compassion are unmatched.

*What does "blessed is the name of the LORD" mean? Why does it matter?*

## PSALM 114

This psalm recounts God's miraculous deliverance of Israel from Egypt. The psalmist describes God's power displayed in the Exodus, when He led His people to freedom. He marvels at nature's obedience to God's command and exhorts the earth to tremble before the God of Jacob, who turns rock into water and flint into a flowing spring.

*What does it mean to you that this marvelous God loves you?*

## PSALM 115

This psalm contrasts the greatness of God with the powerlessness of idols. The psalmist describes the foolishness of trusting in idols—which are works of human hands, incapable of seeing, hearing, or acting. In contrast, God is alive, actively involved in the affairs of His people and deserving of trust and praise.

*How would you define the word idol? What has the potential to be an idol in your life?*

## PSALM 116

This psalm is especially poignant, considering Jesus likely sang it in the hours leading up to His death. Here the psalmist expresses gratitude for God's deliverance from death. He recalls a time when he called on God's name in anguish and despair, and the Lord answered. In response, the psalmist vows to worship and serve God all his days.

*Do you think human death matters to God? Why or why not?*

## Take Your Time and Learn More

- Exalting God's name: LUKE 1:46–55
- God's power over nature: EXODUS 14:21–31
- All glory to God: 1 CORINTHIANS 10:31
- Conditions for answered prayer: 1 JOHN 3:22

*The Bible is countercultural, and so is Bible study.
There's no need to rush through this.*

## PSALM 117

The shortest psalm in the Bible, these two verses call all nations and peoples to extol God's greatness and mercy. They affirm that God's love endures forever and that His faithfulness extends throughout generations. Despite its brevity, this psalm displays the universal scope of God's love and the invitation for all to worship Him.

*Why is God's love for all nations so profound?*

## PSALM 118

This psalm celebrates God's eternal love and deliverance. The psalmist reflects on being rejected by people but upheld by God, emphasizing trust in God over human reliance. He rejoices in God's goodness and salvation, urging all to give thanks and exalt His name.

*Why is nobody more trustworthy than God?*

## PSALM 119

This psalm—the Bible's longest chapter—is an acrostic poem praising God's Word. The Hebrew alphabet contains twenty-two letters, and this psalm contains twenty-two units of eight verses—each section beginning with the next letter of the Hebrew alphabet. The psalmist passionately recognizes God's Word as our source of wisdom, guidance, and delight.

*How has God's Word been a light in your life?*

## PSALM 120

David's lament in this psalm is unique. Unlike his other laments, it doesn't end with hope or praise. David expresses distress living among deceitful people. He's weary; you can hear it in his cry. These are David's honest, broken words being poured out to God.

*God wants us to go to Him immediately and honestly.
What do you need to be honest with God about today?*

### Take Your Time and Learn More

- Paul quotes from Psalm 117: ROMANS 15:11
- Jesus quotes from Psalm 118: MATTHEW 21:42
- Authority and importance of God's Word: 2 TIMOTHY 3:16–17
- Power of the tongue to do harm: JAMES 3:6

*God speaks in the quiet moments.*
*Approach His Word with calm expectation.*

## PSALM 121

Fifteen psalms (120–134) are called "songs of degrees" (or "ascents"), likely sung by the Israelites as they traveled up to Jerusalem for the annual feasts. Because Jerusalem is at a high elevation, all visitors *ascend* to the city. This song acknowledges that help comes from God, who never sleeps nor slumbers.

*How does the promise that God never sleeps help you understand His constant care for you?*

## PSALM 122

This song of degrees was likely sung by travelers on their way to Jerusalem for holy feasts. David expresses joy and longing for Jerusalem, the city of God. He wrote the psalm for what Jerusalem was in his day and for what it would become under his son and his successors.

*Why is corporate worship and fellowship with God's people so important?*

## PSALM 123

This song of degrees expresses humility and dependence on God, looking to the Lord for mercy the way a servant watches the hand of his master. The psalmist is "exceedingly filled" with contempt from the proud (123:4) and he longs for God's compassion. While traveling to Jerusalem, the Israelites likely pass by enemies, so a traveling song about mercy makes sense.

*How does humility deepen our reliance on God's mercy?*

## PSALM 124

This song of degrees expresses gratitude for God's deliverance from enemies. It reflects on how, without God's intervention, Israel's enemies would have "swallowed [them] up alive" (124:3). David praises God as the source of Israel's help, acknowledging that He is faithfully on the side of His people.

*What situation in your life would have turned out very differently without God's intervention?*

### Take Your Time and Learn More

- God's watchful care: Isaiah 40:28–31
- City of the living God: Hebrews 12:22–24
- Humility before God: 1 Peter 5:6–7
- God's rescue and deliverance: Isaiah 54:17

*Before you read, pray. Ask God to*
*speak His truth to your spirit.*

## PSALM 125

This song of ascents celebrates the security of those who trust in God—comparing them to Mount Zion, which cannot be moved. (Remember: Mount Zion is often a poetic reference to Jerusalem since it's the highest point in ancient Jerusalem.) The psalmist affirms God's protection over His people, illustrating the truth that those who do right will remain stable.

*Why is it helpful to sing songs that communicate important truths about God?*

## PSALM 126

This song of degrees expresses joy and gratitude for God's restoration. It recalls the Israelites' return from exile, marveling at God's miraculous deeds. The Israelites' laughter replaces tears as God proves His faithfulness again. He declares that those who sow in tears will reap in joy. The psalm concludes with a prayer for continued restoration and blessing.

*Do you believe emotions should be unhitched from worship? Why or why not?*

## PSALM 127

This song of degrees emphasizes the importance of trusting in God for success and security. The psalmist acknowledges that human effort alone is futile without God's blessing. He affirms that God is the builder and protector of homes and cities and that children are a blessing from Him.

*In what area of your life are you feeling extra stress?*
*Have you talked about it with God?*

## PSALM 128

This song of degrees references God's specific covenant with Israel. It lists many of the blessings that come with fearing the Lord and walking in His ways, describes the prosperity and joy that come to those who fear God, and encourages faithfulness to God.

*Why is context always important when it comes to scripture's promises?*

## *Take Your Time and Learn More*

- God's protection and security: ISAIAH 26:3–4
  - Sowing and reaping: GALATIANS 6:7–9
  - God's provision: 1 CORINTHIANS 3:6–9
  - Family blessings: EPHESIANS 5:22–33

*Don't hurry, don't worry. God's Word provides*
*everything you need for living well.*

## PSALM 129

This song of degrees recounts Israel's difficult history of pain and oppression, yet it also affirms God's gracious deliverance. Despite their enduring affliction, Israel remains undefeated as their enemies' schemes are disrupted by God. Trusting God's righteousness and ultimate victory, the psalmist calls for God's judgment on those who seek Israel's harm.

*How does God's unwavering commitment to Israel shape*
*your understanding of His character?*

## PSALM 130

This song of degrees expresses profound depths of repentance and hope in God's mercy. The psalmist cries out to God from a dark place. Confident in God's "abundant redemption" (130:7), the writer eagerly waits for deliverance and calls others to hope in God's unfailing mercy.

*How do you see God's abundant redemption in*
*the story He is writing with your life?*

## PSALM 131

This song of degrees reflects on the theme of humility. It contains only three verses, yet Charles Spurgeon calls it "one of the shortest Psalms to read, but one of the longest to learn." David renounces pride and ambition, finding peace in quiet trust. He encourages readers to quiet their restless souls and trust in God's providence.

*How does time with God quiet and calm your soul?*

## PSALM 132

This psalm recounts David's vow to build a temple for God. The psalmist recalls David's earnest desire for God's dwelling place and his determination to find a resting place for the ark of the covenant. God affirms this vow, promising blessing on his descendants. The psalmist calls on God to remember David's faithfulness and fulfill His promise.

*Which of God's promises do you need to trust Him to keep today?*

## Take Your Time and Learn More

- God's deliverance from oppressive enemies: ISAIAH 54:17
  - Waiting for the morning: LAMENTATIONS 3:21–26
    - Childlike trust: MATTHEW 18:1–4
  - A dwelling place for the God of Jacob: ACTS 7:45–46

*God loves it when you read and study His Word.*

## PSALM 133

This song of degrees compares unity among believers to precious oil running down Aaron's beard and descending dew on Mount Hermon, symbolizing God's abundant blessing. Mount Hermon is a range of mountains whose melted snow supplies water for the Jordan River. There is richness and significance in unity among believers.

*What are some specific things that threaten the unity of a local church community?*

## PSALM 134

This final song of degrees calls the priests and Levites to continue their faithful service of praise in the temple. Psalm 134 is a fitting conclusion to the collection of travel hymns, affirming the continual worship and adoration of God by His people.

*Which of God's attributes can you worship Him for today?*

## PSALM 135

The psalmist contrasts the true God with idols. Interestingly, almost every verse of this psalm references words or ideas from the Old Testament—including Exodus, Deuteronomy, Jeremiah, and other psalms. The psalmist celebrates God's provision, protection, and salvation—calling all nations to recognize His glory.

*How does worship music both glorify God and benefit you?*

## PSALM 136

This psalm is a hymn of thanksgiving that celebrates God's enduring love and mighty deeds. Each verse repeats the sentence "His mercy endures forever." The psalmist recounts God's creation, deliverance of Israel from Egypt, and victories in battle. The writer marvels at God's miracles, provision, and guidance throughout history. God's unfailing love is the central theme.

*How have you experienced God's enduring mercy in your life?*

## Take Your Time and Learn More

- Brotherly love: JOHN 17:20–23
- Call to praise: REVELATION 7:9–12
- Praise the Lord: DEUTERONOMY 32:3–4
- God's enduring love throughout history: 1 CHRONICLES 16:34–36

*Reading the Bible isn't a race. Let the pages unfold at a pace that allows your spirit to breathe.*

## PSALM 137

This psalm expresses the sorrow and longing of the exiled Israelites in Babylon. The psalmist reflects on his grief by the rivers of Babylon, where he laments the loss of Jerusalem and his inability to sing the songs of Zion. The writer promises not to forget Jerusalem—even amid suffering—and cries out for justice against the oppressors.

*Why can suffering make singing more difficult? Does it always?*

## PSALM 138

The psalmist praises God for answered prayer. He exalts God's steadfast love and faithfulness, declaring praise in the presence of kings. He recalls how God answered his prayers and strengthened his soul. This psalm serves as a testament to the psalmist's unwavering trust in God's goodness.

*Do you believe God has a good plan for your life, even when it doesn't feel that way?*

## PSALM 139

This magnificent psalm celebrates God's intimate knowledge and presence with His people. David marvels at God's omniscience, acknowledging that He knows every thought and action before it occurs. David reflects on God's omnipresence, realizing there is nowhere he can go to escape God. This psalm is a profound meditation on God's intimate relationship with His own.

*What does it mean to you that God knows you entirely and loves you perfectly?*

## PSALM 140

David petitions God for deliverance from evil schemes and violent enemies. Believing his enemies are God's enemies too, he seeks refuge in God's power to shield him from harm. Despite the current threat he is facing, David remains steadfast in his trust of God's protection. His prayer calls for God's justice against his enemies.

*What gives David his confidence that God will maintain the cause of the afflicted (140:12)?*

## Take Your Time and Learn More

- The captives' cry: LAMENTATIONS 1
- Praise for answered prayer: PHILIPPIANS 1:3–6
- God's inescapable presence: HEBREWS 4:13
- Evil's repayment plan: ROMANS 12:17–21

*The greatest truths in scripture are often
revealed in the unhurried moments.*

## PSALM 141

David wants protection from his enemies, but more than that, he wants to live a life of personal integrity and righteousness before God. So he asks God to help him with his speech and actions, requesting discernment to avoid the trap of sin and wickedness. David knows how easily his heart can be led astray.

*What weakness or stubborn sin habit can you ask God to help you overcome?*

## PSALM 142

David cries to God while hiding for his life in a cave. He needs assurance of God's faithful care in the midst of his loneliness. This psalm has been compared to Hannah's prayer in 1 Samuel 1, where she is so deeply distressed that Eli believes she is drunk. Like Hannah, David has been "brought very low" (142:6) and needs God's help.

*On low days, where are you likely to turn first for help?*

## PSALM 143

This psalm is a heartfelt plea for God's mercy and guidance in times of distress. David acknowledges his own unworthiness and appeals to God's righteousness. He recounts his troubles and despair, longing for God's intervention. He recalls past acts of God's faithfulness and expresses trust in His deliverance.

*How would it change your life if you started every morning with prayer?*

## PSALM 144

This is a psalm of praise and petition for God's protection and victory. Acknowledging man's frailty and God's glory, David praises God as his fortress, deliverer, and shield. He prays for rescue from deceitful enemies and for prosperity and peace in the land. He's confident in God's readiness to hear and answer prayer.

*How confident are you that God will hear you when you pray?*

## Take Your Time and Learn More

- Guarding the tongue: EPHESIANS 4:29
- Assurance of God's presence: HEBREWS 13:5–6
- No one is righteous: ROMANS 3:20
- Victory over enemies: 2 SAMUEL 22:2–4

*Bible study is truly a lifelong journey.*
*Relax and enjoy the trip.*

## PSALM 145

David's final entry in the psalms is fittingly called "David's psalm of praise." It's the only psalm with this name. In this hymn, David extols God's goodness, exalts His sovereignty and compassion, and declares His mighty works and abundant grace. He then praises God's unsearchable greatness and steadfast love, recounting His acts of creation and redemption.

*What act (or acts) of faithfulness in your life deserve praise to God today?*

## PSALM 146

This psalm begins the five final songs in the book—the "Hallelujah Psalms." While the book of Psalms is packed with every imaginable category of thought and emotion, these five final psalms are entirely praise. Here the psalmist praises God's compassion for the vulnerable, urging readers to put their hope in God.

*How does God's goodness to you compel you to be good to others?*

## PSALM 147

The psalmist praises God for restoring and sustaining Jerusalem. He celebrates God's power to rebuild the city's walls and gather its dispersed people. He marvels at God's knowledge and care for all creation—from the stars in the sky to the creatures on earth—and affirms God's delight in those who fear and trust Him.

*Have you found it to be true that God heals the brokenhearted and binds up their wounds?*

## PSALM 148

This beautiful psalm calls on all creation to praise God. Humans—from kings to commoners—are called to honor Him. (Note: There is no reference to anything sinful or evil in this psalm. It is simply and profoundly a universal call to worship, affirming that all aspects of the universe play a role in glorifying God as their Creator.)

*What is your favorite thing about God?*

## Take Your Time and Learn More

- Universal praise: REVELATION 5:13
- Care for the oppressed: ISAIAH 61:1–3
- God's faithful care for His people: ISAIAH 40:28–31
- Exaltation of the invisible God: COLOSSIANS 1:15–20

*Try to forget the demands of life for a while.*
*You're spending quality time with God.*

## PSALM 149

This psalm celebrates God's favor upon His people, encouraging the saints to exult in God's victory over their enemies. The psalmist affirms God's pleasure in His people and His vengeance against the wicked. He invites believers to rejoice in God's victory—both present and future.

*How has God given you victory in the past,*
*and how will He give you victory in the future?*

## PSALM 150

This final psalm is a fitting close to the book. It's a crescendo of praise, a resounding exhortation for all creation to worship God with joy. It calls for *all* believers to glorify God with every aspect of their being: "Let everything that has breath praise the LORD" (150:6).

*How can you cultivate a lifestyle of consistent,*
*joyful, and comprehensive praise?*

### Take Your Time and Learn More

- Triumphant praise: REVELATION 19:1–8
- Joyful praise and worship: EPHESIANS 5:18–20

# PROVERBS

*Fearing the Lord results in wisdom and applying practical instruction.*

## SETTING THE STAGE

The book of Proverbs is a collection of wise sayings and teachings primarily attributed to King Solomon—the wisest man in the ancient world.

Comprising thirty-one chapters, Proverbs offers practical and moral insights for pursuing wisdom and righteous living. In many ways, when you read Proverbs, you are learning wisdom from generations of godly people who have gone before you.

Certain themes are repeatedly emphasized throughout the book—including diligence, fear of the Lord, finances, humility, integrity, justice, relationships, righteous living, speech, understanding, and wisdom.

Important to note: the principles in Proverbs are *descriptive*, not *prescriptive*. In other words, they exist to show patterns of human behavior and the consequences that often follow; they don't provide rigid rules or absolute guarantees.

For example, Proverbs 22:6 says, "Train up a child in the way he should go, and when he is old, he will not depart from it." This verse expresses a general truth about the impact of early training on a person's life, but it offers no ironclad promise that every child raised with good instruction will unfailingly follow a righteous path into adulthood.

Like the book of Psalms, Proverbs stands as a timeless guide, offering us practical and enduring wisdom for navigating the complexities of daily life.

## GOOD TO KNOW

Author is primarily Solomon (1:1), with sections attributed to "the wise" (22:17), Agur (30:1), and King Lemuel (31:1). Little is known of the latter two. Solomon reigned approximately 970–930 BC.

*Good things come to those who wait—on the Lord, that is.*

## PROVERBS 1

The book of Proverbs opens with a father instructing his son (and will end with a mother instructing *her* son). Solomon shares the purpose of the book: to impart wisdom, knowledge, and instruction. He stresses the importance of listening to wisdom. . .and the danger of rejecting it.

*Three types of people show up regularly in Proverbs: the wise, the foolish, and the simple. How would you define each?*

## PROVERBS 2

Chapter 2 highlights many of the benefits of wisdom. Wisdom, understanding, and knowledge are like hidden treasures—as such, we should actively seek them. This chapter says God "gives wisdom; out His mouth comes knowledge and understanding" (2:6). Wisdom protects and guides, ultimately shielding a person from evil paths and unrighteousness.

*How do you distinguish between God's wisdom and the world's counterfeit?*

## PROVERBS 3

Chapter 3 encourages trust in God and obedience to His commands. It highlights many blessings of wisdom—including long life, peace, and security. (Note: This chapter illustrates why we should read wisdom literature differently. There are exceptions to these rules. Wise people can die young, and generous people don't always end up rich.)

*Are you seeking God intentionally with your decisions or relying on your own understanding?*

## PROVERBS 4

The writer encourages his son to pursue wisdom and, in two verses, gives six different ways his son can avoid wickedness: "Do not enter into the path of the wicked, and do not go in the way of evil men. Avoid it; do not pass by it; turn from it and pass away" (4:14–15).

*How does culture often glorify or justify behaviors that align with the path of the wicked?*

## Take Your Time and Learn More

- Seeking wisdom: James 1:5
- Seeking wisdom, knowledge, and understanding: Colossians 2:2–3
- God's discipline: Hebrews 12:5–6
- Be on guard: Ephesians 6:10–18

*The Bible is countercultural, and so is Bible study.*
*There's no need to rush through this.*

## PROVERBS 5

This chapter warns against the seductive allure of adultery, emphasizing the consequences of immoral behavior. Speaking to his son, the dad contrasts the fleeting pleasure of sin with the lasting satisfaction of a faithful marriage. He encourages his son to pursue wisdom and self-control, chasing after God's blessings rather than indulging in forbidden pleasures.

*Do you think our entertainment choices impact our perception of immorality? Why or why not?*

## PROVERBS 6

This chapter continues the father's parental warnings to his son, highlighting a list of things God hates. Interesting to note: lying is included on the list twice, emphasizing the severity of deceit and the importance of truth. Being truthful reflects God's character, so people who love God should demonstrate integrity in all aspects of life.

*How do you think honesty impacts your witness as a follower of Christ in the world?*

## PROVERBS 7

This chapter continues warning about adultery and the terrible consequences of yielding to temptation. The dad (presumably Solomon) isn't subtle—he says adultery is a path to death. Solomon had seven hundred wives and three hundred concubines, so he likely knew first-hand the destructive nature of sexual sin. He wants his son to choose the better path.

*What are some steps you can take (or have taken) to protect your relationships from temptation?*

## PROVERBS 8

This chapter is written in praise of wisdom. The writer personifies wisdom as a woman, declaring her value over material wealth and earthly pleasures and inviting everyone to pursue her. Adultery is the path to death; wisdom is the path to life—both are taken by choice.

*If wisdom is life's greatest prize, why are our hearts so tempted to pursue the lesser things?*

## Take Your Time and Learn More

- Warning against immorality: 1 CORINTHIANS 6:18–20
  - Warning against laziness: COLOSSIANS 3:23–25
    - The sin trap: JAMES 1:13–15
  - In praise of wisdom: JOHN 1:1–5

*God speaks in the quiet moments.*
*Approach His Word with calm expectation.*

## PROVERBS 9

This chapter contrasts wisdom and foolishness. Wisdom builds her house, inviting everyone to partake in her feast of understanding. Foolishness, by contrast, is like a woman who sits at the door of her house, calling loudly for the simple to indulge in stolen water and secret bread. Wisdom leads to life. Folly leads to death. You can't simultaneously pursue both.

*Are you surrounding yourself with wise counselors*
*and good influences? Why or why not?*

## PROVERBS 10

Solomon addresses everyone—not just his son—in this chapter, contrasting wisdom and the fear of God with folly and sin. He emphasizes the value of integrity and diligence, which lead to prosperity and blessings. In contrast, deceit and laziness result in ruin and sorrow.

*Proverbs 10:12 says, "Hatred stirs up strife, but love covers all sins."*
*How do you decide between confronting a situation and letting love cover it?*

## PROVERBS 11

The writer of Proverbs 11 contrasts the outcomes of righteousness and wickedness, emphasizing the rewards of integrity and wisdom. He highlights the importance of humility, generosity, and honesty—which, in principle, lead to blessings and honor. In contrast, deceit, pride, and injustice result in ruin and disgrace.

*Considering these verses, why do you think dishonest people often seem to flourish?*

## PROVERBS 12

Much of the book of Proverbs—including this chapter—pertains to the importance of words and how to use them responsibly. Proverbs like this one offer guidance on truthful communication and constructive criticism. A person's speech reflects her character and influences her relationships, shaping the course of her life.

*Can you recall a time you were deeply encouraged*
*(or discouraged) by someone's words?*

## Take Your Time and Learn More

- Wisdom's invitation: MATTHEW 7:24–27
- Earthly versus heavenly wisdom: JAMES 3:13–18
- Sowing and reaping: GALATIANS 6:7–9
- The power of words: EPHESIANS 4:29

*Before you read, pray. Ask God to speak His truth to your spirit.*

## PROVERBS 13

This chapter continues to contrast the outcomes of wisdom and folly. The writer emphasizes the importance of heeding instruction, living with integrity, and seeking wisdom. (Note: Proverbs can sometimes sound like wisdom leads to a life of ease, yet we know wise people suffer too.)

*Can you think of a scriptural example of someone who lived wisely and still suffered?*

## PROVERBS 14

One consistent theme throughout the Proverbs—including this chapter—is the danger of trusting human understanding instead of God's wisdom. When someone stubbornly chooses to "do what feels right" or "follow her heart" even if it contradicts God's Word, things typically end poorly.

*Why do bad decisions look so attractive in the moment, even if we subconsciously understand they will lead to pain or grief?*

## PROVERBS 15

This chapter contrasts the impact of wise and foolish behaviors on a person's life. Gentle speech is an example of wisdom—it can diffuse conflict and bring joy. Wisdom leads to understanding and favor from God, while foolishness invites destruction. The wise seek knowledge and correction while the foolish reject discipline and suffer the consequences.

*What is the difference between wisdom and understanding?*

## PROVERBS 16

This chapter contrasts pride and humility, encouraging humility as the pathway to honor and stressing the many benefits of seeking and understanding wisdom. Solomon extols the virtues of honesty and integrity, contrasting them with the consequences of deceit. He acknowledges the importance of planning and seeking counsel while recognizing God is ultimately in charge.

*How do you actively work to combat pride in your thoughts, attitudes, and actions?*

## Take Your Time and Learn More

- God's discipline: HEBREWS 12:11
- The wisdom of humility: JAMES 1:19–20
- Careful speech: COLOSSIANS 4:6
- Tomorrow: JAMES 4:13–15

*Don't hurry, don't worry. God's Word provides everything you need for living well.*

## PROVERBS 17

This chapter values integrity, wisdom, and discernment in relationships. . .and explains the destructive nature of strife and quarrels. A fool, it says, delights in wrongdoing, but a wise person seeks understanding. This proverb stresses the importance of honesty and trustworthiness in friendships and warns against spreading gossip or aligning with the wicked.

*Why is gossip so appealing or enticing, even though it leads to negative consequences?*

## PROVERBS 18

In this chapter, the writer wisely explains the power of words and attitudes. He says that it's important to listen before speaking—that we shouldn't rush to hasty judgments. He highlights the significance of humility, acknowledging that pride precedes destruction. Words possess the power to bring life or death, so discernment is critical for navigating life's challenges.

*When it comes to friendships, do you believe quality is better than quantity? Why or why not?*

## PROVERBS 19

This chapter addresses various aspects of life and character—emphasizing the importance of integrity, humility, and wisdom. It warns against the pitfalls of laziness and dishonesty, urging diligence and truthfulness in all situations. It touches on the themes of justice, generosity, and the fear of the Lord as essential components for a good life.

*Why is dishonesty so harmful in relationships? Why does lying become easier over time?*

## PROVERBS 20

This chapter covers integrity, justice, and diligence. Warning against the deceitful nature of human hearts, it urges absolute discernment in dealing with others. It lists the consequences of foolishness, laziness, and drunkenness—contrasting them with the blessings of wisdom and righteousness. It advises against greed and dishonest gain.

*Why is human nature so susceptible to the sin of laziness? How do you overcome it?*

## Take Your Time and Learn More

- Restraint: JAMES 1:19–20
- Power of words: EPHESIANS 4:29–32
- Dealing with others: ROMANS 12:17–21
- Earthly wisdom and heavenly wisdom: JAMES 3:17–18

*God loves it when you read and study His Word.*

## PROVERBS 21

This chapter contrasts the righteous and the wicked, highlighting the futility of relying on human wisdom and strength. The writer warns against pride, laziness, and dishonesty—all of which lead to ruin. It is a practical guide for making wise choices and living a life that pleases God.

*How can remembering the gospel help us put pride to death in our life?*

## PROVERBS 22

This chapter advises against pursuing wealth through dishonest means—instead, we should value humility and fear the Lord. The writer lists the benefits of wisdom and understanding, urging parents to train their children in ways that honor God. He warns against associating with the wicked and encourages compassion toward the poor.

*How can we honor God with whatever money He gives us in life?*

## PROVERBS 23

Proverbs 23 is a guide to self-control. The chapter warns against the allure of riches and indulgence, urging moderation and contentment. It highlights the importance of parental instruction and the value of wisdom in decision-making. It cautions against keeping company with the wicked and advises listening to the counsel of the wise.

*Can you think of a time you were generous and God was faithful to meet your need?*

## PROVERBS 24

This chapter warns against envying the wicked and desiring to join them. It also advises against laziness and procrastination, urging diligence and perseverance in all endeavors. It serves as a practical guide for righteous living, encouraging adherence to God's principles for a flourishing life.

*From whom should you seek counsel?*
*Is there ever a time you shouldn't follow counsel?*

## Take Your Time and Learn More

- Humility before God: JAMES 4:6–10
- Godly generosity: LUKE 6:38
- Real treasure: MATTHEW 6:19–21
- Overcoming evil: ROMANS 12:17–21

*Reading the Bible isn't a race. Let the pages unfold
at a pace that allows your spirit to breathe.*

## PROVERBS 25

Solomon encourages his readers to restrain from seeking honor or recognition. He advises wisdom in interpersonal relationships, stressing the value of patience and forgiveness. He also warns against meddling in other people's affairs and urges discretion in speech. Overall, the chapter is a guide for navigating social interactions with wisdom and grace.

*Why is being gentle and honest with our words so important?*

## PROVERBS 26

Solomon uses vivid imagery to illustrate the characteristics of fools—their destructive behaviors and lack of discernment. He urges readers to respond to fools with wisdom and restraint, not to enable or engage with them. He advises against spreading gossip and deceit, explaining the harm it can cause.

*How do you actively pursue truth in a world filled with misinformation?*

## PROVERBS 27

Solomon shares the benefits of genuine friendships and constructive criticism. He tells how valuable humility and patience are when responding to rebuke. He warns against the dangers of pride and self-deception, encourages self-examination and accountability, and stresses the importance of cultivating trustworthiness in relationships.

*Godly friends are willing to wound with truth.
Are you willing to have and be this kind of friend?*

## PROVERBS 28

Solomon lists the blessings of living according to God's principles, contrasting them with the pitfalls of disobedience. He warns against oppressing the poor and pursuing unjust gain, and he highlights the importance of integrity and generosity. Cautioning against pride and stubbornness, he urges humility and teachability instead.

*Practically speaking, what does generosity to the poor look like today?*

### Take Your Time and Learn More

- Humility: LUKE 14:8–11
- Wise communication: JAMES 3:5–12
- The value of adversity: HEBREWS 12:6–11
- Sowing and reaping: GALATIANS 6:7–9

*The greatest truths in scripture are often
revealed in the unhurried moments.*

## PROVERBS 29

Solomon explains how vital discipline is for shaping character. . .and how detrimental stubbornness and rebellion can be. Highlighting the blessings of humility, integrity, and wisdom, he encourages leaders to govern with justice and compassion. They have a responsibility to promote the welfare of their people.

*How do you discern between genuine praise and
flattery in your interactions with others?*

## PROVERBS 30

Proverbs 30 is a collection of wisdom from Agur, known only to this chapter of the Bible. He acknowledges human limitations and the need for dependence on God's wisdom. He contrasts the virtues of integrity and humility with the dangers of pride and greed, urging his readers to seek wisdom and avoid foolishness.

*How should God's view and praise of wisdom shape the way we read the Bible?*

## PROVERBS 31

While scholars don't agree on the identity of King Lemuel, this chapter contains his words, passed down to him from his mother. He paints the image of a virtuous wife—industrious, wise, compassionate, skillful, diligent, strong, resourceful, generous, and God-fearing. Her husband and children praise her, and her community respects her.

*Why is the fear of God foundational to the health of any relationship?*

## Take Your Time and Learn More

- Warnings and instructions: GALATIANS 6:7–9
- Dependency on God's provision: MATTHEW 6:11
- Virtue, wisdom, and strength: 1 PETER 3:3–4

# ECCLESIASTES

*Apart from knowing and trusting God,*
*the meaning of life is elusive.*

## SETTING THE STAGE

Ecclesiastes offers a thought-provoking reflection on the human condition, encouraging us to seek deeper understanding and greater meaning beyond this world's temporary pursuits.

Like an old friend who prefers rich conversation over shallow small talk, the book of Ecclesiastes quickly goes deep, challenging our conventional views of success, purpose, and fulfillment. It invites us to ponder life's complexities and uncertainties.

At times, Ecclesiastes seems to express disillusionment. . .but it actually offers great hope by emphasizing the importance of seeing God's perspective and living in reverent obedience to Him.

The goal of this book is to destroy our godless methods of creating meaning and purpose. Our true significance, it teaches, lies in God. If we read and understand this unique book correctly, Ecclesiastes is a great gift to those of us who want to live with eternity in mind.

The final two verses of Ecclesiastes sum up the book: "Fear God and keep His commandments, for this is the whole duty of man. For God shall bring every work into judgment, with every secret thing, whether it is good or evil" (12:13–14).

## GOOD TO KNOW

Author not stated but probably Solomon. He is identified as "the son of David" (1:1) and "king over Israel in Jerusalem" (1:12), with "more wisdom than all those who have been before me" (1:16). Probably written around the 900s BC.

*Bible study is truly a lifelong journey.*
*Relax and enjoy the trip.*

## ECCLESIASTES 1

Solomon—son of David and wise king of Jerusalem—begins Ecclesiastes with the declaration that "all is vanity" (1:2), setting the tone for the book's exploration of life's big questions. He observes the cyclical nature of life, noting that generations come and go but the earth remains unchanged. He compares human endeavors to chasing after the wind.

*The Preacher indicates that life is repetitive.*
*Do you find this idea positive or negative?*

## ECCLESIASTES 2

Solomon recounts his pursuits—pleasure, wealth, and wisdom—declaring them all meaningless. Despite accumulating great riches and indulging in every pleasure, he finds no lasting satisfaction or fulfillment. He reflects on the inevitability of death, acknowledging that both the wise and foolish will die. He concludes that true contentment comes from fearing God.

*Can you think of a time you achieved a big life goal*
*only to lapse back into dissatisfaction?*

## ECCLESIASTES 3

In the best-known chapter of Ecclesiastes, Solomon reflects on the cyclical nature of life's seasons. He explains that there is a time and purpose for every activity under heaven, including joy and sorrow. He contrasts moments of birth and death, planting and harvesting, love and hate, war and peace—and he acknowledges God's sovereignty over everything.

*Why do you believe people today work so hard to avoid aging and death?*

## ECCLESIASTES 4

Solomon observes the injustices in society—oppression, toil, envy, and loneliness. He specifically criticizes the pursuit of wealth and success at the expense of relationships. What's the point? Ultimately, he concludes that contentment is found not in worldly achievements but in enjoying the simple pleasures of life and pursuing meaningful relationships.

*What would you say are your five most meaningful relationships?*

### Take Your Time and Learn More

- God's goodness in a fleeting life: JAMES 1:17
  - Pursuit of pleasure: MATTHEW 16:26
  - God's sovereignty: ROMANS 8:28
- Life's opposition and God's rest: MATTHEW 11:28–30

*Try to forget the demands of life for a while.*
*You're spending quality time with God.*

## ECCLESIASTES 5

Solomon advises against making hasty vows or speaking impulsively before the Lord. Rather, we should consider the seriousness of our commitments to Him. Ecclesiastes advocates for contentment with life's simple pleasures, recognizing them as gifts from God. Solomon concludes the chapter by reflecting on the fleeting nature of life and the importance of keeping God's commandments.

*How do you primarily view God—as your friend, father, master, or something else? Why?*

## ECCLESIASTES 6

Solomon explores the theme of life's uncertainties and the fleeting nature of human pursuits. He reflects on the paradox of having wealth and possessions but lacking the ability to enjoy them. He emphasizes the importance of contentment and acceptance of life, recognizing it all as a gift from God.

*Why are money and wealth ultimately unable to satisfy the soul?*

## ECCLESIASTES 7

Much like the book of Proverbs, Solomon presents short sayings about wisdom and the nature of life. He contrasts the value of wisdom with the emptiness of foolishness, cautioning against hasty decisions and reckless behavior. He observes the inevitability of suffering and the limitations of human understanding.

*Do you feel an urgency to accomplish any goals,*
*knowing that time is limited? Why or why not?*

## ECCLESIASTES 8

Solomon reflects on the limitations of human wisdom and observes that nobody can fully understand God's ways. He acknowledges the injustices present in the world, recognizing that wickedness often goes unpunished while the righteous suffer. Yet he encourages respect for God's authority as well as the king's.

*How comfortable are you with accepting the mystery of God's ways?*

### Take Your Time and Learn More

- Pursuit of treasure: MATTHEW 6:19–21
- Emptiness of earthly pleasure: LUKE 12:15
- The enigmas of life: ROMANS 8:28
- Obedience to authority: ROMANS 13:1–2

*Good things come to those who wait—on the Lord, that is.*

## ECCLESIASTES 9

Solomon reflects on the unpredictability of life and the certainty of death. He observes that both the righteous and the wicked share the same fate—the equalizing power of mortality. He warns against presuming on the future yet advises diligence and wisdom in everything. He concludes that ultimate satisfaction comes from fearing God and keeping His commandments.

*What are some strategies people use to distract themselves from life's uncertainties?*

## ECCLESIASTES 10

Solomon contrasts wisdom and foolishness, highlighting their respective outcomes. He cautions against making unwise decisions, noting the harm they can bring. He also addresses the importance of good leadership and urges leaders to exercise wisdom and discernment.

*Why do you think Solomon advises against cursing leadership even in our thoughts (10:20)?*

## ECCLESIASTES 11

Solomon offers wisdom on living with a spirit of generosity, diligence, and humility. He encourages sowing seeds of kindness—knowing that they may yield unexpected blessings. He emphasizes the inevitability of both joy and pain in life, urging readers to maintain hope and perseverance through all circumstances.

*How does modern culture view aging? Does it line up with biblical teaching?*

## ECCLESIASTES 12

Solomon finishes this book with a poignant reflection on the fleeting nature of life. He paints a vivid image of old age and its challenges, emphasizing the need to fear God and keep His commandments—"for this is the whole duty of man" (12:13). He concludes with a final exhortation to embrace wisdom and live with respect for God.

*Do you currently find your greatest satisfaction in God? Why or why not?*

### Take Your Time and Learn More

- **Certainty of death:** HEBREWS 9:27
- **Wisdom and foolishness:** JAMES 3:13–18
- **Sowing and reaping:** GALATIANS 6:7–10
- **Living with eternity in mind:** 2 TIMOTHY 4:6–8

# SONG OF SOLOMON

*God intended marital love and intimacy to be beautiful and pure.*

## SETTING THE STAGE

The Song of Solomon—also known as the Song of Songs—contains eight chapters of poetry expressing the beauty of love, desire, and intimacy between a bride and her bridegroom.

Apart from the introduction and conclusion, the book follows no clear storyline or literary organization and isn't intended to be dissected or picked apart. It's simply meant to be read as the passionate and poetic exchanges between two lovers.

The intensity seen throughout the book demonstrates the power of love. When given and received as God designed it, love is life-giving; but when it is taken or abused, passion can be destructive: "Many waters cannot quench love, nor can the floods drown it. If a man would give all the possessions of his house for love, it would be utterly condemned" (8:7).

This book accomplishes three main things with its rich imagery: First, it celebrates pure marital love as ordained by God. Second, it represents God's love for His covenant people, Israel. Third, it pictures Christ's love for His bride, the church.

Whether interpreted as a literal celebration of marital love or an allegorical representation of divine love, this book captures the depth, beauty, and mystery of relationship.

## GOOD TO KNOW

Perhaps written by Solomon (1:1), though some wonder if the song "of Solomon" is like the psalms "of David"—they may be *by*, *for*, or *about* him. Solomon ruled around 970–930 BC.

*The Bible is countercultural, and so is Bible study.*
*There's no need to rush through this.*

## SONG OF SOLOMON 1

Song of Solomon 1 introduces this book of ancient Jewish love poetry with romantic dialogue between a shepherdess and her beloved. The shepherdess acknowledges her skin has been darkened by long hours working in the hot sun, but the shepherd replies by simply praising her beauty. The chapter sets the tone for the passionately intimate exchanges throughout this book.

*Why would Hebrew love poetry be included in the Bible?*

## SONG OF SOLOMON 2

The poetic dialogue continues. The shepherdess will speak more in this book than any other woman speaks in scripture. She compares her beloved to a lily among thorns and expresses her desire for his presence. They delight fully in each other's company, exuding imagery of love and intimacy and illustrating the depth of affection between two lovers.

*Have you ever experienced the joy of restored fellowship*
*with God or someone you love? What happened?*

## SONG OF SOLOMON 3

The shepherdess recalls a nightmare in which she couldn't find her beloved. After searching longingly for him in the city streets, she eventually finds him and brings him to her home. This chapter portrays the intensity of her love for him and the joy of their reunion. It conveys the theme of longing and fulfillment.

*How can the cares of this life drown out your longing for Christ?*

## SONG OF SOLOMON 4

This book likely follows this couple's relationship from courtship to wedding to marriage. The bridegroom praises his bride's physical attributes, comparing her to various elements in nature and expressing his admiration for her beauty. The chapter reflects on the passionate love shared between two lovers.

*Why does genuine love require surrender?*

## Take Your Time and Learn More

- Love and desire: EPHESIANS 5:25–27
- The beauty of the bride: REVELATION 21:2–4
- Joy in the presence of the beloved: JOHN 3:29
- Shared admiration: PROVERBS 5:18–19

*God speaks in the quiet moments.*
*Approach His Word with calm expectation.*

## SONG OF SOLOMON 5

In this chapter, the bride and bridegroom engage in a playful yet passionate exchange. The bride again has a difficult dream about her beloved—which scholars believe indicates a difficulty in their relationship. She searches for him but cannot find him. Eventually, she finds him and they express their love for each other.

*How do love and intimacy in this book differ from*
*modern cultural depictions of marriage?*

## SONG OF SOLOMON 6

This chapter begins with the bridegroom seeking his bride and expressing his desire to be with her. The bride responds by affirming her love for him and expressing her longing for their union. The couple delights in each other's physical attributes and expresses their passion for one another.

*Do you believe God loves and delights over you? Why or why not?*

## SONG OF SOLOMON 7

The dialogue between the bride and her beloved intensifies as they continue expressing their love and desire for each other. The beloved praises the bride's beauty, using vivid imagery to describe her physical attributes. The bride responds with affection, reciprocating his love.

*How is a healthy Christian marriage meant to reflect the*
*relationship between Christ and the church?*

## SONG OF SOLOMON 8

The bride and her beloved share a final expression of love and commitment. The bride longs for intimacy with her beloved, expressing her desire to enjoy his presence. She reflects on the strength of their love, which cannot be extinguished by any force. The couple expresses their devotion to each other and their desire for a love that endures.

*Why does secular culture seem to prefer intimacy over commitment?*

### Take Your Time and Learn More

- Sacrificial love: EPHESIANS 5:25–27
- The beautiful bride: REVELATION 21:2–3
- Love and devotion: PSALM 45:10–11
- A mysterious union: EPHESIANS 5:31–32

# ISAIAH

*Though consequences exist for sin,
God will restore His people to Himself.*

## SETTING THE STAGE

Isaiah, whose name literally means "salvation of the Lord," is known as one of the greatest and most significant writing prophets. His book is the first of the prophetic books.

Comprising sixty-six chapters and spanning a considerable number of themes, it is characterized by its unapologetic messages of judgment, comfort, and the ultimate hope of redemption.

The book begins with messages of judgment, warning Israel and Judah about their disobedience and the consequences of turning away from God. Isaiah calls for the people to repent and return to a right relationship with God.

Notably, the book of Isaiah contains the most extensive and detailed prophecies in the Old Testament about the coming Messiah. These prophecies have had a profound impact in shaping the New Testament understanding of Jesus Christ as the Messiah. The most well-known prophecy: "Therefore the Lord Himself shall give you a sign. Behold, a virgin shall conceive and bear a son and shall call His name Immanuel" (7:14).

While Isaiah's immediate audience is the people of Judah, the themes and prophecies he includes address universal issues of justice, righteousness, and salvation. No other Old Testament book gives us a clearer view of God's grace.

## GOOD TO KNOW

Author is Isaiah, son of Amoz (1:1). He wrote round 740–700 BC, starting "in the year that King Uzziah died" (6:1).

*Before you read, pray. Ask God to speak His truth to your spirit.*

## ISAIAH 1

The book of Isaiah opens with God making a passionate indictment against Israel's rebellion. He accuses them of hypocrisy—offering sacrifices while living in disobedience. At this point, Israel is consumed by sin. Each successive generation continues the corruption. Yet the people continue making religious rituals and offerings. God desires genuine worship.

*Why is hypocritical worship so deeply offensive to God?*

## ISAIAH 2

Isaiah shares a vision of the future exaltation of Jerusalem in which people from all nations flock to worship God. People will finally understand that the Lord of Israel is the one true God. Before this happens, however, there will be a judgment on the proud and arrogant. Isaiah urges people to humble themselves before God.

*How do you cultivate humility in an environment that prioritizes competition and self-promotion?*

## ISAIAH 3

Isaiah describes more of what God will take away from Judah and Jerusalem because of their rebellion against Him. He paints a scene in which God removes wise leaders and competent officials, leading to chaos and oppression. Instead of turning to God, people turn to unreliable leaders and false prophets. But wicked men can't be trusted.

*How do you shift your focus from human strength to daily reliance on God?*

## ISAIAH 4

Isaiah shares a vision of the coming kingdom—a time of blessing after judgment—in Israel's far future, when the people have been made holy by God. The Lord's presence will be a canopy of smoke by day and fire by night. It will serve as a shelter from the heat, offering security and protection. Isaiah provides a hopeful vision of restoration and provision.

*God will eventually make all things right. How does this reality help on difficult days?*

## Take Your Time and Learn More

- Humility before God: MICAH 6:6–8
- Establishment of God's kingdom: MICAH 4:1–5
- Judgment against pride and arrogance: JEREMIAH 9:23–24
- Purification and restoration: ZECHARIAH 13:1–2

*Don't hurry, don't worry. God's Word provides*
*everything you need for living well.*

## ISAIAH 5

Isaiah shares his song about a vineyard. God is likened to a vineyard owner who planted a vineyard expecting good grapes. . .but finds wild ones. This metaphor symbolizes God's disappointment with Israel's unfaithfulness. Despite God's efforts to cultivate righteousness, the people have strayed. Consequently, God will remove their wall of protection.

*What proof of spiritual fruitfulness appears in your life?*
*What about opportunities for growth?*

## ISAIAH 6

Isaiah recounts his vision of the Lord's glory in the temple. He witnesses heavenly beings praising God and acknowledging His holiness. Overwhelmed by his unworthiness, Isaiah confesses his sinfulness. One of the seraphim purifies Isaiah's lips with a burning coal. God asks, "Whom shall I send, and who will go for Us?" Isaiah responds, "Here I am. Send me" (6:8).

*What are your first instincts when overwhelmed by circumstances?*

## ISAIAH 7

Wicked King Ahaz faces a coalition of enemies threatening Judah. God instructs Isaiah to reassure Ahaz that the invasion will fail. Isaiah invites Ahaz to ask for a sign as confirmation, but Ahaz refuses. God promises a sign anyway: a virgin will conceive and give birth to a son who will be called Immanuel.

*What does it indicate about God that He offered this*
*sign even though Ahaz didn't request it?*

## ISAIAH 8

Isaiah continues his prophetic message to Judah, warning of impending judgment. Despite the people's reliance on foreign alliances, Isaiah emphasizes trust in God alone. The prophet condemns seeking guidance from mediums and necromancers, advocating trust in God's Word. Isaiah predicts devastation inflicted by Assyria but assures a remnant will return to God.

*Why is it dangerous to downplay the seriousness of sin?*

## Take Your Time and Learn More

- God's vineyard: MATTHEW 21:33–46
- John references Isaiah 6: JOHN 12:40–41
- Matthew quotes from Isaiah 7: MATTHEW 1:22–23
- Peter quotes from Isaiah 8: 1 PETER 2:6–8

*God loves it when you read and study His Word.*

## ISAIAH 9

Isaiah prophesies the coming of a great light upon those who dwell in darkness. This light will be a child who brings hope and deliverance to the nation. He will be called Wonderful, Counselor, Mighty God, Everlasting Father, and Prince of Peace. Despite the current darkness, Isaiah foretells a future of joy and peace.

*How is God's promise of a Messiah an incredibly gracious answer to His anger over sin?*

## ISAIAH 10

Isaiah describes Assyria as a tool in God's hand to punish Israel's wickedness. Still, he rebukes their prideful intentions—Assyria will be held accountable for their cruelty. God promises to punish Assyria's king and break the yoke placed on Israel. God's power brings both judgment and deliverance.

*When has God used an unlikely instrument to accomplish His good purpose in your life?*

## ISAIAH 11

Isaiah prophesies the coming of a righteous and just ruler from the line of Jesse. This ruler will possess the Spirit of the Lord—bringing wisdom, understanding, and counsel. He will judge with righteousness and equity, restore harmony and peace to the earth, and gather the scattered people of Israel into a unified worship of God.

*What does it mean to delight in the fear of the Lord?*

## ISAIAH 12

Isaiah shares the words of a worshipper, expressing joy and gratitude for God's deliverance and acknowledging His strength. He invites God's people to declare their trust in Him and rejoice in His faithfulness. God is their strength and salvation, and the people should give thanks and proclaim His deeds among the nations.

*What song can you sing in praise of your God today?*

## Take Your Time and Learn More

- Matthew quotes from Isaiah 9: MATTHEW 4:14–16
  - Paul quotes from Isaiah 10: ROMANS 9:27–28
    - Jesus' universal reign: REVELATION 5:5
  - Thanksgiving to the Lord: PSALM 118:14–16

*Reading the Bible isn't a race. Let the pages unfold
at a pace that allows your spirit to breathe.*

## ISAIAH 13

Isaiah tells of God's wrath upon the nations, describing a day of reckoning when the Lord will destroy Babylon and bring devastation upon the land. The imagery shows the severity of God's judgment. Babylon's pride and arrogance will be humbled, and the city will be reduced to desolation.

*How do you make sure you prioritize spiritual wealth over worldly riches in your life?*

## ISAIAH 14

Isaiah prophesies the downfall of Babylon and the restoration of Israel. He shares a taunt against the king of Babylon—who is brought low despite his once-exalted status. The fall of Babylon is similar to the story of Satan, who was overthrown because of pride and rebellion against God. Isaiah prophesies Israel's future freedom and restoration.

*In what practical ways can you live out the promise of God's future, final restoration?*

## ISAIAH 15

Isaiah prophesies judgment against Moab, a neighboring nation of Israel. He describes the devastation that will befall Moab as their cities are destroyed and their people flee in terror. He depicts mourning and lamentation, highlighting the severity of God's judgment on Moab's pride and arrogance. Isaiah emphasizes the need for humility and repentance before God.

*What is the link between humility and repentance?
Can either exist without the other?*

## ISAIAH 16

Isaiah continues the prophecy against Moab, predicting their eventual destruction and lamenting their prideful downfall. Despite Moab's arrogance and rebellion, there is a glimmer of hope for a remnant who will be spared from destruction. Isaiah underscores the importance of humility and reliance on God's mercy.

*In what ways does God's mercy extend beyond simply overlooking faults?*

## Take Your Time and Learn More

- Judgment and destruction of God's enemies: REVELATION 18:2
- The enemy's defeat: LUKE 10:18
- Judgment on Moab: JEREMIAH 48:33–35
- Moab's remnant: JEREMIAH 48:47

*The greatest truths in scripture are often*
*revealed in the unhurried moments.*

## ISAIAH 17

Isaiah prophesies judgment against Damascus, describing the destruction that will reduce the city to a heap of ruins. The imagery portrays the devastation of war and the desolation of once-prosperous cities. Isaiah warns of the consequences of relying on human strength instead of God's. Despite the impending judgment, there is a message of hope for a remnant.

*How do you intentionally stay faithful to God in the midst of life's challenges?*

## ISAIAH 18

Isaiah delivers a message concerning Ethiopia, a major world power and a rival to Assyria. God commands attention to Ethiopia's future, and Isaiah emphasizes God's sovereignty over all nations, regardless of their location or power. Ethiopia will eventually bow before God.

*In what area of your life do you need to relinquish control and trust in God's good plans?*

## ISAIAH 19

Isaiah prophesies judgment against Egypt, describing a time of turmoil, confusion, and division within the nation. Egypt will fall into the hands of a cruel master, bringing suffering and distress. But Isaiah also offers a message of hope, as Egypt will eventually turn to the Lord and He will heal and restore them.

*Why do you think God frequently pairs warnings of judgment with promises of restoration?*

## ISAIAH 20

Isaiah becomes a visible sign to the people. He walks barefoot and wearing only his inner garment—a sign of absolute poverty and humility—to illustrate the shame that will befall these nations. Despite this unusual method, his message is clear: those who trust human strength rather than God will face dire consequences.

*What are some specific indications that a person's trust is in God and not in earthly powers?*

### Take Your Time and Learn More

- Destruction of cities: AMOS 3:15
- Consequences of pride and disobedience: JEREMIAH 13:15–17
- Egypt's future: ZECHARIAH 14:16–19
- Humiliation and shame: 2 KINGS 18:13–16

*Bible study is truly a lifelong journey.*
*Relax and enjoy the trip.*

## ISAIAH 21

Isaiah prophesies the fall of Babylon, using vivid imagery to depict its destruction. He describes watchmen stationed on the walls, anticipating a crisis. Babylon's fall will result in mourning and distress for its people. Isaiah also prophesies the fall of Edom, another nation facing God's judgment. Despite their strength and wealth, these nations will be brought low by God's hand.

*How do you intentionally pursue joy in seasons of trial and uncertainty?*

## ISAIAH 22

Isaiah focuses on the prophecy of Jerusalem's impending fall. He describes the city's inhabitants preparing for defense but ultimately succumbing to defeat. He condemns their lack of repentance and their reliance on human efforts instead of God. Isaiah writes about the role of Shebna—a corrupt official—and the appointment of Eliakim as his replacement.

*What are the differences between godly sorrow and worldly sorrow?*

## ISAIAH 23

Isaiah prophesies judgment against Tyre—a wealthy, influential maritime city that is about to be brought low. He describes Tyre's destruction and desolation as a result of God's judgment. Isaiah emphasizes the fleeting nature of earthly wealth and power, warning against reliance on material riches instead of trust in God.

*Why do you think earthly wealth and power hold such*
*allure, even though they are fleeting?*

## ISAIAH 24

Isaiah portrays a vision of worldwide judgment and devastation. He describes the earth being completely laid waste, with chaos and destruction reigning supreme. Despite the devastation, a remnant will praise God in the midst of the chaos, recognizing His righteousness and power. Isaiah underscores the universal scope of God's judgment and the importance of recognizing His authority.

*How does reading about God's capacity for judgment challenge you in your daily life?*

### *Take Your Time and Learn More*

- **The fall of Babylon:** REVELATION 18:1–3
- **Authority, stewardship, and accountability:** MATTHEW 16:19
- **Major trading city:** NEHEMIAH 13:16–17
- **Judgment on the earth:** 2 PETER 3:10–13

*Try to forget the demands of life for a while.*
*You're spending quality time with God.*

## ISAIAH 25

Isaiah celebrates God as a stronghold for the oppressed, a refuge in times of trouble. He prophesies a day when God will swallow up death and grief, bringing joy and salvation to His people. The righteous will rejoice in God's deliverance while the arrogant will be humbled. Isaiah emphasizes the importance of trusting in God's promises and waiting patiently for Him.

*What are some of God's most precious promises to you?*

## ISAIAH 26

Isaiah composes a prophetic hymn in praise of God's salvation. He exalts God as an everlasting rock and describes the security and peace found in trusting Him. He contrasts the future of the righteous with the downfall of the wicked. He urges God's people to trust Him—even in the midst of adversity—knowing that He will bring justice and deliverance.

*Why is true security and peace only found in trusting God?*

## ISAIAH 27

Isaiah depicts God's ultimate victory and restoration. He describes God as the vineyard keeper, tending to His people and removing what is harmful. Despite His discipline, God's ultimate purpose is to bring about reconciliation and restoration. Isaiah prophesies the defeat of Israel's enemies and the gathering of His scattered people from Assyria and Egypt.

*What does God's role as a vineyard keeper reveal about His involvement in our lives?*

## ISAIAH 28

Isaiah rebukes the pride of Ephraim, a reference to all Israel, warning of impending judgment. Using vivid imagery, he describes a fading crown of beauty and a deceptive covenant with death. Isaiah condemns Ephraim's reliance on false security rather than trusting in God. He emphasizes the importance of a sure foundation in God's righteousness and justice.

*What are some common sources of false security that people rely on today?*

## Take Your Time and Learn More

- Triumph over death: 1 CORINTHIANS 15:54–57
- Security found in God's salvation: ROMANS 5:1–2
- Restoration, pruning, and God's care for His people: JOHN 15:1–2
- Jesus as the cornerstone: 1 PETER 2:4–6

*Good things come to those who wait—on the Lord, that is.*

## ISAIAH 29

Isaiah warns of Jerusalem's impending judgment due to their spiritual blindness, hypocrisy, superficial worship, and failure to obey. Despite their outward piety, their lack of true devotion will lead to their downfall. He condemns those who try to hide their plans from God and promises that their schemes will be thwarted.

*How do you specifically guard against offering lip service to God?*

## ISAIAH 30

Isaiah condemns Judah's reliance on Egypt (instead of God) for protection. He rebukes their refusal to heed God's guidance and warns of their eventual downfall. Despite these warnings, the people reject his counsel, preferring false assurances of safety. Yet God is patient and offers forgiveness to those who repent.

*Why do you think some people prefer to acknowledge only God's mercy, not His wrath?*

## ISAIAH 31

Isaiah again cautions against relying on Egypt's military might instead of God. He warns of the futility of seeking help from human power, emphasizing that God alone is mighty to save. Those who trust in Egypt's horses and chariots will be disappointed since Egypt will be judged.

*How might the warnings of this chapter apply to Western Christians today?*

## ISAIAH 32

Isaiah prophesies a righteous King who will bring peace. He then contrasts the future of the righteous with that of the wicked, promising blessings to those who remain faithful to God. He describes the transformation of society—with justice, peace, and righteousness flourishing. He encourages the people to trust God's sovereignty, even amid uncertainty and distress.

*What steps can you take to avoid becoming complacent in your faith?*

### Take Your Time and Learn More

- Jesus quotes Isaiah 29: MATTHEW 15:8–9
  - God's judgment on disobedience and rebellion: HEBREWS 10:30–31
    - Trust in God's protection: PSALM 20:7
- Rewards for righteousness: JAMES 3:17–18

*The Bible is countercultural, and so is Bible study.*
*There's no need to rush through this.*

## ISAIAH 33

Isaiah prophesies judgment on the nations and delivers a message of hope for God's people. He describes God's sovereignty and power in bringing down the wicked and delivering the righteous. He portrays Jerusalem's eventual restoration and security under God's protection, and he emphasizes the importance of trusting in God's salvation and living uprightly.

*What are some specific ways you can walk righteously and speak uprightly this week?*

## ISAIAH 34

Isaiah prophesies God's judgment on the nations and His vengeance against the wicked. With vivid imagery, he depicts the awful devastation that will come upon the earth. He describes God's wrath as a consuming fire and His judgment as a sword that will slaughter the ungodly. God's justice will be brought against those who rebel against Him.

*Why do you think wicked people persist in their rebellion against God despite the warnings?*

## ISAIAH 35

Isaiah offers a message of hope, describing a time when God will bring restoration and renewal to the land. He pictures a desert blossoming with life, the blind seeing, the deaf hearing, and the lame leaping for joy. He encourages people to be strong and fearless—God will come with vengeance to save them.

*How can the promise of God's judgment actually provide comfort in today's world?*

## ISAIAH 36

Isaiah recounts the events surrounding King Sennacherib's first and second invasions of Judah. The Assyrian commander Rabshakeh comes to Jerusalem, taunting King Hezekiah and the people and urging their surrender. He mocks their trust in God and attempts to create fear and doubt.

*Why do you think some individuals feel compelled to mock those who love and follow Christ?*

## Take Your Time and Learn More

- The new Jerusalem: REVELATION 21:9–27
- Battle of Armageddon: REVELATION 6:15–17
- Arrival of the Messiah: LUKE 7:22
- Invasion of Judah: 2 KINGS 18:13–37

*God speaks in the quiet moments.*
*Approach His Word with calm expectation.*

## ISAIAH 37

Faced with the Assyrian threat, Hezekiah seeks Isaiah's counsel and prays earnestly for God's deliverance. Isaiah reassures him that God will protect Jerusalem. Sennacherib writes a blasphemous letter to Hezekiah, belittling God. So the angel of the Lord kills 185,000 Assyrian solders, causing the rest to flee. Sennacherib is then assassinated by his own sons.

*Do you prioritize prayer in moments in distress and trouble? Why or why not?*

## ISAIAH 38

Isaiah recounts King Hezekiah's illness and miraculous recovery. Facing death, Hezekiah prays earnestly to God, reminding the Lord of his own faithfulness. In response, God gives Hezekiah fifteen more years of life and delivers him from his sickness. Hezekiah expresses his gratitude through a song of praise, acknowledging God's power to save and restore.

*Do you think Christians can argue their own faithfulness before God? Why or why not?*

## ISAIAH 39

Isaiah records King Hezekiah's sin of pridefully showing off his treasures to envoys from Babylon. Isaiah confronts Hezekiah, prophesying that Babylon will eventually conquer Judah and exile its people. Hezekiah responds with indifference, seemingly concerned solely with peace and security in his own time.

*Why do you think God granted Hezekiah more time despite knowing he would sin like this?*

## ISAIAH 40

Isaiah shares a message of comfort and hope for God's people, declaring the greatness of God and His permanent deliverance. Isaiah paints a vivid picture of God's power and majesty, contrasting His eternal nature with humanity's temporary existence. He reassures the people of God's faithfulness and promises strength for those who wait on Him.

*How can you cultivate a spirit of patient trust in God's faithfulness?*

## Take Your Time and Learn More

- Judah's deliverance promised: 2 KINGS 19:20–34
- Hezekiah's healing promised: 2 KINGS 20:1–11
- Hezekiah and the envoys from Babylon: 2 KINGS 20:12–19
- Matthew quotes from Isaiah 40: MATTHEW 3:3

## ISAIAH 41

Isaiah continues comforting and reassuring God's people. He emphasizes God's sovereignty and faithfulness, reminding the Israelites of His past deeds and promises. God challenges the nations and their idols to prove their power, declaring Himself as the one true God. Isaiah urges the Israelites to trust the living God.

*How has God been faithful to you in the past in a way*
*that strengthens your faith for the future?*

## ISAIAH 42

Isaiah prophesies the coming of the Lord, who will bring justice and salvation to the nations. This servant—Jesus Christ—will be characterized by gentleness and humility. He will establish justice on earth and bring hope to the oppressed. Isaiah focuses on God's faithfulness to His covenant promises and His desire for righteousness to prevail.

*Do you find it difficult to praise God during times of adversity? Why or why not?*

## ISAIAH 43

Isaiah reiterates God's steadfast love and faithfulness to His people, promising He will redeem and protect them. Despite their past disobedience, God declares His commitment to them and reminds them that He alone is their Savior and Redeemer. The chapter emphasizes God's power to deliver His people from any situation, including exile and captivity.

*Can you think of a time God delivered you from an "impossible" situation?*

## ISAIAH 44

Isaiah contrasts the foolishness of idolatry with the greatness of God, who alone is worthy of worship. God promises to pour out His Spirit on His people and bless them with His favor. Isaiah encourages the Israelites to remember their identity as God's chosen people and to trust in His power to deliver them.

*In what ways can you express gratitude to God for His forgiveness in your life?*

## Take Your Time and Learn More

- Jesus is the living God: REVELATION 1:17–18
- Matthew quotes from Isaiah 42: MATTHEW 12:17–21
- God's faithfulness to His promises: 1 PETER 2:9–10
- God's redemption: EPHESIANS 2:8–9

*Don't hurry, don't worry. God's Word provides
everything you need for living well.*

## ISAIAH 45

God is sovereign over the nations, orchestrating all events for His purposes. God will even use Cyrus—a pagan king—to fulfill His plan of delivering His people from captivity in Babylon. Despite Cyrus's unawareness of God's role, he will do God's will. This chapter highlights God's ability to work through unlikely means to achieve His purposes.

*Consider ways God has used difficult experiences in your life for His glory.*

## ISAIAH 46

Isaiah contrasts God's power with the powerlessness of idols. He highlights false gods' inability to save or predict the future. By contrast, God is sovereign and reliable, able to declare the end from the beginning. Isaiah reassures the people of God's faithfulness and power to save.

*Do you sometimes rely on your own wisdom instead
of seeking God's direction? If so, when?*

## ISAIAH 47

Isaiah pronounces judgment on Babylon, a symbol of arrogance and oppression. Despite its former glory and power, Babylon will be humiliated by God's righteous judgment. Isaiah exposes the foolishness of pride and idolatry, warning of the consequence of rebelling against God.

*Is it possible for us to cultivate a humble, teachable
heart, or is that something only God can do?*

## ISAIAH 48

Isaiah reminds Israel of God's desire for them to acknowledge Him as their Savior and Redeemer. God promises to refine His people like silver and lead them in righteousness—all they have to do is listen to God's instruction and turn back to Him. Their obedience will bring blessings. . .but their rebellion will bring consequences.

*Why does God refuse to share His glory?*

## Take Your Time and Learn More

- The recognition of God's power: PHILIPPIANS 2:9–11
- God as a refuge and strength: PSALM 46:1–3
- Judgment on Babylon: REVELATION 18:7–8
- God's refining process: PSALM 66:8–12

*God loves it when you read and study His Word.*

## ISAIAH 49

Isaiah continues the theme of restoration and redemption, focusing on the Servant of the Lord—Jesus. Isaiah emphasizes the mission of Jesus to bring salvation not only to Israel but to the entire world. Despite initial rejection and suffering, Jesus' ultimate victory is assured. God promises to restore His people, gathering them from exile and making them a light to the nations.

*How have you personally experienced God's unfailing love?*

## ISAIAH 50

Isaiah speaks of the obedient Servant of the Lord who endures suffering and persecution yet remains faithful to God. Isaiah contrasts the Servant's steadfastness with Israel's stubbornness, emphasizing the importance of listening to God's voice and following His commands. He points to the redemptive work of the Servant, who brings salvation to all who believe.

*How can you develop a greater willingness to obey God's commands?*

## ISAIAH 51

Isaiah calls on Israel's remnant to consider the example of Abraham and Sarah, who trusted God's promises. He encourages God's people to take refuge in Him, reminding them of God's power to save and deliver. Isaiah reassures the Israelites of God's faithfulness and future restoration, and he encourages them to shake off fear and trust God's strength.

*How does the promise of eternal joy and comfort influence your perspective during trials?*

## ISAIAH 52

Isaiah prophesies the redemption of Jerusalem in God's future kingdom. He calls God's people to awaken and clothe themselves in strength because God is coming to deliver them. He portrays the joy of the Israelites as they witness the return of the Lord's presence to Zion. All will realize God's power to save and His faithfulness to His promises.

*How can you intentionally share the good news of God's love with someone this week?*

## Take Your Time and Learn More

- Light to the Gentiles: LUKE 2:29–32
- The Suffering Servant: MATTHEW 27:27–31
- God's persistent love for His people: ROMANS 8:31–39
- Paul quotes from Isaiah 52: ROMANS 10:15

*Reading the Bible isn't a race. Let the pages unfold at a pace that allows your spirit to breathe.*

## ISAIAH 53

Isaiah prophesies about the suffering Servant—depicting Jesus' sacrificial atonement for the sins of humanity and highlighting His rejection, suffering, and eventual vindication. "It pleased the LORD to bruise Him" (53:10). This Servant willingly bears the sins of the world, offering redemption and reconciliation with God.

*How does understanding what Jesus did for you on the cross impact your ability to forgive others?*

## ISAIAH 54

Isaiah continues his themes of restoration and redemption, using the imagery of Israel as the restored wife of the Lord. God promises to extend His covenant love and faithfulness to His people despite past afflictions and exile. God reassures Israel of His enduring commitment and protection. Isaiah encourages Israel to rejoice in anticipation of God's restoration.

*How have you experienced God's everlasting kindness?*

## ISAIAH 55

Isaiah invites all who thirst for spiritual fulfillment to come to God and freely receive His abundant grace, which is available to all who seek Him. He contrasts humanity's futile pursuits with God's eternal promises, urging people to forsake their wickedness and turn to God. He alone offers true satisfaction and joy.

*In what ways do people attempt to satisfy spiritual hunger and thirst apart from Jesus?*

## ISAIAH 56

Isaiah encourages Israel to obey God. He condemns corrupt leaders who lead people astray, and He expresses God's desire for people to uphold His covenant and seek His righteousness. He highlights the importance of genuine worship and obedience to God's commands, affirming that all who seek Him will find joy in His presence.

*How do you prioritize rest, renewal, worship, and fellowship in your weekly rhythm?*

## Take Your Time and Learn More

- Peter quotes from Isaiah 53: 1 PETER 2:22–25
- Galatians alludes to Isaiah 54: GALATIANS 4:27
- Spiritual nourishment and satisfaction: JOHN 6:35
- Blessings for obedience: EPHESIANS 2:19–22

*The greatest truths in scripture are often revealed in the unhurried moments.*

## ISAIAH 57

Isaiah confronts the spiritual adultery of Israel, condemning their empty idolatry and hypocrisy. He exposes their pursuit of false gods and their reliance on worldly alliances instead of God. Yet God offers forgiveness and peace to those who obey.

*How is God gracious even toward the unfaithful?*

## ISAIAH 58

Isaiah challenges the superficiality of religious observance and calls for genuine righteousness and compassion. He critiques fasting that is simply external, saying that it should come from a sincere heart and a commitment to honoring God. He then highlights the blessings that come from obeying God.

*What are some symptoms of false worship?*

## ISAIAH 59

Isaiah discusses the tragic nature of sin and how it creates separation from God. He portrays a society filled with violence, deceit, and corruption, where justice is perverted and righteousness is absent. Nevertheless, "the LORD's hand is not shortened, that it cannot save" (59:1). God is always able to intervene on behalf of His people.

*How does the promise of a Redeemer offer hope in the face of sin and separation from God?*

## ISAIAH 60

Isaiah prophesies the future glory of Zion and the restoration of Israel. He describes a time when God's light will shine brightly upon His people, drawing nations to their splendor. He foretells of prosperity, abundance, and peace. Isaiah envisions the gathering of God's scattered people and the recognition of Israel as a holy nation.

*How can you help other people see God's glory?*

## Take Your Time and Learn More

- God's opposition to the proud: JAMES 4:6–10
- Instructions for righteous living: MATTHEW 25:34–40
- Powers of darkness: EPHESIANS 6:12
- Glorious Zion: REVELATION 21:23–24

*Bible study is truly a lifelong journey.*
*Relax and enjoy the trip.*

## ISAIAH 61

Isaiah presents a glorious vision of restoration and redemption. He portrays the mission of the anointed Servant, who brings good news to the oppressed, binds up the brokenhearted, and proclaims freedom to captives. God will transform mourning into joy and ashes into beauty, fulfilling every good promise through the Messiah.

*How is God the source of every good thing?*

## ISAIAH 62

Isaiah speaks of God's unwavering commitment to His people. . .and His determination to establish Jerusalem as a praise on the earth. He emphasizes the restoration and vindication of Israel, promising a new identity and a name that will reflect God's delight in His children. He urges the people to proclaim the greatness of God's salvation and prepare for His coming.

*How can you live today in light of the future glory promised by God?*

## ISAIAH 63

Isaiah prophesies the Lord's return, picturing Him as a warrior marching from Edom with blood-stained garments. He reflects on God's enduring faithfulness to His people—recalling how He compassionately led them through the wilderness and bore their sorrows. Israel has rebelled and deserves God's discipline, but Isaiah pleads for mercy and restoration.

*Can you recall a time when you experienced God's compassion in an unmistakable way?*

## ISAIAH 64

Isaiah offers a heartfelt plea for God's intervention and restoration. He begins with a cry for God to rend the heavens and come down to His people. They have sinned, but Isaiah appeals to God's compassion and His covenant faithfulness. He longs for God to act on behalf of His people, displaying His power and glory among the nations.

*In what area of your life do you long for God's intervention?*

## Take Your Time and Learn More

- Jesus reads from Isaiah 61: LUKE 4:16–21
- The future glory of Zion: REVELATION 21:2–3
- Jesus' once-for-all-sacrifice that leads to victory: HEBREWS 9:12
- Paul quotes from Isaiah 64: 1 CORINTHIANS 2:9

*Try to forget the demands of life for a while.*
*You're spending quality time with God.*

## ISAIAH 65

This chapter depicts God's judgment on those who persist in idolatry and disobedience, but it also promises blessings to God's faithful servants. Isaiah portrays the new heavens and new earth, where God's people will dwell with Him in peace and prosperity. He emphasizes the fulfillment of God's promises for those who repent.

*How can you pursue deeper dependence on God's provision for your daily life?*

## ISAIAH 66

Isaiah concludes the book with a vision of God's ultimate triumph and judgment. He emphasizes God's desire for true worship from a humble heart. The Lord will not condone hypocrisy, but He promises restoration for the humble and repentant. The book ends with a vision of the new heavens and new earth, where God's people will experience everlasting joy in God's presence.

*What is the source of your hope? Why?*

## Take Your Time and Learn More

- God's promises fulfilled: REVELATION 21:1–5
- God's kingdom will be established: MATTHEW 5:34–35

# JEREMIAH

*God's justice cannot allow evil to go unpunished forever.*

## SETTING THE STAGE

The book of Jeremiah is the second prophetic book. It records a comprehensive record of Jeremiah's ministry as well as the many messages he conveyed to the people of Judah during a tumultuous period in their history.

The book centers on the theme of Judah's impending judgment due to the people's persistent rebellion against God. Jeremiah foretells the Babylonian invasion, the destruction of Jerusalem, and the exile of the people to Babylon as a consequence for their unrepentant sin.

Because of the deeply personal nature of Jeremiah's writing, he is the best-known writing prophet in the Bible.

Often referred to as "the weeping prophet," he is wholly committed to God and to holiness, and he wants the people of Judah to follow this example. Even when his own people persecute him for telling the truth about their impending captivity (19:14–20:18; 37–38), Jeremiah still has compassion on them.

After the fall of Jerusalem, Nebuchadnezzar gives Jeremiah the choice of either going to Babylon or staying with the remnant of his own people. He chooses to stay and minister to his people. While there, he continues to plead with the people to turn back to God.

## GOOD TO KNOW

Author is Jeremiah (1:1), with the assistance of Baruch, a scribe (36:4). Jeremiah wrote approximately 585 BC.

*Good things come to those who wait—on the Lord, that is.*

## JEREMIAH 1

God calls Jeremiah to be a prophet—meaning he has the rare dual title of prophet and priest. His job: "to root out and to pull down, to destroy and to throw down, to build and to plant" (1:10). He is supposed to warn Israel—specifically Judah—about judgment for their persistent idolatry. . .but also to provide them future hope.

*Why are biblical warnings and hope not contradictory?*

## JEREMIAH 2

God gives Jeremiah His first message for apostate Judah. This chapter reads like a lament from God over Judah's rampant unfaithfulness. They've broken their covenant with God and worshipped many Canaanite gods. Jeremiah will compare their idolatry to adultery, prostitution, and promiscuity. Despite God's faithful care, Judah has forsaken their vow.

*How does God's persistent call to repentance prove His unfailing love and care for His people?*

## JEREMIAH 3

God's heart is broken over Judah's unfaithfulness. Despite their ongoing spiritual infidelity, God calls them to return and offers forgiveness and restoration. God's longing for reconciliation is palpable in these pages. Yet in a second message given to Jeremiah for the people, God condemns any superficial apologies and urges only sincere repentance.

*Is an insincere apology worse than no apology at all? Why or why not?*

## JEREMIAH 4

Jeremiah predicts impending judgment upon Judah for their rebellion against God. In no uncertain terms, he warns of impending devastation unless they repent. He describes in great detail the desolation that will result from the invasion, urging people to repent and lament their sin. Even still, God mercifully offers a way to avoid judgment.

*How does considering idolatry as adultery shed light on God's view of unfaithfulness to Him?*

## Take Your Time and Learn More

- Call and commission: ACTS 9:15–16
- Steadfast love and mercy to God's people: HOSEA 2:19–20
- A call to return: HOSEA 14
- Judgment predicted: MATTHEW 24:4–14

*The Bible is countercultural, and so is Bible study.*
*There's no need to rush through this.*

## JEREMIAH 5

Jeremiah gives God's reasons for impending judgment. By turning their backs on God, Judah has tragically abandoned God's commands. Widespread dishonesty, lack of integrity, and ongoing neglect for the needs of the poor and vulnerable run rampant. Jeremiah calls out Judah's corrupt leaders for their role in the wickedness.

*What do you think is a believer's greatest way*
*to resist the pull of moral corruption?*

## JEREMIAH 6

Jeremiah describes a desperate scene in which Jerusalem is overrun by invaders. Despite God's warnings and pleas for repentance, Judah remains stubbornly hardened by sin. So the consequences will be severe. Still, God faithfully calls His people to return to Him—it's the only way they can find rest for their souls (6:16).

*How does verse 16 contradict the idea that*
*following God leads to a difficult, joyless life?*

## JEREMIAH 7

Jeremiah delivers his temple sermon, confronting Judah's blatant hypocrisy. Despite their ongoing, unrepentant sin, they are still coming to God's temple as if nothing is wrong. Meanwhile, after temple worship concludes, they return to pagan pleasures and participate in all manner of sin—including the horrific Canaanite practice of child sacrifice (7:31).

*Do you think insincere worship appears in the church today? If so, in what ways?*

## JEREMIAH 8

A terrible shift takes place—God stops offering repentance. Judgment for Judah is now certain, so instead of issuing warnings, Jeremiah describes the dire consequences: "Death shall be chosen rather than life" (8:3). The way forward is now exile. Jeremiah's words in this chapter serve as a sobering reminder of the consequences that accompany insensitivity to sin.

*Why is it so easy to become desensitized to sin?*

*Take Your Time and Learn More*

- Reasons for judgment: ROMANS 1:18–32
- Warning about destruction: MATTHEW 24:15–22
- Cleansing the temple: MATTHEW 21:12–13
- Insensitivity toward sin: HOSEA 4:1–3

*God speaks in the quiet moments.*
*Approach His Word with calm expectation.*

## JEREMIAH 9

Jeremiah grieves for his people, mourns the spiritual decay of Judah, and laments their refusal to know and obey God. Despite outward displays of zeal, their hearts are hardened. God refers to this hypocrisy as being "uncircumcised in the heart" (9:26).

*In addition to obeying God's commands, how can you cultivate sensitivity to the Holy Spirit's work in your heart?*

## JEREMIAH 10

Jeremiah describes the absurdity of idolatry. He alternates between mocking idols (and their makers) and praising the sovereignty of the one true God. He speaks of how worthless it is to trust idols instead of God, who alone is trustworthy. He then tells God, "Pour out Your fury on the nations who do not know You" (10:25).

*How can you actively guard your heart from loving anything more than God?*

## JEREMIAH 11

Jeremiah delivers a message to the people about their broken covenant. Their pending suffering is not simply punishment; rather, God is keeping His end of His covenant agreement to give blessings for obedience and curses for disobedience (Leviticus 26). During this time, God tells Jeremiah there is a conspiracy to kill him in order to silence his message.

*God's love necessitates His wrath—He cannot have one without the other. Do you agree or disagree?*

## JEREMIAH 12

Likely upset about the conspiracy against him, Jeremiah struggles with the apparent prosperity of the wicked and the suffering of the righteous (12:1-4). God responds by challenging Jeremiah to consider how much worse His people have treated Him (12:7-13). It is important to trust God's wisdom and timing, even when life seems unfair.

*Have you ever had to give up your desire for instant justice in the face of unfair circumstances?*

### Take Your Time and Learn More

- Paul quotes from Jeremiah 9: 1 CORINTHIANS 1:31
- The truth about idolatry: PSALM 115:4–8
- A broken covenant: GALATIANS 3:10–14
- Sign of God's love: HEBREWS 12:5–11

*Before you read, pray. Ask God to*
*speak His truth to your spirit.*

## JEREMIAH 13

God offers two acted-out signs involving a linen loincloth and jars of wine. The loincloth illustrates God's disappointment with Judah. Instead of clinging to Him, they've buried themselves in idolatry. The jars illustrate Judah, and the wine is the wrath of God. He will "smash them against one another" (13:14).

*Jeremiah says he will weep secretly for Judah's pride*
*(13:17). In what ways does pride blind us?*

## JEREMIAH 14

Jeremiah depicts a devastating drought afflicting Judah, resulting in a plea for mercy from the prophet and the people. Despite their fasting and prayers, God rebukes their insincere repentance: their idolatry persists. Jeremiah intercedes on behalf of the people, but God tells him to stop. The prophet laments the ruin of his people.

*Who is most harmed by the worship of idols?*

## JEREMIAH 15

God tells Jeremiah judgment is imminent due to Judah's persistent rebellion and idolatry. Jeremiah expresses his despair and loneliness, feeling like a man of strife and contention. Despite his anguish, God reassures Jeremiah of His protection and promises to deliver the prophet from his enemies.

*How willing are you to speak truth in love to people,*
*even when it's uncomfortable or isolating?*

## JEREMIAH 16

Jeremiah foretells Judah's desolation as a consequence of their idolatry and rebellion. God instructs Jeremiah not to marry or partake in mourning rituals. This chapter gives the consequences of forsaking God—including famine, sword, and exile. Despite Israel's disobedience, God promises to restore His people after judgment, drawing them back to Himself.

*The Israelites keep returning to idolatry. What does this teach you about human nature?*

## Take Your Time and Learn More

- Spiritual blindness: EPHESIANS 4:17–19
- Devastating disasters: JOEL 1:13–20
- The steadfast love of God: ROMANS 8:35–39
- Restoration of Israel: ZECHARIAH 10:6–12

*Don't hurry, don't worry. God's Word provides everything you need for living well.*

## JEREMIAH 17

Jeremiah discusses the deceitful heart, warning against trusting in human strength or turning away from God's commandments. He likens these poor decisions to a parched desert. Those who trust in the Lord, however, are like flourishing trees planted by water. Ultimately, God searches the heart and rewards each person accordingly.

*Why do we make a grave mistake when we assume our hearts are good and trustworthy?*

## JEREMIAH 18

God instructs Jeremiah to go to a potter's house and observe the potter at work. To illustrate His sovereignty over nations, God says He will be as a potter to Israel, tearing it down and shaping it up. This chapter highlights God's willingness to shape His people according to their response to His Word.

*How do you typically respond when God's plans differ from yours?*

## JEREMIAH 19

God instructs Jeremiah to buy a clay jar from the potter and then take some of the elders and priests to the Valley of the Son of Hinnom. There Jeremiah proclaims God's condemnation of the people's idolatry and disobedience. Jeremiah then smashes the clay jar, illustrating God's impending judgment upon Jerusalem. The leaders still refuse to listen, intensifying God's anger.

*In what specific ways can you prioritize God above everything and everyone else?*

## JEREMIAH 20

Jeremiah faces persecution for delivering God's message. Pashhur the priest imprisons and beats him for prophesying against Jerusalem. Jeremiah laments, wishing he were never born. However, despite his anguish, he cannot hold back God's Word—it feels like a burning fire within him. He expresses his distress but acknowledges God's faithfulness.

*How honest are your prayers to God?*

## Take Your Time and Learn More

- Blessings of the righteous: PSALM 1:1–3
- Image of the potter: ROMANS 9:20–21
- Judgment in the Valley of the Son of Hinnom: 2 KINGS 23:10
- Strength in weakness: 2 CORINTHIANS 12:9–10

*God loves it when you read and study His Word.*

## JEREMIAH 21

King Zedekiah begs Jeremiah to plead with God regarding the Babylonian siege of Jerusalem. However, God responds through Jeremiah that Jerusalem's fate is sealed, and He will fight against the city due to its wickedness. Those who stay in Jerusalem will die—either by the sword, famine, or plague. Those who surrender will live.

*How would you define "submission," and why is it so challenging?*

## JEREMIAH 22

God sends Jeremiah to the king's palace to proclaim judgment. So Jeremiah admonishes the officials for their failures in leadership. He calls them to righteousness and to advocate for justice, mercy, and integrity. He warns of impending judgment—stressing the importance of righteous leadership and the dire consequences of unfaithfulness to God's commands.

*Why is obedience to God the best protection against corruption?*

## JEREMIAH 23

Through Jeremiah, God condemns the corrupt shepherds of Israel (both spiritual and political leaders) who have led His people astray. He promises to gather and restore His scattered flock, raising up righteous shepherds—notably the Messiah—who will reign with justice and righteousness. False prophets are condemned for their deceitful messages.

*How do you identify false or deceptive voices in the Christian community?*

## JEREMIAH 24

After Nebuchadnezzar carries off Judah's leaders into exile, God shows Jeremiah two baskets of figs: one contains good figs (representing the exiles God will restore), and the other contains bad figs (symbolizing those who remain in Judah and face destruction). God distinguishes between the faithful and the wicked, promising to restore the repentant and judge the unrepentant.

*What does it mean to have a heart to know God?*

## Take Your Time and Learn More

- True obedience: MATTHEW 7:21–23
- Judgment, warning, and the call to repentance: MATTHEW 23:37–39
- Good versus false shepherds: JOHN 10:11–18
- Restoration and renewal: 2 CORINTHIANS 5:17–21

*Reading the Bible isn't a race. Let the pages unfold
at a pace that allows your spirit to breathe.*

## JEREMIAH 25

Jeremiah has been prophesying for more than twenty years, but nobody is listening. So God promises to use Babylon to completely destroy Judah and the surrounding nations. A seventy-year period of desolation is decreed for Judah. Despite God's patience and repeated calls for repentance, the nation remains obstinate. Severe consequences will follow.

*Do you believe God is still in charge of nations today? Why or why not?*

## JEREMIAH 26

God tells Jeremiah to preach in the temple, delivering a message of impending destruction unless the people repent—echoing similar warnings from earlier prophets. However, instead of repenting, the priests, prophets, and people accuse Jeremiah of blasphemy and seek to have him killed. Eventually the elders intervene, sparing Jeremiah's life.

*Why does it always lead to disaster when a person or nation forgets God?*

## JEREMIAH 27

During the reign of King Zedekiah, God tells Jeremiah to make and wear a yoke—symbolizing submission to Babylon. Babylon's dominance will be God's instrument of judgment. This chapter illustrates God's sovereignty over nations and His use of foreign powers for His purposes. Ultimately, obedience to God is the pathway to preservation.

*Why does it require courage to follow God's will and way?*

## JEREMIAH 28

The false prophet Hananiah contradicts Jeremiah's prophecy of Babylonian captivity. He claims the Lord will break Babylon's yoke within two years and return the exiled articles to Jerusalem. So Jeremiah challenges Hananiah, warning of false hope and death for prophets who speak lies. Within a year, Hananiah dies.

*Where do you typically turn for hope in difficult situations?*

### *Take Your Time and Learn More*

- Seventy-year captivity: DANIEL 9:2
- Rejection and persecution: MATTHEW 21:35–46
- Obedience to government: ROMANS 13:1–5
- Truth for false prophets: 1 KINGS 22:11–28

*The greatest truths in scripture are often*
*revealed in the unhurried moments.*

## JEREMIAH 29

After the first exile, Jeremiah writes a letter instructing the exiles to settle in captivity, build homes, and seek the welfare of their new city. Despite the current circumstances, God promises a future filled with hope and restoration after seventy years. Jeremiah reassures them of God's plans to prosper and not harm them, provided they seek Him wholeheartedly.

*How can times of suffering also become times of blessing?*

## JEREMIAH 30

Jeremiah prophesies hope and restoration for Israel and Judah after their captivity. God promises to bring His people back from exile, heal their wounds, and rebuild their nation. He declares a new covenant with them, offering forgiveness and reconciliation. This chapter describes the intense anguish of the exile but assures a time of redemption and joy.

*What role does repentance play in the process of healing and restoration?*

## JEREMIAH 31

God promises through Jeremiah to bring back the exiles from captivity and rebuild Israel and Judah. He pledges to be their God and to write His law on their hearts, ushering in a new era of intimacy and obedience. Israel will return to being the great nation it was. God loves His people and will bless them abundantly.

*How does God's faithfulness to His people encourage you and give you hope?*

## JEREMIAH 32

Perceiving Jeremiah as disloyal due to his outspoken and unwelcome messages, the king imprisons him. While in prison, God tells Jeremiah that his cousin will come and sell him a piece of land, which he does. This sign signals God's assurance of future restoration despite the current desolation. Jeremiah offers a prayer of praise and gratitude.

*How consistent are you with praising God when you*
*don't fully understand what He's doing?*

## Take Your Time and Learn More

- God knows His plans are good: ROMANS 8:28
- Future healing: REVELATION 21:3–4
- Hebrews quotes from Jeremiah 31: HEBREWS 8:8–12
- God's gracious response: EPHESIANS 3:20–21

*Bible study is truly a lifelong journey.*
*Relax and enjoy the trip.*

## JEREMIAH 33

God speaks again to Jeremiah in prison. He promises to heal and restore His people—bringing back prosperity, joy, and honor. He speaks of a future time when the land will flourish, with Jerusalem rebuilt and renamed "The LORD our righteousness" (33:16). God reiterates His promise to raise up a righteous branch from David's line who will sit on the throne forever.

*Why is God's assurance of forgiveness such a gift?*

## JEREMIAH 34

Jeremiah condemns the hypocrisy of Judah's leaders who made a covenant to release their Hebrew slaves but later violated it by re-enslaving them. God rebukes them for their disobedience and warns of dire consequences, including destruction by the Babylonians.

*How faithful are you to pray about decisions—big and small—before making them?*

## JEREMIAH 35

God tells Jeremiah to invite the Rechabites into one of the chambers of the house of the Lord and offer them wine. They refuse, however, telling him they promised never to drink wine or plant vineyards. God commends their faithful obedience, contrasting it with Judah's disobedience. God promises blessings for the Rechabites' steadfastness.

*Can you think of a time when you chose between peer pressure and personal conviction? What happened?*

## JEREMIAH 36

Jeremiah dictates God's words to Baruch to write on a scroll and read in the temple. Baruch reads the scroll to the people—including the officials—who react with fear and seek the king's counsel. The scroll is brought before King Jehoiakim, who burns it in defiance. God commands Jeremiah to rewrite the scroll, adding more prophecies of judgment.

*How do you make scripture a central part of your life and daily routine?*

## Take Your Time and Learn More

- An everlasting covenant: HEBREWS 7:22–25
- Captivity and release: 2 CHRONICLES 36:12–21
- Call to remain faithful: LUKE 18:8
- Importance of God's Word: 2 KINGS 22:8–20

*Try to forget the demands of life for a while.*
*You're spending quality time with God.*

## JEREMIAH 37

King Zedekiah seeks Jeremiah's counsel during the Babylonian siege of Jerusalem. Jeremiah prophesies that Babylon will capture the city, so he advises surrender to save lives. However, the officials accuse Jeremiah of desertion and imprison him again. King Zedekiah secretly consults Jeremiah again, but the prophet's warnings go unheeded. Jeremiah remains faithful.

*Why is it tempting to conform to the views of other people rather than follow God's guidance?*

## JEREMIAH 38

Officials accuse Jeremiah of discouraging the soldiers and advocating surrender. They persuade King Zedekiah to throw Jeremiah into a cistern, but Ebed-melech appeals to the king for Jeremiah's rescue. Zedekiah grants permission, and Jeremiah is lifted from the pit. Zedekiah privately consults Jeremiah, who says that those who surrender to the Babylonians will live.

*Does withholding truth to spare someone's feelings ultimately benefit or harm that person?*

## JEREMIAH 39

Babylonian forces breach Jerusalem's walls, causing King Zedekiah to flee. Babylon's king executes Zedekiah's sons, blinds him, and carries him into captivity. Jeremiah, spared by Nebuchadnezzar, is given the choice to stay or go to Babylon. He chooses to stay in Judah under the protection of a Babylonian governor. His prophecy of Jerusalem's fall is fulfilled.

*Are you consistently steadfast in your faith, or does it depend on your circumstances?*

## JEREMIAH 40

Babylonian commander Nebuzaradan releases Jeremiah from bondage, giving him the choice to live wherever he chooses. Jeremiah returns to Jerusalem where a governor, Gedaliah—appointed by the king of Babylon—is ruling and establishing peace in the region. However, rumors start to circulate that someone wants to assassinate Gedaliah.

*Today, how do you discern between fearmongering and legitimate warnings?*

## Take Your Time and Learn More

- Zedekiah captured: 2 KINGS 25:1–7
- Peter imprisoned and released: ACTS 12:1–17
- Prophecies fulfilled: 2 KINGS 25:8–21
- Gedaliah: 2 KINGS 25:22–26

*Good things come to those who wait—on the Lord, that is.*

## JEREMIAH 41

A man named Ishmael, along with ten men, murders Gedaliah and others at a feast. Ishmael then captures women, children, and officials—intending to flee to Ammon. Johanan rescues the captives, freeing them from Ishmael's clutches. Then he pursues Ishmael, but Ishmael escapes to Ammon. Johanan leads the rescued captives to safety.

*How much does fear influence your decisions?*

## JEREMIAH 42

Fearing Babylon's revenge, Johanan and other leaders go to Jeremiah for his guidance and prayer. They promise to obey God's instruction, whatever it may be. Jeremiah prays for ten days and then delivers God's response: Stay in Judah and God will offer His protection. Flee to Egypt and face disaster.

*Are there ever positive consequences for unbelief? Why or why not?*

## JEREMIAH 43

Johanan and the people refuse to heed Jeremiah's advice, accusing him of lying. They disobey God's command and journey to Egypt. God tells Jeremiah to take stones to the entrance of Pharaoh's palace and prophesy Egypt's downfall. This chapter highlights the futility of seeking safety outside of God's plan.

*How do you respond when you receive an answer from God that you didn't want?*

## JEREMIAH 44

Jeremiah confronts the Judeans living in Egypt, rebuking them for persisting in idolatry. The people ignore Jeremiah, insisting on continuing their worship of the "queen of heaven." Jeremiah warns of impending judgment, with Egypt facing desolation similar to Judah's. Still, the people remain obstinate, revealing their hardened hearts.

*What are some practical ways to combat blindness to our own sin?*

## *Take Your Time and Learn More*

- The aftermath of Gedaliah's murder: 2 KINGS 25:25–26
  - The remnant of Judah: 2 KINGS 25:22–26
    - Desire for Egypt: EXODUS 14:10–14
  - Consequences of idolatry: DEUTERONOMY 28:15–20

*The Bible is countercultural, and so is Bible study.*
*There's no need to rush through this.*

## JEREMIAH 45

Jeremiah's scribe, Baruch, writes down Jeremiah's words and is deeply distressed by the impending calamity upon Judah. God acknowledges Baruch's faithfulness and promises to preserve his life amid the chaos. However, God warns Baruch not to seek greatness for himself. Baruch is encouraged to seek safety in the midst of impending disaster.

*How would you encourage someone to maintain her faith in an overwhelming season?*

## JEREMIAH 46

Jeremiah issues a clear message to Egypt, foretelling its defeat by Babylon. He depicts Egypt's impending downfall, despite its military might, at the hands of King Nebuchadnezzar as punishment for its arrogance and idolatry. Jeremiah warns of devastation and captivity for Egypt's inhabitants, urging them to prepare for the inevitable judgment.

*Why do people often rely on human strength instead of God for support and guidance?*

## JEREMIAH 47

Jeremiah prophesies against the Philistines, foretelling their destruction by the Babylonians. He vividly describes the Philistines' distress as invaders approach, likening their anguish to the waters rising from the north. God promises to bring disaster upon them, leaving their cities in ruins and their inhabitants in mourning. No idols will save them from God's judgment.

*Why do people turn to idols for help when idols do not save?*

## JEREMIAH 48

Jeremiah prophesies the complete destruction of Moab by the Babylonians. Jeremiah laments this devastation, detailing the loss of Moab's cities and the anguish of its people. Moab's pride and arrogance have brought about its downfall, and the pagan gods prove powerless to help. Jeremiah mourns the destruction and calls for its inhabitants to flee and seek refuge elsewhere.

*Why is God willing to restore His people when they repent?*

## Take Your Time and Learn More

- Warning against pride: PHILIPPIANS 2:3–4
- Prophecy against Egypt: EZEKIEL 29:1–16
- Prophecy against the Philistines: AMOS 1:6–8
- Prophecy against Moab: ZEPHANIAH 2:8–11

*God speaks in the quiet moments.*
*Approach His Word with calm expectation.*

## JEREMIAH 49

Jeremiah prophesies against various nations surrounding Judah. He issues strong warnings to Ammon, Edom, and Damascus, foretelling their downfall due to their pride and violence. He prophesies against Kedar and Hazor, predicting their defeat by the Babylonians. All of these nations—and others—will be severely devastated for their ongoing sin against God.

*Is pride the common denominator of every sin? Why or why not?*

## JEREMIAH 50

Jeremiah prophesies the downfall of Babylon due to her pride and oppression of His people. This chapter describes Babylon's devastation and the restoration of Israel. God promises to deliver His people from captivity, restoring them to their homeland and proving God's faithfulness to His covenant with Israel.

*Is anyone outside the reaches of God's mercy? Why or why not?*

## JEREMIAH 51

God pronounces judgment on Babylon, calling for nations to gather and execute His judgment. In describing Babylon's destruction, Jeremiah likens it to the devastation of Sodom and Gomorrah. Babylon's proud rulers and false gods cannot save it from God's wrath. Jeremiah urges the people of God to flee from Babylon's impending doom.

*What does God's justice in Babylon reveal about Him?*

## JEREMIAH 52

This final chapter of Jeremiah gives a second account of the overthrow of Judah. Gedaliah is assassinated and the Judeans are exiled to Babylon, leaving only the poor to tend the land. The chapter concludes with King Jehoiachin's release from prison and his elevation in Babylon.

*Why do you think God included such specific sins,*
*prophecies, and consequences in the Bible?*

## Take Your Time and Learn More

- Prophecy against Edom: OBADIAH
- Babylon's final doom: REVELATION 18
- Babylon judged: ISAIAH 13
- The destruction of Jerusalem: 2 KINGS 24:18–25:30

# LAMENTATIONS

*God welcomes the brutally honest cries of His
people in response to sin and pain.*

## SETTING THE STAGE

The book of Lamentations, written by Jeremiah about the desolation of Jerusalem, opens with these haunting words: "How the city that was full of people sits solitary! How she has become like a widow! She who was great among the nations, and princess among the provinces—how she has become a forced laborer!" (1:1).

The title Lamentations (the root word being *lament*) is fitting since the book contains five mournful poems that reflect on the destruction of Jerusalem, the desolation of the temple, and the suffering of the people during the Babylonian exile.

Similar in structure to Psalm 119, the first four chapters of Lamentations are written as an alphabetic acrostic, with each of the verses working through the letters of the Hebrew alphabet.

More than simply good literature, the deep significance of the book lies in Jeremiah's great burden to see God's people made right with Him.

Suffering often leads to questions, and the book of Lamentations is filled with many difficult questions and statements directed to God. It reflects a desperate search for understanding in the midst of overwhelming grief.

Lamentations illustrates the important role of lament in the life of God's people. The book is a poignant expression of sorrow, repentance, and restoration.

## GOOD TO KNOW

Author not stated, but the book is traditionally attributed to Jeremiah. Probably written around 586 BC, shortly after Jerusalem fell to the Babylonians.

*Before you read, pray.*
*Ask God to speak His truth to your spirit.*

## LAMENTATIONS 1

Jeremiah mourns Jerusalem following its destruction by Babylon. The once-bustling city now sits in ruins, its people suffering greatly. The chapter personifies Jerusalem as a grieving widow, mourning her desolation and abandonment. She weeps bitterly, with no one to comfort her. Her enemies triumph as she faces God's wrath due to her sins.

*What does Jerusalem's destruction tell you about the*
*consequences of turning away from God?*

## LAMENTATIONS 2

Jeremiah continues lamenting Jerusalem's devastation, portraying the city's downfall as God's judgment for its sins. Jeremiah vividly depicts the severity of the destruction: the temple is desecrated, the walls are broken down, and the people are starved and despairing. In this chapter, "the Lord [is] like an enemy" (2:5), showing no mercy.

*Do you find it hard to reconcile the image of*
*God as judge with the idea of God as Father?*

## LAMENTATIONS 3

Jeremiah moves from deep despair to hope. . .and then from hope to confidence in God's faithfulness. He describes Israel's anguish, feeling trapped and abandoned by God. Yet in the midst of the suffering, he recalls God's steadfast love and mercy. He knows God's discipline is for Israel's good.

*Why do you think Jeremiah chooses to remember*
*God's mercies in the midst of his pain?*

## Take Your Time and Learn More

- The desolation of Jerusalem: PSALM 137:1–6
- Day of the Lord's anger: JEREMIAH 7:31–34
- Personal anguish: PSALM 88

*Don't hurry, don't worry. God's Word provides everything you need for living well.*

## LAMENTATIONS 4

Jeremiah paints a devastating picture of Jerusalem's fall. He shows the once-proud city reduced to desperate conditions. He laments the loss of Jerusalem's honor and dignity, contrasting it with past glory. He highlights the dire consequences of rebellion against God—judgment and exile.

*Why is sin so costly?*

## LAMENTATIONS 5

God's people appeal to Him for mercy and restoration. They confess their sins and acknowledge their consequences. They feel abandoned and forsaken by God, yet even in despair, they cling to God's enduring faithfulness. Lamentations closes with the people praying for God to restore them and bring them back into His favor. They now recognize His power to save.

*Do you find it harder or easier to cling to God in seasons of suffering?*

## Take Your Time and Learn More

- Horrors of the siege: EZEKIEL 5:14–15
- An appeal to God for mercy: PSALM 79

# EZEKIEL

*God's purpose and plan for His people always
surpasses any human limitations.*

## SETTING THE STAGE

The book of Ezekiel was written by a priest.

Ezekiel was living in Jerusalem during the first Babylonian attack, and he was among the first wave of Israelites carried away to Babylon. His book begins five years later. Within is a detailed account of Ezekiel's visions and messages addressed to his exiled community. The writing is filled with symbol and visions.

Unlike previous prophets, Ezekiel's ministry is neither to Judah nor to the ten-tribe kingdom; it is to the entire house of Israel. His job is to keep reminding the people—and specifically children born in exile—why the nation of Israel was brought so low: God abandoned His own temple because of Israel's idolatry and injustice.

At this point, the Babylonian exile is the worst event in Israel's history. In fact, the exile becomes so bleak that it looks like God has eternally removed His hand of blessing from the Israelites.

Thankfully, Ezekiel has two God-given responsibilities in addition to reminding Israel of their sin: to nurture the faith of the people. . .and to eventually give hope.

Even in Israel's bleakest moments, God is making a way for restoration.

## GOOD TO KNOW

Author is Ezekiel, a priest (1:1–3). He wrote around the 590s–570s BC.

## *God loves it when you read and study His Word.*

### EZEKIEL 1

Ezekiel has a vision of a majestic stormy sky and of four living creatures each with four faces and wings. Beside each creature are wheels full of eyes. The vision overwhelms Ezekiel with awe and dread. The scene depicts God's transcendence and authority, preparing Ezekiel for his mission to warn Israel of impending judgment.

*How do you reconcile Ezekiel's terrifying vision with the comforting image of God as your Father?*

### EZEKIEL 2

God commissions Ezekiel to go to the rebellious house of Israel. He warns Ezekiel that the Israelites are stubborn, and though they may resist, he must faithfully proclaim God's message to them. God promises to strengthen Ezekiel and make him bold in delivering His Word. He then presents Ezekiel with a scroll containing lamentations, mourning, and woe.

*Why do you think God sends Ezekiel, even though He knows the people won't listen?*

### EZEKIEL 3

Ezekiel eats the scroll, which tastes sweet. God strengthens Ezekiel, making him bold and fearless. Ezekiel is then carried away by the Spirit to the exiles. He spends seven days among them in mourning, silent and devastated. Then Ezekiel is prompted to repeat what God has told him. . .or be held accountable.

*What might you say to someone who's struggling to prioritize time spent in God's Word?*

### EZEKIEL 4

God tells Ezekiel to do several different things to symbolize Israel's sin. He draws Jerusalem on a brick, for example. He lays on his left side for 390 days—the number of years Israel sinned. He eats limited rations and bakes bread over cow's dung.

*Why do you think God is taking this time to communicate so thoroughly with His people?*

## *Take Your Time and Learn More*

- A vision of the glory of God: REVELATION 4
- Another prophet's commissioning: JEREMIAH 1:7–10
- Another scroll eaten: REVELATION 10
- More prophetic symbolism: HOSEA 1:2

*Reading the Bible isn't a race. Let the pages unfold
at a pace that allows your spirit to breathe.*

## EZEKIEL 5

God commands Ezekiel to shave his head and beard as a picture of the city's humiliation. A portion of the hair is burned, symbolizing the severity of God's judgment through famine, pestilence, and dispersion. Ezekiel is told to scatter the remaining hair, illustrating the scattering of the people among the nations. Jerusalem will become a desolate byword among the nations.

*What does God's commitment to justice tell you about His character?*

## EZEKIEL 6

God directs Ezekiel to prophesy against the mountains of Israel, symbolizing the high places where idolatry thrives. The Lord declares His judgment upon these places of worship, promising to bring devastation and desolation upon them. The people's idols will be destroyed, their altars demolished, and their religious leaders killed.

*How is it possible that Israel had religious leaders who did not love God?*

## EZEKIEL 7

God declares imminent judgment upon Israel for their widespread sin and idolatry. He describes the devastation that will come upon the land, sparing no one but a remnant from His wrath. Even those who seek refuge in fortified places will find no safety; God's judgment will reach them there too. The people's wickedness has reached its peak.

*Reading about God's wrath can be difficult, but why is it important?*

## EZEKIEL 8

The prophet is transported in a vision to Jerusalem, where he witnesses shocking idolatry inside the temple itself. He sees Israel's leaders engaging in detestable practices, offering incense to idols and worshipping creatures painted on the walls. God reveals to Ezekiel the hidden abominations that are prompting Him to pronounce severe judgment on Israel.

*Why do you think it's important for Ezekiel to witness the abominations firsthand?*

## Take Your Time and Learn More

- Prophecy of curses: DEUTERONOMY 28:49–68
- Idolaters to be punished: LEVITICUS 26:27–46
  - Day of reckoning: ZEPHANIAH 1:14–18
  - Spiritual corruption: 2 KINGS 21:1–18

*The greatest truths in scripture are often revealed in the unhurried moments.*

## EZEKIEL 9

Ezekiel sees six men coming toward the city with deadly weapons in their hands. They are accompanied by a man clothed in linen carrying a writing kit. God commands the man to mark the foreheads of those who grieve over the state of the city, sparing them from destruction. The executioners are then instructed to strike down all those without the mark, showing no mercy.

*How much do you value repentance?*

## EZEKIEL 10

Ezekiel sees a throne, and the glory of the Lord fills the temple. He then sees four cherubim—reminiscent of his earlier vision—accompanied by the sound of their wings. As the cherubim move, the wheels beside them also move in unison. The glory of the Lord departs the temple.

*Why doesn't it seem to matter that the Israelites have been warned many times?*

## EZEKIEL 11

The Spirit takes Ezekiel to the east gate of the temple, where he sees twenty-five leaders engaging in wicked counsel. God reveals their evil plans and promises judgment upon them. Meanwhile, Ezekiel intercedes for the people. God assures him of the eventual restoration of Israel—promising a new heart and spirit for the remnant.

*How was the Babylonian exile a sign of God's protection and not just His punishment?*

## EZEKIEL 12

God instructs Ezekiel to pack his belongings and dig through the wall to escape the city. This action represents the exile of Judah's King Zedekiah, who will flee Jerusalem through breaches in the city walls. Despite the people's disbelief, Ezekiel assures them that the prophecies will be fulfilled soon—God will bring judgment upon Jerusalem.

*How can sin keep you from seeing and hearing from God?*

## Take Your Time and Learn More

- Mark of the faithful: REVELATION 7:1–8
- Cherubim: 1 KINGS 6:23–28
- Significance of good leadership: ACTS 1:15–26
- Importance of heeding God's warnings: MATTHEW 24:36–44

*Bible study is truly a lifelong journey.
Relax and enjoy the trip.*

## EZEKIEL 13

Ezekiel condemns false prophets who speak out of their own imagination, promising peace when there is none. These prophets deceive the people, whitewashing spiritual decay and reinforcing the delusion of safety. God vows to judge them, exposing their deceit and punishing them for misleading His people.

*What should we do when we don't like something we read in scripture?*

## EZEKIEL 14

Ezekiel addresses the elders of Israel who have set up idols in their hearts, leading the people astray. God refuses to answer their inquiries, instead calling them to repent. Four judgments are presented: sword, famine, dangerous beasts, and pestilence. This chapter emphasizes personal responsibility and the need to turn away from wickedness.

*In what ways has God pursued your heart (14:5)?*

## EZEKIEL 15

God compares Jerusalem to a useless vine, emphasizing its lack of value compared to other trees. Just as a vine's wood is unsuitable for crafting, Jerusalem's inhabitants have proven unfruitful in their faithfulness to God. God declares judgment, warning that even if they were cast into the fire, they would be of no more use than the wood of the vine.

*Can you accomplish good apart from God? Why or why not?*

## EZEKIEL 16

God compares Jerusalem to an abandoned newborn girl rescued and nurtured into maturity. Then, trusting her own beauty, she turns to prostitution. Despite God's lavish care and blessings, Jerusalem has ungratefully turned to idolatry and promiscuity, forsaking her covenant. This betrayal will lead to God's judgment.

*Why is all sin spiritual adultery?*

### Take Your Time and Learn More

- False prophets condemned: MATTHEW 7:15–23
  - Idolatry condemned: JEREMIAH 14:11–16
  - Metaphor of the vine: JOHN 15:1–8
- God's grace to unfaithful Israel: HOSEA 2:14–23

*Try to forget the demands of life for a while.*
*You're spending quality time with God.*

## EZEKIEL 17

God shares a parable involving eagles and plants. The first eagle, Babylon, takes the top branches of a cedar and plants it in a fertile field. A second eagle, Egypt, entices the vine with promises of protection, causing it to wither. Through Ezekiel, God interprets this allegory, denouncing Zedekiah's alliance with Egypt against Babylon as treasonous.

*Why are we prone to look elsewhere for what can only come from God?*

## EZEKIEL 18

God says individuals will be judged according to their own righteousness or wickedness—children will not die for the sins of their parents. God illustrates this truth with three scenarios: a righteous father whose son turns wicked, a wicked father whose son turns righteous, and a righteous man who turns wicked. Each person bears the consequences of his own choices.

*Why is personal responsibility a critical component of our relationship with God?*

## EZEKIEL 19

Ezekiel records a lament mourning the downfall of two princes of Judah: Jehoahaz and Johoiachin. A lioness raising her cubs symbolizes the hope that Judah has in its royal line. This chapter serves as a warning to future generations about the consequences of unfaithfulness and the importance of righteous leadership.

*How do you see God's heart for His people despite their disobedience?*

## EZEKIEL 20

A group of elders sits down before Ezekiel to inquire of God. He recounts Israel's history of disobedience and God's patience. He reminds Israel's elders of their ancestors' rebellion and idolatry, which led to their exile. And yet the people continued to disobey. Still, God's purpose was not to destroy them completely but to lead them to repentance.

*Why has God held back the full extent of His wrath?*

## Take Your Time and Learn More

- Rebellion and exile of Judah: 2 KINGS 24:8–20
- Personal accountability: DEUTERONOMY 24:16
- Downfall of kings: 2 KINGS 23:31–37
- God's great mercy to Israel: PSALM 78

*Good things come to those who wait—on the Lord, that is.*

## EZEKIEL 21

Ezekiel portrays Babylon as a sword of judgment wielded by God against His people. Jerusalem is likened to a forest that the sword will pass through, bringing destruction. The Ammonites, who rejoiced at Jerusalem's downfall, will also face this sword. Ezekiel highlights the severity of God's judgment on His rebellious people and their enemies alike.

*How do you ensure that you're remaining faithful to God's commands?*

## EZEKIEL 22

Ezekiel condemns the sins of Jerusalem, portraying it as a city filled with bloodshed, idolatry, and moral corruption. The prophet denounces the city's leaders, priests, and prophets for their injustice and hypocrisy. God declares His judgment upon Jerusalem, promising to purify the city through trials and calamities. Despite this, Ezekiel foretells a future restoration.

*Why is it beneficial to have Israel's sin and consequences recorded so specifically?*

## EZEKIEL 23

Ezekiel presents a story of two sister prostitutes—representing Israel's northern and southern kingdoms, whose capitals are Samaria and Jerusalem. Both sisters are portrayed as unfaithful to God, engaging in idolatry and adultery by forming alliances with foreign nations. Despite God's warnings, they persist in their sinful ways, leading to their eventual destruction.

*Is our sin less offensive to God than the spiritual adultery represented in this chapter? Why or why not?*

## EZEKIEL 24

Ezekiel uses a cooking pot to convey the city's impending destruction. The pot—representing Jerusalem—is filled with meat (the people) and boiling water (God's wrath). This symbolizes the city's corruption and its impending judgment. Ezekiel's wife dies but he is instructed not to mourn publicly, just as Jerusalem will be destroyed without the customary rites of mourning.

*How does Ezekiel demonstrate steadfast commitment to God in the face of personal suffering?*

## Take Your Time and Learn More

- Sword of the Lord: JEREMIAH 12:7–12
- Judah's sins avenged: ISAIAH 3:8–11
- Spiritual adultery: HOSEA 2:1–13
- Judgment of Jerusalem: 2 KINGS 25:1–12

*The Bible is countercultural, and so is Bible study.*
*There's no need to rush through this.*

## EZEKIEL 25

God pronounces judgments against various nations—including Ammon, Moab, Edom, and Philistia—for their past antagonism toward Israel. God promises to bring destruction upon them, leaving their cities desolate and their people scattered. Through these judgments, God asserts His sovereignty and righteousness over all nations.

*How does God's judgment against these nations show*
*His love and protection for His people?*

## EZEKIEL 26

Ezekiel prophesies the destruction of Tyre—a wealthy coastal city known for its commerce—due to its arrogance and mistreatment of Israel. Ezekiel details how many nations will come against Tyre, leading to its complete devastation. The once-great city will be reduced to ruins, its glory turned to dust.

*Is it ever good to celebrate someone else's downfall? Why or why not?*

## EZEKIEL 27

God tells Ezekiel to lament Tyre's fall. He portrays Tyre as a magnificent ship adorned with riches from various lands, symbolizing its prosperity and influence. However, it will be destroyed by the Babylonians. This destruction will have far-reaching impact, causing anguish and sorrow among Tyre's trading partners.

*How can you guard against the dangers of pride and self-sufficiency?*

## EZEKIEL 28

Ezekiel addresses the king of Tyre, a proud and arrogant man who boasts of his wisdom and wealth. Ezekiel rebukes the king for exalting himself to the level of a god, and God declares judgment on him. The chapter contains a veiled reference to the fall of Satan, depicting his initial beauty and subsequent rebellion against God.

*What does it look like to "set your heart as the heart of God" (28:2)?*

### Take Your Time and Learn More

- Prophecies against the nations: Amos 1:6–8
- Prophecy against Tyre: Zechariah 9:3–4
- Lamentation and mourning over Tyre: Isaiah 23
- Downfall and humiliation: Isaiah 14:12–15

*God speaks in the quiet moments.*
*Approach His Word with calm expectation.*

## EZEKIEL 29

God pronounces judgment on Egypt for its arrogance and pride. Egypt's punishment includes being conquered and laid waste by Nebuchadnezzar, king of Babylon, as a means for God to show His power and sovereignty over all nations. God promises to make Egypt desolate for forty years, after which He will restore the land and gather its people back.

*How do you discern when you're relying on your own strength and not God's?*

## EZEKIEL 30

Ezekiel prophesies against Egypt, foretelling its downfall at the hands of Babylon. The day of the Lord's judgment will bring devastation upon Egypt, with its cities laid waste and its idols destroyed. The surrounding nations will witness Egypt's downfall and tremble in fear. The judgment will serve as a warning to all nations of God's sovereignty and justice.

*How is the removal of idols (30:13) a demonstration of God's grace to Egypt?*

## EZEKIEL 31

Ezekiel describes Egypt as a towering cedar in Lebanon, majestic and proud among the nations. Pride, however, led to its downfall, and it will be brought low. Egypt's destruction serves as a warning to other nations not to exalt themselves above God. Even Pharaoh is accountable to God.

*In what area of your life are you tempted to rely on your own strength instead of God's? Why?*

## EZEKIEL 32

God tells Ezekiel to lament Egypt's impending downfall. Ezekiel likens Pharaoh to a monster slain by God; now his corpse lies unburied among the nations. The once mighty nation will be plunged into darkness, symbolizing its demise. Egypt's fall serves as a cautionary tale for other nations, demonstrating the consequences of pride and rebellion against God.

*Do you believe God is still involved in world affairs and conflicts today? Why or why not?*

## Take Your Time and Learn More

- Prophecy against Egypt: ISAIAH 19:1–17
- Predicted destruction and desolation: NAHUM 3:5–19
- A great tree destroyed: DANIEL 4:10–17
- Judgment against Egypt: JEREMIAH 46:1–26

*Before you read, pray. Ask God to*
*speak His truth to your spirit.*

## EZEKIEL 33

God appoints Ezekiel as a watchman for Israel, responsible for warning the people of impending danger. God says that the wicked who turn from their ways will live, but the righteous who turn away from righteousness will face judgment. Ezekiel's role as a watchman highlights the responsibility of spiritual leaders to proclaim God's truth and warn of sin's consequences.

*How do you guard against your spiritual*
*disciplines becoming entertainment (33:32)?*

## EZEKIEL 34

God rebukes the shepherds of Israel for failing to care for the flock. God promises to personally shepherd His flock by seeking out the lost, feeding them, and providing safe pasture. God will judge between the fat and the lean sheep, rescuing them from oppression and establishing a covenant of peace. He will bless them with abundance, making them fruitful and secure.

*How have you personally experienced God as your good shepherd?*

## EZEKIEL 35

God condemns Mount Seir—Edom—for rejoicing over the downfall of Israel. He declares judgment upon them, promising to make their land desolate and devoid of life. Their relentless hatred and violence against Israel will be met with God's retribution. God will unleash His fury upon them, demonstrating His sovereignty over all nations.

*In what area of your life do you need to prioritize*
*God's will over your personal ambition?*

## EZEKIEL 36

Ezekiel shares a message of hope. God promises to gather His people from the nations and bring them back to their land. He will cleanse them from their impurities, give them new hearts and spirits, and put His Spirit within them. The land, once desolate, will become fruitful and prosperous. The nations will recognize God's faithfulness in fulfilling His promises to Israel.

*Why are hope and repentance so often tied together?*

## Take Your Time and Learn More

- Warning to repent: LUKE 13:1–5
- Good shepherds: PSALM 23:1–4
- Prophecy against Edom: OBADIAH 10–16
- Restoration of Israel: JEREMIAH 31:31–34

*Don't hurry, don't worry. God's Word provides
everything you need for living well.*

## EZEKIEL 37

In a vision, Ezekiel sees a valley full of dry bones. . .only to watch as God breathes life into them. This symbolizes Israel's restoration and the renewal of hope for God's people. Two sticks (representing the divided kingdom of Israel) are joined, signifying their reunification under God's rule. God will heal His people's despair and division.

*How do you see God's unchanging love in this book and in your life?*

## EZEKIEL 38

Ezekiel prophesies about Gog—the leader of Magog—who will gather a coalition of nations to invade Israel. Ezekiel warns Gog of his impending judgment for his evil intentions against God's people. Despite Gog's large army, God will intervene and defeat him. This defeat will serve as a testimony to God's faithfulness in protecting His people.

*How can you live as a faithful witness of God's love in the midst of uncertainty?*

## EZEKIEL 39

Ezekiel continues sharing the prophecy against Gog, foretelling his ultimate defeat and the subsequent purification of the land of Israel. God promises to bring judgment upon Gog and his armies, causing them to fall upon the mountains of Israel. Gog's defeat will result in a massive seven-month-long burial process to cleanse the land.

*Why is it significant that Israel burns the weapons from this battle (39:9-10)?*

## EZEKIEL 40

After twenty-five years in exile, Ezekiel receives a vision of a new temple and instructions for its construction. This chapter details Ezekiel's guided tour of the temple complex, providing precise measurements for each area. The vision reflects a return to divine order and worship, symbolizing God's presence among His people once again.

*What do the specific temple measurements tell you about God?*

## Take Your Time and Learn More

- Spiritual resurrection: ROMANS 8:11
- Final battle: REVELATION 20:7–10
- Judgment on the enemies of God: REVELATION 19:17–21
- Detailed plans and measurements: REVELATION 21:10–27

*God loves it when you read and study His Word.*

## EZEKIEL 41

Ezekiel continues his visionary tour of the temple, focusing on the inner sanctuary and its surrounding structures. Detailed descriptions convey the temple's grandeur, symmetry, and sacredness. The chambers, walls, and thresholds are all adorned with carvings and decorations. The vision displays the holiness and glory of God's dwelling place among His people.

*Why didn't Ezekiel follow his guide into the inner room while it was measured?*

## EZEKIEL 42

Continuing his detailed tour of the temple, Ezekiel focuses on the chambers for the priests. These chambers—arranged in three stories—provide space for the priests to eat their sacrifices and store their garments and utensils. The measurements and arrangements of these chambers reflect God's concern for order and holiness within His dwelling place.

*Do you think it's important to separate the holy and common today? Why or why not?*

## EZEKIEL 43

Ezekiel sees a vision of the Lord's glory entering the temple through the eastern gate and filling the temple, signifying His presence among His people once again. God instructs Ezekiel to proclaim to the people the temple's design and significance, emphasizing the importance of holiness and obedience in worship.

*Why was the temple so critically important to Israel's relationship with God?*

## EZEKIEL 44

Ezekiel continues sharing his vision of the temple. The eastern gate—previously closed—remains shut because the Lord entered through it. God instructs Ezekiel to describe the temple layout and regulations to the people, emphasizing the importance of holiness. Only the faithful priestly descendants of Zadok are allowed to approach the Lord and serve in the temple.

*What is the role of purity and holiness in worship today?*

## Take Your Time and Learn More

- The Most Holy Place: HEBREWS 9:6–10
- Layout of the temple: HEBREWS 9:1–5
- God's dwelling among His people: HEBREWS 9:11–14
- Access to God: HEBREWS 10:19–22

*Reading the Bible isn't a race. Let the pages unfold at a pace that allows your spirit to breathe.*

## EZEKIEL 45

Through God, Ezekiel describes the division of the land for the people, the princes of Israel, and the temple. God gives more rules for offerings, feasts, and responsibilities. He emphasizes honesty and righteousness in the distribution of the land.

*What do you think the connection is between loving God and treating people fairly?*

## EZEKIEL 46

Ezekiel shares more details regarding the Sabbath and various feasts. Additionally, he shares ideal situations for offerings and sacrifices for various occasions, emphasizing the importance of regular worship and adherence to God's laws.

*How can you cultivate a rhythm of work and rest that honors God and promotes physical and spiritual health?*

## EZEKIEL 47

Ezekiel shares a vision of a stream of water flowing from the temple, its waters increasing in depth as it courses eastward—symbolizing God's gracious blessings and life-giving power. Trees flourish along its banks, representing the fruitfulness of God's provision for His people. Fishermen will cast their nets into the river, and its abundance will sustain them.

*How has God provided for you to work toward His glory and the good of others?*

## EZEKIEL 48

Ezekiel concludes his book with the division of land among Israel's twelve tribes—with special allotments for the temple, the city, and the prince. The city is named "The LORD is there" (48:35), signifying God's presence among His people. This final vision illustrates God's faithfulness to His covenant promises, ensuring that His people will dwell securely under His eternal protection.

*What does God's nearness mean to you today?*

## Take Your Time and Learn More

- Division of land: LEVITICUS 25:23–34
- Invitation to worship: ISAIAH 56:1–8
- River of life: REVELATION 22:1–5
- Fulfillment of God's promises: JOSHUA 21:43–45

# DANIEL

*All nations and rulers on earth will one day
submit to the authority of God.*

## SETTING THE STAGE

When the book of Daniel opens, Babylon has attacked Jerusalem and taken the Israelites into exile. Among them are Daniel and his three friends, whose Babylonian names are Shadrach, Meshach, and Abed-nego.

Despite their many challenges living in a foreign land, Daniel and his friends remain faithful to God. Daniel, though young when taken into captivity, quickly excels in wisdom and rises to become the highest officer in the empire (5:29–6:3).

The first six chapters tell the story of these four men who attempt to do right and maintain hope in a wicked land where evil powers dominate. The second half of the book records Daniel's prophetic visions.

Interesting to note: in the original writing, the first chapter is written in Hebrew, the language of the Israelites; chapters 2–7 are written in Aramaic, the language widely spoken by the ancient empires; and the final five chapters return to Hebrew.

The book of Daniel is the only Old Testament prophecy to set the time of Christ's first advent (9:24–27), and the book is referred to or quoted many times in the New Testament, particularly in the teachings of Jesus and in the book of Revelation. All of this demonstrates the profound influence of Daniel's prophetic visions.

## GOOD TO KNOW

Author is likely Daniel, though some question this. Chapters 7–12 are written in the first person ("I, Daniel," 7:15), while the first six chapters are in third person ("Then Daniel answered," 2:14). Date is apparently the period of the Babylonian captivity, approximately 605–538 BC.

*The greatest truths in scripture are often
revealed in the unhurried moments.*

## DANIEL 1

Babylon has just attacked Jerusalem, taking Daniel and his friends, best known by their Babylonian names—Shadrach, Meshach, and Abed-nego. Pressured in captivity to violate Jewish food laws and eat like Babylonians, they propose a test. They will consume vegetables and water for ten days. Ten days later, they are stronger than ever.

*How can you obey God's commands in the face of opposing cultural expectations?*

## DANIEL 2

King Nebuchadnezzar has a troubling dream and is disturbed. He demands his wise men not only interpret the dream but also tell him what it was. When they fail, he orders their execution—including Daniel and his friends. Through divine revelation, Daniel interprets the dream and gives glory to God. So the king acknowledges God and promotes Daniel.

*How does lip service to God fall short of true devotion and a relationship with Him?*

## DANIEL 3

King Nebuchadnezzar erects a golden statue—displaying his pride and power—and commands everyone to bow down and worship it. Daniel and his friends refuse. Enraged, the king orders them to be thrown into a fiery furnace. God miraculously preserves them, and Nebuchadnezzar witnesses their survival, forcing him to acknowledge the one true God.

*What role do you think a supportive community plays in this story?*

## DANIEL 4

King Nebuchadnezzar has another troubling dream. Again, Daniel interprets it, warning the king of his impending humiliation and advising him to repent. Despite Daniel's counsel, Nebuchadnezzar in his arrogance loses his sanity. He becomes like a beast in the field until he humbles himself before God.

*What do you think was God's goal in humbling Nebuchadnezzar like this?*

### Take Your Time and Learn More

- Daniel and his friends are taken into captivity: 2 CHRONICLES 36:15–20
- God's kingdom versus man's kingdom: REVELATION 19:6–16
- Prohibition against idolatry: EXODUS 20:3–6
- Humility: JAMES 4:6–10

*Bible study is truly a lifelong journey.*
*Relax and enjoy the trip.*

## DANIEL 5

King Belshazzar, son and successor of Nebuchadnezzar, hosts a lavish feast using the sacred vessels from the temple in Jerusalem. During the feast, a mysterious hand appears and writes on the wall, foretelling Belshazzar's downfall because he refuses to humble himself before God. Daniel interprets the writing, warning of God's judgment. This same night, Belshazzar is killed.

*Why is human pride so deeply dishonoring to God, and how does humility exalt Him?*

## DANIEL 6

Jealous officials convince Darius—the current king—to enact a decree forbidding prayer to anyone but him. Despite the threat of punishment, Daniel continues praying openly to God. Officials report him to Darius, who reluctantly orders Daniel thrown into a lion's den. Once again, God protects Daniel and he emerges unscathed. Darius acknowledges God's power.

*Why do you believe Daniel keeps praying publicly instead of in a less risky way?*

## DANIEL 7

This time, Daniel has a vision he can't understand. A messenger explains: "Four great beasts" represent four arrogant empires who will terrorize God's people. Three will be judged; the fourth will be destroyed. The "Ancient of Days" refers to God. The "Son of Man" likely refers to the Messiah, along with the people of God who will share in His rule.

*Why do you think this vision was meant to give Daniel hope?*

## DANIEL 8

Daniel has another vision about two of the beasts from chapter seven—a ram with two horns (representing the Medes and Persians) and a goat (symbolizing Greece). The goat defeats the ram, and its large horn breaks, replaced by four smaller horns. A king will attack Jerusalem, defiling the temple with idols, but he will be destroyed and the temple restored.

*How does hope for future rescue and restoration motivate faithfulness now?*

## Take Your Time and Learn More

- Temporary nature of the powerful: JOB 12:20–25
- Waiting patiently for God to act: PSALM 37:7–11
- Everlasting dominion: REVELATION 5
- Enduring hardships and remaining faithful: 2 CORINTHIANS 4:7–18

*Try to forget the demands of life for a while.*
*You're spending quality time with God.*

## DANIEL 9

Daniel consults Jeremiah's writing, learning Israel's exile will last seventy years (Jeremiah 25:11). Believing seventy years have almost passed, Daniel acknowledges the people's sins and pleads for God's mercy. An angel tells Daniel more time is still needed to atone for their sin.

*When have you wished God's timing were quicker?*
*What did you learn about God during the wait?*

## DANIEL 10

Daniel mourns for three weeks (over what, the text isn't explicitly clear) and denies himself luxuries. Then he receives his final vision. Someone—likely an angel—appears and reveals future events, assuring Daniel of God's favor. Daniel falls to the ground, but the angel strengthens him and tells him that his words have been heard because of his humility before God.

*What does humility in trials look like?*

## DANIEL 11

This chapter contains some of the most detailed prophecy in scripture. Daniel explains his vision, detailing the rise and fall of various kingdoms. He describes key future historical events that have resulted in endless debates among scholars today. The takeaway: God is sovereign over human history, and He knows ahead of time what will happen.

*How can you tell between deceptive experiences and genuine visions from God?*

## DANIEL 12

This final chapter of Daniel includes further prophecies and revelations. Daniel describes a coming tribulation—a time of unprecedented distress—followed by the ultimate deliverance of God's people. He also addresses the resurrection of the dead and the reward of the righteous. He emphasizes perseverance and faithfulness in the face of trouble.

*How does Daniel's unwavering trust in God encourage you to persevere in your own walk?*

## Take Your Time and Learn More

- Confession and intercession for Israel: 2 CHRONICLES 7:14
- Spiritual warfare: EPHESIANS 6:10–18
- Oppression of God's people: REVELATION 13:1–10
- End times: MATTHEW 24:15–28

# HOSEA

*God is faithful and will never forget His people, even in their sin.*

## SETTING THE STAGE

The book of Hosea covers more than twenty years of Hosea's preaching and teaching, full of powerful and symbolic messages. Most of the book is written as poetry.

Most notable in the book is the story of Hosea and Gomer. God instructs Hosea, a prophet, to marry an unfaithful woman named Gomer. This becomes an allegory for God's enduring love toward unfaithful Israel.

Hosea had the right to pursue divorce, but he pursued Gomer instead. Similarly, God had the right to pursue divorce from His covenant people, yet He pursued them.

Three major takeaways from the book of Hosea: God suffers when His people are unfaithful, God will not and cannot condone sin, and God will always love His own.

The final words of the book were likely written by a different author—whoever collected Hosea's writing to be added to scripture. The words speak directly to us today—"Who is wise? He shall understand these things. Prudent? He shall know them. For the ways of the LORD are right, and the just shall walk in them. But the transgressors shall fall in them" (14:9).

There is much to learn about God and His character from this important book.

## GOOD TO KNOW

Author is probably Hosea himself, though the text is in both first and third person. Written between 750 (roughly when Hosea began ministering) and 722 BC (when Assyria overran Israel).

*Good things come to those who wait—on the Lord, that is.*

## HOSEA 1

The prophet Hosea marries a woman named Gomer. They have three children together—symbolically named Jezreel (signifying God's judgment on the house of Jehu), Lo-ruhamah ("she has not received mercy"), and Lo-ammi ("not My people"). These names reflect God's impending judgment on Israel for their spiritual adultery.

*Why couldn't God simply overlook or ignore Israel's sin?*

## HOSEA 2

Israel is portrayed as an unfaithful wife. Though God faithfully rescued her out of Egypt and formed a covenant with her, Israel still engages in spiritual adultery, worshipping the Canaanite god Baal. God demonstrates His enduring love, promising to restore her. Though He warns of the consequences of sin, He also offers a path to reconciliation.

*How does the metaphor of infidelity better help you understand Israel's relationship with God?*

## HOSEA 3

Gomer commits adultery, but God commands Hosea to redeem his unfaithful wife, symbolizing the Lord's relentless love for Israel despite her spiritual adultery. Hosea pays off the debts Gomer owes to her other partners and instructs her to be faithful to him. Just as she must refrain from being with other men, Israel must return to God and forsake her idolatry.

*How does this story already challenge societal norms surrounding betrayal and infidelity?*

## HOSEA 4

Exposing the vile hypocrisy of their worship, God charges Israel with idolatry, spiritual adultery, and moral decay. Israel is plagued by dishonesty, violence, and promiscuity. Both the priests and the people have forsaken the knowledge of God. As a result, God declares judgment and withholds His blessing.

*What does hypocrisy in worship look like today?*

### Take Your Time and Learn More

- Relationship with the unfaithful: 2 KINGS 17:5–23
- Israel's unfaithfulness: JEREMIAH 3:1–5
- Prophetic symbolism to convey God's message: ISAIAH 20:2–4
- Moral corruption and deceit: JEREMIAH 9:2–9

*The Bible is countercultural, and so is Bible study.*
*There's no need to rush through this.*

## HOSEA 5

Hosea describes God's judgment upon Israel and Judah for their spiritual adultery. The leaders and priests are rebuked for leading the people astray, and the nations are warned of impending punishment. Despite their rebellion, God desires their repentance and promises restoration if they return to Him.

*In what ways does spiritual pride hinder genuine spiritual growth?*

## HOSEA 6

Hosea begins with a call to repentance, urging Israel to return to God and acknowledging His righteousness and mercy. The people are reminded of God's desire for steadfast love rather than sacrifices. Despite their temporary displays of repentance, their commitment is as shallow and fleeting as a morning mist or dew. God desires genuine remorse and a lasting change of heart.

*How are you cultivating a more sincere and consistent relationship with God?*

## HOSEA 7

Hosea reveals the depth of Israel's sin and God's disappointment. Despite experiencing God's healing and provision, the people remain unrepentant, indulging in idolatry and political alliances. Their leaders are corrupt, characterized by deceit and drunkenness, and are leading the nation astray. God's desire to heal them is hindered by their refusal to acknowledge their sin.

*Are you sometimes tempted to compromise with the world in opposition to God? If so, when?*

## HOSEA 8

Hosea condemns Israel's continued rebellion against God. The people have forsaken the covenant, choosing idols and kings without consulting God. They sow wickedness and reap injustice, trusting in their military strength and foreign alliances. Despite their outward religious practices, their hearts are far from Him. As a result, God will bring judgment upon them.

*Have you ever relied on something other than God for security, provision, or fulfillment? Why?*

## Take Your Time and Learn More

- Consequences of rebellion: AMOS 5:1–15
- Call to repent and return: MICAH 6:1–8
- Consequences of concealing sin: PROVERBS 28:13
- Reaping the whirlwind: DEUTERONOMY 32:15–21

*God speaks in the quiet moments.*
*Approach His Word with calm expectation.*

## HOSEA 9

Hosea depicts God's judgment on Israel for their persistent idolatry and rebellion. He warns of impending exile and devastation as punishment for their unfaithfulness. Despite their religious ceremonies, God will reject them, making them become wanderers among the nations. Their sin will lead to barrenness, and they will not enjoy the fruits of their labor.

*What are some red flags that warn of spiritual decline?*

## HOSEA 10

Hosea portrays Israel's spiritual decay and God's impending judgment. The people's worship of idols and reliance on their own strength leads to their downfall. They sow wickedness and reap destruction. The Lord will demolish their altars. Hosea's message is clear: "Break up your fallow ground. For it is time to seek the LORD" (10:12).

*How does God's discipline of Israel still show His desire for their ultimate redemption?*

## HOSEA 11

Hosea reveals God's deep love and compassion for Israel despite their persistent rebellion. Like a loving parent, God recalls how He tenderly cared for Israel, teaching them to walk and lifting them up with cords of kindness. Yet Israel turned away, sacrificing to idols and rejecting Him. God's heart is torn with compassion, unable to fully unleash His anger.

*To what do you attribute God's faithfulness in your life despite your sin?*

## HOSEA 12

Hosea admonishes Israel to return to God and live righteously, recalling their forefather Jacob's struggles and eventual reconciliation with God. Israel's deceitful practices, reliance on wealth, and oppression of the poor are condemned.

*Why can material prosperity be a threat to spiritual health?*

### Take Your Time and Learn More

- Forsaking God: DEUTERONOMY 32:15–18
- Call for repentance: JEREMIAH 4:1–4
- God's unceasing love for Israel: JEREMIAH 31:3
- Jacob's struggle with God: GENESIS 32:22–32

*Before you read, pray. Ask God to*
*speak His truth to your spirit.*

## HOSEA 13

Hosea portrays God's judgment on Israel for their persistent idolatry and rebellion. The nation's pride—seen in their refusal to repent—leads to their downfall and destruction. Despite God's past faithfulness in delivering them from Egypt and providing for their needs, Israel has turned away from Him to worship idols. As a result, God announces severe punishment.

*What does the trap of idolatry look like today, and how can you intentionally avoid it?*

## HOSEA 14

In this final chapter, Hosea presents a call to repentance and a promise of restoration. God urges Israel to return to Him, acknowledging their sins and seeking His forgiveness. He assures them of His love and willingness to heal their waywardness if they repent and turn back to Him. He emphasizes genuine repentance and faith in Him alone.

*How does genuine repentance differ from expressions of remorse or regret?*

### Take Your Time and Learn More

- **Forsaking God:** DEUTERONOMY 32:39–43
- **Need for spiritual renewal:** JOEL 2:12–13

# JOEL

*God will not allow evil to corrupt His world forever.*

## SETTING THE STAGE

The book of Joel is brief but powerful. Consisting of only three chapters, it is referenced more than twenty-three times in the New Testament—most frequently by John in the book of Revelation.

The book opens with a description of the devastating locust invasion that has ravaged Judah. But consistent with the other prophetic books, this story is more than the simple retelling of a historical event; it serves as a symbol of God's judgment and call to repentance.

In response to the plague of locusts, Joel issues a powerful call to fast, weep, and repent because—referring back to the book of Exodus—God is "gracious and merciful, slow to anger and of great kindness" (2:13).

Joel leads the priests in repentance and prayer and anticipates a future day when God will intervene, pouring out His Spirit on all people (2:28).

The book concludes with a hopeful vision of restoration and blessing for God's people. The Lord promises to restore Judah's fortune and to judge the nations that mistreated His people. The land will be fruitful, and God's people will dwell securely: "So you shall know that I am the LORD your God dwelling in Zion, My holy mountain. Then Jerusalem shall be holy, and no foreigners shall pass through her anymore" (3:17).

## GOOD TO KNOW

Author is Joel, "the son of Pethuel" (1:1), but little else is known of him. Date is unclear but perhaps just before the Babylonian invasion of Judah in 586 BC.

*Don't hurry, don't worry. God's Word provides everything you need for living well.*

## JOEL 1

Joel begins with a lament over a devastating locust plague, illustrating God's judgment on Israel for their sins. The land lies desolate, the crops have been destroyed, and food is scarce. The priests mourn, and God calls people to fast and pray. Joel urges the elders and inhabitants to lament and call upon the Lord, recognizing the severity of the judgment.

*How do you reconcile the idea of harsh consequences with a loving God?*

## JOEL 2

Joel describes an invading army, likened to a swarm of locusts. He calls for repentance, fasting, and solemn assembly—urging the people to return to the Lord with all their hearts. God's mercy is emphasized, and His restoration and blessings are promised for those who turn to Him.

*What does it look like to "tear your heart and not your garments" (2:13)? Why does this distinction matter?*

## JOEL 3

Joel speaks of a day when God will gather all nations for judgment in the Valley of Jehoshaphat. God will render justice for His people and vindicate His name among the nations. Joel prophesies a time of great upheaval and signs signaling the day of the Lord. Yet amid the chaos, there is hope.

*How do you keep trusting in God's justice in a world where injustice seems to go unpunished?*

## Take Your Time and Learn More

- Devastating consequences: JEREMIAH 9:10–16
- Peter quotes from Joel 2: ACTS 2:17–21
- Gathered for judgment: REVELATION 14:14–20

# AMOS

*God isn't interested in empty religious rituals—He desires sincerity.*

## SETTING THE STAGE

The book of Amos emphasizes social justice, moral accountability, and the consequences of disobedience. Where as the prophet Hosea was burdened over Israel's unfaithfulness, the prophet Amos is burdened by its injustice. The wealthy are exploiting the poor by allowing them to be sold into debt slavery, for example, and corruption is running rampant.

In the first two chapters, Amos delivers a series of stern judgments to Israel. Chapters 3-6 contain poetry about the inevitable consequences of their sin. And then the final three chapters reveal Amos's visions about Israel's coming judgment.

Amos consistently emphasizes the responsibility that comes with being God's chosen people, urging them to repent and to "let judgment run down like waters and righteousness like a mighty stream" (5:24).

He also condemns religious hypocrisy, pointing out how the religious leadership faithfully attends gatherings, makes sacrifices, and gives offerings—all while participating in the ongoing injustice. His message is clear: religion doesn't matter if it doesn't change how we live.

While the book of Amos primarily includes messages of judgment, it concludes with a note of hope. Amos shares a final prophecy that promises restoration and blessing. One day a messianic King will come from David's line to restore and rebuild all that has been broken.

## GOOD TO KNOW

Written by Amos, a shepherd from Tekoa, near Bethlehem (1:1), around the 760s BC.

# God loves it when you read and study His Word.

## AMOS 1

Amos details God's judgments against neighboring nations for their sins. Damascus faces punishment for their cruelty, Gaza for enslaving whole populations, Tyre for betraying an alliance, Edom for ruthless vengeance, and Ammon for barbaric war crimes. These pronouncements set the stage for the impending judgment upon Israel.

*Can secular culture decide what is right or wrong? In what ways do people try?*

## AMOS 2

Amos continues his theme of God's judgment, now focusing on Judah and Israel. Judah is condemned for rejecting God's law and forsaking His commands despite their covenant relationship with Him. Israel faces judgment for their egregious sins—including selling the righteous for silver, exploiting the poor, and committing immoral acts in pagan temples.

*Why is it so easy to forget where our blessings come from?*

## AMOS 3

Amos declares that God's close relationship with Israel brings greater accountability; therefore, they will face judgment for their disobedience. Through a series of rhetorical questions, Amos illustrates the logical connection between calamity and God's intervention. He highlights God's sovereignty in orchestrating events, especially when calamity strikes.

*Why do you think relationship with God brings greater responsibility?*

## AMOS 4

Amos continues his prophetic warnings against Israel's social and spiritual corruption. Despite God's attempts to discipline the people through drought, blight, locusts, plagues, and enemies, Israel remains unrepentant. Amos addresses their insincere worship—criticizing their outward rituals as devoid of true devotion.

*Why is it insulting to God when believers simply go through the motions, spiritually speaking?*

## Take Your Time and Learn More

- Pronouncement of judgment: JEREMIAH 49:7–22
- Judgment for social and moral corruption: ISAIAH 3:13–15
- Refusal to heed God's warnings: HOSEA 8
- Judgment for pride and arrogance: ISAIAH 10:12–19

*Reading the Bible isn't a race. Let the pages unfold*
*at a pace that allows your spirit to breathe.*

## AMOS 5

God pleads with Israel to return to Him. Amos urges the nation to seek the Lord and live, forsaking their idolatry and injustice. He denounces their empty religious practices, demanding instead a genuine pursuit of righteousness and mercy. He laments the inevitability of judgment due to Israel's persistent disobedience.

*How can you prioritize seeking the Lord regardless of what everyone around you is doing?*

## AMOS 6

Amos depicts the luxury and complacency of Israel's elite, contrasting their opulent lifestyle with the impending judgment of God. Amos condemns their indifference toward the suffering of others, particularly in light of the nation's moral decay. Despite the looming threat of invasion and exile, the wealthy remain oblivious, indulging in excess.

*Why is material wealth so often linked to spiritual apathy and moral decline?*

## AMOS 7

Amos receives a series of visions, each revealing impending judgment upon Israel. He sees locusts stripping the land clean. He sees judgment by fire. He sees God standing by a wall holding a plumb line. In each vision, Amos intercedes—pleading for mercy—and God relents. Amaziah the priest tells Amos to go back to Judah, but Amos continues speaking truth.

*Why is human nature typically resistant to hearing messages of repentance?*

## Take Your Time and Learn More

- Hypocrisy in worship: ISAIAH 1:10–20
- Self-indulgence and indifference: JEREMIAH 22:13–17
- Importance of God's Word: 1 KINGS 13:1–10

*The greatest truths in scripture are often*
*revealed in the unhurried moments.*

## AMOS 8

Amos has a vision in which he sees a basket of ripe fruit, symbolizing the imminent end of Israel's prosperity. He prophesies the coming devastation and mourning. The wealthy people who greedily exploit the poor and cheat in business dealings are condemned. God will not forget their sins, and He will punish them accordingly.

*Though genuine worship is for God alone,*
*how and why does it change people's hearts?*

## AMOS 9

Amos concludes the book with a vision of God standing by an altar, declaring judgment upon Israel. God promises not to utterly destroy the house of Jacob, but punishment is inevitable. Even in their exile, God will pursue the sinful, leaving nobody to escape judgment. One day God will restore the altar, the walls, and the vineyards.

*After His people turn their back on Him so many times, why will God still send Jesus?*

## Take Your Time and Learn More

- Scarcity and famine: REVELATION 6:5–6
- James quotes from Amos 9: ACTS 15:14–18

# OBADIAH

*God will eventually destroy every evil,*
*arrogant nation that stands against Him.*

## SETTING THE STAGE

The shortest book in the Old Testament, Obadiah consists of only twenty-one verses. Yet there is still plenty to unpack. Written in a literary form known as a "doom song," the book delivers strong judgment against Edom, the nation descended from Esau.

Edom neighbored Israel on the other side of the Dead Sea. But instead of offering help when Babylon invaded and conquered Israel, Edom took advantage of Israel and actually added to the nation's destruction by capturing and killing Israelite refugees.

In other prophetic books, God held those who'd harmed His people accountable; now, Edom is no exception. The fact that you've probably heard so little about Edom is a testament to the fulfillment of this prophecy.

The first part of Obadiah pronounces doom on Edom, specifically for their pride. But all is not doom. The second part of the book offers a message of hope to Israel, promising deliverance for the house of Jacob. The people will experience God's restoration and blessing (verse 17).

## GOOD TO KNOW

Written by Obadiah (1:1), perhaps a person's name or the title (meaning "servant of God") of an unnamed prophet. Date is unclear but probably within thirty years after Babylon's invasion of Judah in 586 BC.

---

*Good things come to those who wait—on the Lord, that is.*

## OBADIAH

The book of Obadiah is a prophecy against Edom, a nation descended from Esau. It denounces their pride, arrogance, and betrayal against Israel. Despite Edom's false security in their mountain strongholds, God declares their impending judgment and destruction. The chapter warns of Edom's punishment for their violence and mistreatment toward Israel.

*Why do you believe God so faithfully holds accountable those who harm His people?*

## Take Your Time and Learn More

- **Prophecy against Edom:** JEREMIAH 49:7–22

# JONAH

*God's mercy and grace exist for those who
turn to Him in genuine repentance.*

## SETTING THE STAGE

The book of Jonah tells the story of the prophet Jonah, whom God commands to deliver a message of judgment to the city of Nineveh. And though the Bible doesn't explicitly state why Jonah initially refuses, a few reasons are possible.

First, Nineveh is at this time the capital of the Assyrian Empire—the historical enemies of Israel. Second, Jonah might be concerned that if he delivers a message of impending judgment to Nineveh, the people might repent and receive mercy. Third, given the Assyrians' reputation, Jonah might simply fear for his safety.

Regardless of the reason, Jonah attempts to flee from God's presence by boarding a ship bound for Tarshish, in the opposite direction. But he misunderstands one profound truth: it's futile to resist God's will.

A storm ensues, and the sailors on the ship cast lots to decide who's responsible for bringing God's wrath upon them. The lot falls on Jonah, who confesses he is running from God. He advises the sailors to throw him overboard.

After being thrown into the sea, Jonah is swallowed by a great fish that functions as a vessel of God's mercy, preserving his life and giving him the opportunity to reflect and repent.

God speaks to the fish, and it vomits Jonah on dry land (2:10). God gives Jonah a second opportunity to obey; and this time, he heeds the call and goes to Nineveh.

## GOOD TO KNOW

Author is unnamed; the story is Jonah's but written in the third person, probably around 760 BC.

*Bible study is truly a lifelong journey.*
*Relax and enjoy the trip.*

## JONAH 1

The book opens with God telling Jonah to preach in Nineveh, the capital city of Israel's enemy. Not wanting to go, Jonah flees by ship in the opposite direction—but the ship faces a terrible storm. Recognizing God's hand in it, Jonah convinces the sailors to throw him overboard, where a great fish swallows him.

*What can you learn about God's character, given that He didn't let Jonah drown?*

## JONAH 2

In the belly of the great fish for three days and nights, Jonah prays to God. He acknowledges God's sovereignty, seeks His deliverance, and vows obedience. Even stuck in what appears to be a watery grave, Jonah knows God hasn't forsaken him. The fish then vomits Jonah onto dry land.

*How does Jonah's prayer demonstrate God's accessibility?*

## JONAH 3

Once again, God tells Jonah to go preach in Nineveh, warning the people that they're about to be overthrown. This time he obeys, and the people of the city—from the king to the commoners—repent. So God relents from His planned destruction, showing mercy and demonstrating His compassion even toward a pagan nation.

*How can God's eagerness to grant mercy inform your response to those who have wronged you?*

## JONAH 4

Jonah angrily tells God that he disobeyed at first because God is "gracious" and "merciful," (4:2) and he suspected this would happen. Jonah wants God to kill him, but God simply shades Jonah from the sun with a plant. God causes the plant to die, and Jonah again says he wants to die. But God gets the final word.

*What does Jonah's anger over God's mercy to Nineveh reveal?*

## Take Your Time and Learn More

- God's power over all creation, including the sea: PSALM 139:7–12
- Prayer of deliverance: PSALM 18:1–19
- Jesus refers to Jonah: MATTHEW 12:38–41
- Complaining to God: NUMBERS 11:10–15

# MICAH

*Though God is faithful and merciful, He is also just.*

## SETTING THE STAGE

Micah was a prophet during a time of social and moral corruption in Israel. He's the author of the book of Micah, one of the twelve "minor prophets." The name refers to the length of their prophecies, not their importance.

Micah was a contemporary of Isaiah, so it makes sense that several similarities exist between their books (see Micah 4:1-5 and Isaiah 2:2-4, for example).

The book of Micah contains three major themes.

First, Micah declares judgment against Israel and Judah (Micah 1-3), emphasizing the consequences of their idolatry, injustice, and oppression.

Second, Micah prophesies of a future restoration and a coming Messiah (Micah 4-5). The promised ruler will come from Bethlehem and will bring peace to the people of God.

Third, Micah emphasizes the importance of justice, mercy, and humility (Micah 6-7). One of the most beloved verses from the book says, "He has shown you, O man, what is good. And what does the LORD require of you, but to do justice and to love mercy and to walk humbly with your God?" (6:8).

Even as Micah laments Israel's widespread corruption, he expresses confidence in God's forgiveness and faithfulness to His people. Though Israel's sin is great, God's covenant love is greater. It has been God's good plan from the beginning to redeem His people.

## GOOD TO KNOW

"The word of the LORD that came to Micah of Moresheth" (1:1), who either wrote or dictated the prophecies around 700 BC.

*Try to forget the demands of life for a while.*
*You're spending quality time with God.*

## MICAH 1

The book opens with Micah sharing a prophetic message from the Lord, pronouncing accusations and judgment against Israel and Judah "because of the transgression of Jacob and because of the sins of the house of Israel" (1:5). He calls out towns and cities of Israel by name, warning them that God is going to punish them severely.

*How does God's response to His people's sin challenge your own attitude toward sin today?*

## MICAH 2

Micah explains the reasons for God's judgment, condemning the injustice and greed of Israel's corrupt leaders who have grown rich by oppressing the poor. False prophets are preaching peace because the true prophets' constant message of repentance made their listeners uncomfortable (2:6).

*Why are false messages of peace and prosperity often so well received?*

## MICAH 3

Micah continues rebuking Israel's corrupt leaders and false prophets. They operate with bribes and show favoritism to the rich, oppressing the poor and vulnerable—all in the name of God. Micah doesn't mince words when he says, "Therefore, because of you, Zion shall be plowed like a field" (3:12).

*Why is it especially harmful when religious leaders who claim to work for God hurt people?*

## MICAH 4

Despite his unapologetic pronouncements of judgment up to this point, Micah now prophesies a future of peace, envisioning a time when God will establish His kingdom on earth. Nations will seek God's wisdom and justice, and war will end. God will gather the scattered remnant and restore them, ruling over them from Zion.

*Considering the current state of the world, what do you think of a time of future peace and restoration?*

## Take Your Time and Learn More

- Impending invasion: ISAIAH 10:28–32
- Corruption and greed: JEREMIAH 6:13–15
- Faithless leaders rebuked: EZEKIEL 34:1–10
- Future exaltation: ISAIAH 2:1–5

*Good things come to those who wait—on the Lord, that is.*

## MICAH 5

Offering more hope, Micah prophesies the birth of a messianic King from David's line, born in Bethlehem, who will rule over the restored people in Jerusalem. He will be exalted, and His reign will extend to the ends of the earth. God will bring final justice to rid the world of evil.

*How can you cultivate hopeful expectation for the fulfillment of God's future promises?*

## MICAH 6

Micah returns to prophesying God's accusations against Israel. As if in a courtroom, God reminds Israel of everything He has done for them, then accuses them of breaking their covenant obligations. Micah famously explains what the Lord requires of man—"to do justice and to love mercy and to walk humbly with your God" (6:8). Israel has done the opposite.

*What do you think it looks like, practically speaking, to "walk humbly with your God"?*

## MICAH 7

Israel is steeped in corruption and betrayal, and God's message to them is severe—Israel will eventually be exiled to Babylon. Yet the book still ends with hope. This last chapter affirms God's mercy and redemption. Its final words are "You will give truth to Jacob and mercy to Abraham, which You have sworn to our fathers from the days of old" (7:20).

*Which do you believe is more powerful—human evil or God's covenant love?*

## Take Your Time and Learn More

- Matthew quotes from Micah 5: MATTHEW 2:1–6
- What God requires of man: ISAIAH 1:10–17
- God's faithfulness and mercy: PSALM 27

# NAHUM

*God is sovereign over all nations and will
bring justice to the oppressed.*

## SETTING THE STAGE

The book of Nahum was written by the prophet Nahum and is considered to be the sequel to the book of Jonah. Both books contain strong prophetic warnings and messages focused on the city of Nineveh, the capital of the Assyrian Empire.

The Assyrian army was the Israelites' most formidable and feared adversary—a truly evil empire known for its military might, ruthless tactics, and relentless conquests.

God's people were waiting for Him to bring judgment on their enemy, but Nineveh's repentance upon hearing Jonah's message of impending destruction delayed God's judgment for nearly a hundred years.

The book of Nahum is written as lyric poetry. Nahum is clear and unapologetic as he declares the certainty of God's judgment and delivers words of comfort and hope to the people suffering under Assyrian oppression—"The LORD is good, a stronghold in the day of trouble, and He knows those who trust in Him" (1:7).

Far more than an angry rant against Israel's enemy, the book of Nahum serves to remind God's people that God is committed to justice and will eventually make everything right: "The LORD is slow to anger and great in power and will not at all acquit the wicked" (1:3).

## GOOD TO KNOW

"The book of the vision of Nahum the Elkoshite" (1:1), who either wrote or dictated the prophecies between 663 and 612 BC.

*The Bible is countercultural, and so is Bible study.*
*There's no need to rush through this.*

## NAHUM 1

The prophet Nahum pronounces God's righteous judgment on the oppressive Assyrian empire. Through Nahum, God communicates His great power, promising justice against the wicked. Yet while God destroys arrogant empires, He also offers refuge to those who trust in Him. God's judgment against evildoers is certain, but so is His care for His people.

*Practically speaking, what does it mean to seek refuge in God?*

## NAHUM 2

Nahum vividly depicts the upcoming destruction of Nineveh, the capital of the ancient Assyrian Empire. He portrays the city under siege—its walls breached, its fortifications destroyed, and its people fleeing in terror. Despite its former strength and glory, Nineveh will be powerless against the overwhelming force of God's judgment.

*How do you reconcile God's love with His wrath seen in this book?*

## NAHUM 3

Nahum condemns Nineveh for its wickedness and predicts its destruction. Using vivid imagery, Nahum describes Nineveh as a city full of deceit, violence, and exploitation—a city built on the blood of the innocent, now doomed to shame and defeat. Nahum affirms the certainty of God's justice and the downfall of wicked nations.

*How does God's wrath toward Nineveh impact your understanding of the seriousness of sin?*

## Take Your Time and Learn More

- God's compassion for those who trust Him: Exodus 34:6–7
- Salvation and deliverance: Isaiah 52:7–10
- Cause of destruction: Jeremiah 50:29–32

# HABAKKUK

*God will deal with evil in His way and in His time.*

## SETTING THE STAGE

The book of Habakkuk is unique in its format because—while it is authored by a prophet—it is not written as a message to be shared on behalf of God to His people. Rather, it is written as a direct discourse between the prophet Habakkuk and God.

The book of Habakkuk is a deeply tender and personal record of Habakkuk's journey to trust that God is good, even when there is so much evil in the world.

Written during an extremely dark time of moral decay in Judah, the book records Habakkuk's questions about the apparent injustice and violence all around him—"O LORD, how long shall I cry, and You will not hear, even cry out to You, 'Violence!' and You will not save?" (1:2).

In the book's three short chapters, God graciously answers each of Habakkuk's questions and complaints, assuring the prophet that Judah's enemies will ultimately face judgment. He also reminds the prophet that the righteous are called to live by faith and wait patiently for the fulfillment of God's promises.

The final chapter records a beautiful prayer in which Habakkuk rehearses God's faithfulness through history and then declares his love for God. It's one of the clearest and most profound demonstrations of faith in the Bible.

## GOOD TO KNOW

Little is known of Habakkuk (1:1); his prophecy dates to approximately 600 BC.

*God speaks in the quiet moments.*
*Approach His Word with calm expectation.*

## HABAKKUK 1

Habakkuk cries out to God, upset by the evil he sees in Judah. He questions why God allows the wicked to prosper while the righteous suffer. God reveals His plan to raise up Babylon—a ruthless nation—to execute judgment. Troubled, Habakkuk wonders why God would use a more wicked nation to punish a less wicked one.

*Can you think of a time you received an answer to prayer that surprised you?*

## HABAKKUK 2

Habakkuk waits for God's response—watching and listening. God answers, instructing him to write down a vision that will be fulfilled in time. The vision contrasts the fate of the arrogant (whose greed and violence will lead to their downfall) with the destiny of the righteous (who will live by faith). God's glory will spread throughout the world.

*What sins of your nation are deplorable to you?*
*How much do you pray about them?*

## HABAKKUK 3

Habakkuk prays in song for God's mercy amid impending calamity. He recalls God's past deeds and power, acknowledging His sovereignty over all creation. Despite the impending destruction, he knows God will ultimately deliver. With imagery of thunderstorms and earthquakes, this chapter beautifully describes God's majesty and His power to save His people.

*How can you intentionally strengthen your*
*faith while waiting for an answer from God?*

## Take Your Time and Learn More

- **Impending judgment:** JEREMIAH 5:6–9
- **Eventual triumph of righteousness:** ISAIAH 2:1–4
- **Faith in adversity and uncertainty:** PSALM 77

# ZEPHANIAH

*There is coming a day when God will make all things right.*

## SETTING THE STAGE

The book of Zephaniah contains a clear message of judgment against various nations, as well as a call to repentance and a promise of restoration for the remnant of God's people.

Zephaniah was the great-great-grandson of King Hezekiah (1:1). He prophesied during the reign of King Josiah of Judah, addressing a period of great moral and spiritual decline.

One of the clear themes of the book is "the day of the LORD," a term Zephaniah uses throughout to describe the future day of reckoning when God executes judgment again on the nations and Jerusalem: "The great day of the LORD is near; it is near and in a great hurry, even the sound of the day of the LORD. The mighty man shall cry bitterly there" (1:14).

Interesting to note: nowhere does Zephaniah ever mention which army will be used to bring judgment. We know from the other minor prophets that the answer is Babylon, but Zephaniah is drawing attention to the reality that it is God—not an opposing army—who will ultimately enact justice against evildoers.

Yet even amid his clear messages of judgment, Zephaniah faithfully calls the people of Judah to repent. He encourages them to seek the Lord, do what is right, and humble themselves before the day of God's wrath.

God cannot tolerate evil, and He will deliver justice. However, He also sees those who are faithful.

## GOOD TO KNOW

Zephaniah (1:1) wrote 640–620 BC, during the reign of King Josiah.

*Before you read, pray. Ask God to*
*speak His truth to your spirit.*

## ZEPHANIAH 1

During Josiah's reign, God tells Zephaniah that He is going to bring judgment upon Judah and Jerusalem for their disobedience and idolatry. Zephaniah warns of a day of reckoning when God will sweep away everything from the land, leaving it desolate. This chapter describes the horrors of God's wrath, employing images of destruction and devastation.

*What role do community and fellowship play*
*in maintaining faithfulness to God?*

## ZEPHANIAH 2

Zephaniah continues his prophecy of judgment, urging the nations surrounding Judah to repent. Despite their arrogance, these nations will face the same fate as Judah if they do not turn to God. Zephaniah also promises restoration for the remnant of God's people who seek refuge in Him.

*Why does God deliver judgment? Is judgment for sin necessary?*

## ZEPHANIAH 3

Zephaniah condemns Jerusalem for its rebellion and corruption. Despite God's past judgments and calls to repentance, the city remains unrepentant and continues in its wickedness. However, amid the impending destruction, there is a promise of future restoration. God pledges to gather and establish a remnant of faithful and humble people who will trust in Him alone.

*How should Christians today trust God for*
*redemption, restoration, and ultimate victory?*

## Take Your Time and Learn More

- God's wrath poured out: JEREMIAH 4:23–28
- Call for humble repentance: JOEL 2:12–17
- Restoration and blessing: ISAIAH 12

# HAGGAI

*Someday God will build a new Jerusalem and live with His people.*

## SETTING THE STAGE

The short but powerful book of Haggai addresses the returned exiles in Judah. Written about seventy years after the Babylonian exile—during a period of spiritual apathy and neglect for God—Haggai rebukes the community for taking so long to rebuild the temple. He seeks to motivate them to prioritize its reconstruction: "Is it time for you yourselves to dwell in your paneled houses and this house to remain desolate?" (1:4).

In response to Haggai's rebuke, the people repent and renew their commitment to rebuild, so Haggai's tone turns from admonishment to encouragement. He assures them that God is with them and will help them. Obedience to God, Haggai reminds the people, is what ultimately leads to His blessing.

As they rebuild, it becomes clear to the people that the new temple is unimpressive—nothing like the temple Solomon built five hundred years before, with its interior walls lined with cedar and its floors overlaid with gold. And this is discouraging.

So Haggai prophesies that the glory of the future temple will surpass that of the former—hinting at a future Messianic fulfillment and anticipating a time when God will shake all heaven and earth and bring about a kingdom of eternal peace (2:9).

## GOOD TO KNOW

Haggai wrote in 520 BC—a precise date because he mentions "the second year of Darius the king" (1:1), verifiable against Persian records.

*Don't hurry, don't worry. God's Word provides
everything you need for living well.*

## HAGGAI 1

The prophet Haggai opens this short book by rebuking the people for their misplaced priorities. While investing in their own fancy houses, they've neglected the temple. Haggai urges them to reconsider, calling for a renewed commitment to God's house. Haggai's message makes an impact, and Zerubbabel and Joshua lead the people to resume constructing the temple.

*Do you ever prioritize personal comfort over
spiritual responsibility? If so, in what areas?*

## HAGGAI 2

The people rebuilding the temple are discouraged. This version is nothing compared to the structure Solomon built hundreds of years earlier. Haggai responds to the people's disappointment by reassuring them of God's presence and promising greater glory for the new temple. He clarifies that the temple's significance lies not in its grandeur but in its God.

*In what area of your life do you need to
persevere in the face of disappointment?*

### Take Your Time and Learn More

- Rebuilding God's house: Ezra 5:1–2
- Future glory of the temple: Zechariah 4:6–10

# ZECHARIAH

*God is always patiently guiding history
toward His eternal purpose.*

## SETTING THE STAGE

The book of Zechariah, like the book of Haggai, begins after the return of the exiles from Babylon. And like the prophet Haggai, Zechariah seeks to motivate the people to prioritize rebuilding the temple.

The book of Zechariah begins with a solemn warning and a call to repentance.

Zechariah then shares eight visions—symbolic and vivid images that relate a message from God. These visions include the man among the myrtle trees, the four horns and four carpenters, the measuring line, the high priest Joshua, the golden lampstand and two olive trees, the flying scroll, the woman in an ephah (basket), and the four chariots (1:7–6:8). These visions represent restoration, judgment, and God's plan for Israel, but they are also the reason readers sometimes find the book of Zechariah difficult to read and understand.

Despite these challenges, Zechariah is rich in theological depth, offering us profound insight into God's redemptive plan, the role of the coming Messiah, and the ultimate fulfillment of God's promises.

No other Old Testament prophet shares more prophecy in such a short space. One of Zechariah's most well-known prophecies involves Jesus' triumphal entry: "Rejoice greatly, O daughter of Zion; shout, O daughter of Jerusalem. Behold, your King comes to you. He is just and has salvation, lowly, and riding on a donkey, and on a colt, the foal of a donkey" (9:9).

## GOOD TO KNOW

Author is Zechariah, son of Berechiah (1:1); some believe a second, unnamed writer contributed chapters 9–14. Written approximately 520–475 BC.

*God loves it when you read and study His Word.*

## ZECHARIAH 1

During the reign of Darius, the prophet Zechariah receives a series of visions from the Lord. The first vision depicts a man riding on a red horse among the myrtle trees—symbolizing God's watchful presence and His intention to restore Jerusalem. In response to Zechariah's plea for mercy, God promises to restore Jerusalem and comfort His people.

*What does repentance to God look like in your life?*

## ZECHARIAH 2

Zechariah sees a vision of a man with a measuring line going to measure Jerusalem—indicating its expansion. God declares His intentions to return to Jerusalem and dwell among His people. He promises to protect them like a wall of fire, calling for the nations to come to Zion, where He will dwell.

*Why is it such a profound idea that God wants to dwell among His people?*

## ZECHARIAH 3

Zechariah sees Joshua the high priest—dressed in filthy rags and standing before the angel of the Lord, with Satan accusing him. The Lord rebukes Satan and declares Joshua to be a brand plucked from the fire, symbolizing his purification and restoration. Joshua's filthy clothes are replaced with clean robes, signifying his forgiveness and righteousness.

*Do you think there is still a connection today between obedience and blessing? Why or why not?*

## ZECHARIAH 4

Zechariah sees a vision of a golden lampstand with seven lamps and two olive trees. Zerubbabel will complete the rebuilding of the temple, not by might or power but by the Spirit of the Lord. The two trees represent Zerubbabel and Joshua, leaders in the restoration, receiving God's help to complete their tasks.

*What are some practical ways you can rely more on God's Spirit and less on human strength?*

### Take Your Time and Learn More

- Call to repentance: DANIEL 9:1–19
- Future glory of the city: ISAIAH 54:1–3
- Forgiveness and restoration: REVELATION 12:10–11
- Completion of the temple: EZRA 6:14–15

*Reading the Bible isn't a race. Let the pages unfold
at a pace that allows your spirit to breathe.*

## ZECHARIAH 5

This chapter contains two visions. The first involves the flying scroll, representing God's judgment and curse on those who steal and swear falsely. The second reveals the ephah (basket) with a woman in it—symbolizing the people's wickedness. These visions depict God's justice against sin and His removal of wickedness from the land.

*Do you believe Christian culture is becoming desensitized to sin? Why or why not?*

## ZECHARIAH 6

Zechariah sees four chariots coming out from between two bronze mountains, each with different colored horses representing God's angels carrying out His will on earth. Zechariah receives a command to take silver and gold from exiled Jews and make a crown for Joshua the high priest, symbolizing his role as a priestly king and foreshadowing the coming Messiah.

*What do Old Testament visions and prophecies teach
you about God's care for His people?*

## ZECHARIAH 7

People from Bethel ask about continuing the tradition of fasting during the fifth month, commemorating the destruction of the temple. God responds, questioning their sincerity and urging them to prioritize justice, mercy, and compassion over ritual observance. He reminds them that their ancestors' refusal to listen led to their downfall.

*What are the dangers of practicing religious rituals without genuine devotion?*

## ZECHARIAH 8

God promises to restore Jerusalem, transforming it into a city of truth and righteousness where people of all nations gather. Despite past hardships, God pledges to dwell among them and assures them of His unwavering commitment. The streets will fill with children playing—symbolizing peace and joy. Once-hostile nations will seek God's favor.

*Do you have any painful moments in your life that you can now look back on with joy?*

## *Take Your Time and Learn More*

- God's judgment on the wicked: REVELATION 6:5–8
  - Future glory of David's throne: PSALM 132:17
- Rebuke against empty religious rituals: ISAIAH 58
  - God will restore Israel: ISAIAH 2:1–5

*The greatest truths in scripture are often revealed in the unhurried moments.*

## ZECHARIAH 9

Zechariah prophesies the triumphal entry of the Messiah into Jerusalem, heralding peace and salvation. He describes the humility and gentleness of the coming King, contrasting Him with the proud rulers of the world. The Lord promises to establish His dominion.

*How does the accuracy of Old Testament prophecies increase trust in God's Word?*

## ZECHARIAH 10

God urges His people to seek Him for rain and spiritual nourishment instead of relying on false idols or diviners. He promises to provide abundant showers, lush pastures, and fruitful crops as a sign of His favor and restoration. The Lord pledges to gather His scattered flock from the nations and bring them back to their land. They will flourish under His care.

*How does the gospel lead to authentic joy?*

## ZECHARIAH 11

Zechariah symbolically acts out the rejection of Judah. He portrays himself as a shepherd appointed to care for the flock, but they despise him. This represents God's relationship with His people, who reject His guidance and protection. Zechariah breaks two staffs, symbolizing the end of the covenant with God. He demands payment for his service, signifying the people's betrayal.

*How does disobedience reflect a lack of trust in God's wisdom and guidance?*

## ZECHARIAH 12

God declares His intention to make Jerusalem a cup of trembling and a burdensome stone to all the surrounding people. He promises to protect Jerusalem and defeat its enemies. The people will mourn and recognize Jesus, whom they've pierced, leading to repentance and salvation. God will pour out His Spirit on the house of David and Jerusalem.

*Despite the benefits of conviction, why do our hearts so often despise it?*

## Take Your Time and Learn More

- Matthew describes the fulfillment of Zechariah 9's prophecy: MATTHEW 21:1–11
- The good shepherd: JEREMIAH 23:3–4
- Matthew describes the fulfillment of Zechariah 11's prophecy: MATTHEW 27:3–10
- Future recognition of Jesus as Messiah: REVELATION 1:7

*Bible study is truly a lifelong journey.*
*Relax and enjoy the trip.*

## ZECHARIAH 13

Zechariah prophesies a day when a fountain from the house of David will cleanse and refine the people from sin. False prophets and idols will be banished. Even the wounds of false prophets will bear witness against them. Two-thirds of the people will die while one-third will be refined in fire. These will be God's people.

*What are some examples of modern idols that compete with our devotion to God today?*

## ZECHARIAH 14

Zechariah prophesies the ultimate victory and reign of the Lord over the nations. Jerusalem will be besieged, but the Lord will come to its defense, standing on the Mount of Olives. The Lord will become King over all the earth, and the city will be transformed into a holy place. People from all nations will worship the Lord there.

*What role does God have in shaping the course of human history?*

### Take Your Time and Learn More

- Matthew describes the fulfillment of Zechariah 13's prophecy: MATTHEW 26:31–32
- Restoration and exaltation of Jerusalem: REVELATION 22:1–5

# MALACHI

*Though God must consistently handle sin,
He never abandons His people.*

## SETTING THE STAGE

The book of Malachi, the final book of the Old Testament, was written by Malachi about a hundred years after the Israelites returned from their Babylonian exile.

The temple has been rebuilt by this point, but—true to human nature—the Israelites are becoming just as unfaithful as their ancestors, who brought the exile upon themselves in the first place.

Malachi desperately wants this new generation to be faithful to God, so he delivers a series of rebukes, challenges, and messages to the people. He speaks specifically of how the people are bringing shameful offerings—including sick or blemished animals—that God calls "polluted bread on My altar" (1:7). This corrupt form of worship ultimately dishonors God, so Malachi addresses the priests who are participating in it and urges the people to return to God with genuine hearts.

Malachi prophesies the coming of the forerunner, John the Baptist, with words that will be repeated or referenced multiple times in the New Testament: "Behold, I will send My messenger, and he shall prepare the way before Me" (3:1).

The final chapter concludes with a vision of the day of the Lord, highlighting the coming judgment for the wicked and the blessing for the righteous.

With their growing anticipation for the Messiah's arrival, Malachi's words serve as a fitting conclusion to the Old Testament.

## GOOD TO KNOW

Author is Malachi (1:1), meaning "my messenger"; no other details are given. The book dates to approximately 450 BC.

*Try to forget the demands of life for a while.*
*You're spending quality time with God.*

## MALACHI 1

Malachi condemns the contempt and lack of respect shown by the priests. They offer blemished animals to God instead of giving their best. God is not pleased. Malachi warns of the consequences of their disobedience, indicating that God will no longer accept their sacrifices.

*How do you ensure that your worship of God is genuine and honorable to Him?*

## MALACHI 2

Malachi continues rebuking the priests for their failure to honor God and uphold His covenant. He condemns the priests for their corrupt practices—including showing partiality in their judgments and marrying foreign women who worship other gods. God warns them of the consequences, promising to curse their blessings and shame them before the people.

*Why are corruption and hypocrisy in the lives of religious leadership so offensive to God?*

## MALACHI 3

God promises to send a messenger who will prepare the way for the Lord's coming. This messenger will purify the people like a refiner's fire or launderer's soap, ensuring they are worthy of God's favor. God calls the people to return to Him with their tithes and offerings, promising abundant blessings in return. He warns of judgment for those who persist in sin.

*How might you respond to people who—like the Israelites—question God's justice?*

## MALACHI 4

Malachi prophesies the coming day of the Lord, when the wicked will face destruction like stubble consumed by fire. For the righteous, however, the Sun of righteousness will rise with healing in its wings, bringing joy and restoration. Elijah will precede the great and dreadful day, turning hearts of fathers to their children—and vice versa.

*Is God's Word an encouragement to you? Do you read it out of duty or delight?*

## Take Your Time and Learn More

- Paul quotes from Malachi 1: ROMANS 9:13
- Image of the marriage covenant: EPHESIANS 5:21–33
- The coming of the forerunner: MATTHEW 3:1–12
- Jesus references Malachi: MATTHEW 17:10–13

# MATTHEW

*Jesus is the glorious fulfillment of every Old Testament prophecy.*

## SETTING THE STAGE

Matthew, the first book in the New Testament and the first of the four Gospels, introduces us to Jesus, the answer to Israel's prayers and the central figure in God's unfolding redemptive plan for the world.

The book is a rich, eyewitness account of the life, death, and resurrection of Christ. While the book is technically anonymous, it is believed to have been written by Matthew (also called Levi), a former tax collector and disciple of Jesus.

The book emphasizes Jesus as the long-awaited Messiah and King.

The opening chapters contain a genealogy that establishes Jesus' royal lineage by connecting Him to David. This genealogy also connects Jesus to Abraham, fulfilling the Messianic prophecy that through Abraham, all the world would be blessed (Genesis 12:3; 18:18).

The book highlights Jesus' teachings, notably His Sermon on the Mount (chapters 5–7). With its entirely unique perspective on Christian living, Jesus' profound message turns the world on its head.

But even as Jesus' work—including His miracles and healings—affirms His divine authority, strong opposition from religious leaders culminates in His crucifixion.

Matthew concludes with Jesus triumphing over death through His resurrection and then giving the Great Commission, where He instructs His disciples to go out into the world and make disciples of every nation.

## GOOD TO KNOW

The first Gospel's author is not stated but traditionally attributed to Matthew, a tax collector (9:9) also known as Levi (Mark 2:14). Matthew was written around AD 70, when Romans destroyed the temple in Jerusalem.

*Good things come to those who wait—on the Lord, that is.*

## MATTHEW 1

The book begins with the genealogy of Jesus, tracing His lineage from Abraham through David to Joseph. After highlighting key figures in Israel's history, it tells how the angel visits Joseph, confirming Mary's conception by the Holy Spirit and giving Him the name *Jesus*. Jesus is no ordinary person. He is the God of Israel in human flesh.

*Why is it helpful when studying scripture to have access to this genealogy?*

## MATTHEW 2

The long-awaited Messiah is born in Bethlehem. Wise men, guided by a star, come to worship Him. The family flees to Egypt, fulfilling the prophecy in Hosea 11:1. After they leave, King Herod orders the brutal massacre of all male children in Bethlehem two years old and younger as an attempt to kill Jesus.

*Why did King Herod react so violently to the news of Jesus' birth?*

## MATTHEW 3

Just as heralds made public announcements for kings at this time in history, so John the Baptist heralds Jesus as the rightful King of the Jews. John preaches repentance and baptizes people in the Jordan River. He declares truth about Jesus and warns of judgment. Jesus is baptized by John, signaling the start of His earthly ministry.

*Why do you believe Jesus insisted on being baptized?*

## MATTHEW 4

Jesus faces temptation in the wilderness, where Satan makes multiple (unsuccessful) attempts to deceive Him. Jesus consistently responds with scripture, affirming His commitment to obey God completely. John the Baptist has been arrested for confronting evil (Matthew 14:3–4), and Jesus begins His ministry in Galilee, preaching repentance, healing diseases, and calling disciples.

*Can you recall a time when you relied on scripture to resist temptation?*

### Take Your Time and Learn More

- Prophecy about Immanuel: ISAIAH 7:14
- Prophecy about Bethlehem: MICAH 5:2
- Prophecy about John the Baptist: ISAIAH 40:3
- Man does not live by bread alone: DEUTERONOMY 8:3

*The Bible is countercultural, and so is Bible study.*
*There's no need to rush through this.*

## MATTHEW 5

Jesus begins His famous Sermon on the Mount, explaining what it looks like to follow Him. He discusses topics such as anger, adultery, divorce, retaliation, and love for enemies—all new information for these eager listeners. He clarifies that He hasn't come to destroy the law of Moses but to fulfill it.

*Why do you think it's important that Jesus clearly says He didn't come to destroy the law?*

## MATTHEW 6

Jesus teaches on the subject of righteousness practiced in the context of worship. He talks about righteous deeds (such as giving, praying, and fasting), explaining that these actions are only righteous if done for God and His approval. Doing these deeds to receive recognition from people makes them self-righteous and not at all glorifying to God.

*Why is it so tempting to prioritize human approval over God's approval?*

## MATTHEW 7

Jesus continues teaching His Sermon on the Mount, covering topics such as judgment, discernment, prayer, and obedience. He emphasizes the need for authentic faith, warning against hypocrisy and false teaching while urging listeners to build their lives on the foundation of His words.

*Matthew 7:1 is easily one of the most misinterpreted verses in the Bible. What are the potential consequences of misunderstanding this verse?*

## MATTHEW 8

After concluding Jesus' Sermon on the Mount, Matthew records nine stories in which Jesus impacts real people living their real lives. In this chapter, Jesus heals a leper, a centurion's servant, and Peter's mother-in-law, revealing both His compassion and power.

*Huge crowds followed Jesus, but mostly for His miracles more than His message. How does this compare with today?*

## Take Your Time and Learn More

- Sermon on the Mount: LUKE 6:20–26
- Instruction on prayer: LUKE 11:1–13
- Self-awareness and humility: LUKE 6:37–42
- Jesus heals a centurion's servant: LUKE 7:1–10

*God speaks in the quiet moments.*
*Approach His Word with calm expectation.*

## MATTHEW 9

Jesus goes to Capernaum, a city of Galilee, where He interacts with several individuals. He heals a paralytic man, a woman who has been bleeding for twelve years, and the dead daughter of a synagogue ruler. He also heals two blind men and frees a demon-possessed man, demonstrating compassion and the power to make the broken whole.

*What can you learn about Jesus just by observing the people He chooses to heal?*

## MATTHEW 10

Jesus commissions His twelve disciples, empowering them to preach, heal, and cast out demons. He instructs them to go "to the lost sheep of the house of Israel" (10:6), warning that because Israel's leaders stand to lose so much if people follow Jesus, the disciples should be ready for persecution.

*For the disciples, what is the cost—and compensation—for following Jesus?*

## MATTHEW 11

Still in prison, John the Baptist wants to verify that Jesus is the long-awaited Messiah, so he sends his messengers with questions. Instead of replying in anger, Jesus assures John with the miracles He's performing. John's messengers return with confidence that John's ministry hasn't been in vain. (In Luke 7:28, Jesus calls John the greatest of the prophets.)

*How does it encourage you to see how Jesus responded to John's questions?*

## MATTHEW 12

Jesus challenges the religious leaders' understanding of the Sabbath. He defends His disciples' actions, heals a man's withered hand, and addresses accusations that He's being empowered by demons. Amid escalating conflicts with the religious leaders, Jesus continues teaching truth.

*Given that Jewish religious law devotes twenty-four chapters to Sabbath regulations, how is Jesus' message of "Come to Me. . .and I will give you rest" (11:28) revolutionary?*

## Take Your Time and Learn More

- Jesus heals a paralyzed man: MARK 2:1–12
- Jesus commissions disciples: LUKE 10:1–12
- Jesus affirms John the Baptist: LUKE 7:18–23
- Lord of the Sabbath: MARK 2:23–28

*Before you read, pray. Ask God to*
*speak His truth to your spirit.*

## MATTHEW 13

This chapter contains many of Jesus' parables about the Kingdom—including the sower, the mustard seed, the pearl, and the hidden treasure. Each parable illustrates important aspects of the kingdom of God. Some listeners accept Jesus wholeheartedly; others reject Him outright.

*What do the responses Jesus received during*
*His life say about the effect of teaching?*

## MATTHEW 14

Several important events take place in this chapter: John the Baptist is executed at Herod's birthday celebration. Jesus feeds the five thousand with five loaves of bread and two fish. Jesus walks on water during a storm—inviting Peter to join Him. And Jesus continues healing the sick.

*Jesus was deeply impacted by the news of John the Baptist's death*
*(14:13). What insight does this provide about His relational nature?*

## MATTHEW 15

Jesus confronts the religious elite over their hypocritical adherence to traditions and their neglect of God's commands. The heart, He says, is far more important than external rituals. He also heals a Canaanite woman's daughter, demonstrating that faith knows no cultural boundaries.

*The Pharisees mistakenly equated their traditions with God's*
*Word. How are we tempted to do the same?*

## MATTHEW 16

Jesus teaches His disciples more about His identity, asking them, "Who do you say that I am?" Peter answers, "You are the Christ, the Son of the living God," and Jesus says He will build His church on this correct answer (16:15-19). Jesus foretells His death and resurrection, rebuking Peter when he denies this prediction.

*Following Jesus means denying ourselves just as He*
*did (16:24). What does this look like today?*

## Take Your Time and Learn More

- Teaching of parables: PSALM 78:2
- Feeding of the five thousand: MARK 6:31–44
- Hypocrisy rebuked: ISAIAH 29:13
- Son of Man: DANIEL 7:13–14

*Don't hurry, don't worry. God's Word provides
everything you need for living well.*

## MATTHEW 17

This chapter records Jesus' transfiguration on a mountain, where He reveals His divine glory to Peter, James, and John. Again, Jesus predicts His death and resurrection. He heals a boy from demonic possession and performs a miracle by helping Peter pay the temple tax with a coin found in a fish's mouth.

*Why wouldn't Jesus simply produce a coin for the tax? Why send Peter out?*

## MATTHEW 18

Jesus continues teaching truths that turn culture's value system on its head, beginning with the concept that childlike faith is necessary to enter heaven. He then teaches His disciples more about humility and forgiveness, sharing His process for how to handle conflict in the church. Jesus' followers should resolve disputes in a way that honors God and preserves unity.

*Do you typically approach conflict resolution biblically? Why or why not?*

## MATTHEW 19

Jesus addresses the Pharisees on the topic of divorce. He emphasizes the sanctity of marriage, condemning divorce except in cases of adultery. His disciples rebuke people for bringing their children to Jesus, but He overrules them, inviting the children closer. He talks to a wealthy young man about gaining true wealth by giving it away.

*Do you believe wealth is a stumbling block to the
gospel in Western culture? Why or why not?*

## MATTHEW 20

Jesus continues teaching, interacting, and healing as He moves closer to Jerusalem. He shares a parable about laborers in a vineyard; tells His disciples for the third time that He will die and resurrect; and interacts with the mother of James and John, who seeks promotion for her sons. Jesus says that to be great is to become a servant.

*How does modern culture contradict Jesus' invitation to be a servant?*

### Take Your Time and Learn More

- The Transfiguration: MARK 9:2–8
- Jesus and children: MARK 10:13–15
- God's original design for marriage: GENESIS 2:18–25
- True greatness and servanthood: MARK 10:35–45

*God loves it when you read and study His Word.*

## MATTHEW 21

Jesus fulfills a prophecy (Zechariah 9:9) by triumphantly entering Jerusalem on a donkey as crowds gather to welcome Him with shouts of "Hosanna!" and lay palm branches before Him. He enters the temple, driving out merchants who are profiting from the spiritual needs of people. Jewish leaders question Him, but Jesus challenges their authority and exposes their hypocrisy.

*What do the Jewish leaders teach us about religious knowledge that lacks genuine faith?*

## MATTHEW 22

Jesus shares the parable of the wedding feast, illustrating salvation by grace. Israel's religious leaders are offended, so they conspire to trap Him. Instead, Jesus responds with wisdom, answering their questions about the greatest commandments: love God and neighbor. He asks challenging questions of His own, and the outraged leaders determine to kill Him.

*What do you observe about the way Jesus interacts with His enemies?*

## MATTHEW 23

This chapter is almost entirely Jesus' words. He delivers scathing rebukes to the religious leaders who have failed in leading the people. He criticizes how they outwardly display piety while neglecting justice, mercy, and faithfulness. The people, He warns, should not imitate their hypocrisy. After He laments over Jerusalem, Jesus is finished speaking publicly.

*Jesus says the Pharisees are driven by wrong motivations. How often do you examine your motives?*

## MATTHEW 24

Jesus leaves the temple with His disciples and heads toward the Mount of Olives, where He begins His famous Olivet Discourse. Sitting on the mount—the temple in view—He answers the disciples' questions and prophesies about the end times, urging the disciples to remain faithful.

*What does it look like to stay faithful to God on a daily basis?*

## Take Your Time and Learn More

- Triumphal entry: ZECHARIAH 9:9
- Greatest commandment: DEUTERONOMY 6:4–5
- Rebuke for religious hypocrisy: JEREMIAH 7:1–15
- End-times outline: DANIEL 9:24–27

*Reading the Bible isn't a race. Let the pages unfold at a pace that allows your spirit to breathe.*

## MATTHEW 25

This is one of the few chapters in the Bible containing only Jesus' words. Continuing His Olivet Discourse, Jesus shares two parables to teach about being prepared: the parable of the ten virgins and the parable of the talents. He emphasizes that when He has gone away, the disciples should live ready for His return.

*How does considering Christ's return offer hope in the midst of challenges?*

## MATTHEW 26

Jesus celebrates Passover, reveals that one of His disciples will betray Him, and institutes the Lord's Supper. Moving to the Garden of Gethsemane, Jesus asks His disciples to watch while He prays. He returns three times to find them sleeping. Jesus is betrayed by Judas, arrested, and brought to trial. Peter denies Him.

*Jesus' whole life has built toward this moment. Why did He allow it?*

## MATTHEW 27

Jesus stands trial before Pilate, who finds no fault in Him yet yields to the crowd's demand for crucifixion. Jesus is mocked, beaten, and led to Golgotha, where He is crucified between two criminals. Darkness descends, and Jesus cries out to God before dying. The earth shakes. The temple curtain is torn in two. Jesus is buried in a tomb, and guards are placed to secure it.

*Was Jesus' death a failure? Why or why not?*

## MATTHEW 28

Two women visit Jesus' tomb, but it's empty. Jesus is risen! Filled with fear and joy, these two faithful followers run to tell the disciples. Meanwhile, the chief priests bribe the guards of Jesus' tomb to say His body had been stolen. Jesus appears to His disciples and commissions them to make disciples of all nations.

*In what specific ways does Jesus' resurrection shape your view of life, death, and eternity?*

## Take Your Time and Learn More

- Faithful stewardship and accountability: LUKE 19:11–27
- The Lord's Supper instituted: MARK 14:22–25
- Isaiah's prophecy of Jesus' death: ISAIAH 53
- Resurrection of Jesus: MARK 16:1–8

# MARK

*Jesus did not come to meet expectations, but to meet needs.*

## SETTING THE STAGE

The book of Mark is the shortest of the four Gospels, providing a fast-paced, first-person account of Jesus' life, death, and resurrection from the perspective of John Mark.

The book opens with a quick beginning sentence and then quotes the ancient prophet Isaiah to introduce the ministry of the famous forerunner to Christ—John the Baptist. John prepares the way for Jesus, identifies Him as Messiah, and calls people to repent. He helps set the stage for the unfolding events of Jesus' ministry, death, and resurrection.

The book of Mark is filled with stories that show Jesus' power to heal the sick, broken, and oppressed. (One example: Jesus heals a leper in Mark 1:40–45). Most profoundly, though, Mark shows Jesus doing something the Jewish people believe only God in heaven can do: forgive people of sin.

Mark's writing gives us a glimpse of Jesus as both powerful and compassionate in His ministry on earth. Caring for the marginalized and suffering, Jesus uses His divine power to bring transformation and healing.

As in the book of Matthew, the book of Mark concludes with Jesus' death and resurrection, as well as Christ's Great Commission to the remaining eleven disciples.

## GOOD TO KNOW

The second Gospel's author is not stated but traditionally attributed to John Mark, a missionary companion of Paul and Barnabas (Acts 12:25) and an associate of the apostle Peter (1 Peter 5:13). Probably written in the AD 60s, during the Roman persecution of Christians.

*The greatest truths in scripture are often revealed in the unhurried moments.*

## MARK 1

Jesus is baptized by John the Baptist. He begins His public ministry and calls His first disciples, who immediately follow Him. He performs miracles, healing the sick and casting out demons. News of Jesus' teachings and miracles spreads like wildfire throughout the region.

*God says He is "well pleased" with Jesus. . .and then Jesus is immediately tested in the wilderness. How can this challenge assumptions about trials as punishment for sin?*

## MARK 2

Mark records four stories that show Jesus' absolute authority: He heals a paralyzed man, demonstrating His authority over sin. He calls Levi the tax collector to follow Him, showing His authority over public opinion. He tells a parable about wineskins, illustrating His authority over tradition, and He confronts religious leaders, illustrating His authority over the Sabbath.

*Why do you think the religious leaders opposed Jesus so vehemently?*

## MARK 3

Jesus heals a man with a withered hand on the Sabbath, angering the Pharisees, who already want to destroy Him. Jesus appoints twelve apostles, empowering them to preach, cast out demons, and heal the sick. Jesus faces accusations of being demon possessed; He responds by warning against blaspheming the Holy Spirit.

*How do you distinguish between what is right in God's eyes versus what is socially acceptable?*

## MARK 4

Jesus teaches parables, communicating spiritual truths with earthly examples. He tells the parables of the sower, the candle, the growing seed, and the mustard seed. He then calms a storm, demonstrating His power over nature. He challenges His disciples to trust Him in every situation.

*Why do you think the crowds seem to prefer Jesus' miracles over His teaching?*

## Take Your Time and Learn More

- Ministry of John the Baptist: ISAIAH 40:3–5
- Jesus heals the paralyzed man: LUKE 5:17–26
- Jesus heals a man with a withered hand: MATTHEW 12:9–14
- The parable of the sower: MATTHEW 13:1–23

*Bible study is truly a lifelong journey.*
*Relax and enjoy the trip.*

## MARK 5

Jesus and His disciples encounter a demon-possessed man on the eastern shore of the Sea of Galilee. Jesus casts the demons into pigs, and the local people are so distraught that they beg Jesus to leave immediately. Jesus raises Jairus's daughter from the dead and heals a woman with a bleeding issue. Word about Jesus continues to spread.

*Jesus' most common type of miracle is healing. What might this indicate?*

## MARK 6

Jesus takes His disciples to His hometown of Nazareth, where He sends them out to preach and heal in His name. Jesus famously uses a boy's lunch—five loaves and two fish—to feed thousands. Jesus then walks on water and heals many people in Gennesaret.

*Do you ever catch yourself wanting what God can do more*
*than you want God Himself? What is the remedy?*

## MARK 7

Jesus confronts the Pharisees and scribes—the religious elite—for prioritizing human traditions over God's commands. He exposes their hypocrisy, criticizing how they neglect the heart (where sin originates) while adhering to external rituals. He heals a Gentile woman's daughter and restores a man's hearing and speech. Jesus continues calling people to genuine faith.

*Why is it typically easier to fix external behavior rather than internal motives?*

## MARK 8

Again, Jesus feeds a multitude, publicly disagrees with the Pharisees, and heals a blind man. When Jesus questions His disciples about His identity, Peter confesses Him as the Christ. Jesus predicts His death and resurrection, challenging His disciples' expectations of a worldly Messiah. He then teaches about the cost of discipleship.

*Have you ever been torn between worldly*
*success and spiritual growth? How did that go?*

## Take Your Time and Learn More

- Jesus drives out demons: LUKE 8:26–39
- Feeding of the five thousand: MATTHEW 14:13–21
- Diagnosis of the heart: MATTHEW 15:1–20
- Peter confesses Christ: MATTHEW 16:13–20

*Try to forget the demands of life for a while.
You're spending quality time with God.*

## MARK 9

Jesus takes Peter, James, and John on a high mountain to reveal His divine glory. (This is called His "Transfiguration.") Jesus becomes so radiant that His disciples are terrified. Once they come down from the mountain, Jesus heals a demon-possessed boy. He then predicts His death and resurrection, warns against causing others to stumble, and urges people to repent.

*Jesus teaches that humility is the secret to greatness.
Why is it undervalued in secular culture?*

## MARK 10

Jesus teaches on marriage, divorce, and the value of children. He encounters a rich young ruler, challenging him to sell his possessions and follow Him. Jesus warns of how hard it is for the wealthy to enter the kingdom. James and John request positions of honor, but Jesus teaches about servant leadership. He heals blind Bartimaeus.

*How can wealth be a stumbling block to knowing and following Jesus?*

## MARK 11

Jesus makes His triumphant royal entry into Jerusalem for Passover, fulfilling prophecy. He curses a fig tree for bearing no fruit and clears the temple of money changers, condemning their exploitation of worshippers. He outwits the religious leaders with His questions, teaches on faith and forgiveness, and emphasizes the power of prayer.

*Do you believe religious leaders can still exploit worshippers today? If so, how?*

## MARK 12

Jesus takes one last public opportunity to highlight the problems with Jewish religious leaders. Through a parable about a vineyard owner and a series of debates with the religious elite, He identifies ways they use religion to gather honor for themselves. These are the greatest commandments: love God and neighbor. Jesus praises the widow's sacrificial offering.

*How is the widow's offering of two coins meant to
challenge our understanding of generosity?*

## *Take Your Time and Learn More*

- The Transfiguration: MATTHEW 17:1–13
- God's original intention for marriage: GENESIS 2:24
- Jesus' triumphal entry: ZECHARIAH 9:9
- The stone that the builders rejected: PSALM 118:22–23

*Good things come to those who wait—on the Lord, that is.*

## MARK 13

Jesus' teaching in this chapter is called the Olivet Discourse because He takes His disciples up to the Mount of Olives to talk. He predicts the temple's destruction, warns of false messiahs, explains future events, and emphasizes the certainty of His return. He cautions the disciples against becoming spiritually lazy when He's gone.

*What are practical ways to overcome spiritual laziness and press forward in pursuit of God?*

## MARK 14

Jesus shares a final Passover meal with His disciples. But He takes the bread and cup and gives them new meaning, instituting the Lord's Supper. Jesus and His disciples go to Gethsemane, where Jesus prays in anguish and accepts God's will. Judas betrays Jesus, leading to His arrest, and Peter denies Jesus three times, as predicted.

*How does Jesus' prayer in Gethsemane exemplify how we should approach God during trials?*

## MARK 15

After three years in public ministry, Jesus is brought before Pilate, who finds no fault in Him. But because Pilate cowardly yields to the crowds' demands, Jesus is mocked, beaten, and crucified. Darkness covers the land. Jesus cries out to God and dies. The temple curtain is torn, and Jesus is buried in a borrowed tomb.

*What do you think causes the centurion near the cross to say Jesus is God's Son (15:39)?*

## MARK 16

When the women arrive on Sunday morning, they find the stone rolled away and the tomb empty. Jesus has risen, just as He said! An angel tells them about Jesus' resurrection, and the women leave to tell the disciples. The disciples will now carry on Jesus' work after His resurrection and ascension.

*Why is it helpful that multiple writers of scripture include the same events from Jesus' life?*

## *Take Your Time and Learn More*

- The Olivet Discourse: Matthew 24
- The Lord's Supper instituted: Matthew 26:17–30
- Isaiah's prophecy of Jesus' death: Isaiah 53
- Women find the tomb empty: Matthew 28:1–10

# LUKE

*In God and the gospel, all power structures are
reversed and everyone is welcome.*

## SETTING THE STAGE

The Gospel of Luke, written by the physician Luke, gives us a comprehensive and distinctive account of Jesus' life, death, and resurrection.

Written with meticulous detail and an eye for historical accuracy, the book includes a list of chronological stories, parables, and teaching not found in the other Gospels—contributing to a fuller view of Jesus' mission.

But Luke's goal isn't simply to record Jesus' life as ancient history. He wants us to see the Messiah as the fulfillment of a promise. And like the book of Mark, Luke shows Jesus as a tender and compassionate Savior who's deeply concerned for the marginalized, poor, and outcasts.

Since Luke emphasizes themes of mercy, forgiveness, and compassion, his Gospel is sometimes called "the Gospel of compassion." In it, we see Jesus as a gracious healer and a friend of sinners.

Unique to this book, we meet the good Samaritan and the prodigal son—symbolizing God's relentless love and call to repentance. Also, unique to this time in history, Luke highlights the role of several women—including Mary and Martha, a poor widow, and the women at Jesus' tomb.

Consistent with the previous two Gospels, Luke's final chapters record Jesus' crucifixion, resurrection, and commission to go make disciples of all the nations.

## GOOD TO KNOW

The third Gospel's author is not stated but traditionally attributed to Luke, a Gentile physician (Colossians 4:14) and a missionary companion of the apostle Paul (2 Timothy 4:11). Possibly written in the AD 70s-80s, as the gospel was spreading throughout the Roman Empire.

*The Bible is countercultural, and so is Bible study.*
*There's no need to rush through this.*

## LUKE 1

The angel Gabriel appears to Zechariah, announcing that his wife, Elizabeth, will conceive a son despite her old age. Gabriel also visits Mary, revealing she will conceive and bear the Messiah. Mary visits Elizabeth, and her baby leaps in her womb. Mary sings the Magnificat, praising God's mercy. John the Baptist is born.

*What does Mary's willingness to accept the angel's message say about her faith?*

## LUKE 2

Caesar Augustus announces a census, leading Joseph and Mary to visit Bethlehem. There, Jesus is born. Angels announce His birth to nearby shepherds, who visit the newborn Messiah. Jesus is circumcised and presented at the temple, where Simeon and Anna recognize Him as the promised Savior. Jesus grows and, at age twelve, visits the temple in Jerusalem.

*Why is it significant that shepherds are the first to hear the news of Jesus' birth?*

## LUKE 3

Alternating between the stories of Jesus and John the Baptist, Luke returns to writing about John the Baptist in this chapter. John prepares the way for Jesus (Malachi 3:1; Isaiah 40:3) by predicting the Lord's arrival and preaching repentance. John baptizes Jesus. Luke then provides a detailed genealogy of Jesus.

*Why do you think Luke chose to trace Jesus' genealogy all the way back to Adam?*

## LUKE 4

Jesus is led by the Spirit into the wilderness, where He is tempted by the devil. He resists, however, with scripture. He then begins His ministry in Galilee, teaching in synagogues and creating a stir. He casts out demons and heals the sick. He preaches in Capernaum and performs miracles. The people reject Him in His hometown.

*How does Jesus' response to rejection encourage you to persevere no matter what?*

### Take Your Time and Learn More

- Song of praise: 1 SAMUEL 2:1–10
- Isaiah's prophecy of a special child: ISAIAH 9:6–7
- Prophecy of John the Baptist's duties: ISAIAH 40:3–5
- Jesus refers to Isaiah: ISAIAH 61:1–2

*God speaks in the quiet moments.*
*Approach His Word with calm expectation.*

## LUKE 5

Jesus calls His first disciples—Simon Peter, James, and John—after performing a miraculous catch of fish. Jesus then cleanses a man with leprosy, heals a paralyzed man lowered through the roof by his friends, and challenges religious leaders' objections. Amid criticism for associating with sinners, Jesus declares His mission to call sinners to repentance.

*On whom do you think Jesus had more compassion—*
*sinners or religious hypocrites? Why?*

## LUKE 6

After spending a full night praying, Jesus calls His final seven apostles, including Judas Iscariot. Jesus challenges societal norms with countercultural teachings known as "the Beatitudes." He preaches love for enemies, non-retaliation, and generosity. He emphasizes the importance of internal character over external appearances and warns against hypocrisy.

*Why do you think Jesus treated Judas Iscariot kindly, even knowing he was a betrayer?*

## LUKE 7

Jesus heals a centurion's servant from a distance, commending the centurion's faith. To the amazement of the crowd, Jesus raises a widow's son from the dead. John the Baptist sends messengers to inquire about Jesus' identity, and Jesus responds by commending John's role in preparing the way. Jesus continues contrasting religious hypocrisy with true humility.

*Why is religious hypocrisy so offensive to Jesus?*

## LUKE 8

Jesus continues traveling and teaching. He tells parables to communicate important spiritual truths, and He performs miracles to demonstrate His divine power. He heals a demon-possessed man and a woman with a bleeding issue, and He raises a synagogue leader's daughter from the dead. He consistently emphasizes the need for genuine faith.

*Why do you think Jesus asked who touched His garment*
*(8:45), considering He is all-knowing?*

## Take Your Time and Learn More

- Calling of Matthew: MATTHEW 9:9–13
- Sermon on the Mount: MATTHEW 5–7
- Jesus heals the centurion's servant: MATTHEW 8:5–13
- Parables: MARK 4:1–34

*Before you read, pray. Ask God to*
*speak His truth to your spirit.*

## LUKE 9

Jesus commissions His twelve apostles, empowering them to preach, heal, and cast out demons. He feeds the five thousand, predicts His death and resurrection, and teaches about the cost of discipleship. He is transfigured in the presence of Peter, James, and John, revealing His glory. He rebukes religious leaders and challenges His followers.

*In general, do you think today's Christian community values and practices self-denial?*

## LUKE 10

Jesus commissions seventy-two of His followers to go ahead of Him to every town and village, preaching what they've learned from Him. The seventy-two followers return "with joy" (10:17), reporting successful interactions. Jesus teaches the parable of the good Samaritan (highlighting love for neighbors), then visits Martha and Mary (emphasizing eternal priorities).

*How do you prioritize personal worship in a world full of distractions?*

## LUKE 11

Jesus teaches His disciples how to pray, demonstrating persistent prayer that trusts God's provision. He rebukes the Pharisees for their hypocrisy and lack of inner purity, and He warns against rejecting the truth. He continues teaching in parables—all while moving toward Jerusalem. . .and the culmination of His ministry on earth.

*How do you cultivate a consistent and meaningful prayer*
*life in the midst of your busy schedule?*

## LUKE 12

Jesus warns His disciples and the crowds against hypocrisy, fear, and greed—urging people to trust God's provision and prioritize eternal treasure. Through parables, He teaches about the folly of materialism, and He reassures His disciples that God's work is worth the sacrifice. He urges His disciples to be vigilant and ready for His return.

*How can material possessions serve as temporary*
*substitutes for deeper spiritual needs?*

## Take Your Time and Learn More

- Feeding of the five thousand: MATTHEW 14:13–21
- Greatest commandment: MATTHEW 22:34–40
- Instruction about prayer: MATTHEW 6:5–15
- Trust in God's provision: MATTHEW 6:25–34

*Don't hurry, don't worry. God's Word provides*
*everything you need for living well.*

## LUKE 13

Jesus urges people to repent. Along with teaching other parables, He uses the parable of the fig tree to emphasize the importance of bearing fruit. He heals a disabled woman on the Sabbath, illustrating His compassion and authority, and He laments Jerusalem's ongoing rejection of Him.

*How does Jesus' lament over Jerusalem reflect His heart for the lost?*

## LUKE 14

Jesus shares a series of parables, illustrating who will enter the kingdom of God. He then stresses the cost of discipleship, urging followers to carefully consider whether they're ready to forsake everything. He compares this commitment to counting the cost before building a tower or going to war. He emphasizes the demands and rewards of true discipleship.

*When sharing the gospel, why is it easy to overlook the cost of following Jesus?*

## LUKE 15

Jesus shares three parables (the lost sheep, the lost coin, and the lost son) about the joy of finding what was lost. These stories all illustrate God's relentless pursuit of sinners and the celebration in heaven over their repentance. This chapter is packed with illustrations of God's great love and extravagant mercy.

*How have you witnessed God's extravagant mercy in your own life?*

## LUKE 16

Jesus continues teaching about choices that honor God. He talks about the proper use of wealth, warning against serving money over God. He tells the story of the rich man and Lazarus, contrasting earthly wealth and heavenly reward. He urges listeners to avoid the pitfalls of greed and self-indulgence, instead prioritizing faithful stewardship.

*In what specific ways can you be faithful to God in the small things this week?*

## Take Your Time and Learn More

- True and false faith: MATTHEW 7:13–23
- Parable of the wedding feast: MATTHEW 22:1–14
- Parable of the lost sheep: MATTHEW 18:10–14
- Faithful stewardship: MATTHEW 6:19–24

*God loves it when you read and study His Word.*

## LUKE 17

Jesus teaches about forgiveness, faith, and humility. He warns against causing others to stumble and calls for a radical response to sin. He heals ten lepers—highlighting the importance of gratitude and faith. He addresses His second coming and the need for readiness. He compares the last days to the days of Noah and Lot, urging vigilance and faithfulness.

*What is the relationship between gratitude and forgiveness? How are they insepurubly linked?*

## LUKE 18

This chapter is a study in contrasts. Jesus tells the parable of the persistent widow and the unjust judge. Next, He contrasts the prayers of the Pharisee and the tax collector. Lastly, He contrasts earthly wealth and heavenly reward. Jesus blesses little children, predicts His own death and resurrection, and heals blind Bartimaeus.

*Why do you think children matter so much to Jesus?*

## LUKE 19

Jesus encounters Zacchaeus, a tax collector, and changes His life. He tells the parable of the ten pounds, explaining the importance of good stewardship. Jesus then triumphantly enters Jerusalem, where He's welcomed as a king. Still, He laments Jerusalem's impending destruction. He cleanses the temple and teaches daily. The religious leaders' opposition escalates.

*How have you experienced God's love in unexpected or transformative ways like Zacchaeus did?*

## LUKE 20

The religious leaders question Jesus' authority, generating a series of debates. The leaders attempt to trap Jesus with questions about paying taxes on earth and marrying in eternity, but Jesus always answers wisely. He warns against hypocrisy and condemns the scribes' pride.

*How does pride impact our relationship with God and our experience of His grace, love, and forgiveness?*

## *Take Your Time and Learn More*

- Jesus warns against false prophets: MATTHEW 24:23–28
  - Teaching on humility: MATTHEW 18:1–14
  - Triumphal entry of Jesus: MARK 11:1–11
- Jesus' authority is questioned: MATTHEW 21:23–27

*Reading the Bible isn't a race. Let the pages unfold
at a pace that allows your spirit to breathe.*

## LUKE 21

Jesus praises the poor widow's offering and contrasts her genuine devotion with the ostentatious displays of wealth by others. Jesus then gives His Olivet Discourse, teaching on the destruction of Jerusalem and the end times. He speaks of persecution and betrayal, ultimately encouraging His disciples to be ready for His return.

*Jesus warned that following Him will not be easy.
So why are believers still surprised by hardship?*

## LUKE 22

Jesus celebrates the Passover meal with His disciples, taking the bread and cup and instituting the Lord's Supper. He predicts Peter's denial and instructs His disciples to prepare for persecution. In the Garden of Gethsemane, He prays fervently, ultimately submitting to God's will. Judas betrays Jesus with a kiss, leading to His arrest and trial.

*Why was Judas's choice to betray Jesus with a kiss especially offensive?*

## LUKE 23

Jesus stands before Pilate and Herod, but neither man finds Him guilty. The crowds demand His crucifixion, so Jesus is mocked, beaten, and led to Golgotha. There He is crucified between two criminals. Jesus forgives His executioners and promises Paradise to the repentant thief. Jesus dies, and the temple curtain tears, signifying access to God through Jesus.

*What is the significance of Jesus dying on the day after Passover?*

## LUKE 24

On Sunday morning, women find the tomb empty and encounter angels who announce Jesus' resurrection. Meanwhile, Jesus suddenly appears, incognito, beside two of His disciples as they walk to Emmaus. They don't recognize Him until later. Jesus appears to His disciples and tells them to preach repentance and forgiveness. The book ends with the disciples worshipping God.

*How does Jesus' life inspire you to worship and praise Him?*

### Take Your Time and Learn More

- Olivet Discourse: MATTHEW 24:1–35
- The Lord's Supper instituted: MATTHEW 26:17–30
- Trial and crucifixion of Jesus: MATTHEW 27:1–56
- Jesus' resurrection: MARK 16:1–20

# JOHN

*Jesus, the Son of God, came to bring
eternal life to those who believe.*

## SETTING THE STAGE

The book of John is the fourth and final Gospel, written by the apostle John. It offers a distinctly theological perspective on Jesus' life, death, and resurrection. Unlike the other three Gospels, John focuses on the divinity of Jesus and His identity as the eternal Word made flesh.

Throughout the book—in addition to recording Christ's many miracles and teachings—John presents his readers with a list of Jesus' "I am" sayings: I am the bread of life (6:35); the light of the world (8:12); the door (10:9); the good shepherd (10:11); the resurrection and the life (11:25); the way, the truth, and the life (14:6); and the vine (15:5). More than simple symbolism, these names communicate the truth that in Jesus we find everything we need.

Near the end of his book, John clearly states his reason for writing it: "But these are written that you might believe that Jesus is the Christ, the Son of God, and that believing you might have life through His name" (20:31).

Ultimately, John wants his readers to move beyond a superficial understanding of Jesus and embrace a deep, personal, and transformative relationship with Him—one that will last for all of life and eternity.

## GOOD TO KNOW

The fourth Gospel's author is not stated but traditionally attributed to John, "that disciple whom Jesus loved" (John 21:7), brother of James and son of Zebedee (Matthew 4:21). Written around the AD 90s, as the last of the Gospels.

*The greatest truths in scripture are often
revealed in the unhurried moments.*

## JOHN 1

John introduces Jesus as the eternal Word—existing before creation—and the source of all life and light. He then segues to the ministry of John the Baptist, testifying to Jesus' identity as the Messiah, the Lamb of God who takes away sin. By the end of this chapter, Jesus has called His first five disciples.

*Why do you think the disciples are willing to follow
despite knowing so little about Jesus?*

## JOHN 2

John records two major events in Jesus' life. First, he writes about Jesus' first public miracle at a wedding in Cana, where He turns water into wine to reveal His power and authority. Second, he writes about Jesus driving out the money changers from the temple—rebuking their misuse of God's house for profit.

*Why is misusing God's house—and specifically worship—for profit so offensive?*

## JOHN 3

In this chapter, Jesus speaks with Nicodemus, a Pharisee who seeks to understand spiritual matters, teaching about being born again. Also, the last testimony of John the Baptist is given, reaffirming Jesus' authority. This chapter contains the most famous Bible verse: John 3:16.

*John the Baptist willingly becomes lesser so that Jesus will
become greater. How can you guard against jealousy?*

## JOHN 4

John records Jesus' gracious encounter with the Samaritan woman at the well. Jesus breaks social barriers by speaking to her, offering living water that symbolizes eternal life. The woman believes and shares her testimony, leading many Samaritans to faith. Jesus then heals an official's son, demonstrating His power to bring healing.

*Who in your life needs to hear your testimony of faith?*

### Take Your Time and Learn More

- In the beginning: GENESIS 1:1–5
- Cleansing of the temple: MATTHEW 21:12–13
- Cleansed and made new: EZEKIEL 36:25–27
- Fountain of living water: JEREMIAH 2:13

*Bible study is truly a lifelong journey.*
*Relax and enjoy the trip.*

## JOHN 5

Most of this chapter is Jesus' spoken words. He confronts His enemies and responds to His critics. He heals a man by the Pool of Bethesda on the Sabbath, stirring controversy among the Jewish leaders. He claims authority as the Son of God and teaches about the resurrection of the dead.

*Why do the Jewish leaders, who have studied the scriptures so diligently, still miss who Jesus is?*

## JOHN 6

John records several important moments in this chapter. He narrates Jesus' feeding of the five thousand and His walking on water, demonstrating His power over nature and provision for physical and spiritual needs. John shows many people struggling with Jesus' teachings and abandoning Him. When Jesus affirms His divinity, people must believe or reject.

*What do most crowds—then and now—want from Jesus?*

## JOHN 7

Jesus begins the end of His public ministry by going to Jerusalem and teaching in the temple. He provokes debate about His identity and authority. Conflict arises among the crowds regarding His origin and message, and the Pharisees send officers to arrest Him. However, they end up captivated by His words. Nicodemus defends Jesus against unjust accusations.

*Do you think Jesus debated simply to stir up controversy? Why or why not?*

## JOHN 8

Jesus declares Himself the light of the world, exposing sin and offering freedom to those who believe in Him. He debates with the Pharisees, asserting His divine authority and confronting their spiritual blindness. He reveals His identity as the eternal "I AM," prompting belief or rejection.

*What can you learn from Jesus' reaction to false accusations against Him?*

## Take Your Time and Learn More

- Jesus heals: MARK 2:1–12
- Bread from heaven: EXODUS 16
- Feast of Tabernacles: LEVITICUS 23:33–43
- Light of the world: ISAIAH 9:2

*Try to forget the demands of life for a while.*
*You're spending quality time with God.*

## JOHN 9

Tension is growing. Jesus heals a man born blind, sparking controversy. The Pharisees interrogate the healed man, but he testifies to Jesus' miraculous power. The healed man's parents confirm his identity, even though they fear expulsion from the synagogue. Jesus confronts the Pharisees' spiritual blindness, and the healed man worships Jesus as the Son of God.

*In what ways is the story of Jesus literally healing the blind man also metaphorical?*

## JOHN 10

Jesus is still speaking to the critics who are upset about the healing of the man born blind. Jesus presents Himself as the good shepherd, contrasting His care for His sheep with the destructive intentions of thieves and hired hands. He asserts His authority and lays down His life for His flock. Jesus confronts the Pharisees, challenging their unbelief.

*How does considering Jesus as your good*
*shepherd impact your relationship with Him?*

## JOHN 11

John recounts one of the most famous stories in the Bible: Jesus raising Lazarus from the dead. Traveling from a distance, Jesus arrives in Bethany, where Lazarus has been dead for four days. He comforts Martha and Mary, weeping with them. He then commands Lazarus to come forth. Many people believe; others report His actions to the Pharisees.

*Why do you think Jesus seems to let Lazarus's situation worsen before He acts?*

## JOHN 12

This chapter records the last of Jesus' public teaching prior to His death. Jesus enters Jerusalem amid praise, fulfilling prophecy as the King of Israel. Despite the people's initial enthusiasm, Jesus predicts His death, highlighting its purpose for salvation. He also foretells His glorification through death, challenging His disciples to follow His example of sacrificial service.

*How will Jesus' death ultimately glorify God?*

### Take Your Time and Learn More

- Jesus heals a blind man: MARK 8:22–26
- The good shepherd: PSALM 23
- The dead come to life: EZEKIEL 37:1–14
- King of Israel: PSALM 2

*Good things come to those who wait—on the Lord, that is.*

## JOHN 13

To demonstrate servitude, Jesus humbly washes His disciples' feet. He also predicts Judas's betrayal, prompting astonishment and denial among His disciples. Jesus instructs them to love one another as He has loved them—a defining characteristic of a follower of Jesus. He foretells Peter's denial, demonstrating His knowledge of future events.

*Which specific person can you serve today, based on Jesus' example of humble service?*

## JOHN 14

Knowing what's coming, Jesus comforts His disciples, explaining His return to His Father's house and promising to prepare a place for them. He identifies Himself as the way, the truth, and the life. He promises that the Holy Spirit will come, comforting and guiding them in His absence. He encourages obedience as evidence of love for God.

*If obedience reveals love for God, what does disobedience reveal?*

## JOHN 15

John 15 is one of the few chapters in the Bible composed almost exclusively of Jesus' direct words. Here Jesus teaches on the vine and branches, illustrating the importance of abiding in Him for spiritual fruitfulness. He urges His disciples to remain in His love through obedience, commanding them to love one another as He has loved them—the mark of true discipleship.

*How is abiding in Christ the opposite of self-reliance?*

## JOHN 16

Jesus gives final instructions to His disciples before His crucifixion, predicting persecution and the coming of the Holy Spirit. He warns of sorrow at His departure but promises joy in His return. He foretells the disciples' scattering, but He promises victory over the world. He encourages prayer by promising to answer. He also encourages faith despite tribulation.

*In what ways is the presence of the Holy Spirit a great gift to believers?*

### Take Your Time and Learn More

- Humility and servanthood: LUKE 22:24–30
- God's presence and protection: ISAIAH 43:1–3
- The vine and the branches: PSALM 80
- God's comfort: ISAIAH 54

*The Bible is countercultural, and so is Bible study.*
*There's no need to rush through this.*

## JOHN 17

While Matthew, Mark, and Luke record more of Jesus' anguish in Gethsemane, John chooses to record more about Jesus' prayer—often called "Christ's High Priestly Prayer." John records Jesus' intimate communion with His Father and His concern for His disciples' unity and growth. Graciously, Jesus even prays for future believers.

*What did Jesus specifically pray for you in John 17:20-23?*

## JOHN 18

John recounts Jesus' betrayal, arrest, and trial before the Jewish leaders and Pontius Pilate. Judas leads soldiers to Jesus in the Garden of Gethsemane, where Jesus willingly surrenders. He rebukes Peter's violence and heals Malchus's ear. Jesus appears before Pilate, who finds no guilt but succumbs to pressure and condemns Jesus to crucifixion.

*Why do you believe Pilate ultimately agrees to Jesus' crucifixion?*

## JOHN 19

John records Jesus' trial, crucifixion, and burial. Soldiers mock Jesus, dressing Him in a purple robe and crowning Him with thorns. Jesus carries His cross to Golgotha. On the cross, Jesus entrusts Mary to John and declares, "It is finished" (19:30). Then He surrenders His spirit and dies. Jesus' side is pierced, confirming His death, and He is buried in a borrowed tomb.

*When Jesus said, "It is finished," to what was He referring?*

## Take Your Time and Learn More

- Jesus intercedes: HEBREWS 7:25
- Jesus' arrest: MATTHEW 26:47–56
- Suffering Savior: PSALM 22

*God speaks in the quiet moments.*
*Approach His Word with calm expectation.*

## JOHN 20

John recounts Jesus' resurrection. Mary Magdalene discovers the empty tomb and informs Peter and John, who find the linen cloths but no body. Mary encounters Jesus, mistaking Him for a gardener until He reveals Himself. Jesus commissions her to tell the disciples of His resurrection. That evening, Jesus appears to the disciples, showing them His wounds.

*How does Jesus' resurrection bring hope to your current circumstances?*

## JOHN 21

Jesus appears to His disciples by the Sea of Galilee. He instructs them to cast their nets on the other side of their boat, resulting in a miraculous catch of fish. After breakfast, Jesus questions Peter's love and restores him after his denial, commissioning Peter to feed Jesus' sheep. He predicts Peter's martyrdom and John's long life.

*Jesus shows great grace to Peter in this chapter.*
*How has Jesus shown great grace to you?*

## Take Your Time and Learn More

- **Victory over death:** LUKE 24:1–12
- **Another miraculous catch of fish:** LUKE 5:1–11

# ACTS

*In commissioning His followers to spread
the gospel, Jesus initiates the church.*

## SETTING THE STAGE

The book of Acts is sometimes called the "Acts of the Apostles." It could actually be called the "Acts of the Holy Spirit" since the Holy Spirit is referenced more than fifty times.

Because Acts picks up where the book of Luke leaves off, many scholars and theologians believe these writings should be two parts of a single work instead of two distinct books.

Acts provides us with a rich historical account of the early church's growth and the spread of the gospel following Jesus' instructions shortly before His ascension—"But you shall receive power after the Holy Spirit has come on you, and you shall be witnesses to Me both in Jerusalem and in all Judea and in Samaria and to the farthest part of the earth" (1:8).

Luke then records the remarkable event of Pentecost, when three thousand people are saved and baptized. This marks the birth of the church and the beginning of its extraordinary mission to spread the gospel.

Acts contains the missionary journeys of Paul, Barnabas, and other apostles as they carry the good news of the gospel across the Roman Empire, facing ongoing challenges, brutal opposition, and miraculous interventions.

The book serves as a helpful bridge between the Gospels and the Epistles, offering a historical foundation for understanding the development of the early church and the global mission given by Christ.

## GOOD TO KNOW

Author not stated, but Acts is traditionally attributed to Luke, Gentile physician (Colossians 4:14), missionary companion of the apostle Paul (2 Timothy 4:11), and author of the third Gospel. Covering events of the AD 30s–60s, it was probably written between AD 62 and 80.

*Before you read, pray. Ask God to
speak His truth to your spirit.*

## ACTS 1

Luke details Jesus' final instructions to His disciples. Jesus commissions them to be His witnesses, spreading the gospel from Jerusalem to the ends of the earth. He promises the Holy Spirit and then—forty days after resurrecting—ascends into heaven. Acts 1 sets the stage for the birth of the church and the spread of the gospel worldwide.

*What are some practical ways to rely on the Holy Spirit in daily life?*

## ACTS 2

On the day of Pentecost, the Holy Spirit descends upon 120 of Jesus' followers, fulfilling His promise. Peter boldly preaches the gospel to the crowd who has gathered to celebrate—proclaiming Jesus as the crucified and risen Messiah. By nightfall, about three thousand people have repented, been baptized, and joined the infant church.

*How boldly do you speak about Jesus? Why?*

## ACTS 3

Peter and John encounter a lame man begging at the temple gate. Peter, filled with the Holy Spirit, heals him. The man leaps to his feet and praises God, thus attracting a crowd. Peter preaches, calling people to repent—bringing the new church to the attention of the Sanhedrin (the Jewish ruling court). The religious leaders grow hostile.

*How is Peter so bold after recently fearfully denying Jesus?*

## ACTS 4

Peter and John are arrested for preaching about Jesus' resurrection. They are warned and freed, but this is just the beginning. Filled with the Holy Spirit, the apostles continue speaking the Word of God with great courage. They demonstrate an unwavering commitment to proclaim the gospel no matter what happens.

*Why do you think the early believers incorporated
scripture (Psalm 2:1-2) into their prayer?*

### *Take Your Time and Learn More*

- Wait for the Holy Spirit: LUKE 24:49
- Outpouring of the Holy Spirit: JOEL 2:28–32
- Healing: LUKE 5:17–26
- Peter quotes from Psalms: PSALM 118:22

*Don't hurry, don't worry. God's Word provides*
*everything you need for living well.*

## ACTS 5

Ananias and Sapphira withhold part of the proceeds from a land sale, lying to the apostles and the Holy Spirit. God strikes them both dead for their deception. Regardless, the church continues to grow. Persecution from unbelievers continues to accelerate. The apostles are beaten and released, rejoicing that they are counted worthy to suffer for Jesus.

*What is hypocrisy and how do you guard against it in your Christian life?*

## ACTS 6

Greek-speaking widows are being overlooked in the daily distribution of food. So the apostles delegate the responsibility of caring for them to seven men of good reputation, including Stephen. Stephen is a skilled debater, which draws attention. He's falsely accused and brought before the Sanhedrin.

*Stephen is described as "full of faith and of the Holy Spirit" (6:5). What does this look like today?*

## ACTS 7

Stephen powerfully defends the faith before the Sanhedrin, recounting Israel's history. He accuses the religious leaders of resisting the Holy Spirit, just as their ancestors did. Angered by his words, they stone him to death, laying their garments at the feet of a man named Saul. Stephen's martyrdom marks the beginning of widespread persecution against the church.

*What do you think motivated Stephen to forgive those who martyred him?*

## ACTS 8

The church faces persecution following the martyrdom of Stephen, leading believers to scatter from Jerusalem. Now the gospel will travel to the ends of the earth, just like Jesus instructed. Philip, one of the seven chosen with Stephen to serve, encounters an Ethiopian eunuch. Philip explains the scriptures to him, and he believes in Jesus and is baptized.

*How can you intentionally share the gospel within your sphere of influence this week?*

### Take Your Time and Learn More

- Seriousness of deception and disobedience: Joshua 7
- Appointing of leaders: Exodus 18
- Israel's history recounted by Stephen: Genesis 12–50
- Isaiah quoted in Acts: Isaiah 53

# God loves it when you read and study His Word.

## ACTS 9

Saul travels to Damascus to arrest believers, but Jesus appears to him in a blinding light, and Saul is dramatically converted. He becomes a fervent follower of Christ, preaching Jesus and confounding the people who once feared him. Saul transforms from persecutor to apostle before the eyes of those he once sought to harm.

*Do you believe your salvation testimony is as powerful as Saul's? Why or why not?*

## ACTS 10

Cornelius, a devout Roman centurion, receives a vision telling him to send for Peter. Peter comes to Cornelius's house and preaches the gospel—salvation through faith—and the Holy Spirit falls on all who hear the word. Peter baptizes these new believers, marking a significant moment in the spread of the gospel to the Gentiles.

*Why is it a great gift that Gentiles are welcome—by grace through faith—into God's family?*

## ACTS 11

Peter defends his actions to the Jewish believers in Jerusalem who at first don't understand why he is willing to baptize Gentiles. Peter explains what happened, and the believers in Jerusalem praise God for granting repentance to the Gentiles. As a result, the gospel continues to spread, even as persecution by the Roman government rises.

*How can differing religious convictions lead to conflicts among sincere Christians?*

## ACTS 12

Herod arrests Peter, planning to deal with him after Passover. An angel frees Peter from prison the night before his trial. Peter goes to the house where believers are praying for him. When he knocks, a servant girl recognizes his voice but is so excited that she forgets to let him in. The believers rejoice.

*How do you discern whether your prayers are earnest or spoken out of a sense of duty?*

## Take Your Time and Learn More

- Dramatic conversion: 1 KINGS 21:25–29
- God's desire for people to repent: JONAH 3
- God includes Gentiles: MATTHEW 15:21–28
- Miraculous rescue: DANIEL 3

*Reading the Bible isn't a race. Let the pages unfold at a pace that allows your spirit to breathe.*

## ACTS 13

Barnabas and Saul are set apart for missionary work. They begin their journey, preaching the gospel in Cyprus and continuing on from there. Many Jews and Gentiles believe the gospel, but opposition from Satan leads to Paul and Barnabas's expulsion from the region. Just as Jesus instructed, the gospel is traveling to the ends of the earth.

*Whose responsibility is it to prove the truth of salvation to people? Why?*

## ACTS 14

Paul and Barnabas continue their journey. Opposition arises, prompting them to flee to Lystra and Derbe, where they heal a crippled man. The crowds mistake them for gods, leading to a confrontation with the locals. Paul is stoned and left for dead. He survives and continues preaching. Paul and Barnabas return to cities they've visited, strengthening the believers.

*Why do you think persecution doesn't dampen Paul's zeal for preaching the gospel?*

## ACTS 15

This chapter is similar to Acts 11, where Peter had to explain why he ministered to the Gentiles. Now Paul and Barnabas are testifying that Gentiles are coming to faith in Christ. So the leadership debates whether or not the Gentiles should be commanded to follow Mosaic law. They decide the law is not required for salvation.

*What are some potential dangers of imposing cultural practices on believers from other places?*

## ACTS 16

Paul and Silas begin their second missionary journey, revisiting churches established during their first journey. In Lystra, they meet Timothy, who joins them in ministry. In Macedonia, a Philippian jailer is converted after an earthquake miraculously releases Paul and Silas from prison yet they refuse to escape. The church is growing.

*What is Christian hospitality, and how does it reflect the gospel?*

### Take Your Time and Learn More

- Paul and Barnabas fulfill prophecy: ISAIAH 49:6
- Preaching leads to repentance: JONAH 3
- Gentile inclusion in the church: GALATIANS 2
- God's plan to bless all nations: GENESIS 12:1–3

*The greatest truths in scripture are often*
*revealed in the unhurried moments.*

## ACTS 17

Paul and Silas travel to Thessalonica and preach in the synagogue, leading to both Jewish and Greek conversions. Jewish opponents stir up trouble, forcing them to flee to Berea. Everywhere they go, some oppose them while others believe. In Athens, Paul engages with philosophers in the Areopagus, proclaiming the gospel to the intellectual elite.

*How does the gospel threaten power systems that exploit others?*

## ACTS 18

Paul travels to Corinth, where he meets Aquila and Priscilla—fellow Christian tentmakers. Paul preaches in the synagogue, but Jewish opposition prompts him to focus on Gentile converts. Despite threats, Paul remains in Corinth for eighteen months, establishing a strong church. He sails for Syria, stopping briefly in Ephesus.

*How do you prioritize fellowship and deeper relationships with local believers?*

## ACTS 19

Paul returns to Ephesus for a nearly three-year stay. After establishing the church there and watching it grow, he returns to Macedonia and Greece. Demetrius, a silversmith who fears economic loss due to the decline of idol worship, incites a riot against Paul. The gospel is spreading. . .and the opposition is growing.

*What are some examples of cultural opposition to the gospel today?*

## ACTS 20

Paul finishes his third missionary journey. In Troas, he preaches late into the night, and a sleepy young man named Eutychus falls from a window. . .but is miraculously revived by Paul. In Miletus, Paul delivers a poignant farewell address, warning of future dangers to the church and committing them to God's care. Tears are shed and goodbyes are spoken.

*How can you prepare for potential gospel opposition?*

## Take Your Time and Learn More

- Superiority of the living God over man-made idols: JEREMIAH 10:11
- Preaching Christ crucified: 1 CORINTHIANS 2
- Prohibition of idolatry: EXODUS 20:3–6
- Paul's final instructions: 1 TIMOTHY 4:11–16

*Bible study is truly a lifelong journey.*
*Relax and enjoy the trip.*

## ACTS 21

Paul travels to Jerusalem despite warnings from fellow believers of impending danger. Tensions arise when Jews express concern over his teaching regarding Gentiles and the law. When Paul is falsely accused of bringing a Gentile into the inner courts, a riot erupts. Paul is seized by the crowd and rescued by Roman soldiers.

*How do you discern between genuine opposition, constructive criticism, and mere disagreement?*

## ACTS 22

Paul addresses a Jewish mob in Jerusalem, recounting his conversion on the road to Damascus. He describes his encounter with Jesus, his blindness, his healing, and his baptism. Paul explains his former zeal for persecuting Christians and his subsequent call to preach the gospel to the Gentiles. The crowd listens until he mentions the Gentiles, inciting their anger.

*Have you ever shared your faith in the face of opposition? What happened?*

## ACTS 23

Paul appears before the Sanhedrin, declaring his innocence but causing a dispute over the resurrection. Fearing for Paul's safety, the Roman commander transfers him to Caesarea for trial before Governor Felix. Paul is accused of inciting a government overthrow, but he defends himself by proclaiming his adherence to the law and his faith in the resurrection.

*Is it possible to accept the gospel without believing in the resurrection? Why or why not?*

## ACTS 24

After years of traveling and preaching, Paul stays in custody for two years. He continues to affirm his innocence and commit to peace, but Felix keeps postponing his trial, hoping for a bribe. Felix and his wife, Drusilla, listen to Paul's message, but they remain undecided.

*Can you think of a time when you felt stuck—yet looking back, you can see God's hand at work?*

## Take Your Time and Learn More

- Facing persecution: MATTHEW 10:16
- Saul's conversion: ACTS 9
- Trial rules: EXODUS 23:1
- Speaking truth with integrity: PSALM 15

*Try to forget the demands of life for a while.*
*You're spending quality time with God.*

## ACTS 25

Paul's case is transferred to Festus, the new governor of Judea, and the Jewish leaders present their accusations against Paul. Festus, unable to find sufficient charges against Paul, asks if he would be willing to go to Jerusalem for trial. However, Paul appeals to Caesar, exercising his right as a Roman citizen to have his case heard by the emperor.

*How likely are you to stay true to your convictions, regardless of circumstances?*

## ACTS 26

Paul defends himself before King Agrippa, recounting his conversion and his mission to preach the gospel. He explains how his zeal for Judaism led him to persecute Christians until his encounter with Jesus on the road to Damascus. Paul emphasizes his commitment to Christ's resurrection. Agrippa acknowledges the persuasiveness of Paul's testimony.

*Why do you believe Paul's testimony is so intriguing, even to nonbelievers?*

## ACTS 27

As a prisoner, Paul sets sail for Rome. The ship faces fierce winds and a severe storm. Paul reassures the passengers and crew—275 people—of God's protection and predicts their survival, warning against abandoning ship. They shipwreck on a reef off the island of Malta, where Paul miraculously survives a viper bite and heals many.

*In what ways does Paul's journey prove that God's plans are not ruined by human decisions?*

## ACTS 28

Paul arrives in Rome, where he is permitted to live under house arrest. Despite his imprisonment, Paul boldly proclaims the gospel to Jewish leaders, explaining Jesus' fulfillment of Old Testament prophecies. Some believe; others reject his message. Paul continues teaching and preaching for two years, sharing Jesus' offer of forgiveness to anyone who will listen.

*Who in your life needs to hear your testimony of when you came to faith in Christ?*

## *Take Your Time and Learn More*

- God's protection over a faithful servant: DANIEL 6:16–23
  - Bold proclamation of God's truth: PSALM 119:46
    - God's sovereignty over the sea: JONAH 1
  - Preaching the gospel to the spiritually blind: ISAIAH 6

# ROMANS

*In place of the law, Jesus offers a new and
better covenant, available to all.*

## SETTING THE STAGE

The book of Romans is a letter written by the apostle Paul, previously known as Saul of Tarsus,
to the diverse Christian community in Rome. At this time in church history, believers were
growing increasingly divided over debatable issues in the Christian life, and Paul wanted to
help restore unity.

The book could accurately be subtitled "the Gospel of God" since it takes the deepest dive
in scripture into key Christian doctrines and the implications of faith.

Paul begins his letter by establishing that the whole world is hopelessly guilty before a
righteous God (3:19, 23). He then explains how justification is available to slaves of sin—Jew
and Greek alike—by faith in Jesus, apart from works of the law. Nobody is able to perfectly keep
the hundreds of commands God gave Moses in the Old Testament. . .and that was by design.

The apostle addresses the tension between grace and works, illustrating that salvation is
a gift that leads to a life of obedience and holiness. He then explores the role of faith—using
Abraham as an example—as well as the certainty of Israel's restoration.

After navigating several complex topics—including predestination, sovereignty, and the
relationship between Jews and Gentiles—the book concludes with a beautiful benediction of
praise: "To the only wise God be glory forever through Jesus Christ. Amen" (16:27).

## GOOD TO KNOW

Written by the apostle Paul (1:1), with the secretarial assistance of Tertius (16:22). Written
approximately AD 57, near the conclusion of Paul's third missionary journey.

*Good things come to those who wait—on the Lord, that is.*

## ROMANS 1

Paul introduces himself as a servant of Jesus, called by God to preach the gospel. Launching into his message, he says God's existence and power are evident in creation, leaving humanity without excuse for unbelief. Regardless, people still choose to suppress the truth, leading to moral decay and idolatry. So God's wrath is revealed against sin.

*How does the beauty and majesty of creation compel you to worship and glorify God?*

## ROMANS 2

Paul warns of God's impartial, righteous judgment. God judges every person based on the same standard of truth and works, granting mercy to the repentant. Paul explains that the external sign of circumcision is only meaningful if accompanied by obedience, highlighting the heart over rituals. Righteousness is about faithfulness, not heritage.

*Why is it a great gift that God shows no partiality (2:11)?*

## ROMANS 3

Paul asks and answers important questions in this chapter. He establishes humanity's universal guilt before God, regardless of religious heritage, and refutes Jewish claims of superiority. Nobody is righteous—all have turned away from God. The law serves to reveal sin, not justify it. God's righteousness is made available through faith in Jesus to all who believe.

*Why does pride make absolutely no sense in the life of a believer?*

## ROMANS 4

Paul illustrates his point with an example familiar to his audience: Abraham. Many Jewish people believed Abraham was righteous because he obeyed God through circumcision. Paul cites Genesis 15:6, affirming that Abraham's faith was credited to him as righteousness many years before he was circumcised or before the law. Justification is a gift received by faith.

*How does this era of self-sufficiency pose challenges to accepting salvation as a free gift?*

## *Take Your Time and Learn More*

- Creation reveals God's existence: PSALM 19:1–6
- The new covenant changes hearts: JEREMIAH 31:31–34
- Universal nature of sin: PSALM 14:1–3
- Faith as the basis for justification: GALATIANS 3:6–9

*The Bible is countercultural, and so is Bible study.*
*There's no need to rush through this.*

## ROMANS 5

Paul highlights the benefits that come from being justified by faith. Through Jesus, believers have peace with God, access to grace, and hope of glory. Paul contrasts Adam's sin (which brought condemnation and death) with Christ's righteousness (which brings justification and life). Jesus makes it possible to be reconciled with God.

*Practically speaking, how does being right with God change the way you suffer (5:3)?*

## ROMANS 6

Paul asks and answers an important question: If believers are declared righteous by God, why stop sinning? Why not take full advantage of God's grace? Paul explains that believers are no longer slaves to sin but slaves to righteousness, called to live in obedience and holiness. What's true about Jesus should be true about those who follow Him.

*How does knowing you already have victory encourage you as you battle sin?*

## ROMANS 7

Paul uses the metaphor of marriage to illustrate believers' relationship with the law. Just as a woman is free to remarry if her husband dies, so believers are freed from the law's obligations through Jesus' death. Despite desiring to obey God, Paul acknowledges his own personal weakness and dependence on God's grace (7:7–25).

*What does it look like to rely daily on God's grace?*

## ROMANS 8

Paul presents the power and assurance of life in the Spirit. Those in Christ are freed from condemnation, empowered to fulfill God's righteous requirements. The Spirit enables believers to overcome the flesh, leading to life and peace. Believers are adopted as children of God, crying out, "Abba, Father!" (8:15). Despite present suffering, believers eagerly await redemption.

*How does the concept of future glory shape your perspective on current struggles?*

## Take Your Time and Learn More

- Sin and death enter the world through one man: GENESIS 3
- Baptism: COLOSSIANS 2:12–13
- The law's role in revealing sin: GALATIANS 3:19–25
- New creation in Christ: 2 CORINTHIANS 5:17

*God speaks in the quiet moments.*
*Approach His Word with calm expectation.*

## ROMANS 9

Paul explains God's sovereign wisdom and grace in working out His good purposes. Paul expresses anguish over Israel's rejection of Christ. He explains that not all descendants of Israel are true Israelites, highlighting God's freedom to choose individuals for His purposes. Quoting from the Old Testament, Paul illustrates God's sovereign choice in Jacob and Esau.

*How can you cultivate a sincere burden for people around you who need Jesus?*

## ROMANS 10

Paul explains Israel's misunderstanding of righteousness, given that they're seeking it through the law rather than faith. He writes that salvation comes to those who confess Jesus as Lord and believe in their hearts that God raised Him from the dead. Both Jews and Gentiles who call upon the name of the Lord will be saved. There is no distinction between them.

*Why is zeal without knowledge so dangerous?*
*Have you ever witnessed this combination?*

## ROMANS 11

Paul writes about God's relationship with Israel. He addresses the question of whether God has rejected His people. God has not rejected Israel, as evidenced by Paul himself—a Jew who believes in Christ. However, the majority of Israel has stumbled in unbelief, leading to the inclusion of the Gentiles in God's salvation plan.

*How should we respond when God's plan (in our lives or in His Word) is difficult to understand?*

## ROMANS 12

While describing practical Christian living, Paul urges believers to present their bodies as living sacrifices, transformed by the renewing of their minds. Paul emphasizes humility and the use of gifts for the benefit of the body of Christ. Love should be genuine—shown through hospitality, kindness, and forgiveness. Paul encourages believers to live in harmony.

*What does it mean—practically—to present your body as a living sacrifice?*

### *Take Your Time and Learn More*

- God shows mercy to whom He chooses: EXODUS 33:19
- Paul quotes from Joel: JOEL 2:32
- Hosea's prophecy fulfilled: HOSEA 2:23
- Genuine worship and right living: ISAIAH 1:11–20

## ROMANS 13

Paul addresses the Christian's relationship with authority. He urges believers to submit to governing authorities because they are established by God to promote order and punish wrongdoing. Christians are called to obey laws and pay taxes as a matter of maintaining a good witness. Love for one another promotes peace.

*How do you reconcile the instruction to submit to authority*
*with the fact that authority often opposes God?*

## ROMANS 14

Paul writes about debatable matters, encouraging believers not to judge each other based on personal convictions regarding food, drink, or observance of special days. Instead, Christians are called to accept and encourage each other in the faith. All people are accountable to God, and their actions should be motivated by faith and obedience.

*What are some specific ways you seek to live for the Lord in your daily life?*

## ROMANS 15

Paul expresses the importance of unity and mutual encouragement among believers, urging the strong to be patient with the weak and to seek to build them up. Quoting scripture, he shows that God's heart is for both Jews and Gentiles to praise Him together. Paul recounts his ministry among the Gentiles and his desire to visit Rome. He prays for hope.

*How does unity among believers specifically reflect God's character and purposes?*

## ROMANS 16

Paul closes his letter by greeting numerous people, warning against divisive teachings, and encouraging the Romans to remain faithful. He sends greetings from fellow workers and urges readers to be wise. He concludes with a doxology praising God's power to strengthen believers according to the gospel.

*How can you personally help foster unity within your own church community?*

## *Take Your Time and Learn More*

- Love fulfills the law: MATTHEW 22:34–40
- Disputable matters: 1 CORINTHIANS 8
- Everyone should praise the Lord: PSALM 117
- Aquila and Priscilla: ACTS 18:2–3

# 1 CORINTHIANS

*Jesus' resurrection means His followers can
have abundant life now and forever.*

## SETTING THE STAGE

The book of 1 Corinthians, written by the apostle Paul, is an intensely practical letter addressed
to the Corinthian church during a time of deep division.

Paul has received a letter from the Corinthians, and this epistle is his response. In it, he
wants to provide guidance to this first-century Christian community on matters of doctrine,
conduct, and church life.

In 1 Corinthians, we get a glimpse into the challenges faced by the church in Corinth nearly
twenty-five years after Jesus ascended back to heaven. And perhaps surprisingly, we learn
that their challenges aren't so different from ours today.

In the book, Paul will address such topics as division within the church, immorality, lawsuits
among believers, questions about marriage and celibacy, instructions on worship, the Lord's
Supper, and spiritual gifts.

First Corinthians 13 is the oft-quoted "love chapter." Consistent with the rest of Paul's letter,
we know love is core to the gospel and should therefore be central to the Christian life.

Toward the end of this book, Paul emphasizes Christ's resurrection as critically important
to the Christian faith. At first, this may feel like a departure from his writing about the Christian
life; but in reality, it's Jesus' resurrection that gives Christians victory over sin and the ability
to do what God commands.

## GOOD TO KNOW

Written by the apostle Paul, with Sosthenes (1:1). Written approximately AD 55–57.

*Don't hurry, don't worry. God's Word provides
everything you need for living well.*

## 1 CORINTHIANS 1

Paul writes a letter to a church that he helped establish—meaning he knows them well. In his letter, he emphasizes unity and wisdom, urging the church to avoid divisions and quarrels. He contrasts God's wisdom with worldly wisdom and reminds them that their calling and salvation are by God's grace.

*What are some potential dangers of forgetting that salvation is God's grace in our lives?*

## 1 CORINTHIANS 2

Paul emphasizes the gospel's simplicity and power, reminding the Corinthian church that he preached with humility and reliance on the Spirit, not with eloquent words or clever arguments. Paul explains that only those who are spiritually discerning can understand God's truth.

*How effectively do contemporary preachers follow Paul's example?*

## 1 CORINTHIANS 3

Paul addresses the Corinthian Christians' immaturity and division, rebuking them for their quarreling and allegiance to human leaders. Warning against worldly wisdom, he reminds them of the importance of building on the foundation of Christ. Paul also reminds them that they are God's temple and that God will judge their work.

*How are your attitudes, words, and actions
contributing to your church's unity (or disunity)?*

## 1 CORINTHIANS 4

Paul urges humility and single-minded devotion to Christ. He defends his apostolic authority, explaining that he and his fellow workers are servants entrusted with the gospel. Paul emphasizes the importance of faithfulness and integrity in stewardship, reminding readers that God will judge their motives and actions. Therefore, they should imitate Christ.

*In what ways can pride lead to division and conflict within the church community?*

## Take Your Time and Learn More

- Boasting only in the Lord: JEREMIAH 9:23–24
- Revealing spiritual truths: PSALM 119:18
- Christ as the foundation of the church: ISAIAH 28:16
- God as the ultimate judge of hearts: JEREMIAH 17:10

## *God loves it when you read and study His Word.*

### 1 CORINTHIANS 5

Paul confronts the Corinthian Christians for their tolerance of immorality. Specifically, he rebukes them for allowing a man involved in open sexual sin to remain in fellowship. Paul commands the church to remove the offender, emphasizing the importance of purity and discipline within the body of believers. He warns of the corrupting influence of sin. God's standard is holiness.

*How do sincerity and truth (5:8) serve as guardrails for the Christian life?*

### 1 CORINTHIANS 6

Paul admonishes his readers for taking legal disputes before secular courts rather than resolving them within the church. He urges them to settle disagreements among themselves with wisdom and integrity. He reminds them of the importance of honoring God with their bodies—which are temples of the Holy Spirit, purchased by Christ's blood.

*How does knowing that your body is a temple of the Holy Spirit impact your daily decisions?*

### 1 CORINTHIANS 7

Paul addresses marriage, singleness, and Christian living. He acknowledges both the advantages of singleness for devotion to God and the gift of marriage. He encourages believers to remain in the marriage they were in when they trusted Christ, even if their partner hasn't yet believed. He urges his readers to remain in the situation in which they were called.

*How can you steward your current status—married or single—for the glory of God?*

### 1 CORINTHIANS 8

Because idol temples are integrated into daily life in Corinthian society, avoiding all contact is nearly impossible. So Paul addresses the issue of eating food sacrificed to idols. He explains Christian liberty, cautioning against using it to cause other believers to stumble. He emphasizes love for others over asserting personal rights.

*Can you think of a decision in your life that was guided by the principle of love over liberty?*

## *Take Your Time and Learn More*

- Condemnation of sexual immorality: Leviticus 18:6–28
- Quarreling: 2 Timothy 2:23–24
- Jesus teaches on singleness and marriage: Matthew 19:10–12
- Food sacrificed to idols: Acts 15:20

*Reading the Bible isn't a race. Let the pages unfold
at a pace that allows your spirit to breathe.*

## 1 CORINTHIANS 9

Paul defends his apostleship and right to be financially supported by the people he serves, but then he explains why he's refusing to benefit from this right: he doesn't want to hinder the gospel. He uses his own example of self-discipline and perseverance to encourage his readers to run the Christian race with endurance.

*What are some similarities between running a physical
race and living out the Christian faith?*

## 1 CORINTHIANS 10

Paul warns the Corinthians against repeating the mistakes of Israel, who fell into idolatry and immorality. He tells them to avoid anything even close to idol worship, encouraging them to flee from temptation and to participate in the Lord's Supper with reverence. He concludes the chapter with an exhortation to do everything for the glory of God.

*How do you practically prioritize God's glory above everything else in life?*

## 1 CORINTHIANS 11

Paul addresses two issues that need correction: head coverings for women and how to observe the Lord's Supper. He emphasizes the importance of maintaining proper order and respect during gatherings, and he urges believers to participate in the Lord's Supper in a worthy manner. He warns against irreverence and division.

*How do you ensure that you observe the Lord's Supper worthily?*

## 1 CORINTHIANS 12

Paul explains that the Holy Spirit distributes spiritual gifts among believers for the common good. He describes the church as a body with distinct, essential, interdependent parts. He emphasizes the importance of unity and mutual care, regardless of gifts or roles—all functioning together for God's glory and the edification of believers.

*How does Paul's metaphor of the church as a body challenge individualism?*

## Take Your Time and Learn More

- The laborer deserves his wages: 1 TIMOTHY 5:18
- Warning against idolatry: EXODUS 32:1–10
- Humble service: JOHN 13:4–17
- Unity and diversity within the body of Christ: ROMANS 12:4–5

*The greatest truths in scripture are often
revealed in the unhurried moments.*

## 1 CORINTHIANS 13

Often called the "love chapter," 1 Corinthians 13 emphasizes the importance of Christian love. Paul describes love's attributes, explaining that without love, even the most extraordinary gifts and actions are meaningless. Believing love is the greatest virtue, he exhorts his readers to pursue love above all things, as it reflects God's nature and is essential for Christian living.

*How has the assurance that "the greatest of these is
love" (13:13) been proven in your own life?*

## 1 CORINTHIANS 14

Having begun his instructions about spiritual gifts in chapter 12, Paul concludes them in this chapter. He stresses the importance of orderly worship, with each gift being useful for building up the body of believers. He encourages understanding and clarity in community, rather than confusion—ensuring everything is done for the edification and unity of the church.

*How does disorder in the church discredit the true work of God (14:40)?*

## 1 CORINTHIANS 15

Paul now presents the foundational truth for the gospel: Christ's resurrection. Without it, faith is futile, preaching is worthless, and believers are stuck in sin. He describes the victory over death and sin through Christ's resurrection, which brings hope and assurance of future resurrection for believers.

*Which holiday do you believe is more significant: Easter or Christmas? Why?*

## 1 CORINTHIANS 16

Paul concludes his letter with practical instructions and personal greetings. He encourages the Corinthians to set aside offerings for the saints in Jerusalem, demonstrating their unity and support for fellow believers. He discusses his travel plans and urges readers to extend hospitality. He encourages the church to be diligent, steadfast, and loving.

*How do you pursue true Christian love in your relationships?*

## Take Your Time and Learn More

- Two greatest commandments: MATTHEW 22:37–39
- Edification, order, and discernment: 1 THESSALONIANS 5:11–22
- Jesus as the resurrection and the life: JOHN 11:25–26
- Cheerful giving: 2 CORINTHIANS 9:7–8

# 2 CORINTHIANS

*Followers of Christ should live counterculturally, as Jesus did.*

## SETTING THE STAGE

The book of 2 Corinthians, by the apostle Paul, is a letter written shortly after 1 Corinthians.

However, though it is called "2 Corinthians," we find several clues throughout the book that this isn't actually the second time Paul has written to this church. The clues suggest the possibility of a sequence of additional communication—not included in the Bible—between Paul and the Corinthians believers.

After receiving the letter known as 1 Corinthians, people in the Corinthian church have developed distrust in Paul. Some say he is insincere; others question his authority as an apostle. So Paul's response in this letter is deeply vulnerable and transparent.

Paul defends his authority and integrity by candidly sharing his experiences of hardship and persecution in service to God. He also talks about his thorn in the flesh (12:7–10), emphasizing a central theme of His letter—God's grace is sufficient for the Christian life (12:9).

Second Corinthians addresses the themes of suffering, comfort, reconciliation, and ministry. It concludes with Paul's practical, pastoral advice: "Finally, brothers, farewell. Be perfect, be of good comfort, be of one mind, live in peace. And the God of love and peace shall be with you" (13:11).

## GOOD TO KNOW

Written by the apostle Paul, with Timothy (1:1). Dated to approximately AD 55–57, shortly after 1 Corinthians.

*Bible study is truly a lifelong journey.*
*Relax and enjoy the trip.*

## 2 CORINTHIANS 1

Writing to the church in Corinth, Paul expresses comfort in affliction, highlighting God's role as the Father of compassion. He shares his own experiences of suffering and deliverance, affirming that trials equip him to comfort others. Paul expresses the importance of unity in prayer and recalls the Corinthians' support during his hardships. God is faithful to fulfill His promises.

*Why is self-reliance dangerous in the Christian life?*

## 2 CORINTHIANS 2

Paul addresses the issue of discipline in the Corinthian church, urging readers to forgive and restore a repentant member. He discusses his previous letter's impact, expressing relief at its outcome. He reaffirms his commitment to the gospel. He highlights believers' role as a pleasing fragrance of Christ, contrasting it with the odor of death for those who reject the gospel.

*What are some symptoms of unforgiveness in the heart?*

## 2 CORINTHIANS 3

Paul contrasts the ministry of the old covenant—engraved on stone tablets—with the ministry of the new—written on hearts by the Spirit. The old covenant brought condemnation; the new one brings righteousness and life. He affirms that believers are being transformed into Christ's image by the Spirit, enabling them to serve with boldness.

*Why is a believer's spiritual health so closely associated with involvement in the local church?*

## 2 CORINTHIANS 4

Paul emphasizes the glorious nature of gospel ministry despite hardships. He contrasts the hiddenness of the gospel's light with the veiled minds of those who reject it. Despite facing afflictions, Paul affirms that the power to persevere comes from God. He sees his struggles as temporary, far outweighed by the eternal glory awaiting believers.

*Why is it so easy to focus on earthly issues to the exclusion of eternal ones?*

## Take Your Time and Learn More

- God's comfort in times of affliction: PSALM 23:4
- The light of the world: MATTHEW 5:14–16
- Transformed into the image of Christ: ROMANS 12:2
- Future glory awaits: 2 CORINTHIANS 4:16–18

*Try to forget the demands of life for a while.*
*You're spending quality time with God.*

## 2 CORINTHIANS 5

Paul discusses the glorious hope and assurance Christians have in the resurrection. He describes the temporary nature of earthly bodies compared to the eternal glory awaiting believers. He emphasizes the longing for heaven and the transformation that comes with it. Paul stresses the urgency of accepting God's grace and the responsibility of living for Christ.

*In what specific ways can you be an ambassador for Christ in your local community?*

## 2 CORINTHIANS 6

Paul encourages believers to live lives that reflect the grace they have received. He urges them not to receive God's grace in vain but to live as servants of God. He tells his readers to remain faithful amid trials, avoiding unequally yoked relationships with unbelievers. He expresses his deep affection for the Corinthians.

*Would you describe holiness as more of a pursuit or an achievement? Why?*

## 2 CORINTHIANS 7

Paul continues expressing his great affection for the Corinthians, rejoicing in their repentance, which brought godly sorrow leading to salvation. He contrasts godly sorrow with worldly sorrow, highlighting its transformative power. He commends his readers for their response to his previous letter and the comfort they brought to Titus. He expresses godly confidence in them.

*What are some differences between godly sorrow and worldly sorrow?*

## 2 CORINTHIANS 8

Paul encourages the Corinthians to excel in giving, using the Macedonian churches' generosity as an example. Despite their own poverty, they gave generously—even beyond their means. Paul sees this as proof of their love for God and urges the Corinthians to follow suit. Generosity not only meets the needs of others but also reflects the grace of God.

*In what ways does giving reflect our understanding of the gospel?*

## Take Your Time and Learn More

- Gospel transformation: GALATIANS 6:15
- In the world, not of it: 1 CORINTHIANS 5:9–13
- Godly sorrow: PSALM 51:17
- Humility and sacrificial love of Jesus: PHILIPPIANS 2:5–8

# Good things come to those who wait—on the Lord, that is.

## 2 CORINTHIANS 9

Paul continues writing about giving. Generosity should be voluntary and not forced, he says, since God loves a cheerful giver. Paul assures readers that their generosity will not only meet the needs of the saints but produce thanksgiving to God and glorify Him. He acknowledges God's abundant provision.

*What does it mean to be a "cheerful giver" (9:7)?*

## 2 CORINTHIANS 10

Paul defends his authority against detractors who question his credentials. He explains that while his weapons are not of the flesh, they are powerful for tearing down strongholds and arguments against God. Paul urges the Corinthians to obey Christ, addressing disobedience in their midst. When he arrives, he will confront those who challenge him.

*How can you consistently ensure that your confidence is in God and not in your own abilities?*

## 2 CORINTHIANS 11

Paul passionately defends his apostleship, recounting his suffering for the gospel. He contrasts himself with false apostles who seek to deceive the Corinthians. Paul boasts—not in himself but in his weakness for Christ's sake. He warns the Corinthians not to accept a gospel different from the one he gave them. Despite suffering, Paul remains vigilant in his commitment to Christ.

*How does Paul's suffering help authenticate his claim to be an apostle?*

## Take Your Time and Learn More

- Cheerful giving: LUKE 6:38
- Spiritual warfare: EPHESIANS 6:12–13
- Warnings about false prophets: MATTHEW 7:15–20

*The Bible is countercultural, and so is Bible study.*
*There's no need to rush through this.*

## 2 CORINTHIANS 12

Paul humbly acknowledges a thorn in his flesh—a constant reminder of his weakness. He has begged God to remove it. . .but has learned that God's grace is sufficient. Paul boasts in his weaknesses because through them, Christ's power is made perfect. Paul expresses his love for the Corinthians, longing for their spiritual well-being.

*Have you ever asked God to change something in your life. . .*
*yet found His grace sufficient? What happened?*

## 2 CORINTHIANS 13

Paul tells his readers to examine themselves and to strive for unity, peace, and holiness. Paul desires their spiritual growth, affirming his authority as an apostle and warning the people against disobedience. He promises to act decisively against unrepentant sinners when he arrives. Paul concludes his letter with blessings, encouraging them to rejoice and comfort one another.

*Why are isolation and self-reliance dangerous in the Christian life?*

## Take Your Time and Learn More

- **Strength in weakness:** PHILIPPIANS 4:13
  - **Heart exam:** PSALM 139:23–24

# GALATIANS

*What the law could never accomplish,*
*the gospel provides through Jesus.*

## SETTING THE STAGE

The book of Galatians, written by the apostle Paul to a group of churches in Galatia, is a passionate defense of the gospel.

At the time this letter was written, the Galatians were facing a double threat: impure doctrine and impure conduct.

At this point in history, Christianity had spread and many non-Jewish people were coming to faith in Christ. Yet some Jewish Christians were mistakenly convinced that salvation would only be extended to those who obeyed the laws in the Torah—eating only kosher food, for example, and circumcising males.

So Paul opens the book of Galatians with a fervent declaration of the gospel's freedom from legalistic bondage. He emphasizes justification by faith alone: "Knowing that a man is justified not by the works of the law but by the faith of Jesus Christ, even we have believed in Jesus Christ, that we might be justified by the faith of Christ and not by the works of the law, for by the works of the law no flesh shall be justified" (2:16).

Paul's letter will culminate in an exhortation to live by the Spirit rather than falling back into legalistic bondage.

Galatians is particularly helpful in understanding the relationship between faith and works, law and grace, and the freedom found in the gospel of Christ.

## GOOD TO KNOW

Author is the apostle Paul (1:1); possibly written around AD 49, as one of Paul's earliest letters.

*God speaks in the quiet moments.*
*Approach His Word with calm expectation.*

## GALATIANS 1

Paul begins this dearly loved book by defending his apostolic authority—meaning his words are trustworthy. He warns his readers against any deviation from the gospel, reminding them that salvation is by grace through faith alone. Paul recounts his conversion testimony and early ministry, reminding the people that his terrible past didn't hinder God's call on his life.

*How do you discern daily between genuine gospel truth and false teaching?*

## GALATIANS 2

Paul defends his trustworthiness. He wants people to hear his message and knows he must first demonstrate he is a legitimate apostle. He recounts his affirmation from other apostles in Jerusalem, asserting unity in their message. He describes a time he confronted Peter over hypocrisy, emphasizing the importance of remaining faithful to the true gospel.

*Have you ever noticed discrepancies between your public and private behavior? What did you do about it?*

## GALATIANS 3

Paul argues why justification is only possible through Christ. He reasons that Abraham was justified by faith, so anyone who believes is his spiritual heir. He argues that anyone under the law is cursed because nobody can perfectly obey it. He explains that Jesus bore the curse of the law by becoming a curse for those who believe.

*How does understanding that your salvation is a gift impact your relationship with God?*

### Take Your Time and Learn More

- Warning against accepting a different gospel: 2 CORINTHIANS 11:1–4
- Buried with Christ and raised in new life: ROMANS 6:4–6
- Equality of believers in Christ: COLOSSIANS 3:11

*Before you read, pray. Ask God to
speak His truth to your spirit.*

## GALATIANS 4

Paul uses the analogy of a child under guardianship until the appointed time to illustrate how humanity was under the law before Christ. He explains that—through Christ—believers are now sons and heirs of God, no longer slaves to the law. Paul urges the Galatians to embrace their freedom in Christ.

*Are there any areas of your life where you are
tempted to rely on your own works or merit?*

## GALATIANS 5

Paul begins this chapter by emphatically stating, "Stand fast, therefore, in the liberty by which Christ has made us free" (5:1). Paul contrasts the works of the flesh with the fruit of the Spirit, highlighting the importance of walking in the Spirit to overcome sinful desires. He encourages believers to love each other, serving each other humbly.

*Who can you love sacrificially and serve humbly today?*

## GALATIANS 6

Paul says Christians should bear each other's burdens, thus fulfilling the law of Christ. He explains that when a fellow Christian is sinning, other Christians should step in and help with gentleness and humility. He urges personal responsibility, encouraging people to examine their own actions and never become conceited.

*How does humility reflect Jesus' character and His approach to helping people?*

### Take Your Time and Learn More

- Christ's humility and obedience: PHILIPPIANS 2:6–8
  - Free from the law of sin: ROMANS 8:1–2
    - Importance of community and mutual support: 1 THESSALONIANS 5:11

# EPHESIANS

*God wants His church to live and love like Jesus.*

## SETTING THE STAGE

The book of Ephesians was written by Paul and is considered the first of his letters sent from a Roman prison. This powerfully written letter addresses the identity and unity of the Christian community.

Ephesians can easily be divided into two sections—the first half reiterates the gospel; the second half applies it. The book addresses such topics as predestination, adoption, and the mystery of God's will. It offers practical instructions for holy living and calls believers to walk in love and in the fullness of the Spirit.

Also included in the book is the well-known armor-of-God imagery (6:10–18), which provides a powerful metaphor for spiritual warfare. This section encourages believers to "take the whole armor of God, that you may be able to withstand in the evil day, and having done all, to stand" (verse 13).

Specifically, this book presents a rich theology of the church as the body of Christ, emphasizing both the unity and diversity represented within the community of believers. Every believer is necessary and contributes to the overall health of the body.

Ephesians includes so much practical wisdom that it continues to encourage and instruct the church today. It provides believers with a clear understanding of our identity in Christ, made possible by the grace of God.

## GOOD TO KNOW

Written by Paul (1:1), around AD 62, toward the end of the apostle's life.

*Don't hurry, don't worry. God's Word provides
everything you need for living well.*

## EPHESIANS 1

After a short introduction, Paul describes God's spiritual inheritance for believers. He praises God for choosing believers in Christ before the foundation of the world. He then prays for his readers—that they can grasp the hope of God's calling and the riches of His inheritance.

*If you are a follower of Christ, how does knowing you were chosen "according to the good pleasure of His will" (1.5) affect you?*

## EPHESIANS 2

Paul writes about the method of salvation, explaining that it is by grace through faith in Christ. He highlights how Christ's death and resurrection transform believers, reconciling Jews and Gentiles into one body. Through Christ, believers are made alive, seated with Him in heavenly places. Salvation is by grace apart from works, and believers are God's workmanship.

*Salvation is transformative. How has your relationship with God changed your life?*

## EPHESIANS 3

Paul explains his role as a steward of God's grace, proclaiming the incomprehensible riches of Christ's love and the fullness of God's glory. Paul prays for the Ephesians' understanding to be rooted in Christ—that they will be able to grasp the dimensions of God's love. He concludes with a doxology of praise to God.

*What does it mean for you to be "rooted and grounded in love" (3:17)?*

## Take Your Time and Learn More

- God calls believers according to His purpose: GALATIANS 1:15–16
- Salvation based on God's mercy: TITUS 3:4–7
- Rooted and built up in Jesus: COLOSSIANS 2:6–7

*God loves it when you read and study His Word.*

## EPHESIANS 4

Paul calls believers to live in unity, emphasizing the importance of humility, gentleness, patience, and love. Paul writes about the new hope believers have in Christ. He exhorts followers of Jesus to speak truthfully—avoiding lies and anger—and work diligently, sharing with people in need.

*What does it mean to live a life "worthy of the vocation to which you are called" (4:1)?*

## EPHESIANS 5

Paul tells his readers to imitate Christ. He warns against sexual immorality, impurity, and greed—instead urging thanksgiving, purity, and self-control. He contrasts the fruitless deeds of darkness with the fruitful life in the Spirit, and he encourages worship and Christlike love in marriage. The believer's responsibility is to reflect Christ's love in all relationships.

*Paul tells readers to imitate God (5:1).*
*Why is comparing ourselves to other people insufficient?*

## EPHESIANS 6

Paul addresses the reality of spiritual warfare and the believer's armor of God. He instructs masters to act with fairness and integrity, children to honor their parents, and parents to nurture their children in the Lord. He concludes his letter by urging believers to stand firm and pray for each other.

*How consistently do you pray for the people in your life?*
*How could you do even more?*

## Take Your Time and Learn More

- Diversity of gifts given for the common good: 1 CORINTHIANS 12:4–11
- Husbands should love their wives: COLOSSIANS 3:19
- Firm in the faith: 1 PETER 5:8–9

# PHILIPPIANS

*God wants His children to find joy
and contentment in every season.*

## SETTING THE STAGE

The book of Philippians, another letter written by Paul during his first imprisonment, was in part a thank-you for a gift of money given to Paul by the church at Philippi—a vibrant community of mature believers faithfully following Christ. This letter is uniquely tender and relational since its recipients are especially close to Paul's heart.

Often referred to as the "epistle of joy," Philippians is packed with instruction for practical Christian living, with words such as "joy" and "rejoicing" appearing frequently. The theme verse seems to be Philippians 4:4: "Rejoice in the Lord always, and again I say, rejoice."

Philippians urges believers to imitate Christ's humility, to rejoice in the Lord, and to pursue unity within the church. Paul explains that a relationship with Jesus is always personal and transformative. As Nero's prisoner, Paul shares his own example of daily reliance on Christ's strength: "I know both how to be cast down and I know how to abound. . . . I can do all things through Christ who strengthens me" (4:12–13).

Philippians beautifully communicates the message that our enduring joy comes from a deep and ongoing relationship with Jesus, regardless of external circumstances.

## GOOD TO KNOW

Written by Paul, with Timothy (1:1), probably in the early AD 60s.

*Reading the Bible isn't a race. Let the pages unfold at a pace that allows your spirit to breathe.*

## PHILIPPIANS 1

Paul expresses gratitude for the Philippian believers' partnership in the gospel and their steadfast faith. Despite being in prison, he rejoices in the spread of the gospel. Paul's desire for the Philippians is that their love will expand and that they will grow in knowledge and discernment. He models joy in adversity and partnership in ministry.

*Paul undoubtedly loved his Christian friends. How do you show love for yours?*

## PHILIPPIANS 2

Paul encourages humility and unity among believers, pointing to Christ as the ultimate example. He urges his readers to emulate Christ's selflessness—considering others as more significant than themselves. He highlights Jesus' obedience, calling believers to be obedient, knowing that it is ultimately God who works in them.

*What is the link between humility and unity?*

## PHILIPPIANS 3

Paul warns against false teaching, emphasizing the surpassing value of knowing Christ. He shares his own once-prized credentials and achievements, which he now considers loss compared to the surpassing worth of knowing Christ. Paul's desire is to be found in Christ, attaining righteousness through faith. His greatest prize is eternal life in Christ Jesus.

*How does anticipating eternity impact your daily decisions and actions?*

## PHILIPPIANS 4

Paul writes about strength in suffering, encouraging believers to rejoice always and cultivate a spirit of gentleness and prayerfulness. Emphasizing the importance of contentment in all circumstances, he tells readers to bring their anxieties to God through prayer and thanksgiving. Believers should find their joy and peace in Jesus.

*Can you think of a difficult time in which you experienced the incomprehensible peace of God? What happened?*

### Take Your Time and Learn More

- God's faithfulness to complete the work He started: 1 THESSALONIANS 5:24
- Christ's humility and obedience: LUKE 22:42
- Forsaking everything to know Christ: MATTHEW 16:26
- Anxiety: 1 PETER 5:7

# COLOSSIANS

*Christ is supreme. False teaching is*
*dangerous. Church unity matters.*

## SETTING THE STAGE

The book of Colossians—like Ephesians and Philippians—was written by Paul during his Roman imprisonment. But unlike his previous letters, Colossians was not written to a group of people he knew nor to a church community that he began.

Paul had received word that someone in the Christian community in Colossae was teaching an alluring but dangerous philosophy—that there is hidden or secret knowledge that, when acquired, leads to salvation. (We now know this belief as "Gnosticism.")

Not only does Paul want to help protect believers in Colossae, he wants to protect the church at large, given that it's always at risk of deception.

This letter stresses the sufficiency and supremacy of Christ over any human tradition or philosophy: "Beware lest any man take you captive through philosophy and vain deceit, according to the tradition of men, according to the rudiments of the world, and not according to Christ" (2:8).

In addition to addressing the dangers of false teaching, Paul also encourages his readers with some helpful thoughts on practical Christian living. He urges believers to set their minds on heavenly things, demonstrate compassion and forgiveness, and maintain unity within the body of Christ. More than anything, Paul wants his readers—then and now—to pursue Christ with greater devotion.

## GOOD TO KNOW

Written by Paul, with Timothy (1:1), probably in the early AD 60s.

*The greatest truths in scripture are often
revealed in the unhurried moments.*

## COLOSSIANS 1

Paul praises the Colossians' faith and love, attributing their growth to the gospel's transformative power. He highlights Christ's role in creation, redemption, and reconciliation. Paul describes his ministry to make Christ known, warning against false teaching and presenting Christ as the source of all wisdom and knowledge.

*What practical steps can you take to continue in
your faith "grounded and settled" (1:23)?*

## COLOSSIANS 2

Paul warns against various deceptive philosophies and traditions that are threatening Colossian believers and undermining the sufficiency and supremacy of Christ. He encourages believers to remain rooted and built up in God, guarding against worldly ideologies and legalistic practices. Completeness is found in Christ alone.

*Which worldly ideologies threaten the health of
the church and individual believers today?*

## COLOSSIANS 3

Paul encourages believers to set their minds on heavenly things, putting to death earthly desires and embracing new life in Christ. He urges readers to reflect Christ's character, telling them to let the peace of Christ rule in their hearts. Paul addresses various relationships, instructing each to live in accordance with God's will.

*What does it mean for your life to be "hidden with Christ in God" (3:3)?*

## COLOSSIANS 4

Paul reminds believers to commit themselves to prayer, remaining watchful and thankful. He requests prayers for his ministry and encourages readers to share the gospel every chance they get. He says to behave wisely toward outsiders, and always carefully use gracious speech.

*How does gracious speech reflect Christ's character and
contribute to the gospel's testimony in our lives?*

## Take Your Time and Learn More

- Christ is the glory of God: HEBREWS 1:2–3
- Rooted and grounded in love: EPHESIANS 3:17
- Citizenship in heaven: PHILIPPIANS 3:20–21
- Instructions for the Christian life: 1 THESSALONIANS 5:16–18

# 1 THESSALONIANS

*Jesus will return, gathering His own to Himself.*

## SETTING THE STAGE

First Thessalonians was written by Paul to the church community in Thessalonica. Believed to be Paul's earliest letter in the Bible, it emanates pastoral warmth, offers deep encouragement, and provides a glimpse into the concerns of the early Christian community.

In it, Paul expresses deep affection for the Thessalonian believers and commends them for their faith and perseverance in the face of persecution. At this time in history, believers are being accused of transferring their loyalty from Caesar to Jesus, and they are paying dearly for it.

Paul, therefore, wants to strengthen their faith during these ongoing challenges.

Eschatology (the study of the end times) is a prominent theme in this letter. Paul addresses concerns about believers who have died, assuring this community of the hope and resurrection that await all followers of Jesus. One passage in this book is often quoted at Christian funerals. It begins, "I do not want you to be ignorant, brothers, concerning those who are asleep, lest you sorrow as others who have no hope" (4:13).

Like Paul's previous letters, this one emphasizes practical Christian living, inviting believers to a life of holiness, love, and diligence. Paul encourages the community to be steadfast and to live in anticipation of Christ's return.

## GOOD TO KNOW

Written by Paul, along with Silas and Timothy (1:1), in the early AD 50s.

*Bible study is a journey. Relax and enjoy the trip.*

## 1 THESSALONIANS 1

Despite persecution and trials, the church in Thessalonica is thriving. Paul commends the believers for their work produced by faith, their labor inspired by love, and their endurance driven by hope in Christ. Paul commends changed lives and evangelistic zeal.

*How do you cultivate and maintain a vibrant relationship with Christ?*

## 1 THESSALONIANS 2

Paul recalls facing opposition and suffering while ministering in Philippi. Yet he boldly preached the gospel with sincerity and purity, avoiding flattery and seeking only to please God. He expresses his gentle care for the Thessalonians.

*Why do you think humans tend to prioritize pleasing man over pleasing God?*

## 1 THESSALONIANS 3

Paul tells his readers that he sent Timothy to strengthen and encourage them in their faith. Timothy's report of their steadfastness and love brings joy and comfort to Paul during his own trials. He prays fervently for them to grow in love and holiness.

*How does understanding God's character impact the way we respond to suffering?*

## 1 THESSALONIANS 4

Paul instructs the believers on sexual purity and brotherly love, encouraging them to control their bodies in holiness and honor. He addresses the hope of Christ's return, comforting them about believers who have died and assuring them of their resurrection and reunion with Christ.

*How can believers maintain sexual purity in a sex-crazed culture?*

## 1 THESSALONIANS 5

Paul discusses Christ's return, encouraging believers to be ready. He contrasts the fate of those who are spiritually asleep with those who are living for Christ. He urges believers to build each other up, honor their leaders, live in peace, and rejoice, pray, and give thanks continually.

*Which do you find most challenging: rejoicing, praying, or giving thanks?*

### *Take Your Time and Learn More*

- Triad of virtues: 1 CORINTHIANS 13:13
- Word of God: HEBREWS 4:12
- Prayer for the believers: JUDE 24–25
- Christ's return: 1 CORINTHIANS 15:52
- Rejoice, pray, give thanks: PHILIPPIANS 4:4, 6

# 2 THESSALONIANS

*God wants His children to be faithful until He returns.*

## SETTING THE STAGE

Second Thessalonians, authored by Paul, is a follow-up to 1 Thessalonians and was likely written shortly after the first letter. Paul had received word that the problems he addressed in his first letter had gotten worse. The persecution had intensified and the community was struggling.

So Paul builds on the themes established in his first letter, addressing three specific ideas:

First, Paul offers hope amid suffering. He reminds this precious community of believers that they are suffering because they love Jesus—"This is evidence of the righteous judgment of God that you may be counted worthy of the kingdom of God, for which you also suffer" (1:5).

Second, Paul offers clarity about Christ's return. Just as eschatology was a prominent theme in 1 Thessalonians, Paul returns to the topic in this second letter due to misunderstandings among the readers who were scared about the return of Christ. Paul reassures them by providing additional insight into the events preceding "the day of the Lord."

Finally, Paul admonishes the believers to be diligent in their daily work. He expresses some concern about individuals in the community who are being idle, disruptive, and unwilling to contribute through productive work.

He closes the letter with a prayer for peace "always by all means" (3:16).

## GOOD TO KNOW

Written by Paul, along with Silas and Timothy (1:1), in the early AD 50s.

*Try to forget the demands of life for a while.*
*You're spending quality time with God.*

## 2 THESSALONIANS 1

Paul expands on many of the themes from his previous letter. He commends the Thessalonians for their perseverance amid persecution. He assures them of God's righteous judgment, offering comfort and rest to those who suffer and endure affliction. He prophesies Christ's return—bringing retribution to those who reject the gospel and relief to believers.

*How is it possible for churches or Christians to thrive in the midst of persecution?*

## 2 THESSALONIANS 2

Paul addresses some concerns and misunderstandings about the day of the Lord. He urges believers not to be unsettled by wrong teaching on this topic. Before God's judgment arrives on the earth, there will be a rebellion and a "man of sin" (2:3) who opposes God and exalts himself. Paul encourages believers to stand fast in the truth.

*How can you avoid harmful misunderstandings of scripture or biblical teaching?*

## 2 THESSALONIANS 3

This chapter begins with a prayer request and ends with a prayer. First, Paul urges believers to pray for him and his companions—that God's Word will spread quickly and be honored. He warns against idleness, saying that those unwilling to work shouldn't eat. He urges readers not to tire of doing good, especially toward fellow believers. He then closes with a benediction.

*How does prayer contribute to endurance?*

## Take Your Time and Learn More

- Future judgment and the return of Christ: MATTHEW 25:31–34
- The coming of the man of sin: DANIEL 7:25
- Importance of diligence: PROVERBS 10:4

# 1 TIMOTHY

*Through Paul, God gives instructions to be faithful in ministry.*

## SETTING THE STAGE

The book of 1 Timothy was written to Timothy, a young leader and companion whom Paul is mentoring in ministry, in the last few years of Paul's life. Paul calls Timothy "my own son in the faith" (1:2).

Together with 2 Timothy and Titus, 1 Timothy is referred to as a "pastoral letter."

Paul writes this letter to address problems existing in the church in Ephesus that are creating controversy and division in the Christian community. He commissions Timothy to confront these problems and restore order: "I write these things to you hoping to come to you shortly, but if I remain long, that you may know how you ought to behave yourself in the house of God, which is the church of the living God, the pillar and ground of the truth" (3:14-15).

First Timothy is viewed by many in ministry today as a manual for leadership, offering guidance on leadership qualifications, sound doctrine, conduct of worship, and the role of men and women in the church.

Additionally—and highly unique to this time in history—Paul discusses social concerns, including the treatment of widows and elders as well as the appropriate use of wealth.

Paul's message throughout 1 Timothy is consistent: faithful adherence to scripture will result in genuine faith and Christian love.

## GOOD TO KNOW

Written by Paul, around AD 63.

*Good things come to those who wait—on the Lord, that is.*

## 1 TIMOTHY 1

Paul encourages Timothy to stay in Ephesus and confront the false teaching that is plaguing the Ephesian church. Paul recounts his own transformation from persecutor to apostle, acknowledging his need for forgiveness and the grace and mercy of Christ. He charges Timothy to guard the gospel entrusted to him.

*How can you actively guard your heart and mind against false teachers and teaching?*

## 1 TIMOTHY 2

Paul instructs Timothy to pray for leaders and for all people, as God desires all to be saved and come to the knowledge of the truth. Paul affirms Christ as the mediator between God and humanity, giving Himself as a ransom. Paul encourages men to pray without anger or quarreling, and he encourages women to be modest.

*Is it possible to have a modest outward appearance and yet not please God? Why or why not?*

## 1 TIMOTHY 3

Paul gives the qualifications for overseers and deacons in the church. He emphasizes the importance of moral character, integrity, and leadership skills for those in positions of authority. Their wives should be worthy of respect, not slanderers, and faithful in all things. Paul explains the significance of these roles in maintaining order and spiritual health within the church.

*Why is integrity required in the lives of Christian leaders?*

### Take Your Time and Learn More

- The gospel: JOHN 3:16
- Jesus as mediator between God and humanity: HEBREWS 9:15
- Calling of leadership: TITUS 1:7

*The Bible is countercultural, and so is Bible study.*
*There's no need to rush through this.*

## 1 TIMOTHY 4

Paul warns against false teaching that departs from the faith. He describes a time when people will abandon the truth to follow deceiving spirits and liars. Paul advises Timothy to be nourished on the words of faith and sound doctrine, rejecting any teaching that contradicts truth. He encourages Timothy to set an example in speech, conduct, love, faith, and purity.

*How can you identify and overcome obstacles to your spiritual growth?*

## 1 TIMOTHY 5

Paul gives practical instructions on how to treat different groups within the church. He advises Timothy on how to interact with older and younger members, widows, and elders. He stresses the importance of showing respect and honor to those deserving, especially widows who have no family to care for them. Paul also instructs Timothy on dealing with accusations against elders.

*Why are widows consistently important to God throughout scripture?*

## 1 TIMOTHY 6

Paul addresses various issues concerning godliness. He warns against the desire for riches, which can lead to harmful temptations and spiritual destruction. He emphasizes contentment, instructing Timothy to flee from greed and urging the wealthy to be generous. Finally, he charges Timothy to guard the gospel faithfully, avoiding worldly teaching that can lead astray.

*Why is God the only source for truth and trustworthiness?*

## Take Your Time and Learn More

- **Example of the believer:** MATTHEW 5:16
- **Caring for family:** 2 CORINTHIANS 12:14
- **Danger of loving money:** ACTS 5:1–10

# 2 TIMOTHY

*Following Jesus requires willing sacrifice and personal risk.*

## SETTING THE STAGE

The book of 2 Timothy is believed to be the final letter written by Paul. Likely authored during his second imprisonment in Rome, it was written to Timothy at the end of Nero's reign.

In addition to being filled with rich spiritual wisdom, this book stands as a poignant testimony to Paul's enduring love for Jesus, his commitment to the gospel, and his concern for the church. At this point in Paul's life, he is not only in prison but has been abandoned by those who once declared loyalty to him (1:15; 4:16).

Understanding that his time is limited, Paul addresses Timothy in this letter with a tone of urgency, emphasizing his need for unwavering faithfulness and perseverance in the face of adversity.

This book is often referred to as "Paul's farewell." In the final lines of his letter, he writes, "I have fought a good fight, I have finished my course, I have kept the faith" (4:7).

Paul shares his final, practical advice on leadership, resilience, and the importance of sound doctrine. Notably, he identifies Timothy's source of stability as scripture—profitable for teaching, rebuking, correcting, and training in righteousness (3:16-17).

He acknowledges the challenges inherent in Christian ministry, stresses the importance of passing on the faith to future generations, and reminds Timothy of the enduring power of God's Word in guiding and sustaining the Christian life.

## GOOD TO KNOW

Written by Paul, around the mid-60s.

*God speaks in the quiet moments.*
*Approach His Word with calm expectation.*

## 2 TIMOTHY 1

Paul writes to Timothy, his beloved disciple, encouraging him to fan into flame the gift of God in his life. He urges Timothy not to be ashamed of the gospel, or of Paul's suffering for it, but to join in suffering for the gospel. Paul reminds Timothy that it is God who enables believers to endure hardship.

*Paul recalls Timothy's sincere faith. What makes faith sincere?*

## 2 TIMOTHY 2

Paul encourages Timothy to entrust the things he learns to other faithful people who will then pass them on to others. He likens the Christian life to that of a soldier, athlete, and farmer—emphasizing the importance of discipline, endurance, and diligence. Paul urges Timothy to flee youthful passions. He emphasizes the importance of handling God's Word accurately.

*Why do you think Paul instructed Timothy to stay away from disputes and quarreling?*

## 2 TIMOTHY 3

Paul warns Timothy about the difficult final days, when people are characterized by love for themselves, money, and pleasure. He describes these individuals as having a form of godliness but denying its power, and he urges Timothy to avoid them. Paul emphasizes the importance of scripture. He reminds Timothy to continue in what he has learned and firmly believes.

*Why does Jesus deserve your love more than anything or anyone else in the world?*

## 2 TIMOTHY 4

Paul warns Timothy about the rise of false teaching that will deceive many. He emphasizes the importance of holding firmly to the truth of God's Word, and he encourages Timothy to train himself in godliness—physical exercise has value, but godliness is eternal. He instructs Timothy to set an example for others in speech, conduct, love, faith, and purity.

*How have you experienced God's grace in your own Christian race so far?*

### *Take Your Time and Learn More*

- Power and confidence through the Holy Spirit: ROMANS 8:15
  - Importance of discipleship: PSALM 78:4
    - Authority of scripture: 2 PETER 1:21
    - Steadfast faith: HEBREWS 12:1–2

# TITUS

*God, through the gospel, transforms people
and cultures from within.*

## SETTING THE STAGE

The book of Titus is a letter to Titus, one of Paul's most reliable travel companions and ministry partners (1:5).

Without understanding much of the backstory, we know that the network of churches in Crete has come under the influence of corrupt teaching and leadership. Believers are apparently merging their new understanding of Jesus with their old ideas of the Greek gods they previously worshipped.

And we know anything added to the gospel makes it no gospel at all.

So Paul is sending Titus to fix the situation. This letter provides Titus with Paul's instructions: "Therefore rebuke them sharply, that they may be sound in the faith, not giving heed to Jewish fables and commandments of men who turn from the truth" (1:13-14).

Specifically, Paul entrusts Titus with the crucial task of appointing qualified elders who will lead with integrity and counteract the harmful influence of false teaching that has impacted the Cretan Christian community.

The book of Titus lists the qualifications of elders, stresses the importance of sound doctrine, warns against false teaching, and describes the Christian's moral responsibility to various groups such as older men and women, younger men and women, and servants.

Paul's message in the book of Titus can be summed up simply: embrace what God calls good and reject what God calls evil. It's still a reliable message for us today.

## GOOD TO KNOW

Written by Paul around AD 63.

*Before you read, pray. Ask God to*
*speak His truth to your spirit.*

## TITUS 1

Paul instructs Titus, his fellow worker, regarding appointing elders in every town. He emphasizes the qualifications required for these elders—including being blameless, faithful, hospitable, and good with family management. Paul warns against those who teach false doctrine, urging Titus to rebuke them sharply. He stresses the importance of living a godly life.

*Why are qualifications and disqualifications so important for church leaders?*

## TITUS 2

Paul outlines instructions for various groups within the church community—including the older men, older women, younger men, younger women, and slaves. Paul emphasizes the importance of Titus setting a good example in all his teaching. He stresses the need for godly living and adherence to sound doctrine within the church.

*Are you investing in intergenerational relationships within your church family? If so, how?*

## TITUS 3

Paul reminds believers to be submissive to authorities. He says true transformation is an act of God's mercy, but he also stresses the importance of maintaining good works, avoiding foolish controversies, and rejecting divisive individuals. He instructs Titus to avoid engaging in pointless arguments and to focus on promoting unity and godly living.

*Why is it easier to judge people's spirituality by their actions rather than by their hearts?*

## *Take Your Time and Learn More*

- Importance of good doctrine: 2 TIMOTHY 3:16–17
- Transformative power of God's grace: EPHESIANS 2:8–10
- Salvation through God's mercy and grace: EPHESIANS 2:4–5

# PHILEMON

*God's grace means believers are equals in His work and family.*

## SETTING THE STAGE

The book of Philemon is a short, unique letter written by Paul to Philemon, a wealthy Christian from Colossae, about a runaway slave named Onesimus. And despite it being Paul's shortest letter, it packs a powerful punch.

Onesimus, a slave, had likely robbed his master and fled to Rome where he heard the gospel being taught through Paul's ministry and came to faith in Christ. And even more than that, he became helpful to Paul in ministry (verses 11–13).

By choosing to follow Christ, Onesimus knew he needed to return to Philemon—but slaves who fled their masters often faced harsh physical consequences and brutal legal retribution. So a slave returning to his master of his own choice was countercultural in every way.

In this letter, Paul pleads with Philemon to reconcile with Onesimus. But more than that, he asks Philemon to do something culturally revolutionary—to embrace Onesimus "not now as a servant, but above a servant—a brother beloved" (verse 16).

This reconciliation would create a model for how Christian communities should navigate issues of conflict, inequality, and societal norms. Just as God has lavishly poured out His grace on us, we should be quick to extend grace to others.

## GOOD TO KNOW

Written by Paul (1:1), probably around AD 63, when he was imprisoned in Rome.

---

*Bible study is a journey. Relax and enjoy the trip.*

## PHILEMON 1

Paul and Timothy write to Philemon about Onesimus, Philemon's runaway slave. Paul appeals to Philemon to receive Onesimus back as a beloved brother, not as a slave. He offers to pay any debts and asks Philemon to forgive Onesimus, suggesting that God may have allowed him to run away for a greater purpose.

*What are some specific ways the gospel transforms relationships among believers?*

### Take Your Time and Learn More

- Christian love and fellowship: COLOSSIANS 1:3–8

361

# HEBREWS

*Jesus is better than any Old Testament person or sacrifice.*

## SETTING THE STAGE

Hebrews is a unique and profound book, likely addressing a community of Jewish Christians facing challenges to their faith.

For centuries, the authorship of the book has been a subject of debate. And though we still don't know with certainty who wrote it, we know its rich theological content continues to leave an enduring impact.

Blending Old Testament imagery with the New Testament person and work of Jesus, Hebrews celebrates the superiority of Christ compared to the Old Testament rituals, priesthood, and covenant.

Hebrews reaffirms the reality that Jesus is the fulfillment of the Old Testament promises and prophecies. . .and that in every way, Jesus as our new High Priest is better.

Key concepts include the role of faith, the perseverance of believers, and the supremacy of Christ's sacrifice. The book also includes the well-known "faith chapter"—Hebrews 11.

We know from chapter 10 that the recipients of the letter are facing ongoing persecution because of their faith; as a result, some in the community are abandoning the Lord.

So this book offers practical exhortations and deep encouragement for Christian living, encouraging readers to persevere in faith, to draw near to God with confidence, and to endure trials by "looking to Jesus, the author and finisher of our faith" (12:2).

## GOOD TO KNOW

Author is not stated; Paul, Luke, Barnabas, and Apollos have all been suggested. Probably written before AD 70, since Hebrews refers to temple sacrifices. Romans destroyed the Jerusalem temple in that year.

*Don't hurry, don't worry. God's Word provides everything you need for living well.*

## HEBREWS 1

Hebrews begins by affirming Jesus' nature, importance, and role in God's plan of salvation. Jesus is portrayed as the final, ultimate revelation of God, far surpassing the prophets. This chapter emphasizes Christ's position as God's Son, appointed heir of all things, and the Creator of the universe. The chapter concludes by highlighting Christ's exaltation at God's right hand.

*Why do you think the New Testament references Old Testament passages so frequently?*

## HEBREWS 2

Chapter 2 encourages readers to pay close attention to the message of salvation proclaimed by Jesus; drifting away from it will bring serious consequences. Through Jesus' incarnation and suffering, He tasted death and conquered it, freeing believers from fearing death and eternity.

*Practically speaking, how do you guard against drifting away from God?*

## HEBREWS 3

This chapter encourages believers to fix their thoughts on Christ, who is faithful. Drawing parallels with Israel's rebellion in the wilderness, the writer warns against hardening hearts through unbelief. He emphasizes the importance of maintaining faith and obedience—encouraging mutual accountability to prevent falling away.

*How do you fix your thoughts on Jesus during the mundane moments of everyday life?*

## HEBREWS 4

Again drawing parallels with Israel's failure to initially enter the Promised Land, this chapter emphasizes the importance of perseverance and obedience, warning against falling short of God's rest due to disobedience and unbelief. Thankfully, God's Word is far more than a dusty collection of books—it is living and life-changing.

*How have you personally experienced the Bible to be a living book?*

### Take Your Time and Learn More

- Beginning of all things: JOHN 1:1–3
- Christ's experience with temptation: MATTHEW 4:1–11
- Importance of Christian accountability: GALATIANS 6:1–2
- Power and effectiveness of God's Word: ISAIAH 55:11

*God loves it when you read and study His Word.*

## HEBREWS 5

This chapter discusses the qualifications of a high priest, highlighting the priesthood of Christ. It emphasizes Jesus' obedience and suffering, enabling Him to empathize with human weaknesses (5:2). It warns against falling away from the faith and encourages perseverance in following Christ.

*Why is it important to have a High Priest who can sympathize with our weaknesses?*

## HEBREWS 6

A warning against apostasy, urging believers to move beyond basic teachings and press on to maturity. Agricultural imagery illustrates the consequences of fruitful growth versus barrenness. Believers are urged to imitate the faith and patience of those who inherit God's promises.

*How can you encourage fellow believers who struggle with their faith?*

## HEBREWS 7

This chapter elaborates on the priesthood of Melchizedek, presenting him as a type of Christ, superior to the Levitical priesthood. Christ's perfection and the unchanging nature of His priesthood are emphasized. He is the ultimate High Priest who mediates between God and man.

*How does knowing that Jesus is "something better" (11:40) encourage your faith?*

## HEBREWS 8

This chapter contrasts the old and new covenants, affirming the superiority of Jesus as the mediator of a better covenant. This new covenant, established through Christ's sacrifice, promises a changed heart and forgiveness of sins.

*What are some specific ways the new covenant improves upon the old covenant?*

## HEBREWS 9

Christ's death was necessary for the forgiveness of sins, contrasted with the temporary nature of animal sacrifices under the old covenant. Jesus' once-and-for-all sacrifice offers people eternal life. He will appear again to those who eagerly await Him.

*How can you urge others to eagerly await Jesus' return?*

## Take Your Time and Learn More

- Jesus as our eternal High Priest: HEBREWS 4:14–16
- Christ's role as intercessor: ROMANS 8:34
- Superiority of the new covenant: JEREMIAH 31:31–34
- Christ's sacrifice: 1 PETER 3:18

*Reading the Bible isn't a race. Let the pages unfold at a pace that allows your spirit to breathe.*

## HEBREWS 10

This chapter highlights the superiority of Christ's sacrifice over the old sacrificial system. Christ's sacrifice cleanses believers from sin once and for all, granting them access to God's presence. The chapter encourages believers to hold fast to their confession of faith without wavering—persevering in faith despite trials.

*How have trials shaken or strengthened your own faith?*

## HEBREWS 11

This chapter is often called the "Hall of Faith" because it includes many examples of believers who persevered in faith even in the face of incredible adversity. This chapter says faith is the foundation of our relationship with God, guiding us through trials and enabling us to please Him.

*Does it surprise you that individuals such as Gideon and Samson are included in Hebrews 11? Why or why not?*

## HEBREWS 12

This chapter encourages believers to endure trials by fixing their eyes on Jesus, the author and finisher of their faith. It compares the Christian journey to a race, urging readers to persevere and lay aside every hindrance. God disciplines those He loves, shaping them into obedient children. The chapter highlights the importance of holiness and warns against rejecting God's grace.

*In what specific ways is the spiritual life like a race?*

## HEBREWS 13

This final chapter exhorts believers to love one another and show hospitality. Marriage is honored, and believers are urged to be content, to remember their leaders, and to imitate their faith. Jesus Christ is the same yesterday, today, and forever. This chapter advises against being carried away by strange teachings and emphasizes the importance of grace.

*How do you cultivate contentment in a culture that constantly promotes consumerism?*

## Take Your Time and Learn More

- Confidence to approach God through Jesus: EPHESIANS 3:12
- Faith in action: 2 CORINTHIANS 5:7
- Call to perseverance: PHILIPPIANS 3:14
- Security in God's presence and provision: PSALM 118:6

# JAMES

*Genuine faith is demonstrated by God-glorifying actions, not just words.*

## SETTING THE STAGE

The book of James, often called the "Proverbs of the New Testament," is a letter written to the Christian Jews scattered throughout the Roman Empire.

James's goal in writing this letter is not to convey any new theological truth—it's to remind readers what they should already know. The book of James is very practical and wisdom-filled, focusing on Christian living and genuine faith.

James begins his letter by urging believers to count trials as opportunities for growth, emphasizing the difficult reality that—though we would prefer our faith flourish in seasons of comfort—faith is actually tested and strengthened through challenges.

James then repeatedly communicates to his readers that faith is not simply intellectual or passive; rather, genuine faith will transform both the heart and the life. He emphasizes throughout his letter the necessity of putting faith into action—"Be doers of the word and not hearers only, deceiving your own selves" (1:22).

James emphasizes the importance of bridling the tongue, showing mercy, and acting justly. James passionately calls for Christians to express their faith through good works because while good works do not earn salvation, they help validate genuine faith.

The book of James is a call to authentic Christian living, where faith is not just professed but demonstrated.

## GOOD TO KNOW

Author is James (1:1), probably a brother of Jesus (see Matthew 13:55; Mark 6:3). Written approximately AD 60.

*Great truths are often revealed in unhurried moments.*

## JAMES 1

James encourages his readers to count trials as joy because they produce endurance. He promises wisdom to those who ask God for it in faith without doubting. He says trials test faith, leading to the crown of life for those who endure. And he says the unchanging God gives every good gift.

*How do trials reveal what is actually in our heart?*

## JAMES 2

James explains the necessity of genuine faith expressed in actions, not merely words. He condemns favoritism toward the rich, contrasting it with God's impartiality. He highlights the inseparable link between faith and works: true faith produces fruit in obedience.

*How is partiality shown in the church today?*

## JAMES 3

James cautions against the danger of the tongue, comparing it to a small but mighty flame that can create immense destruction. Stressing the importance of self-discipline in speech, he explains how absurd it is to use the tongue to both praise God and speak negatively about others.

*Why can the tongue be so difficult to control?*

## JAMES 4

James addresses the root of quarrels and urges humility. He says friendship with the world is enmity with God. We should submit to God, resist the devil, and draw near to God through repentance. James cautions against boasting about future plans without considering God's will.

*How does engagement with unbelievers differ from friendship with the world?*

## JAMES 5

James accuses the rich of hoarding wealth and being corrupt. He encourages patience and endurance in suffering, as well as confessing sins to one another. He highlights the effectiveness of fervent prayer, using Elijah as an example. He tells believers to love one another.

*In what ways can wealth distract people from focusing on eternal matters?*

## *Take Your Time and Learn More*

- Seeking wisdom from God: PROVERBS 2:6
- The importance of love for others: LEVITICUS 19:18
- Characteristics of wisdom from God: PHILIPPIANS 4:8
- Submitting to God and resisting temptation: 1 PETER 5:8–9
- Importance of confessing sin: 1 JOHN 1:9

# 1 PETER

*God's people always have hope in the midst of suffering.*

## SETTING THE STAGE

First Peter was a letter written by Peter in fulfillment of the instruction Jesus gave him in Luke 22:32. Remember, Peter denied Christ on the night of His death, but Jesus said to him, "And when you are converted, strengthen your brothers." Some Bible scholars believe this letter is one way Peter obeyed that instruction.

Peter is called "the apostle of hope."

First Peter was written to discouraged believers during a dark period of intense persecution. The purpose of the book is to provide encouragement and guidance to Christians navigating the challenges of faithfully living for Jesus in a hostile environment.

The book addresses suffering, perseverance, and identity. In it, Peter passionately invites followers of Christ—"a chosen generation, a royal priesthood, a holy nation" (2:9)—to imitate Jesus' example of how to faithfully endure suffering—not by rebelling but by lavishing the love of Christ on those who do not yet know Him.

Peter encourages his readers to maintain steadfast faith, rooted in the resurrection of Christ, promising hope amid persecution.

He concludes his letter with a beautiful benediction: "May the God of all grace, who has called us to His eternal glory in Christ Jesus, after you have suffered a while, make you perfect and establish, strengthen, and settle you" (5:10).

What hope!

## GOOD TO KNOW

Written by Peter (1:1), along with Silas (5:12), approximately AD 65.

*Bible study is truly a lifelong journey.*
*Relax and enjoy the trip.*

## 1 PETER 1

The apostle Peter addresses believers scattered throughout Asia, describing their heavenly inheritance and the hope they have in Christ. He encourages them to rejoice in their salvation, though they face difficult trials that refine their faith.

*Is participation in your local church an important part of your life? Why or why not?*

## 1 PETER 2

Peter encourages believers to crave God's Word. He describes Jesus as the living stone, rejected by humans but chosen by God, urging believers to build their lives on Him. Since they are God's own—shown mercy through Christ—Peter calls them to endure unjust suffering like Jesus did.

*Why do you think many Western Christians today dislike the concept of submission?*

## 1 PETER 3

Peter instructs wives to respect their husbands, pursuing inner beauty over outward adornment. He tells husbands to understand and honor their wives, showing consideration and respect. Believers should live in harmony, extending sympathy, love, and compassion.

*How is "modesty" typically defined in Christian culture? What all should it include?*

## 1 PETER 4

Peter calls believers to live for God's will, no longer pursuing worldly desires but living according to Christ's example. He tells them to prepare to endure suffering and to love one another deeply—extending hospitality and serving each other.

*How can you live in greater harmony with people this week?*

## 1 PETER 5

Peter addresses the elders, encouraging them to shepherd God's flock with humility, not for personal gain but out of eagerness to serve. He reminds believers to humble themselves under God's mighty hand, casting their anxieties on Him and knowing He cares for them.

*What is an example of a time when God's care for you was especially obvious?*

## Take Your Time and Learn More

- Hope of eternal life: TITUS 3:7
- Identity and purpose of God's people: EXODUS 19:6
- Enduring trials with joy: JAMES 1:2–3
- God's care and provision: PSALM 55:22

# 2 PETER

*Watch carefully for corrupt teachers who distort God's truth.*

## SETTING THE STAGE

Second Peter and 2 Timothy—though written by two different authors—have much in common, including the fact they were written by men awaiting martyrdom. Both letters are joyful, yet both are written as farewell addresses.

This second letter from Peter was likely written to the same audience as the first. It serves as a guide for Christian living and a warning against false teaching that always threatens the health and faith of the church.

Knowing his time is short, Peter gets right to the point, addressing issues that are crucial for the spiritual growth and stability of the church. First, he seeks to strengthen the foundation of the Christian life by emphasizing seven Christlike traits that should define believers: faith, virtue, knowledge, self-control, patience, godliness, brotherly kindness, and love (1:5–7).

Next, he warns readers about false teachers. Deeply concerned about the preservation of sound doctrine, Peter addresses both the corrupt lifestyles and the distorted theology of wicked teachers who are increasingly leading believers astray.

The final verse in the book—and Peter's last recorded words—sum up his solution to the church in the face of ongoing challenges and false teaching: "But grow in grace and in the knowledge of our Lord and Savior Jesus Christ" (3:18).

## GOOD TO KNOW

Written by Peter in the late AD 60s, shortly before his execution.

*Try to forget the demands of life for a while.*
*You're spending quality time with God.*

## 2 PETER 1

Peter encourages believers to grow in their faith, reminding them of the precious promises of God. He urges them to add virtue, knowledge, self-control, patience, godliness, brotherly kindness, and love. By cultivating these qualities, believers will be fruitful in their knowledge of Jesus. Peter affirms the reliability of scripture and warns against false teachers.

*How can you incorporate regular reminders of the gospel into your daily routine?*

## 2 PETER 2

Peter warns about false prophets and teachers who will introduce destructive heresies, exploiting believers with deceptive words. He cites examples from history and says these false teachers will face judgment. Peter emphasizes God's ability to deliver the godly and punish the unrighteous.

*How can you distinguish between genuine believers who struggle with doubts and false teachers who actively promote doctrinal error?*

## 2 PETER 3

Peter addresses scoffers who doubt Christ's return, reminding believers of God's past judgments and His promise of a future day of reckoning. Emphasizing that God's timing is not bound by human expectations, he urges patience and godliness as they await Christ's coming. He concludes with a call to steadfastness, growth in grace, and vigilance against false teachers.

*Why does flawed doctrine almost always lead to flawed living?*

## Take Your Time and Learn More

- **Blessings of belonging to Christ**: EPHESIANS 1:3–14
- **God's judgment on the ungodly and rescue of the righteous**: JUDE 5–7
- **God's patience for the salvation of many**: ROMANS 2:4

# 1 JOHN

*Every true believer will demonstrate the love of Christ.*

## SETTING THE STAGE

First John is attributed to John, the son of Zebedee and one of Jesus' disciples. Together with Peter and James, John was one of Jesus' three closest friends during His earthly ministry. So John's writing in all five books he authored—John; 1, 2, and 3 John; and Revelation—reveal him as a man who knew and loved Christ in a personal way.

To John, Jesus was not an academic subject or a mere topic of discussion. Jesus was a personal friend. Multiple times in his writing, John refers to himself as the disciple whom Jesus loved (John 13:23, 19:26).

Unlike the other disciples, John is given the gift of a long lifetime and old age. By the time 1 John is written, the other disciples have likely died difficult deaths. But John has lived to be an old man and is the last surviving apostle.

And now, writing to several Gentile congregations, John wants his readers to know and love the same Jesus he knew and loved when Christ walked the earth.

In this book, John's writing is clearly shaped by the urgency he feels in his later years. In just five chapters, he will write about love, fellowship, and our assurance of salvation.

## GOOD TO KNOW

Though the author is not stated, church tradition says John wrote 1, 2, and 3 John around AD 92.

*Good things come to those who wait—on the Lord, that is.*

## 1 JOHN 1

John explains that fellowship with God is contingent on walking in the light—characterized by righteousness and truth. John calls believers to live authentic Christian lives marked by intimacy with God, honesty about sin, and obedience to scripture.

*Why does giving and seeking forgiveness improve all our relationships?*

## 1 JOHN 2

John urges believers to obey God's commands as a demonstration of their love for Him. He distinguishes between those who walk in darkness, lacking understanding of God's truth, and those who walk in the light, guided by Christ's teachings. John emphasizes loving one another.

*Do you have any unresolved bitterness in your heart? What should you do?*

## 1 JOHN 3

John emphasizes the profound love God has bestowed on believers as His children. He explains that this love is not merely expressed in words but through actions, and he urges followers to live in righteousness and refrain from sin. John contrasts the children of God and those of the devil.

*What does it mean—practically speaking—to abide in Christ?*

## 1 JOHN 4

John says that God is love and that those who abide in love abide in God. He emphasizes love's transformative power, stating that it casts out fear and enables believers to reflect God's character. He underscores the necessity of loving one another as evidence of knowing God.

*Who can you specifically demonstrate Christ's love to this week?*

## 1 JOHN 5

John reaffirms the core belief in Jesus as the Son of God, emphasizing that faith in Him is essential for salvation. He encourages believers to pray confidently, knowing that God hears and answers their prayers according to His will.

*In what area do you currently struggle to trust God's promises? Why?*

## Take Your Time and Learn More

- Children of light: Ephesians 5:8–14
- Warning against loving the world: Romans 12:2
- Love one another: John 13:34–35
- Characteristics of love: 1 Corinthians 13
- Overwhelming victory through Christ: Romans 8:31–39

# 2-3 JOHN

*Walk in truth. Avoid deceivers. Demonstrate love.*

## SETTING THE STAGE

The books of 2 and 3 John are short yet powerful letters written by John.

Second John is the shortest book of the Bible by word count and was written to "the elect lady and her children." The exact identity of this lady is not clearly stated, leading many to debate whether she was an actual woman or a metaphor for the church. Her children could potentially be a reference to members of the community or to followers of the faith.

Regardless of the letter's recipient, it addresses the themes of truth, love, and obedience to God's commands. It emphasizes the importance of walking in the truth and avoiding false teachers: "And this is love: that we walk according to His commandments. This is the commandment, that, as you have heard from the beginning, you should walk in it" (verse 6).

Third John is the shortest book of the Bible by verse count and was written to a man named Gaius. John is writing to commend Gaius for his hospitality and support of traveling missionaries. The book addresses hospitality, truth, and the contrast between positive and negative examples within the church.

Both 2 and 3 John are personal and practical, focusing on specific situations within the early church.

## GOOD TO KNOW

Though the author is not stated, church tradition says John wrote 1, 2, and 3 John around AD 92.

*The Bible is countercultural, and so is Bible study.*
*There's no need to rush through this.*

## 2 JOHN

John addresses the importance of walking in truth and love. He commends his readers for their faithfulness to God's commands, encouraging them to continue. He warns them not to support false teachers but to show discernment instead. He stresses the need to abide in Jesus' teaching.

*Why do you think Jesus showed more compassion to tax collectors,*
*prostitutes, and outcasts than He did to false teachers?*

## 3 JOHN

John commends Gaius for his hospitality and faithfulness to truth. He praises Gaius for supporting missionaries. However, he criticizes Diotrephes, a church leader who did not welcome him but instead spread malicious gossip. He urges Gaius to imitate what is good and not what is evil. John plans to address these issues further in person.

*How can we balance maintaining unity and confronting*
*problematic behavior in the church?*

## Take Your Time and Learn More

- Truth in love: EPHESIANS 4:15
- Commendation of faithful workers: PHILIPPIANS 2:25–30

# JUDE

*The church must defend the faith and stay faithful to God.*

## SETTING THE STAGE

Though this letter is short—only one chapter—it is severe in its tone and content since it was written in response to apostasy in the church.

Because of the prevalence of false teachers, Jude writes: "Beloved, when I gave all diligence to write to you of the common salvation, it was necessary for me to write to you and exhort you that you should earnestly contend for the faith that was once delivered to the saints" (verse 3).

Jude begins with a quick introduction, continues with a long warning about the corrupt teachers who are influencing the church, and concludes with a clear charge to the church about how they should respond.

Yet despite the strong warnings and confrontational tone, Jude concludes with a message of hope, encouraging readers to build themselves up in the faith and anticipate Christ's mercy and eternal life: "Now to Him who is able to keep you from falling and to present you faultless before the presence of His glory with exceeding joy, to the only wise God, our Savior, be glory and majesty, dominion and power, both now and ever. Amen" (verses 24–25).

## GOOD TO KNOW

Jude (1:1), possibly Jesus' half brother (see Matthew 13:55; Mark 6:3), wrote his letter around AD 82.

---

### *God loves it when you read and study His Word.*

## JUDE

Jude writes a short letter stressing the urgency of opposing false teachers. He encourages believers to contend earnestly for the faith despite ungodly influences. He warns of immoral infiltrators who pervert God's grace into a license for sin. He urges that steadfastness, prayer, and mercy be shown to the wavering, but he also urges caution and separation from the corrupt.

*What does it look like in today's context to "earnestly contend for the faith"?*

## *Take Your Time and Learn More*

- **God will complete what He started:** PHILIPPIANS 1:6

# REVELATION

*God will triumphantly return to judge evil and gather His own.*

## SETTING THE STAGE

The book of Revelation, the final book of the New Testament, offers a profound glimpse into the culmination of God's redemptive plan.

Written by John, the book can rightly be called "the Revelation of Jesus" or "the Revelation to John" as it records everything seen and heard by John in a series of visions. John uses symbolism extensively, and he frequently references Old Testament events and prophecies.

The book was written as a letter to seven churches in Asia. The number seven, which John weaves throughout the entire book, is significant because it's often associated with completeness or perfection. Therefore, its repeated use symbolizes the fulfillment of God's promises and the completion of His redemptive plan.

The book serves as both a source of comfort for believers facing persecution and a call to persevere in the midst of challenges. It concludes with an invitation to all who thirst to come and partake of the water of life, emphasizing the eternal hope offered through faith in Christ.

And then come these hopeful words: "He who testifies these things says, 'Surely I come quickly.' Amen. Even so, come, Lord Jesus" (22:20).

Ultimately, the book reveals God's divine plan for the culmination of history and the ultimate victory of God's kingdom.

## GOOD TO KNOW

Author is John (1:1), probably the apostle. Written approximately AD 95.

*God speaks in the quiet moments.*
*Approach His Word with calm expectation.*

## REVELATION 1

Exiled on Patmos, John declares that God has given him a revelation of Jesus Christ. Jesus identifies Himself as the Alpha and Omega, the Almighty, and the Living One who conquered death. John's vision reaffirms Christ's supremacy over time, space, and all creation, laying the foundation for the messages to follow.

*Why do you think Revelation is so deeply encouraging to persecuted Christians?*

## REVELATION 2

John delivers Jesus' messages to seven churches in Asia Minor—addressing their strengths and weaknesses, and offering warnings. This chapter contains Christ's words to four of the seven churches: Ephesus, Smyrna, Pergamum, and Thyatira. Jesus calls each church to repent—offering promises to those who overcome and emphasizing the importance of perseverance in the face of trials.

*How does a church congregation lose its love for Jesus (2:4)?*

## REVELATION 3

John continues Jesus' messages to the final three churches: Sardis, Philadelphia, and Laodicea. He commends the faithful church in Sardis and praises the perseverance in Philadelphia, but He rebukes Laodicea for their lukewarmness and self-sufficiency. These messages emphasize the importance of faithfulness and readiness for Christ's return.

*How can you combat spiritual apathy in your own life?*

## REVELATION 4

John transitions from talking about the past to describing the future. He depicts his vision of the heavenly throne room, where he sees God seated, surrounded by elders and living creatures. He provides a glimpse into the heavenly worship that transcends time and space, inviting believers to join in praising God for His holiness and power.

*In what ways can we prove our genuine love for Jesus in worship and in life?*

### Take Your Time and Learn More

- Revelation of Jesus Christ: DANIEL 7:13–14
- Discernment in the church: MATTHEW 24:4–5
- The enduring nature of the church: MATTHEW 16:18
- God seated on the throne: ISAIAH 6:1–4

*Before you read, pray. Ask God to
speak His truth to your spirit.*

## REVELATION 5

John describes a scroll, sealed with seven seals, in the right hand of God. John weeps when nobody is found worthy to open it. But then one of the elders comforts him, telling him the Lion of Judah is the only one worthy. Jesus, symbolically seen as a Lamb, takes the scroll, and the heavenly hosts worship Him.

*How does seeing Jesus as both lion and lamb shape
your understanding of His character?*

## REVELATION 6

John describes the opening of the first six seals, unleashing various apocalyptic events on the earth. The imagery becomes more elaborate. The first four seals bring conquest, war, famine, and death—widespread chaos and suffering. The fifth seal reveals the souls of martyrs crying out for justice. The sixth seal delivers the terror of humanity facing God's wrath.

*How does Revelation impact your understanding of justice and vengeance?*

## REVELATION 7

John describes a scene that seems to occur between the opening of the sixth and seventh seals. He shares a vision of God's faithful servants sealed for protection before the impending judgments. John sees 144,000 sealed—as well as a vast multitude from every tribe and nation—praising God. This chapter holds both great mercy and impending judgment.

*How should believers' and unbelievers' experience of suffering differ?*

## REVELATION 8

John unveils the opening of the seventh seal, signaling the beginning of the seven trumpet judgments. Silence in heaven precedes the prayers of saints, mingled with incense, ascending before God. Seven angels are given trumpets, heralding devastating judgments upon the earth. These events symbolize God's righteous judgment upon a rebellious world.

*What comfort does God's promised judgment provide?*

## Take Your Time and Learn More

- Lion of the tribe of Judah: GENESIS 49:9–10
- Vision of horsemen: ZECHARIAH 1:8–11
- Great multitude that no one could number: DANIEL 12:1
- Day of the Lord: ZEPHANIAH 1:7

*Don't hurry, don't worry. God's Word provides*
*everything you need for living well.*

## REVELATION 9

John describes the fifth and sixth trumpet judgments that unleash excruciating pain and destruction. Despite the catastrophic events, humanity refuses to repent of its idolatry, sorcery, immorality, and violence. These events serve as warnings of impending judgment on callous hearts hardened against God's mercy.

*Why do you think people who survive these calamities still do not repent?*

## REVELATION 10

During a short interlude between the sixth and seventh trumpet judgments, John shares a vision of a mighty angel descending from heaven, holding a small scroll and proclaiming divine mysteries with a thunderous voice. This chapter highlights the significance of God's Word in prophetic revelation and the impending fulfillment of God's purposes.

*What has it cost you so far to follow Jesus? What are you willing to pay?*

## REVELATION 11

John introduces two witnesses who will prophesy for 1,260 days until they are killed by a "beast." Their bodies will lie in the street for three and a half days, but God will resurrect them, striking fear into the hearts of observers. The seventh trumpet sounds, announcing Christ's reign and eliciting worship from heaven.

*How does Revelation disprove the idea that people would trust in God if they saw His miracles?*

## REVELATION 12

John takes a detour from narrating end-time events to share a vision of a woman (symbolizing Israel) clothed with the sun, crying out in the pain of childbirth. The woman gives birth to a male child who defeats a dragon (Satan) and ascends to heaven. War breaks out in heaven, portraying spiritual battle.

*Do you think the church is facing any unique threats in the twenty-first century?*

### *Take Your Time and Learn More*

- The grave is naked before God: JOB 26:6
  - No more delay: DANIEL 12:7
  - Two witnesses: ZECHARIAH 4
  - War in heaven: DANIEL 12:1

*God loves it when you read and study His Word.*

## REVELATION 13

John introduces the beasts rising from the sea and the earth, representing political powers aligned with Satan. The first beast—with blasphemous authority—receives worship and persecutes God's people. The second beast enforces the mark of the first beast and symbolizes allegiance to Satan. Those refusing the mark face persecution.

*How often do you pray for the persecuted church around the world?*

## REVELATION 14

John shares visions of the Lamb standing on Mount Zion with His redeemed, who are singing a new song. Three angels loudly call for worship of God, warn against the mark of the beast, and pronounce judgment on Babylon. John contrasts the fate of the faithful and the rebellious, emphasizing the certainty of God's judgment.

*Is it ever appropriate to rejoice over the defeat of God's enemies? Why or why not?*

## REVELATION 15

John shares a vision of seven angels carrying the final judgments of God's wrath during the tribulation. The sanctuary fills with smoke, signifying God's glory and power. This scene is a celebration as redeemed believers join in worship, singing praises to God. These visions indicate the culmination of God's judgment on earth and the response of His faithful followers.

*Why do you think certain narratives and teachings are repeated throughout scripture?*

## REVELATION 16

John resumes recording God's judgments. He describes the bowl judgments—God's final wrath poured out on the unrepentant. These judgments include painful sores, a sea that becomes blood, rivers and springs that turn to blood, scalding fire, global darkness, a dried-up Euphrates, and earthquakes and hail.

*How do you explain the fact that the wicked curse God rather than repent when they are judged?*

## Take Your Time and Learn More

- Beasts rising out of the sea: DANIEL 7:3–8
  - Like the Son of Man: DANIEL 7:13–14
    - Sea of glass: EXODUS 24:10
- Water turned to blood: EXODUS 7:17–21

*Reading the Bible isn't a race. Let the pages unfold
at a pace that allows your spirit to breathe.*

## REVELATION 17

John describes a prostitute riding a scarlet beast, symbolizing a corrupt religious system and its alliance with worldly powers. The woman is drunk with the blood of martyrs. The angel reveals the downfall of the prostitute and the beast's ultimate destruction. John contrasts the corrupt systems of the world and the purity of God's kingdom.

*How have you seen Satan use elements of God's truth
to create counterfeit religious systems?*

## REVELATION 18

John describes the fall of a different "Babylon"—symbolizing corrupt, idolatrous systems. A mighty angel declares Babylon's destruction. John describes the city's destruction in vivid detail, symbolizing the end of all worldly glory and power. He emphasizes the fleeting nature of human achievement and the inevitability of God's judgment on unrepentant sin.

*Which worldly pleasures look appealing, even though
you know they'll never truly satisfy?*

## REVELATION 19

John hears a multitude in heaven praising God—including the twenty-four elders mentioned in Revelation 4:4. The marriage supper of the Lamb is announced, and Christ returns on a white horse, leading the armies of heaven to defeat the beast and the false prophet. It culminates in the establishment of Christ's reign and the defeat of His enemies.

*How does thinking about future rejoicing encourage you to rejoice in God right now?*

## REVELATION 20

John describes Christ's millennial reign, when Satan is bound for a thousand years. Faithful believers reign with Jesus, participating in His kingdom. After the thousand years, Satan leads the nations in rebellion against God; however, he is ultimately defeated. The final judgment occurs: the wicked face eternal punishment and the righteous receive eternal life.

*Why is it hard to see the ugliness of sin the way God sees it?*

## Take Your Time and Learn More

- Ten horns: DANIEL 7:7–8
- Downfall of Babylon: JEREMIAH 51
- Singing praise to God for His righteous judgment: PSALM 96
- Reign of Christ: ISAIAH 24:21–23

*The greatest truths in scripture are often revealed in the unhurried moments.*

## REVELATION 21

John shares his vision of a restored earth—free from sin and evil—where God dwells among His people. John sees the holy city, the New Jerusalem, descending from heaven. God wipes away every tear, and death, sorrow, and pain cease to exist. The city is brilliant and beautiful, housing God and His redeemed creation.

*What do you most look forward to about eternal life with God?*

## REVELATION 22

John depicts the beauty of New Jerusalem. He describes the river flowing from God's throne and talks about the tree of life that bears twelve kinds of fruit. The angel confirms the authenticity of John's vision, warning against adding to or subtracting from the book of Revelation. Jesus promises His imminent return, urging His people to be ready and faithful.

*Why is God entirely worthy of your worship both now and forever?*

### Take Your Time and Learn More

- **New heaven and new earth:** ISAIAH 65:17–25
  - **Tree of life:** GENESIS 2:8–10

# FOR YOUR BIBLE
# READING OBSERVATIONS

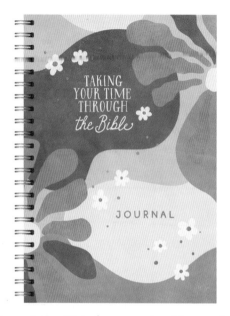

It's great to read through the Bible in a year—but it's even better to slow down and savor your time in God's Word. This pretty, spiral-bound journal makes a wonderful record of your time in scripture, providing space to record observations, interpretations, and applications.

Spiral-bound Paperback / 978-1-63609-995-8

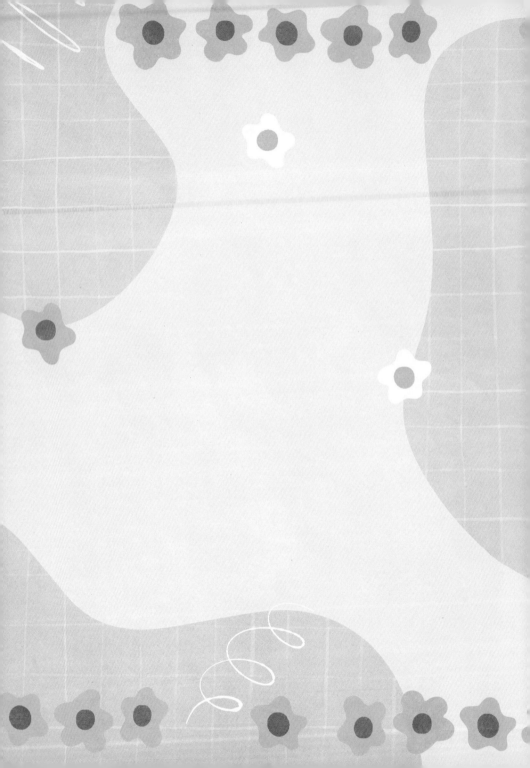